The Wealth of Man

PETER JAY

PublicAffairs
NEW YORK

The pictures in this volume were taken by Peter Jay in the course of his travels while writing this book and, at the same time, filming the BBC's television series, of which he is also the author, on the same subject. The purpose of the pictures is not to provide scholarly support for the main run of the text of the book. Rather, it is to illustrate a more personal and subjective subplot, the story of his journey in pursuit of the larger history. The author hopes this purpose may excuse his amateur efforts with the camera (a mini-DV).

The photos can be identified as follows: Introduction: Home Economicus, Chapter 1: Money, Chapter 2: Athens, Chapter 3: Islam, Chapter 4: Florence, Chapter 5: Sea Lanes, Chapter 6: Steam, Chapter 7: Arms Race, Chapter 8: Wars, Chapter 9: Marx & Engels, and Chapter 10: Your Way.

Published in the United States by PublicAffairs™, a member of the Perseus Books Group.

Printed in the United States of America.

Book design by Jenny Dossin.

LIBRARY OF CONGRESS CATALOGING-IN-PUBLICATION DATA
Jay, Peter.
The wealth of man / Peter Jay.
p. cm.
Includes bibliographical references and index.
ISBN 1-891620-67-3
1. Wealth—History. 2. Economic man—History. 3. Economic development—History.
I. Title.
HC79.W4 J39 2000
330.9—dc21
00–037362

FIRST EDITION
1 3 5 7 9 10 8 6 4 2

For Emma, Tamsin, Alice, Patrick, Nicky,

Tommy, Sammy, Jamie and Lara

CONTENTS

The Idea of the Book

PERHAPS NO STORY IS MORE RIVETING THAN MAN'S EVOLUTION, his battle for survival in competition with other species and in interaction with his environment, and the natural selection—so far—of the species with the most successful brain. The account of mankind's perennial and ubiquitous urge to reproduce, to obey the prompting of the selfish gene and to subdue every threat to survival, has us on the edges of our intellectual seats.*

But equally exciting is mankind's struggle to satisfy his second imperative, the individual's craving, separately and collectively, for material betterment, which for brevity we may call wealth or welfare. It is, in fact, part of the same story, man's success in the evolutionary stakes (construed in the broad sense that includes biological and social evolution, since there has been little or no development in man's purely genetic evolution over the last 40,000 years) being linked to his success as an economic agent.[1]

This economic quest is nonetheless a distinct tale within the total story. It is distinct because its subject is critically different, namely, the individual human being, whether acting privately or collectively, rather than the species or the genome that defines it.[2] The geneticist, like the nature that he studies, is "careful of the type . . . careless of the single life."[3] For the historian, specific men and women are the protagonists. And for

*Let it be stipulated at the outset that our usage of terms such as "mankind," "man" and the like embraces male and female equally wherever the context requires.

the economist it is the individual human who is both the sole ultimate beneficiary—or victim—of the whole process and the mainspring of its workings, whether he or she be guided by the invisible hand of market forces or by more overt political direction.

The tale is also distinct because its characteristic academic disciplines are different—history and economics rather than biology, genetics and psychology, although as we shall see the two approaches overlap, borrow from each other and are perhaps currently converging. This means essentially that events are looked at through different or differently focused lenses, lenses that see not the genes we carry fighting the battle for selection and survival, but man working, producing, accumulating, saving, investing, trading, owning and inventing and, more profoundly, organizing, regulating, governing, politicking, legislating, judging, moralizing, ideologizing and theorizing, struggling to survive and, in a different way, finding his more successful innovations selected for survival by their own success.

The story of the wealth of man is our economic history. It is the story of how over about the past 10,000–15,000 years modern humans—walking, talking, big-brained animals who had been around for perhaps 100,000–135,000 years—began as one not particularly important species among many, disputing the earth's fruits and spaces with countless other bigger, stronger, infinitely more ancient and far more numerous species, and arrived at the position in which we now find ourselves at the start of the third Christian millennium.[4]

To the best of our knowledge, at about the time the middle stone age (Mesolithic period) was beginning in Europe, say 8,000 years B.C., the human population on earth was perhaps 6 million, already spread throughout all the continents, including Australia and the Americas, though not Antarctica.[5] They lived in small bands of perhaps half a dozen families and supplied their essential wants—food, clothing, warmth and shelter—directly from nature.* Their life expectancy at birth was about thirty years, although once individuals survived to thirty they could expect to reach sixty.[6]

A few rude tools, treasured stones and garments apart, they owned no property, had no savings, passed on no inheritance, used no money and

*Thomas Robert Malthus (1766–1834), English economist, author of *Essay on Population* (1798) and other works, defined the necessities of life as "food, clothing, lodging and firing."

held few regular exchanges with others of their kind beyond their immediate group. Their standard of living, as we would use the term today, was in the most literal sense at subsistence level, though there is some argument whether their lives were nasty as well as solitary, poor, brutish and short, as the English seventeenth-century philosopher Thomas Hobbes (1588–1679) observed.[7] Leften Stavrianos has even suggested a rather idyllic life in balance with nature, with labor (hunting and gathering) restricted to a comfortable twenty hours a week and what seems an enviable absence of the characteristic evils and annoyances of modern life.[8] This view is rather contradicted by a recent report on findings by Larry Barham, a cave archaeologist at Bristol University who studied evidence of hunter-gatherers inhabiting the Cheddar Gorge 12 kya.* An excavation of a group of adults and children at the site in the 1980s showed that "all the bodies had been neatly butchered—the first solid evidence in Britain of cannibalism."[9]

Today we live differently. There are more than 6 billion of us, more than 1,000 for every one 10,000 years ago, though we still inhabit much the same geographical space. We—men and women, the global average—now expect to live past our sixty-fifth birthdays.[10] Nearly half of us live in great cities and towns, indeed in elaborate civilizations, and supply our wants—essential as much as optional—at the end of long chains of cultivation, extraction, production and distribution, paying in money that for the most part we earn in specialized work. The standard of living of very large numbers in the more affluent societies, and even of the considerable minorities living in less-developed economies, would have been unimaginable to our Mesolithic ancestors. It flows broadly from the fact that such people have produced what they need for subsistence very early, as it were, in the week, the remainder being surplus to that minimum.

In other words human productivity—output per person per week or per hour—has increased much faster than the population. And in dimensions that we cannot reduce to demonstrable numbers we conceive ourselves to have separated utterly and forever from our fellow species of 10,000 years ago—in knowledge, self-knowledge, art, science, medicine, mastery of nature, governance, social development, the very perception of right and wrong, in fact in everything that defines what (at least until

*The abbreviation "kya" stands for "thousand years ago" and is used to specify very early or prehistoric times. A date given as "12 kya," for example, could also be written as "10,000 B.C."

very recently) we confidently and proudly referred to as "civilization." We see ourselves as indisputably the master species, controlling the destiny of ourselves and all other species, arbitrating the distribution of earth's plenty and adjusting its scarcities, reigning in self-conscious majesty over our conquered kingdom.

And yet it is not a straightforward or uninterrupted story of "progress," nor even of "economic progress," though it may sometimes seem like that in America in the last half millennium. The present conclusion of the story may only be the end of chapter one in a longer and different story. Man's economic advance has occurred in fits and starts, has been punctuated by long periods of stagnation and in some cases retreat and has encountered frequent cul-de-sacs.

The driving forces have been the natural selection of innovations that work and the invisible hand that, under the right conditions, channels private appetite into the attainment of social ends or at least of widely shared advantage.[11] Both are ethically blind, indifferent alike to individual happiness and social justice. The enjoyment of the progress that has been achieved has been distributed with extreme and generally growing inequality (partly because the peaks of wealth become higher whereas the floor remains always the same).

It is for all that a gripping story—of triumph and calamity, of benevolence and iniquity—in which the visions of genius regularly confront the rankest folly, and it poses a stupendous puzzle: How and why did it happen? What were the decisive moments and advances? Why was progress so uneven? Was there a single recipe for progress? Was it a matter of science or society, knowledge or attitude, luck or policy, climate or race, culture or structure? Is the answer to be found in economics or politics or sociology or demography? Or in philosophy, art or indeed religion? Have we at last inherited the earth? What limits, moral and practical, are there to our enjoyment of this patrimony? Are we, and must we remain, the fittest to survive?

These questions have taxed historians, including economic historians, almost since men began to think.

HOW IT LOOKED A CENTURY AGO

When Alfred Marshall (1842–1924), widely celebrated as the father of what he himself called "economic science," wrote his classic volume, *Principles of Economics* (1890), he provided immediately following the introductory chapter "two short sketches: the one related to the growth of free enterprise and generally of economic freedom, and the other to the growth of economic science. They have no claim to be systematic histories however compressed; they aim only at indicating some landmarks on the routes by which economic structure and economic thought have travelled to their present position."[12]

Although in later editions these sketches were relegated to appendices, they still provide fascinating insights into how one of the greatest of all economists—and one of the most humane and civilized among them—thought economic change and development was really caused. The sketch of how "economic structure" reached the position it held in Marshall's day, at the end of the nineteenth century, is a breathtakingly bold and heroically sweeping account of man's whole economic story from the time when "we find savages living under dominion of custom and impulse; scarcely ever striking out new lines for themselves; never forecasting the distant future, and seldom making provision even for the near future; fitful in spite of their servitude to custom, governed by the fancy of the moment; ready at times for the most arduous exertions, but incapable of keeping themselves long to steady work."[13]

Here we find the inventor of the driest of microeconomics, the creator of marginal utility and elasticities of demand and supply, the man who made the differential calculus the chief weapon in the social scientist's armory, speaking the language of the classical historian, almost of the journalist. His picture of early man seems to owe more to late-nineteenth-century English assumptions of the kind that also influenced Kipling's *Jungle Book* than to any laborious archaeology or anthropology.[14] And his discussion of race as the key variable in the story, together with climate and inherited institutions, would today have terminated his academic career in short order.[15]

Marshall's picture is indeed based quite explicitly on the Darwinian notion of selection of the most successful; when applied to economic history, the races are seen as playing the role that species play in biology.[16] Speaking of the "mutual debts of biology and economics," Marshall notes that Darwin borrowed his key concept of the "struggle for existence" (Darwin later adopted Herbert Spencer's name for it, "the survival of the fittest") from "Malthus' historical account."[17] Marshall adds that "since that time biology has more than repaid her debt" to the extent that the analogies between the disciplines "have at last established their claim to illustrate a fundamental unity of action between the laws of nature and in the moral world."* [18] This, he says, is manifested in economics in "the law that the struggle for existence causes those organisms to multiply which are best fitted to derive benefit from their environment."[19] Thus, Marshall argues,

> the struggle for existence causes in the long run those races of men to survive in which the individual is most willing to sacrifice himself for the benefit of those around him; and which are consequently the best adapted collectively to make use of their environment . . . on the whole, and subject to grave exceptions, those races survive and predominate in which the best qualities are most strongly developed.[20]

Marshall's concept of "race" is clearly not genetic, since he remarks that "race qualities themselves are, however, mainly caused by the action of individuals and physical causes in more or less remote times" and that "the usages which make a race strong in peace and war are often due to the wisdom of a few great thinkers who have interpreted and developed its customs and rules."[21] Indeed, as we discuss in this book, there may be more than a mere overlap between Marshall's concept of "race" as the primary actor in the drama of human economic history and the concept of "culture" advanced as the main explanatory tool in David Landes's modern inquiry into why some nations are so rich and some so poor.[22]

In yet another of his gasp-inducing generalizations, Marshall adds that "none of these things [race qualities] are of any permanent avail if the climate is unfavourable to vigour: the gifts of nature, her land, her waters, and her skies, determine the character of the race's work."[23] In this too, as we shall see, his ideas in their broadest conceptual outline are to a

*Marshall always insisted that economics was a moral science.

degree vindicated by Landes, who having reviewed the evidence concludes that "life in poor climes, then, is precarious, depressed, brutish. The mistakes of man, however well intentioned, aggravate the cruelties of nature. Even the good ideas do not go unpunished. No wonder that these zones remain poor; that many of them have been growing poorer," though Landes cautions that "it would be a mistake to see geography as destiny."[24]

THE MISSION OF HISTORY: TO EXPLAIN

This digression on Marshall is germane for several reasons. For a start, no one can read his thirty-page economic history of man, "The Growth of Free Industry and Enterprise," without marveling at its range, audacity, lucidity, language and ambition. In that, it is a model.

The appeal of any work of history lies in its ability to convince readers that they understand its subject, better at least than they did before they read it. To understand is to see events as manifestations of forces, regularities, causes, general truths that we recognize as pervasive and that appear believable to our educated intelligence. To explain is to show that the events are indeed manifestations of such forces and so on. Yet to identify and expound such forces and general truths always makes the historian vulnerable to the next scholar who finds an exception and to the chroniclers and investigators who deplore the very idea of general truths, let alone laws of history.

Some historians take refuge in the pure collection of facts, supposedly theory-free, and relish what they piously call their "rich particularity." Others do not shrink from seeking to explain what they report but somehow pretend that the explanations do not rely on any generalizations. This in practice means that they rely on implicit and usually rather banal generalizations that most readers may be expected to assume without recognizing them as anything so suspect as "theories" or "laws."

Marshall ducks none of these challenges. In today's argot he goes right out there and tells it like he thinks it is. His theories and his explanations cannot be ours. But his model of a history that really tries to explain, to give the reader understanding, to paint the big picture with a bold brush and to think his way through the tangle of events so as to uncover the deeper and more lasting forces that shape the stage on which we strut and play, is as valid today as ever.

More than 100 years ago he wrote, "Although the proximate causes of the chief events in history are to be found in the actions of individuals, yet most of the conditions which have made those events possible are traceable to the influence of inherited institutions and race qualities and of physical nature."[25] Today we reject his particulars, but we must emulate his program—to explain and to understand man's economic story, where we came from and why and how we are where we are today, and to understand it in themes and language that are believable and clear.

THE MISSION OF ECONOMIC HISTORY: TO EXPLAIN GROWTH

Marshall inaugurated more than a century of economic historiography, which has reached, especially in America, a crescendo of energy, argument and fundamental rethinking. All of it is carrying us further and further away from "straight" economics as it has been mainly taught in the English language, in particular further and further away from the "neoclassical" theory of economic growth. It is ironic that this theory has many of its roots in those parts of Marshall's *Principles of Economics* which dealt not with economic history and man's economic advance, but with the specification of various kinds of static equilibria under prescribed conditions of scarcity, freedom, competition and perfect information.

Individuals, in the neoclassical model, are assumed to wish to maximize their "utility"—or wealth—by choosing the combination of their various wants, including their desire for leisure, that gives them the best outcome. More wants in total can be satisfied if more goods and services are produced. That can happen only if extra capital is invested. The stock of capital is composed of human capital (labor), physical capital (machines and other man-made aids to production) and natural resources. These in turn depend on technology, seen as man's command of nature, because it determines the skills of labor, the qualities and capabilities of the machines and so on and what counts usefully as a natural resource. Technology itself, or at least gains in it, is seen as flowing from inventions/innovations that in turn reflect and depend on the stock of knowledge (what man knows about nature).

Accordingly, maximizing man forgoes some current consumption in order to create those additions to the capital stock that will best add to the future satisfaction of wants. Where the greatest gain will be made by investing in new kinds of machines and skills rather than in more machines and skills of the existing kind, new inventions will be exploited. If the number of people in the labor force rises in relation to the size of the (nonhuman) capital stock, then the optimum combination of human and nonhuman capital shifts in favor of less capital per person. Likewise for natural resources.

In such a world the ultimate determinants of how much is produced and how much is produced per head (the indicators of economic performance) are the rate of growth of the population and the amount of consumption forgone in each period (which is the same thing as the percentage of income saved by the society). A higher rate of savings than of population growth produces rising output per head (and therefore, since they are the same thing, of income per head and of living standards)—and vice versa.

As the American Nobel prizewinner Douglass North remarks, "From the viewpoint of the economic historian this neoclassical formulation appears to beg all the interesting questions."[26] Nobody, one supposes, is going to argue that investment does not play a pervasive role in affecting future output levels, nor that investment can take place without savings defined as current production not immediately consumed, in other words as what Marshall himself referred to as "surplus . . . over the necessaries of life."[27] Still less will it be claimed that population—or to put it more broadly, demographic change—cannot influence performance and living standards in both directions.

What, however, seems so obvious that it is hard to understand how neoclassical theorists managed to ignore it for so long is that population trends and the savings ratio (the unconsumed portion of current output) offer us absolutely no satisfying explanation of many of the major issues in economic history, such as why some peoples and regions at some times seem to have advanced very rapidly while others have not. It is hard to resist completely the suspicion that the persistence of the neoclassical model, like that of other scholastic devices, lay more in its potency to preserve the ascendancy of its professors. It had, after all, the necessary characteristics of obscurity and difficulty as well as being amenable to mathematics, even if it promised no illumination of the human economic story.

ANOTHER MODEL

At the opposite intellectual extreme as a tool of economic history stands narrative, plain, vivid and highly suggestive storytelling. Its supreme expression—and arguably the best, most penetrating and enjoyable textbook of the nature of economic growth—is not an economics book at all or even a formal history, but a personal family story, Jung Chang's *Wild Swans.*[28] It tells the tale of twentieth-century China as a seesaw alternation between the irrepressible enterprise, inventiveness and productivity of the Chinese people and the successive insane assaults upon their prosperity and achievements by degenerate, desperate and/or deluded rulers, successively imperial, nationalist and communist.

No phase illustrates this theme more spectacularly than the cycle of Mao Zedong's Great Leap Forward. In 1956, Jung Chang tells us, China was, relative at least to the wars, privations and traumas of the previous half century, momentarily stable and free of starvation, bandits, inflation and war. In a moment of apparent lucidity, Mao had even decided that the "industrialization" of the economy required the support of China's educated citizens. He had therefore announced the Hundred Flowers Policy—"let a hundred flowers bloom"—as a result of which "the country enjoyed a year of relative relaxation." For a moment, the economy prospered as people put their skills, energies and such assets as they had managed to conceal through the bad times to work to ameliorate their lot. Then, in 1958, when Jung Chang was six years old, came the next assault from the center: "All around me," Jung Chang recalls,

> uplifting music blared from loudspeakers, and there were banners, posters, and huge slogans painted on the walls proclaiming "Long Live the Great Leap Forward!" and "Everybody Make Steel!" . . . Mao . . . ordered steel output to be doubled in one year. . . . Nearly 100 million peasants were pulled out of agricultural work and into steel production. They had been the labor force producing much

of the country's food. Mountains were stripped bare of trees for fuel. But the output of this mass production amounted only to what people called "cattle droppings" ... meaning useless turds....

Mao's fixation on steel went largely unquestioned, as did his other obsessions. He took a dislike to sparrows—they devour grain. So every household was mobilised. We sat outside ferociously beating any metal object, from cymbals to saucepans, to scare the sparrows off the trees so they would eventually drop dead from exhaustion.... That summer [1958] all of China was organised into these new units ["people's communes"], each containing between 2,000 and 20,000 households.... In 1958 the regime effectively banned eating at home. Every peasant had to eat in the commune canteen.... The peasants filed into the canteens every day after work and ate to their hearts' content. . . . They consumed and wasted the entire food reserve in the countryside. . . . With no incentive to work they just went to the fields and had a good snooze.

Agriculture was also neglected because of the priority given to steel. Many of the peasants were exhausted from having to spend long hours finding fuel, scrap iron, and iron ore and keeping the furnaces going. The fields were often left to the women and children, who had to do everything by hand, as the animals were busy making their contribution to steel production. When harvest time came in autumn 1958, few people were in the fields.

The failure to get in the harvest in 1958 flashed a warning that a food shortage was on its way.... As the sixties began a great famine spread across the whole of China. . . . An accepted estimate for the death toll for the whole country is around 30 million [which would make it the greatest calamity in man's career on earth, excepting only the Yellow River floods in the early 1930s, Stalin's purges and World War II]. . . . By the beginning of 1961, tens of millions of deaths had finally forced Mao to give up his economic policies. Reluctantly, he allowed the pragmatic president Liu and Deng Xiaoping, general secretary of the Party, more control over the country.... Things began to improve.

The pragmatists put through a succession of major reforms. It was in this context that Deng Xiaoping made the remark: "It doesn't matter whether the cat is white or black, so long as it catches mice." There was to be no more mass production of steel. A stop was put to crazy economic goals, and realistic policies were introduced. Public canteens were abolished, and peasants' income was now related to their work. They were given back household property, which had been confiscated by the communes, including farm implements and domestic animals. They were also allowed small plots of land to till privately. In some ar-

> eas land was effectively leased out to peasant households. In industry and commerce, elements of a market economy were officially sanctioned, and *within a couple of years the economy was flourishing again.*[29]

The same rapid and spontaneous recovery of economic life after years of destruction and desolation took place at the end of the Cultural Revolution in the early 1970s, when Mao

> had no choice but to turn to the old, disgraced officials again. . . . Zhou Enlai . . . set about getting the economy going. The old administration was largely restored, and production and order were emphasised. Incentives were reintroduced. Peasants were allowed some cash sidelines. Scientific research began again. Schools started proper teaching, after a gap of six years. . . . With the economy reviving, factories began to recruit new workers.[30]

In those stories are such theory and ideology as this book contains. It is not a crude plea for laissez-faire. The stability of the mid-1950s depended much too clearly and critically on the success of government (albeit the government of Mao Zedong) in terminating the physical chaos, both civil war and banditry, that had plagued China for most of the first half of the century for the experience of this era to support any anarchic theory of economic progress.

What it does support, at least as a description of China in the twentieth century but also as an approximation to the general experience of mankind over as many as 100 centuries, is the axiom that given half a chance to improve their lot, including that of their family and near community, people will put forth extraordinary cunning, diligence and persistence in pursuit of that goal. It also supports a second axiom, namely, that mankind's political failures expose human societies to the chronic risk—and intermittent certainty—of progress reversed and prosperity dissipated. Over the whole period of our story, those failures consist in man's inability to resolve for good a conundrum: Economic success requires good government, but all government breeds misgovernment, and misgovernment destroys prosperity.

THE WALTZ

Out of this picture emerges the waltz motif (one, two three; one, two, three) that runs through our history. There are those who will want to see in this the mark of the Hegelian beast, a resurrection of the dreaded dialectic of thesis, antithesis and synthesis. Nothing so portentous—or so flawed—is intended. The waltz motif simply asserts as a frequently encountered pattern, though certainly not an iron law, that

1. From time to time an economic advance is made (e.g., the development of agriculture), by chance opportunity or by a development in knowledge or technique, that apparently enables more mouths to be fed or existing mouths to be better fed or living standards to be raised in one way or another.

2. This advance provokes predatory threats from one or another species of outsider (external raiders) or free rider (internal idlers) who hopes to secure the fruits of the advance for himself without the costs or effort required to support the advance.

3. These threats invite—and may or may not attract—a social-political solution (e.g., structured settlements with rulers) whereby the original advance is protected from predation by rules prohibiting or discouraging such conduct and/or by direct policing and defense.

It is the stability or otherwise of the social-political solutions achieved in the third step that frequently determines how far, where and for how long the fruits of the original purely economic advance are enjoyed. It is because step 1 provokes step 2 and because step 3 can always fail that whole civilizations, as well as lesser economic units, frequently retrogress economically and sometimes fail altogether, although of course natural calamity can do the job without the aid of human political incompetence or military inferiority.

It is for this reason that economic historians who wish to explain man's economic advance and its frequent interruptions and failures are necessarily drawn deeply into the observation and description of the social, cultural and political structures and values that man has devised to facilitate and protect his economic progress. Without them, purely economic advance is not enough and soon fails, and however much economic historians seek to confine their agenda to economic events and their explanation, they are rapidly obliged to concern themselves with the total organization and governance of societies, if not for their own sake, at least as necessary ingredients in the understanding of the purely economic story.

Adam Smith (1723–1790) went before us in this as in so much else.[31] Indeed, he diagnosed a version of the waltz motif at the very heart of his explanation of the wealth of man and of nations and of why they should grow, which he called "the natural progress of opulence."[32] It all starts, he believed, in the nature of man, in his innate curiosity and competitiveness allied to a perpetual disposition to ameliorate his material condition, in other words to seek wealth.[33] This, Smith thought, led to the division of labor and the growth of knowledge, similar in broad concept to step 1 of our waltz motif.

This "thesis" immediately ran into its antithesis in the form of what Smith saw as the practical inhibitions to growth, mainly predation by the powerful within a society and by outside invaders, as well as by the monopolistic tendencies of merchants and manufacturers and by slavery. Synthesis was then found, where success occurred, in social and political developments such as the emergence of towns and markets, the evolution of the middle class, the political matrix of citizenship, state power, rents and taxes and the reinforcing legitimization of these structures by value systems based on kinship, status, the state and religion.

THE TASK DEFINED

Thus we find in Adam Smith, as we find in such contrasting observers as Alfred Marshall and Jung Chang, the same conviction that the heart of the matter, the key to understanding how and why the wealth of man advanced and retreated, lies in a rounded view of man's total social context, political, psychological and ethical as well as economic. It is a view to which economic historians in the modern era have returned in growing numbers after a phase of what now seem unduly mechanistic, economics-based attempts to explain economic history in neoclassical categories (technological change, surplus production, savings and investment).

Nonetheless, the modern swing back to more seemingly relevant categories of explanation, while bringing the subject much closer again to Marshall's actual writings as distinct from his formal theories of supply, demand and marginal utility, does run the risk of sacrificing rigor to rather casual pontification and anecdote. Savings propensities may be irrelevant, but at least they can be measured. "Cultural factors" may be decisive, but it is hard to prove them, and nasty prejudices may lurk in their undergrowth camouflaged in respectable language.

All this points to a challenge confronting *The Wealth of Man:* the need to provide real explanations through explicit and in principle refutable theses while rejecting glib rationalizations for our own wishful thinking. Historians will never become pure social scientists because the need for narrative, the complexity of the matter they study and the impossibility of repeatable experimentation all ensure that the human story will never be finally boiled down to a finite list of statable laws. But historians can—and we must try to—tell their stories in ways that help readers to feel they understand what happened because they are able to recognize patterns of cause and effect that recur consistently, not just when it suits the author's convenience. This discipline I try to obey.

So, we invite readers to board our craft near the source of that river of mankind's economic history that rises just over ten millennia ago and to sail with us downriver, tracing bends and cataracts, reaches and meanders, to the immense delta of the global economy at A.D. 2000. In the process we hope to show a little more about the behavior of the currents that give this river its life and its drama.

The Wealth of Man

CHAPTER ONE

The Discovery of Value

BY 12 KYA,* OR MAYBE A MILLENNIUM OR TWO EARLIER, THERE were in the world perhaps a few million people, fewer probably than the seven million or so who live in London today.[1] They were members of the species *Homo sapiens sapiens.* They were spread throughout almost all the earth's inhabitable areas, excluding only the then ice-bound areas of Antarctica, most of modern Canada and northern Europe and remote islands such as Madagascar and New Zealand. This chapter will take us to 1000 B.C. (3 kya), by which time the human population of the planet had increased above 40 million, possibly well above that number, and had extended the range of its habitation to include the no longer ice-bound areas of modern Canada and northern Europe.[2]

In terms of evolutionary time, even for man, it was a very short moment before 10 kya when our hero sets out on his economic odyssey. To put it all into quick chronological perspective, the earth was formed 4,600 million years ago (mya). First life began about 600–400 mya, and the first mammals appeared about 170 mya.[3] The dinosaurs suddenly became extinct 70 mya, and about 10 mya (toward the end of the Miocene

*In this chapter we use "kya" to mean "thousand years ago" and "mya" for "million years ago," measured back—where it is important—from precisely A.D. 2000; thus we show the sack of Babylon in 1595 B.C. as "3.595 kya." we use "B.C." and "A.D." referring to the conventional pre-Christian and Christian eras only where they are necessary in order to chime with dates already too familiar to readers (e.g., 1200 B.C. for the fall of Troy) to be sensibly converted to kya. No cultural bias or offense is intended against those who use other systems of dating.

Epoch) the earth began to cool, forming ice caps at the poles. The first humans appeared less than 10 mya.

The first hominids (man's ancestors as they first evolved from the apes) descended from the trees to walk upright on the dry grasslands of Africa that were emerging from the forests as climate change lowered the rainfall, probably by 4 mya, though they may go back as far as 7 or even 9 mya.[4] They included *Australopithecus ramidus, Australopithecus afarensis* (known as "Lucy"), *Australopithecus africanus, Homo habilis* and *Homo erectus,* each possibly evolving from the other in that order.[5] The first stone tools were being used, in Ethiopia, about 2.4 mya.[6] About 1.8 mya the first of a series of up to eleven ice ages began, forming ice sheets over high latitudes.[7] The earliest evidence of fire being used by humans (in modern Kenya and South Africa) dates to 1.6 mya.[8] The first men (*Homo erectus)* to appear outside Africa were "Java Man" about 1 mya (possibly 1.8 mya), and the first to appear in Europe were not later than 0.5 mya (500 kya).[9] *Homo sapiens* (distinguished by his larger, rounder skull) appeared in Africa and Europe at this time. The European branch of the "family" evolved from about 230 kya into the Neanderthals *(Homo sapiens neanderthalensis),* who peopled Europe and western Asia until 40–30 kya.[10] They actually had larger brains than ours today and were well adapted to ice-age Eurasia.[11]

Meanwhile, in Africa we ourselves, anatomically modern humans styled *Homo sapiens sapiens,* evolved 135 kya. From 100 kya we began to migrate out of Africa, reaching the Near East by 90 kya.[12]* This migration may have been deflected eastward by the onset of the penultimate ice age (71–59 kya), with early modern humans reaching China and Southeast Asia about this time.[13]

Then, between about 60 and 30 kya, an extraordinary event appears to have occurred, the last major event to date in modern man's long genetic evolution and arguably the foundation for everything that has followed in man's economic story.[14] Something changed radically in the human brain, enlarging human intelligence in ways that transformed man's ca-

* We use "Near East" in the traditional English sense to refer to areas bordering upon (or nearly so) the eastern end of the Mediterranean: in broad terms the modern territories of Turkey, Cyprus, Syria, Lebanon, Palestine, Israel, Jordan and Egypt. We use "Middle East" broadly to refer to countries bordering upon the Persian Gulf, today's Iraq, Iran, Kuwait, Saudi Arabia and sundry Gulf states, and to other countries in the Arabian peninsula, such as Yemen and Oman.

pacities and, equally important, his appetites. Of course, this did not occur overnight in one amazing mutation, but by the standards of evolutionary time it happened quickly, and we can date it from the extraordinary performance of the species from that time.

From about 40 kya the types of tools used by man proliferated, and man himself spread very rapidly across the world, frozen ice caps apart. As William McNeill and John McNeill remark, "No comparably global expansion of a large-bodied life form, leaping across both climatic and water barriers, had ever occurred before."[15] By 50 kya *Homo sapiens sapiens* had reached, in modern terms, Japan (then part of the Asian mainland) and Java (also part of the mainland). By 40 kya he was in Europe, Borneo, Australia and New Guinea. By 30 kya he had reached southwest Australia, Tasmania, Okinawa, central Asia (Kazakhstan) and Siberia; and a couple of millennia later he had seen the extinction of the last Neanderthal in Europe and had crossed the sea to the Solomon Islands east of New Guinea. By 10 kya he had crossed the Bering land bridge (in about 15 kya), passed through the corridor between the ice sheets of the Canadian west coast and the main bulk of Canada, spread throughout the rest of North America from Nova Scotia to Mexico and penetrated into the Amazon basin and all the way down the west coast of South America to Patagonia. He had also left remains at Cresswell Crags in Britain.[16]

Adaptability to marked climate changes and tolerance of a widely varying diet had given evolutionary advantages to premodern man during the previous nearly 2 million years of intermittent ice ages. His erect posture and two-legged walk left his hands free to wield tools and weapons—basically sticks and stones—and the sticks and stones for capturing and preparing his prey left room for smaller teeth and jaws and eventually for an all-important rearrangement of the larynx. Meanwhile, from a very early time premodern man had learned to use fire for heat, light, cooking, frightening large predators and driving them toward traps and burning dry landscapes so as to accelerate the recycling of nutrients into new growth. Finally, brains had been getting bigger as *Homo erectus* and later the varying subspecies of *Homo sapiens* evolved.[17]

But none of this accounts for what has been called the "big bang of human culture" and "our great leap forward" about 50 kya.[18] Historians are not agreed about what exactly happened. In the *Cambridge Ancient History* we are told:

> It is now becoming more and more probable that spoken languages were already well developed at least 100,000 years ago [100 kya], probably as early as the functionally superb stone tools fashioned by the craftsmen of the Lower Palaeolithic (Abbevillian, etc.) in Western Europe. After all, languages are as much tools of communication as artifacts are tools for making articles of wood, bone and stone, used for a large variety of purposes by primitive man. Even without this obvious parallel, the fact that such different animals as bees and dolphins are now known to have most elaborate communication patterns should give us pause.[19]

McNeill and McNeill believe that the "most plausible explanation" of man's rapid spread across the habitable areas of the globe 40 kya "is to suppose that marked improvements in communication and co-operation were what allowed roving *Homo sapiens sapiens* bands to colonise the habitable globe and establish themselves everywhere as a dominant species. The key innovation was probably the full deployment of language to create symbolic meanings."[20] Jared Diamond thinks this leap forward was the result of "the perfection of the voice-box and hence for the anatomical basis of modern language on which the exercise of human creativity is so dependent."[21]

The English archaeologist Steven Mithen believes that some kind of social language binding early man's communities together dates much further back, to 250 kya, and that the really significant change from about 60 kya was more in the way the brain works. Specifically, he argues that without any further enlargement the brain of *Homo sapiens sapiens* acquired an ability for abstract thought based on a form of synthesis of the preexisting simpler thought processes, such as elementary understanding of the physical world about us, ability to handle immediate social relations and ability to make and use—and teach others how to make and use—tools and weapons. Thus, he argues, natural history intelligence was combined with social and technical intelligence to yield a higher intelligence capable of using man-made images and objects with symbolic meanings to communicate, through art, religion and otherwise.[22] This may in fact be closer to what McNeill means by "the full deployment of language" than at first appears.

Dramatic behavioral changes followed this supposed intellectual advance. Tools, formerly made mainly from stone, began to be fashioned from all sorts of new materials, such as bone and ivory. Stone blades began to be used. People began purposely to construct places to live and to decorate both their homes and their bodies with paint and ornaments.[23]

More important than any of these specific manifestations of man's new mental agility, apart perhaps from his diaspora throughout the habitable globe, would turn out to be the agility itself. A being who can think abstractly, who can express, convey and perhaps record useful knowledge in a language of specific symbolic meanings and who can conceive—and then similarly convey and transmit—by pure imagination aided by verbal reasoning states that surpass his own direct experience, is a being who can both dream of great wealth (a dream that can, we suppose, be dreamt by no other animal) and set about devising the means of realizing the dream (means that no other animal can design). And thus our stage is suddenly occupied by the protagonist whose greed and cunning—or if you prefer, whose imagination and intelligence—make him the hero, or villain, of our story.

The last ice age began about 24 kya and was ending just before our story begins, about 13 kya.[24] The end of the ice ages shortly preceded the beginning of the Neolithic Age, at least in Eurasia (10.5 kya), and man's first great economic leap forward.

The life of the hunter-gatherer has been variously depicted as "poor, nasty, brutish and short," if not actually "solitary," and as almost idyllic, involving a well-balanced diet, a twenty-hour workweek and high living standards.[25] L. S. Stavrianos, quoting Sahlins, writes that each one of Hobbes's adjectives has been replaced by its opposite, and that "food-gathering society is now viewed as 'the original affluent society,' whose members work 'bankers' hours' and enjoy healthy diets, economic security and a warm social life."[26]

We have little direct evidence of how they lived, and Stavrianos's view rests heavily on modern research into the life-styles of contemporary hunter-gatherers in southern Africa, the Arctic, the Amazon and the Australian deserts. But modern hunter-gatherers are not a good model, since they are forced to occupy marginal lands, though this does imply that early hunter-gatherers may have lived better. Such evidence as we have suggests that their physical stature was as variable as our own today. Their body weight was on average lower than people whose staple food is carbohydrate cereal, that is, most of modern Western society, though higher than malnourished Africans. Their probably high protein intake would have given them a high bone and muscle mass.

Life expectancy was below today's but not as bad as commonly supposed. If we accept the conventional view that the human metabolic rate indicates for creatures of our body and brain size a potential life expectancy of ninety years, the only thing that has changed in the last 10,000 years—and most of the change has been in the last 100—is the number of people who actually reach that potential. The highest mortality then as now would have been in early childhood, with a remission thereafter until people reached their fifties, when the immune system begins to wear out. As noted earlier, this might have meant a life expectancy at birth of thirty and at thirty of sixty.[27]

Most hunter-gatherers were nomadic, moving from site to site as supplies of suitable prey and/or gatherable foods ran low, though these migrations may have been circular, leaving time for each location to renew itself, sometimes assisted by the firing of dry landscapes. They may also on occasions have practiced cannibalism.[28] The hunting, which we presume to have been mainly done by the men because of their greater strength, relied on sticks, stones, spears, lances, javelins, slings, bows and arrows and, after 15 kya, blades, traps and fire. Man's ability to find food and shelter in new places was a precondition of his explosive diaspora around the world during the fifty millennia leading up to 10 kya. Large animals presented an attractively economic target because they were not necessarily more difficult to kill and their carcasses yielded a big return. There is some evidence that this effect was particularly marked in those areas, like the Americas, where man arrived somewhat suddenly and already equipped with mature hunting skills and developed weapons. The large animals had no previous experience of this threat and may have succumbed more easily and more rapidly than their like in Eurasia who had learned to fear man as man's skills evolved. For example, if you are being stalked by a hunter who has a bow and arrow, then you need to know that it is dangerous to let him come within arrow range, a much greater distance than that over which animals had previously been threatened by other animals (except perhaps plummeting birds of prey). Either way, large-bodied animals (elephants, horses, lions, cheetahs, camels, giant bison with a 6-foot horn spread, giant ground sloths, stag moose, musk oxen, mastodons and three types of mammoth) died off abruptly at about the time man arrived in the Americas.[29] Virtually all large creatures disappeared in Australia (giant kangaroos, rhinolike marsupials called diprotodonts as big as cows, marsupial leopards, a 400-pound ostrichlike flightless bird and large reptiles such as 1-ton lizards, giant pythons and land-dwelling crocodiles). In the main areas of Eurasia the die-off was less extreme, with extinction mainly reserved for mammoths and woolly rhinoceroses, but even the surviving species appear to have become scarcer and harder to hunt.[30]

This nearly worldwide (though apparently not in Africa) fall in the numbers of large animals coincided with sharp climate changes (especially sharp in Africa), which could account for the die-off. But the comparative immunity of big animals in Africa, where they had had the longest experience of human predators and therefore the longest opportunity to develop defensive strategies (e.g., running away at the first appearance of men) and where man's impact was most blunted by his own vulnerability to disease, suggests that man may have been the main agent of the destruction.[31] The discovery in modern Arizona of many mammoth skeletons with spearheads between their ribs and the coincidence within 100 years of the arrival of Clovis hunters in that area and the extinction of both mammoths and ground sloths look suspicious.*[32] If early American man in effect ate the available horses into extinction, he paid a terrible price 12,500 years later when Europeans arrived mounted on—and seemingly growing out of—their well-trained steeds.[33]

Early man had long been a proficient fisherman, and catching fish is the form of the hunting-gathering economy that survives most strongly to this day, since modern fisheries still predominantly depend on wild stocks and play little or no part in the breeding, protection and husbanding of species (pockets of fish-farming notwithstanding). Migratory fish

*Clovis hunters, so called because their large stone spearpoints were first found at a site near Clovis, New Mexico, have been proposed as the first "Americans." Their earliest sites so far discovered date from 14-13 kya, and the evidence suggests that they penetrated the whole of the Americas, North and South.

and sea creatures such as salmon and whales became over the next several millennia the focus of whole settled communities on the Pacific coast of North America. With weirs, nets, harpoons, bone hooks and other devices, these communities were able to harvest sufficient fish at the seasonal peaks to provide food year round.[34] Other sedentary or semipermanent communities in the era of predominant hunting-gathering were based on

- the regular migration routes of large herds of animals such as reindeer, horses and mammoths (possibly the economic base of the Magdalenian and Cro-Magnon societies that produced the cave paintings of southern France and northern Spain)[35]

- the harvesting, for example, by the Natufians in the Near East, of wild cereal crops such as wheat in exceptionally favorable locations, mainly in the western sector of the Fertile Crescent[36]

- established trade routes, again conspicuously in the Near East, for example at Jericho[37]

While the men were hunting and fishing, it seems probable that most of the gathering was done by the women, accompanied by their children. The exceptionally long period of the human child's dependence on its parents (possibly itself the basis, with language, for the transmission of extraordinary quantities of information and skills from generation to generation) disqualified women from the dangers and speed of the hunt. Gathering required highly developed knowledge of what to gather, where to find it and what its nutritive and medicinal uses might be. This division of labor in winning food also cemented the mutual dependence of the family members, since food from whichever source needed to be shared. This, too, may have tied the men more closely into the rearing and instructing of children, thereby again giving man an evolutionary advantage by sending the young forth into the world better prepared to survive.

It may well have been the women who made at least one of the two epochal discoveries that began the total transformation of man's economy from about this time (10 kya), namely, cultivation in the sense of the deliberate sowing, weeding, safeguarding and harvesting of specific crops, which thus became domesticated, being naturally selected to favor man's uses. There is no precise agreement among historians about exactly how, let alone with what motivation, man achieved this breakthrough. Climatic changes leading at least in the Near and Middle East to warmer and moister conditions followed the end of the ice ages. But in the 11–10 kya millennium much drier weather put a premium on helping nature to yield a harvest that no longer occurred in the wild. At the same time and across other parts of Eurasia, the developing scarcity of large game may have obliged man to look for substitute foods.[38] Most probably the development of cultivation was sparked by the natural observation and experimentation of those who were already engaged in gathering wild crops, reinforced perhaps by an increased dependency of the family group on new food sources. The change was intimately bound up with the progressive adoption at about this time of a settled or sedentary life-style and with population growth.

A plausible reconstruction of how settlement, cultivation and population trends may have interacted during this period might go as follows: Hunter-gatherer societies were geared to very low or nil population growth, but the species itself could and did grow (at slightly under one person annually per 10,000 of population 12 kya) by expanding into new habitable territories through the formation of new bands and communities.[39] In exceptionally favorable locations—astride early trade routes, by abnormally well-endowed fishing grounds and where climate and soil conditions offered such an abundance of vegetable food that supplies were never exhausted and there was no need to move on in search of new supplies—a few communities did settle, enjoying the advantages of sedentary life in larger families and permanent homes and other installations. Some of these began to notice the natural habit of certain forms of plant life, notably wheat, and discovered how to support it by sowing, weeding, watering and selecting. When the climate grew colder and drier in the Near East, these communities were forced to intensify their efforts at cultivation in order to feed already settled communities, which would have been reluctant and ill equipped to return to a nomadic life. Cultivation thus became a necessity rather than just an embellishment of nature. Its success in raising output, in supporting preferable life-styles of settled communities and in encouraging population growth combined to recommend it to the much larger groups of hunter-gatherers who had not yet converted to agriculture and to spread the new economic system by purely Darwinian selection: Those who did it survived and prospered more than those who did not.

The cultivation of crops was only one of the two developments that supported what has come to be known as the agricultural revolution from about 10 kya. The other, which may have followed as much as a millennium later and in which the men may have joined more actively with the women, was the domestication of animals as an aid to man's economic requirements, both as a source of food and materials in themselves and as otherwise useful to carry, to pull, to guard, to be milked, to be ridden in battle and in the hunt and to befriend. Experience was to prove that only a limited number of large (over 100-pound) animals were suitable for domestication, probably because few species exhibited all the essential characteristics:

- They had to be herbivorous (carnivores require too much food per unit of edible carcass). Dogs are omnivorous and not normally eaten. Cats were domesticated not for food but as solitary hunters of vermin and as pets.
- They had to grow quickly enough to give the farmer a return within a reasonable period.
- They had to be willing to breed in captivity.
- They could not be likely to kill their keepers (otherwise the hippopotamus could have been a prolific source of milk).
- They could not be likely to destroy themselves in their efforts to escape captivity.
- They had to have a social structure, such as the herd, that made them easily led and managed by men.

Lack of one or more of these qualities disqualified 134 out of 148 seemingly eligible large mammal species, leaving only what have turned out to be the "major five" (sheep, goats, cattle, pigs and horses) and the "minor nine" (Arabian and Bactrian camels, donkeys, llamas, reindeer, water buffalo, yak, Bali cattle and mithan).* All were domesticated between 10

*Bali cattle and mithan are relatives of the aurochs and are still used as domestic animals in India and Southeast Asia.

and 4.5 kya, and no species has been added since. Wolves had been bred into dogs a little earlier, 13 kya.[40]

This double revolution—the cultivation of the land and the herding of edible and useful animals—transformed man's primary systems for feeding himself and supplying his other needs. Its effect was to increase manyfold the energy—food, drink, fuel and animal muscle power—that man could extract from his physical environment, thereby laying the foundations for two decisive strategic consequences:

- the sustenance of a hugely increased and rapidly increasing global population
- the generation of surpluses, that is, of more food and other energy than was required simply to sustain the effort of producing it, thus providing energy for other human activities and food for specialists in those activities, which then became the early stirrings of what we recognize as civilization

The agricultural revolution was first seen, so far as we know, in the Fertile Crescent, which stretched in an arc from the head of the Persian Gulf northwest through the higher ground north of the Tigris, then westward and southward through southern Turkey and western Syria before passing through Lebanon and Israel to the headwaters of the Gulf of Aqaba. But this was not the only place where agriculture was invented. It seems to have evolved quite separately and with equal inventiveness in China (c. 9 kya), Central America (c. 5 kya), South America (Andes and Amazon basin, c. 5 kya), sub-Saharan Africa (c. 4 kya) and Southeast Asia (date uncertain, somewhere between 9 and 3 kya).[41] These independent but similar occurrences at the hands of a single species spread out through the habitable world chime elegantly, if not definitively, with our picture of modern man, having survived the last of the ice ages and newly equipped with his transformed brain, developed language(s) and conspicuous adaptability, setting about subduing his environment so as to extend his own success, whether by multiplying his own number or by enhancing his individual control, comfort and—the word begins to thrust itself forward—wealth. In short, an improved species begins to fulfill its potential at the first climatic opportunity.

It is important, however, not to become teleological about how and why all this happened, in other words not to assume or imply that it happened because people consciously saw an opportunity for economic advance and therefore took it. That, by and large, is not how things happen in human affairs, as Charles Darwin and Adam Smith in their different ways—with natural selection and by the invisible hand—were later at pains to explain. Macrochange is not induced by conscious design and intent, not anyway until human intelligence and the relevant social science have advanced to the point where man can be conscious of such things and at least dream of influencing them (although even then, as we Fall know, the best-laid plans of macromen and macromice "*gang aft agley*"). The agricultural revolutions of the post-ice-age, early Neolithic Period—and its equivalents in places other than the Fertile Crescent—did not bring immediate improvements in living standards. Although we may presume that each individual was doing what made sense to him, subject to the customs and rules of the band and wider community within which he lived, it is clear that for many people the new methods of food production meant deterioration in diet. The agricultural revolution seems to have brought an end to the bankers' hours reported by Sahlins and the beginning of a crushing work burden that has remained the lot of most people for the rest of human prehistory and history.[42]

The forces that actually caused agriculture gradually to replace hunting and gathering as man's primary economic activity were impersonal and unconscious. We have already seen that supplies of wild food, especially huntable animals, declined, and there is plenty of evidence from Pacific islands in more recent times that it was only when men had exterminated the available sea and land animals and birds that they turned to more intensive methods, domesticating chickens and cultivating crops. Second, climate changes greatly encouraged the growth, originally in the wild, of cereals that could be harvested in bulk, and these in due course lent themselves to the first domestication (e.g., wheat and barley) in places like the Fertile Crescent. These natural supplies had already encouraged technological developments—methods of harvesting, dehusking and storing grain—that in turn fostered the cultivation of such crops. Fourth, population growth both raised the demand for food and resulted from increased supplies as agriculture became more productive, thus reinforcing the demand for yet more production in a self-propelling cycle.

Last, of course, the agricultural life led people to live in more concentrated settlements that, if nothing else, equipped them through sheer numbers to overpower any of the more thinly spread hunter-gatherers with whom they came into conflict.[43]

At this point in the story, as the agricultural revolution was fulfilling itself over several millennia from about 10 kya, we encounter the beginnings of the next great departure in human economic history: concentrated dwelling arrangements starting with the village. There had, of course, been villages in preagricultural societies, where particular forms of hunting (such as trapping migratory reindeer and seasonal fishing) and gathering (in especially fertile locations) or habitual trade routes permitted the nomadic life to be abandoned. But it was the spread of agriculture that made the village the archetype of man's abode for the rest of history. One hunter-gatherer needed something like 10 square miles of favorable territory to make a living, whereas even the earliest agriculture could support over fifty people on a single square mile, a ratio of more than 500:1. The concentration and fixity of food supplies naturally led to permanent residences and denser numbers in each community—in other words to the village. Where hunter-gatherer society typically consisted of migrating bands of thirty to fifty people, simple farming could support villages of hundreds—and in due course more intensive farming (based on plowing and irrigation) supported towns of thousands.[44]

This development both enabled and was reinforced by the beginnings of specialization. Again, the very first specialists doubtless go back well before village life, with recognized members of the band having special authority on such matters as the spirit world and its propitiation, the medicinal use of herbs and other natural materials and the telling of the time and the seasons from observation of the heavens. But a village, particularly if the surrounding fields are generating a surplus of food above what is necessary to feed the families of those working in them, provides a convenient place where people supplying some service other than food production can both live and find a market for their services sufficient to furnish them with a full-time, or perhaps at first part-time, living.

If each farmworker in a village of 100 workers devotes 1 percent of his produce to feeding the family of the man who keeps the spirit world happy or the sick suitably dosed, or who builds the best shelters or makes the best clothes, then the division of labor has begun, and it is the size and fixity of the village compared with the dispersed and moving band that has made this possible. Temples and those who served them were an obvious priority in a world where man seemed powerless in the face of gigantic impersonal forces dominating almost every aspect of his welfare. As Philip Curtin has pointed out, temples attract crowds, which in turn attract those who want to do business with the crowds, merchants and retailers. Before long they attract politicians, too, but we run a little ahead.[45]

Permanent settlements in favorable locations swiftly followed the first agriculture from about 9 kya in the western part of the Fertile Crescent. Settlements in dry farming areas, together with more far-reaching trade and the first kiln-fired pottery, start less than 1,000 years later both in the central Fertile Crescent at Hassuna close to the Tigris and further east, thus establishing in the northeastern corner of the crescent the Hassuna culture (8.5–8 kya), which was supported by barley, sheep, goats, pigs and cattle and distinguished by fine painted pottery and specially built kilns. This was displaced about 8 kya by the Halafian culture (8–7.4 kya), which embraced the whole northern section of the crescent and was ruled by chiefs who amassed considerable personal wealth in the form of pottery, jewelry, sculpture and tools of both flint and obsidian. We are told that as a result of the Neolithic/agricultural revolution, the population of the area that is modern Iraq increased "from something under 10,000 to something over 100,000, though as the change was spread over the whole of the period from the 7th to the 5th century [9–6 kya] it is better described as evolutionary than revolutionary."[46] We should not, however, lose sight of the importance of the continuing hunter-gatherer communities that interacted with the new settlements and diffused raw materials and ideas, especially in the crescent:

> Their regular cycles of movement, taking their flocks to new grazing, brought them in contact with different groups of people in different ecological niches and seem to have provided a crucial channel of communication through which goods and ideas could flow, linking more isolated groups of people over considerable distances. Later, with the development of more complex societies and of writing, this role was to a large extent taken over by urban specialists, merchants, scribes, messengers.[47]

The simultaneous Samarran culture (8–7.5 kya) to the immediate south of Hassuna pioneered large-scale irrigation, including canals that opened up the dry plains of central Mesopotamia to settlement. The Ubaid culture (7.9–6.3 kya), cultivating the flood plain of the Tigris and Euphrates from the future site of Ur in the east to the Mediterranean coast in the west, replaced the Halafian culture in the north from 7.4 kya, though the population was not yet totally dependent on irrigation, and a considerable section was still seminomadic.[48]

Places like Eridu, near the future site of Ur on what were then the headwaters of the Persian Gulf, were centers of religion for surrounding villages and may have exercised special authority either through a priesthood or more prosaically through control of trade and/or irrigation. They became the first towns from about 7 kya. Not long after 7 kya local centers appeared in the Near East, and by 6.5 kya regional centers appeared on the eastern extremities of the crescent.

At this time productivity was boosted by the invention of the plow.[49] The sail and the potter's wheel were also in use. Farming became intensive, and villages multiplied, some of them with temples of increasing size. As important as, and in some ways much more so than, the invention of the plow was the development before 6.3 kya of an accounting system recorded on clay tokens, which can fairly be regarded as the origin of writing. The quickening pace of change and its importance in man's whole economic story is emphasized by Crawford, who writes of the Uruk period (6.3–5.2 kya): "Technologically, it was a time of rapid and important changes. . . . The Uruk period was arguably the most innovative and important of any in the history of Mesopotamia and its influence was felt as far as the Mediterranean and the Anatolian plateau."[50]

The scene was set in southern Mesopotamia for the next leap forward. From about 5.5 kya a little to the north and west of Eridu but still in southern Iraq, the world's first city, Uruk, appeared. Its population grew from 10,000 to perhaps 50,000 by about 4.9 kya. The largest of several cities, it became the seat of the first empire, Sumeria.[51] We are told that "during the middle centuries of the 3rd millennium [c. 4.5 kya] the population of Sumer surged up to the half-million mark, its villages became towns and the towns became the political powers of the area."[52]

Climate changes contributed, perhaps decisively, to this rapid development, according to Nissen:

> The climatic changes documented for the middle of the fourth millennium [c. 5.5 kya] seem, within a space of two to three hundred years, to have stemmed the floods that regularly covered large tracts of land and to have drained such large areas that in a relatively short period of time large parts of Babylonia, particularly throughout the south, became attractive for new permanent settlements. . . .
>
> The net result was that Babylonia was now much more densely settled than any other part of the Near East had ever been. . . . This was one result of the necessity to employ irrigation, the basic techniques of which had long been known, but which never previously had to be used so systematically. As noted, however, irrigation in the earlier periods looked quite different from the way we usually imagine it to have looked in Babylonia. Even though by this time the water had receded so much that the land had become habitable, there was nonetheless for some considerable time so much water still available that nearly every arable plot had easy and direct access to it. This fact, together with Babylonia's extremely fertile soil, must have produced a "paradise," with multiple, high-yield harvests each year.[53]

Crawford is clear that water supply was determining the location of the new permanent settlements:[54] "Because of the imperatives of irrigation techniques, early settlement tended to concentrate in fairly narrow bands along the river courses, sometimes three or four towns quite close together, sometimes one large city, like Uruk, with a necklace of smaller satellite towns or villages."[55]

In other parts of the world, too, cities were developing. They appeared in the Nile valley from 5.1 kya, and by 4.575 kya Snofru's fourth dynasty had founded the Old Kingdom of Egypt at Memphis.[56] Villages appeared in Baluchistan, west of the Indus basin, from 8 kya; cities emerged in the Indus valley from 4.6 kya, and shortly afterward (4.3 kya) Sumerian records suggest that trade was flowing between the Indus and the Euphrates. In China wet-rice farming villages spread from 8.5–6 kya; towns and complex fortifications developed from about 5 kya. From the foundation of the Shang dynasty by King Tang (3.766 kya) cities with monumental buildings indisputably appeared, though Chinese tradition unsupported by archaeological finds pushes Chinese "civilization" back to the first emperor Hung Di (4.7 kya).[57] In the Americas Peru had permanent fishing villages from 5.5 kya and Mexico had permanent farming villages from 4.3 kya. Temples and ceremonial centers were grafted onto villages from about 4.6 kya at Aspero in Peru, though true towns and cities seem to be unknown before the Olmec civilization in Mexico (3.25–2.4 kya).

The history of the early cradle of human development (the Fertile Crescent plus Egypt and eastern Anatolia) was dominated for about three and a third millennia from 6.3 kya by a new and—to the eye of the fastidious economic historian—nasty phenomenon: politics, in the sense of a struggle for power within and between communities. Of course, something that we might be willing to call politics must have been commonplace in every human gathering larger than the family (and indeed within families) as long as what we recognize as modern man, with his enhanced brain capacity and command of language and abstract thought, had been around, since about 30 kya.

But equally obvious, the whole business of human relationships in terms of command over people (politics) and things (economics) changes radically once (1) the number of people involved in a typical living and working location rises from tens to hundreds and then to thousands and tens of thousands and (2) the production system is generating a substantial surplus of output above what is necessary simply to keep the food producers and their families going. Suddenly, as it were, the numbers to argue with are multiplied and the number of arguments increases geometrically. Suddenly also (we are still speaking of millennia), there is real surplus wealth to argue about; and argument leads to conflict. People start to specialize in the whole embryonic business of politics, government and war—in short, proto-rulers, proto-politicians and proto generals arise. Crawford puts it this way: "Specialisation of this sort led in its turn to a more stratified society with an unequal distribution of wealth and status, a development which can be traced both in the architecture and in the graves. There also seems to have been an increase in the scale of warfare as the concentration of resources led some communities to become noticeably richer than their neighbours."[58]

Fights, skirmishes, raids and even minor battles were no doubt normal throughout the era of the hunter-gatherers, however idyllic their lifestyle may mostly have been. But war is something else. War takes organization, substantial forces, big disputes, sustained leadership and, in today's language, money, that is, command over more men and materiel than lie to the hand of the village elder rushing out of his hut at the first sound of alarm and calling upon his neighbors to form a posse. War is political, in its goals, in its causes, in its conduct, in its financing and in its consequences.

We are now face to face with the first manifestation of the waltz motif in economic history. By the agricultural revolution man had taken the first step, a step forward in his economic capacity. From the surplus wealth that engendered and from the possibility of concerted human military effort concentrated village and town life permitted flowed the second step: war. As a means of advancing the attainment of human economic goals more rapidly than waiting for the next breakthrough in production technology, war offered swifter and more ample returns.

The opportunity was seized. Between the early Uruk period (5.5 kya), when the Sumerian empire first exhibited to men the possible fruits of city- and town-based civilizations, and 3 kya, when recorded history conventionally begins and this chapter ends, the three-pointed star of the Levant, Anatolia and Mesopotamia managed numerous empires and numberless warlike campaigns. It is hard not to sympathize with Douglass North's resigned admission that Mesopotamia in this period was "invaded and overrun by Indo-Europeans (Hittites) and Semites (Amorites); *as a result there was a bewildering succession of rulers and empires of varying size.*"[59]

The main empires were

- Sumeria (6.3–4.35 kya) in southeastern Iraq
- Akkadia, founded by Sargon the Great, from 4.334 to 4.004 kya, when its chief city, Ur, was sacked
- the Old Babylonian and Old Assyrian periods under different rulers from 1.9 to 1.7 or 1.6 kya in southern and northern Mesopotamia, respectively
- the Middle Assyrian empire from 3.4 to 3.0 kya, when, neatly enough for the historian, desert Arameans and Chaldeans from the empty area within the arc of the Fertile Crescent invaded Mesopotamia, overthrew the Assyrian empire and, in 1000 B.C., occupied Ur

Neo-Assyrian and Neo-Babylonian empires appeared in the next millennium. But already the previous millennium had produced countless military campaigns (though far fewer and far less destructive than those of the next millennium in that area, let alone those that hypermodern man has achieved in the last century, not to mention the last millennium). Not least of these were

- Hammurabi setting out to all points of the compass from Babylon between 3.787 and 3.757 kya
- Hittite campaigns from Anatolia against Babylon around 3.595 kya
- Suppiluliumas's Hittite campaigns west, south and southeast from Anatolia into western Turkey, northern Mesopotamia and the Levant 3.334–3.323 kya
- Adad-nirari's Assyrian campaigns in today's northern Iraq (3.305–3.274 kya)
- Shalmeneser I's campaigns north from Assyria toward the Caucasus (3.273–3.244 kya)
- Tukulti-Ninurta I's campaigns eastward and southeast to Babylon (3.243–3.207 kya)
- Tiglath-pileser I's Assyrian campaigns northwest as far as Turkey's modern borders, west to the Mediterranean in modern Lebanon and southeast to Babylon (3.115–3.076)[60]

The third step of the waltz was, as it always tends to be, the political settlement that for the time being adjusts—or fudges—the conflict between the original step forward and the sideways or backward step forced upon the dancer by the darker temptations to which the step forward has exposed him. Wealth is created. Wealth is a magnet for theft and violence. Society tries to make rules. This three-step movement led to the establishment of empires that lasted for hundreds of years. Unprecedented economic achievements were registered and used to support religious, artistic and political endeavors that man had never seen or dreamt before.

In an economic history we have no need to describe these in detail. Nonetheless it should command our wonder that up to 3,000 years before Homer, twice as long before Christ as he was before us and six times longer ago than William the Conqueror, a great city existed. It stood at the crossroads of sea- and land-borne trade near the head of the Persian Gulf. Thousands of people not directly engaged in farming were being supported by an intensively farmed hinterland. Produce was being daily carried to the city and exchanged, formally or in effect, for services obtained there, or perhaps as a form of tribute to priestly and other rulers. We have evidence of markets and fluctuating prices in Mesopotamia by 5 kya, possibly alongside other forms of exchange such as reciprocal giving and swapping. And this economic activity was orchestrated through the central agency of a temple, which received tribute and supplied those it considered deserving.[61]

Prices presuppose money, and although we find no coins before about 2.65 kya, it is clear that precious metals measured by weight were being used as a medium of exchange and settlement, as well as a store of wealth and a measure of value, as of 4.3 kya.[62] Crawford spells it out more precisely, and we can see that words like "money" and "price," when applied to these remote times, have at best a metaphorical force:

> A money economy was not in use during the fourth and third millennia, but there was a well regulated system of exchanges. The value of one article was expressed in terms of its worth in some standard commodity such as copper. At the beginning of the Early Dynastic period [5 kya] goods were "priced" in terms of copper, but later in the third millennium [4–5 kya] silver became the medium of exchange. And we know from archaeological finds that silver was hoarded (store of wealth).[63]

By the beginning of the fourth millennium ago (4 kya), we find silver being used in Mesopotamia as money, with local laws laying down penalties, benchmark prices for common goods and lending rates (at 20 percent per annum). To facilitate their use as money, silver and other metals were made into large ingots, cut into small scraps or drawn out into thin wire and made into rings of fixed weight so that they could be easily measured out in the settlement of transactions.[64]

Monumental architecture, essentially temples and palaces, already existed by about 5.2 kya in Uruk where the Eanna temple enclosure within an encircling wall boasted three temples, a palace, a pillared hall, a great court and other buildings. Temples at Eridu and Uqair were erected on massive terraces and richly decorated with geometric designs and mosaics. The value obviously attached to these huge constructions—and the agricultural surplus required to provide the resources to put them up—attests to the conscious pride that these communities and in particular their rulers must have invested in the building and rebuilding over the centuries of ever bigger and better ziggurats.

Indeed, temples were the key to much of the economic life of Sumerian civilization. In some cities the priests were the rulers. But even where distinct secular rulers had been established in a neighboring palace and the temple merely housed the god of the city and his priests, it still seems often to have been a prime mover in the cultivation of crops, vegetables and fruit trees, in organized irrigation and the management of sheep, goats and fisheries and in both manufacturing and trade beyond the immediate vicinity. Thus the earliest development of what we can recognize as city and regional states must have begun, with some kind of political authority emanating from the hold that the god and his temple exercised over the minds of simple people.

Less spiritual factors may also have been at work. McNeill writes:

> Lassitude and chronic malaise . . . of the kind induced by blood fluke and similar parasitic infections, conduce to successful invasion by the only kind of large-bodied predators human beings have to fear: their own kind, armed and organized for war and conquest. . . . How important parasitic infection of agricultural field workers may have been in facilitating the erection of the social hierarchies of early river civilizations cannot be estimated very plausibly. But it seems reasonable to suspect that the despotic governments characteristic of societies dependent on irrigation agriculture may have owed something to the debilitating diseases that afflicted field workers who kept their feet wet much of the time, as well as to the technical requirements of water management and control which have hitherto been used to explain the phenomenon.[65]

Uruk's White Temple to the west of the Eanna complex was certainly a focus of what was then the largest human settlement in the world.[66] Its inhabitants were very different people, economically, culturally and politically, from the simpler hunter-gatherers who had first begun to domesticate animals and crops five millennia earlier. They had accumulated wealth that was previously inconceivable, and though it originally belonged to the community or its rulers or to families rather than individuals, the concept and the fact of private ownership spread between 5 and 4 kya. By the end of that millennium, private enterprise had taken over much of the trade that was previously the preserve of the state.[67]

The people of Uruk had also stumbled upon the division of labor and the investment of saved surpluses in objects, chiefly tools and structures, of future utility. They had developed and expanded exchange and trade to the point where markets, money and prices hugely enhanced their efficiency by radically reducing the costs of each transaction (costs of finding a customer or supplier, of judging value and of settling) and where cities as well as towns were supported by surrounding rural areas as well as by more distant sources such as quarries for stone to build their temples and palaces. Exotic materials like alabaster, carnelian, chlorite, mother of pearl, lapis lazuli, marble, obsidian, turquoise and copper were imported into Mesopotamia over many hundreds of miles from the Caucasus, modern Iran and Afghanistan.[68] Aesthetic sensibility, allied to religious feeling, had expanded from the cave art of the earliest beneficiaries of *Homo sapiens sapiens*' improved brain to encompass architecture, sculpture, mosaics, jewelry, curious stone engraving and fine bronze and other metalworking.[69]

Most importantly, they had mastered the miracle of irrigation, both the engineering disciplines and the human and political organization required to build and operate a system requiring a colossal initial investment and a breathtakingly wide coordination of the conduct of thousands of communities. North notes the first: "The capital involved in an irrigation system must be acquired; canals, for example, dug and maintained; drainage systematically organized; and sluices and floodgates arranged so water is distributed over the area to be irrigated."[70] McNeill, whose perspective is global, notes the second:

> Insofar as early agriculture depended on irrigation, as was the case in Mesopotamia and Egypt as well as in the Indus River valley and in the Peruvian coastal region, more elaborate social controls than those ordinarily needed in a simple, more or less isolated village, were required. Planning of canals and dykes, cooperation in their maintenance, and above all, allocation of irrigation water

among competing users, all invited or required some sort of authoritative leadership. Cities and civilizations resulted, characterized by far wider co-ordination of effort and specialization of skills than anything village life permitted.[71]

After about 5 kya Mesopotamia became drier. This and other climate changes altered the economic geography of the area in ways that contributed to the development of the first city-state empires. Nissen explains:

As the recession [of the waters] continued . . . it must finally have had a tremendous effect on an agricultural economy that relied exclusively on artificial irrigation, so that during the Early Dynastic I period [5–4.75 kya] settlements were no longer scattered over wide areas of the whole country, but assembled along a few water courses. In addition the river courses not only seem to run in a straightened line, but, in some cases, water courses branch off them that are so straight that they resemble, for the first time, the lines of canals.[72]

From 4.8 to 4.25 kya, the level of the gulf fell. Rivers cut more deeply into the plain, and more effort was needed to irrigate the land, leading eventually to the development of the enormous Mesopotamian canal system. Crawford sums up the centralizing effects this eventually had on Mesopotamia. She explains that the Early Dynastic period (periods I–III, i.e., 5–4.35 kya) is

usually regarded as when the political concept of the city-state first took shape. The history of the time, in so far as it is possible to reconstruct it, is marked by the shifting of political power from one to another of the major cities on the Sumerian plain. The cities seem to have been ruled by governors or princes, possibly with the help of some sort of assembly of citizens. The ruler had military, judicial and religious duties and the power of the temple is apparently less than it had been in the Uruk period [6–5.2 kya], though the temple continued to be a major landowner and a vital part of the economy. The secular and religious aspects of the state seem to have been in some sort of balance. In the Agade period which followed [4.35–4.15 kya], it was, for the first time, the secular power which was the dominant influence: for the first time, too, the whole of the Sumerian plain was united under one conqueror, the great Sargon of Agade.[73]

Although the evidence is far from clear-cut and varies from city to city, it seems that what we would recognize as more secular rulers, separate from the temples, appeared somewhat later than this Uruk period, most notably King Sargon the Great of Agade, close to the later Babylon, the founder of the Akkadian empire (4.334–4.193 kya). But however political authority was shared between temple and palace, they played between them the dominant role in the economic life of the society until Mesopotamia was infiltrated by the Amorite people from the south after about 4 kya, though some authorities see their arrival as simply a consequence of an underlying deterioration in the fertility of southern Mesopotamia as the saltwater table rose too close to the surface and killed the crops. Sumerian societies certainly failed, and their language was progressively displaced by newly arriving Semitic speakers, becoming a dead language by 3.8 kya.

The Amorites established a dynasty at Babylon, launching the Old Babylonian period, and produced as their sixth king Hammurabi (3.792–3.750 kya), to whom is attributed the legal code whose 282 clauses were carved on a rock column in Babylon. Under this dispensation the economic role of the state shrank, and temples were no longer the main source of funds for investment. Independent merchants called *tamkaru* became the chief players in trade, moneylending and other entrepreneurial activities. Although the ruling government levied taxes and still traded directly in food, most trade was now conducted by these private merchants, if not the first private sector in history, then after the people of Uruk certainly the second.[74] Indeed, Runciman has drawn a bold and striking comparison between Babylon in this period and England a century before the Norman conquest. State and private roles were interwoven in these agrarian societies:

> Two large, literate, prosperous agrarian societies which are quite remarkably alike, despite being many hundreds of years and miles apart in time and place, are England in the tenth century A.D. and Babylonia in the eighteenth century B.C. An Anglo-Saxon king, bishop, landowner, merchant, peasant, craftsman, soldier, priest, clerk, tax-collector, schoolteacher, servant or slave would be immediately at home in Hammurabi's Babylon, and vice versa. In both societies, there were royal and ecclesiastical estates side by side with private land-holdings, taxes paid to the king as well as dues to the church or temple, private cap-

> italists engaged in long-distance trade for profit, an active land market, tenancy and serfdom as well as slavery and the possibility of manumission for debt-slaves, written law codes, local agents of royal power liable for military or auxiliary service, administration of justice at village level, and for women, subordinate though they generally were, a right to retain a dowry and bequeath it in due course to a child or children.[75]

Yet it was not the Amorite dynasty in old Babylon but the Assyrians in Ashur, about 215 miles to the north and west, who took the next step down this road, institutionalizing the merchants as a powerful estate of the realm. There are written records of an Assyrian ruler after 4 kya whose power was shared with three groups: the elders, the "town" and the *karum,* or quay. Evidently the latter were the merchants, gathered as it were on the local rialto, and they administered the city's commerce, levied taxes on the local copper trade, lent funds to individuals and rented out space in their warehouses. In this we can see, if we like, the first deposit bank, "world" trade center, clearinghouse and chamber of commerce, as well as a guild both exercising quasi-governmental powers and seeking the private interests of its members. Perhaps it was indeed the first quasi-nongovernmental organization, blurring the modern distinction between the supposedly accountable sphere of the state and the nonaccountable sphere of private action.[76]

The Ashur *karum* was at the center of a trade network reaching through merchant settlements as far away as Kanesh in Anatolian Cappadocia, which were in turn hubs of local networks of as many as twenty other settlements throughout their regions. Gold, silver and copper drew the Assyrian merchants to the Anatolian highlands, while the tin that was essential for making bronze was brought from the Iranian plateau and textiles from Babylon. The relationship between these essentially state-sanctioned private enterprises and the state itself expressed fundamental economic logic, namely, that by a variety of means the palace got paid for the official protection it gave to the traffic. As today, the state policed the roads, helped creditors to get paid, borrowed from (and occasionally lent to) affluent citizens and insisted on being supplied at the best prices. At the same time the state was aware that if it bore too heavily upon local business, that business would migrate elsewhere. This is perhaps the earliest example of what is currently called "regulatory competition."[77]

In short, supply and demand ruled through the signals emitted by highly sensitive prices, while political authority sought to tap into the flow of wealth without extracting too much more than the market value of the protection it provided. Much of the subsequent history of political economy and the relationship between the public and private sectors of more recent economies was prefigured in this Old Assyrian period in northern Mesopotamia. The later history of this region up to 3 kya witnesses the Hittite sack of Babylon (3.595 kya), inaugurating a "dark age" succeeded by the Middle Assyrian empire, which lasted until 3.076 kya with little significant economic innovation.

Since noting the early spread of villages in other parts of the world between 8 and 9 kya, we have focused almost exclusively on the civilizations of Mesopotamia and its neighboring areas. We have as yet said nothing about the contribution to man's economic march of two millennia of Egyptian history, from the founding of the First Dynasty at the beginning of the Early Dynastic period (5.1 kya), through the Old and Middle Kingdoms to the fall of the Twentieth Dynasty at the end of the New Kingdom in 3.069 kya.[78] Nor have we yet touched on events in China at this time, or indeed on the Indus valley civilization between 4.6 and 3.8 kya.

Ancient Egypt depended entirely on the Nile. The river's narrow floodplain, which is never more than a few miles wide, was probably the most favorable area for agriculture anywhere in the ancient world. The annual floods subsided by the late summer, enabling crops to be grown in the fertile soil during the warm winter and harvested in spring before flooding resumed. The river was also Egypt's main highway, while the desert on either side protected Egypt from invaders. Indeed, Egyptian civilization had existed for 1,300 years before it suffered its first invasion.[79] Its relative isolation, however, also explains why Mesopotamia, which had much greater contact with other peoples from the outset, had a bigger impact on mankind's early economic development.

The Nile valley's first farmers date from before 8 kya, with the first chiefdoms and towns originating about 5.3 kya. Egypt's emergence as a single state dates back to the period between 5.1 and 4.686 kya, when it seems that desertification and the growing concentration of population along the Nile increased the need for irrigation. This, in turn, encouraged the rise of local rulers and eventually, as their territories merged, to two coalitions or kingdoms, based respectively in Upper and Lower Egypt.

About 5 kya, the ruler of Upper Egypt, Narmer, conquered Lower Egypt. The foundation of the capital at Memphis, in Upper Egypt, consolidated Egypt's unification.[80]

What we now regard as the hallmarks of Egyptian civilization—hieroglyphic script and massive pyramid tombs—date from the first 500-year phase of Egyptian unity during the Old Kingdom, 4.686–4.181 kya. The construction of the 482-foot-high Great Pyramid, for the pharaoh Khofu, marked the climax of pyramid building. In addition to bearing graphic testimony to the immense power that the pharaohs had over their subjects and to the efficacy of their governmental bureaucracy, the pyramids exerted an enormous strain on the resources of an agrarian economy. Although pyramid construction was subsequently scaled down, the latter half of the Old Kingdom saw the diversion of massive resources into the construction of temples that were inspired by worship of the sun-god, Ra.[81]

Nobody knows for certain why the Old Kingdom collapsed, although a period of low floods around 4.150 kya brought famine and starvation and helped to undermine the monarchy's already dwindling authority. Egypt endured about a century of civil war before unity was restored 4.060 kya under Mentuhotep II. During the next 300 years (known as the Middle Kingdom period), Egypt expanded its economic and political horizons, trading and building contacts with the Levant and launching military expeditions to the south. But central rule again broke down 3.730 kya, and during 3.648–3.552 kya most of Egypt, apart from a small independent southern kingdom at Thebes, fell to the invading Hyksos, a Semitic people from the Levant. The foreign influences introduced by the Hyksos enhanced Egypt's economic development. Bronze-working and two-wheeled chariots were probably introduced during this period, as were new weapons (the composite bow and scale armor), new fashions, musical instruments, domestic animals and crops.[82]

The demise of the Hyksos 3.552 kya and the return to Egyptian self-rule ushered in the New Kingdom, which lasted for almost 500 years and during which ancient Egypt reached its political and economic zenith. The militaristic leader Tuthmosis I (who ruled 3.507–3.494 kya) conquered the Levant, making the Euphrates his easternmost frontier and thereby creating a vast buffer zone against invasion from the Middle East. In the south, however, his motives for expansion were economic. Nubia's rich gold deposits prompted Tuthmosis to reconquer Lower Nubia; Kush was occupied as far south as the Nile's fourth cataract. A quarter of a century later, the Egyptian quest for riches prompted Queen Hatshepsut to send a trading expedition to east Africa.[83] Today the fabulous treasures of Tutankhamen (who reigned 3.333–3.323 kya) provide us with a compelling evocation of the wealth and artistic richness of the New Kingdom.

But despite enjoying the material benefit of Nubian wealth, the Egyptians struggled to maintain their grip on the Levant, and they were eventually ousted by the Hittites ten years after the end of Tutankhamen's reign.[84] Even Rameses II, "the Great" (who ruled 3.290–3.224 kya), during whose leadership ancient Egypt probably achieved its greatest wealth and influence, had to make peace with the Hittites after his advance on the Levant had been halted at Qadesh.[85] Only twenty years or so after the end of Rameses II's reign, the entire Near East was disrupted by great migrations of peoples. Around 3.180 kya Egypt was invaded by a coalition of sea peoples from the Aegean, Anatolia and the Levant who eventually settled at Gaza after Rameses III defeated them off the Nile Delta. But internal disputes further weakened the New Kingdom, and the empire was lost by 3 kya. After the period covered in this chapter there followed more than 300 years of disunity and foreign rule.[86]

All in all, the Sumerian and subsequent civilizations of the Near and Middle East must rank among mankind's most spectacular achievements. At the beginning, however much we now disdain the word and acknowledge the subtleties and felicities of the hunter-gatherer's life-style, men were savages. At the end they were civilized, and they had established a platform of human progress from which subsequent developments to the east in Persia and India and to the west in Europe were launched, either literally or figuratively.

CHAPTER TWO

Citizenship

BY 1000 B.C. (THE END OF CHAPTER 1), THE HUMAN RACE HAD progressed, we estimated, to a global population of about 40 million distributed throughout almost all the world's habitable regions (apart from Madagascar and New Zealand).[1] Best guesses at the population of Europe by this time put it at about 10 million, a quarter of the global total.

By 400 B.C. Europe's population was probably almost 20 million, within a global total of 150 million. [2] Four centuries later, Europe's population had risen to about 25 million in an even more rapidly growing global total of 250 million.[3]

But the next millennium produced sharp fluctuations. The world's population in A.D. 1000 was much the same as it had been ten centuries earlier. But it fell to just over 200 million in A.D. 600. In Europe, the numbers rose to 36 million in A.D. 200, then fell by about a quarter by A.D. 600, before ending the millennium at much the same level as they had started, 36 million. Over the same period, Asia saw its population fall from 170 million to 134 million in A.D. 600 before partially recovering to 152 million by A.D. 1000. In short the widespread progress of the species, as measured by its numbers, seems to have been dramatically interrupted for the next eight centuries.

The thread of economic advance and leadership in the central Eurasian area, which seemed to have been lost in Mesopotamia and Egypt during the second millennium B.C., passed for a while to the Phoenicians.* They were a seafaring people, who reputedly linked Sumer to Upper Egypt via the Persian Gulf, the Indian Ocean and the Red Sea; circumnavigated Africa; and fetched tin from Cornwall.

They had established themselves as formidable merchants from as early as the third millennium B.C., and from 1000 B.C. they began to colonize the central and western Mediterranean from their bases in Tyre and Ugarit on the eastern Mediterranean coast. Before being defeated—first by the revived Neo-Babylonian empire under King Nebuchadnezzar in the sixth century B.C., then by Alexander the Great in the fourth century B.C. and finally in their new capital of Carthage by the Romans in 146 B.C.—they had, in about 1400 B.C., invented an alphabet that was an improvement on the previous hieroglyphics and cuneiform writing as a tool of commerce. They bequeathed this alphabet via Greece and Rome to the modern world.[4]

Greece meanwhile was experiencing heavy inward migration from the north, as indeed was the rest of the civilized world as far east as Mesopotamia. Greece itself was occupied by Dorian people who came south from the Balkans. The migrants were motivated by the desire for loot and more fertile land, and they were encouraged by the decline of Mycenaean power. Since they came intending to settle with their families and as they displaced lesser tribes, they were perhaps responding to overpopulation in their own homeland and to pressure from Balkan peoples behind them.[5] But whatever the cause of their migration, they finally destroyed the Mycenaean civilization that gave the world the fair Helen of Troy and the supposed historical basis for Homer's epics.[6] By 1000 B.C., Dorians occupied most of the Peloponnese, Crete, southwest Asia Minor and its islands; Ionians inhabited Attica, Euboea, most of the Aegean islands and the central coast of Asia Minor; and a mixture of peoples generally known as Aeolian were to be found in the north, in Lesbos and in northwest Asia Minor.[7] Thucydides, the great fifth-century Athenian historian, later described the almost Hobbesian state of nature in which these waves

*In the previous chapter we used "kya" to mean "thousand years ago" and "mya" for "million years ago," measured back—where it was important—from precisely A.D. 2000. This enabled us to use a consistent system for the whole of the earlier period more than 3 kya. But in this chapter and the rest of the book we use the traditional B.C./A.D. dates, since the artificiality of contriving "years ago" dates and unfamiliar numbers for familiar events would try the patience of most readers. No cultural bias or offense is intended against those who use other systems of dating.

of immigrants clung to existence on the fringes of the mountainous Greek mainland:

> The country now called Hellas had no settled population in ancient times; instead there was a series of migrations, as the various tribes, being under the constant pressure of invaders who were stronger than they were, were always prepared to abandon their own territory. There was no commerce and no safe communication either by land or sea; the use they made of their land was limited to the production of necessities; they had no surplus of wealth and no regular system of agriculture.[8]

From this unpromising beginning the glories of Greek civilization began to emerge over the ensuing centuries. Geography played a part. The topography of Greece, like that of Japan and Norway, separates communities by huge masses of arid and scarcely passable mountains but links coastal settlements by the great highway of the sea. Any people arriving in Greece from the north would have been constrained to settle in the lowland areas and to supplement the limited agricultural opportunities by resort to the sea, well furnished with harbors and islands, both for fishing and trade.

This at the very least appears consistent with what we find developing by the eighth century B.C., namely, a series of fairly independent valley and coastal communities sharing a common Hellenic identity and language, as a direct result of the disruption caused by the large-scale migrations.[9] This combination—strong local independence within a freely communicating wider association—seems initially to have encouraged a quasi-Darwinian political economy of more or less random experimentation moderated by a kind of natural selection of successful solutions.

We are forced to speculate because we do not know precisely how Greece in the Archaic period found the fork in the road that took at least some of its communities away from the Mesopotamian model—of societies sharply polarized between a landowning governing elite and a poor and exploited taxpaying peasantry—toward something entirely new. But it is clear that after about 800 B.C. a new idea began to catch on: that governance, though indispensable in any community in order to provide justice and organize defense, derived its legitimacy and authority from law, conceived as unchanging rules that men could discover and that were part of the natural order of things. Since these laws, codified by lawgivers like Solon, were eventually agreed to by assemblies of the citizens, the underlying rationale for executive power came over time to acquire a less undemocratic spin, markedly different from earlier societies, where authority belonged to those who said they spoke for god and who could demonstrate that they wielded the greatest might.

The practicalities of government were recognized in the election of magistrates with executive powers. But their accountability to their fellow citizens was also recognized in a formalized process of selection or election for a limited period of time, usually a year, and the conduct of their duties was continuously negotiated in public argument.[10]

All of this was a very long way from any kind of perfect democracy or egalitarian society. Differences of wealth and economic status were marked, and access to the councils that increasingly arbitrated the affairs of the developing communities was far from universal. Upper classes and elites existed, exercising disproportionate influence and power.

Nonetheless the door was open to the concept and the fact of citizenship, even if this was very far from being open to all. Slaves, women and foreigners, deemed unable to fight for their community, the first duty of a citizen, were not eligible. But the seed was planted of the idea that a society or community was, to a degree, a contract of mutual convenience among its members and that this fact needed to determine the way its affairs were managed and the way in which the rights and interests of individuals were protected.

In itself this was obviously a political idea, but it was also pregnant with economic significance. It implied in the longer run the recognition that economic processes, as one form of social activity, exist for nothing more than the fulfillment of individuals' goals and wants. It also implied that individuals should have the presumptive right to pursue those goals and to hold onto the fruits of their endeavors. These notions, it is now widely recognized, are fundamental to the purposes and dynamic of successful economies, though not to the exclusion of the equally important principle that all can fail if the proper functions of the community in providing a stable framework, necessary investment and appropriate incentives are unfulfilled.

The development of this Greek institution, the idea we know as politics—the very word derives from the Greek word for city, *polis*—begins to explain why such attention and importance is given to events that affected at the time the merest fraction of the human species in a place that must still have appeared a backwater to contemporaries. But it soon came to claim the first place in the ancient Greek's sense of who he was, not least because he was expected to stand in battle shoulder to shoulder with his fellow citizens, each knowing that his life depended on the courage and discipline of the next man in his phalanx. The leadership of temporary lay magistrates, replacing the mystique of theocratic and hereditary rulers, further emphasized the mutuality of the relationship between the citizen and his community or city.

Nonetheless, such beautiful thoughts could be no guarantee against the ordinary pressures and crises of political and economic life in a free community. The great divide between rich and poor, privileged and weak, persistently asserted itself and threatened to consign the society either to bondage or chaos.

We are here once again in the grip of the waltz motif that we saw at work in Chapter 1 as the agricultural revolution led to village, town and city life with their social and political problems, which in turn were solved by new rules and structures. Here we encounter, as the first step in the figure, the development of the successful Mycenaean civilization and, as the second step, the wave of immigration, seemingly attracted by the relative prosperity and opportunities of the Mediterranean shoreline.

The resolution in the third step is the settlement of the Dorians and other peoples in their new home. Then the next figure begins with the growth of prosperity as conditions became more stable, migration from the north ceased, trade developed in the Aegean and eastern Mediterranean and the technical advance of iron metallurgy became more widespread, all contributing to rising wealth and population in the eighth century B.C.[11] The challenges and resolutions to which this led in the second and third steps of the figure will be seen in the developments of the next two centuries. The actual principal settlements (they may be called "cities" without any implication that these politically structured independent rural communities and towns had yet achieved substantial urban development) of Greece in 700 B.C. included Corinth, Athens, Thebes, Sparta, Argos and many others. They added up eventually to 200 in the Aegean, to say nothing of another 1,300 elsewhere in the Mediterranean and Black Seas as a result of Greek colonization from the late eighth century or beginning of the seventh century onward, mainly for agriculture but also to accommodate surplus population and to trade with the metropolis.[12]

Attica at the dawn of our period was a small, self-sufficient agricultural region, bounded by mountains and the Aegean. It was depopulated, isolated and relatively poor compared to what it had been during the Mycenaean period and consisted of decentralized villages, independent neighborhoods, kinship groups and local cults.[13]

Aided by geography, climate and a developing mastery of the Aegean and Black Seas, expanding trade extended specialization and the division of labor. By the middle of the fifth century B.C., Athens had become the prosperous center of an empire, deriving its main food supplies—grain—from the shores of the Black Sea while exporting wine, olives and manufactured goods throughout the two seas as well as to much of the eastern Mediterranean.

This process was accompanied by the usual political strains and convulsions associated with managing economic change. Early systems of personal rule gave way to class struggles between aristocrats and both farmers and urban artisans; and a brief tyranny was the result of excessive disorder.

But Athens' story rose above the usual oscillation between autocracy and anarchy through the contribution of three exceptional men, Solon (c. 638–558 B.C.), Cleisthenes (c. 570–500 B.C.) and Pericles (c. 500–429 B.C.), who among them established what we know as Athenian democracy at home and built the external economic system, based on sea power, which was the heart of the Athenian empire.

Solon created the laws that established the ordinary individual and his freedom and protection as, at least in theory, the chief beneficiaries of society. He made it illegal for a man to sell—or pledge—his own person into bondage. He allowed anyone to seek redress from the courts on behalf of any victim of wrong, not just himself. He gave a right of appeal in important exceptional cases to a people's court, in which the verdict was given by the people as a whole, or at least by a sort of grand assize of several thousand citizens.[14] He canceled at a stroke the debts of the farming population, so reestablishing them as freeholders owning their farms. He created throughout his laws a deliberate bias in favor of the weak and helpless, allowing any citizen or the state itself to act on their behalf in the courts. Solon is thus celebrated, even if anachronistically, as the founder of Athenian democracy and as the author of a system of justice that put the individual citizen in the place of honor as both the ultimate dispenser of fair play and the ultimate owner of the *right* to fair play.

Cleisthenes did for the political organization of Attica what Solon had done for its laws, reducing the political importance of the ancient tribes based on kinship and establishing over 100 geographically defined demes (local communes). In this and other ways, he destroyed forever the old exclusive patriarchal idea of the state as a corporation and confirmed both the principle of active democracy, engaging the sovereign citizens in every aspect of government, and the principle of free intercourse between Athenians and strangers, welcoming immigrants and giving them opportunities to acquire citizenship even when they arrived as slaves. These aliens, and the free trade that went with Athens' outward-looking attitude, became cornerstones of Athenian prosperity in the fifth century. The historian Herodotus, for example, who came from Halicarnassus (Bodrum), was an "outlander" in Periclean Athens from 466 to 443 B.C.

For thirty years in the middle of the fifth century (c. 460–429 B.C.), the golden period of Athenian civilization and empire, the dominant figure was Pericles. As general, statesman and thinker, he built the Athenian empire, the sea power that sustained it and the economic system that supplied it. He expressed—most memorably in his famous funeral speech—its values and principles, he masterminded the construction of the Parthenon and other great buildings of the Acropolis, and he led the Athenians into the disastrous Peloponnesian War with Sparta, which long after his death destroyed it all.

The extraordinary fascination and admiration that classical Athens continues to arouse two and a half millennia after its brief glory was extinguished are due to the power of its two defining ideas, freedom and democracy (though the majority of its population, the women and the slaves, enjoyed neither), and to the brilliance of the surviving accounts of its story, above all that by Thucydides (c. 460–400 B.C.).

Just as the architects of the British Empire never stopped to invent a theory of the empire but left it to late-nineteenth-century academic historians like J. R. Seeley at Cambridge to provide the rationale, so the justification of the Athenian empire was written by its historian. Although he put much of it into the mouth of Pericles in his account of the funeral oration, Thucydides' justification is exactly the same as Seeley's: the overriding benefits of the imposed civilization, above all its supreme celebration of freedom, the very thing an empire denies to its subject peoples:

> Our government is not copied from those of our neighbours: we are an example to them rather than they to us. Our constitution is named a democracy, because it is in the hands not of the few, but of the many. But our laws secure equal justice for all in their private disputes, and our public opinion honours and welcomes talent in every branch of achievement. . . . Moreover, the city is so large and powerful that all the wealth of all the world flows into her, so that our own Attic products seem no more homelike to us than the fruits of the labours of other nations. . . . For you now it remains to rival what they have done and, knowing the secret of happiness to be freedom and the secret of freedom a brave heart, not idly to stand aside from the enemy's onset.[15]

This, more than anything else, captures the positive part of the spirit of Athens and the beliefs, political values, social organization and open attitude to the external world that, with sea power, underlay Athens' economic achievements and the ends to which they were put: "We are lovers of beauty without extravagance . . . wealth to us is not mere material for vainglory but an opportunity for achievement; and poverty we think no disgrace to acknowledge but a real degradation to make no effort to overcome."

It is this emphasis on the sovereignty of the individual (provided he is male and a freeman) rather than on the corporate state that lies behind our special focus on citizenship as the key contribution of classical Athens to the story of the wealth of man.

Previous civilizations did not in the same way or to the same degree establish such a primacy for the individual and such citizens' rights. This was the special contribution of the classical period. Like all generalizations it is no doubt arguable, but the claim here is that it is also illuminating. It shows again the waltz motif asserting itself through two complete figures:

- (step 3 of the previous figure) first time round, Solon's and, the second time round, Cleisthenes' reforms resolving previous tensions

- (step 1) a new figure on each occasion beginning with a surge of prosperity in the resulting political and economic space
- (step 2) threats caused by the extreme inequalities that economic growth can easily generate through the concentration of new wealth and power in very few hands, as well as threats from other cities that resented, feared or coveted the new wealth (and perhaps arrogance) of Athens
- (step 3) the need for a new resolution, which in the first case was Cleisthenes' reforms and in the second case the Peloponnesian War and the simultaneous outbreak of a lethal infectious disease, which proved a total catastrophe for Athens

Before we turn to Rome and its concept of citizenship, we need to note other, more down-to-earth aspects of Greek economic history in the first millennium B.C. The first coins used by man, as far as we can tell, were minted from electrum in western Asia Minor in what was in 650 B.C. the large kingdom of Lydia, though within fifty years something similar was being created in bronze both on the shores of the Black Sea and in China.

Electrum is a natural alloy of gold and silver, which the Lydians found in the local Pactolus River and extracted from mines. The coins were roughly oval and were graduated in weight from just over 17 grams (0.6 oz.), nearly the weight of a British £1 coin today, down to just over one-hundredth of the largest coin, offering a wide choice. The largest collection has been found at the Temple of Artemis at Ephesus, where overland trade from the east reached the sea routes of the Aegean and the Mediterranean.

The original purpose of this coinage is uncertain and may not have flowed directly from what may seem to us with hindsight to be the self-evident convenience of a medium of exchange with self-declaring face value. The earliest coins were stamped but still needed to be weighed, like bullion, before being used as money; in themselves, therefore, they represented no great advance on the bullion money that had been in use in the Near East for thousands of years. But like many events in history, it was not the *reason* why they happened but the consequences to which they led that changed the world.

Over the next century Greek cities discovered the economic use of coins as a standard of value and a medium of exchange. From almost the earliest coins (though the very earliest may have been minted by individuals for religious purposes or as gifts to be made in the course of business and politics), the designs that differentiated them from mere lumps of metal were stamped by some kind of public authority, so identifying the issuing community. There seems to be widespread agreement among historians that civic consciousness—or political vanity—was a primary motive for the issue of coinage that was so much beloved by the rapidly developing Greek city-states on both sides of the Aegean from the late seventh century onward.

In words that might have inspired the authors of the articles in the Maastricht Treaty in 1992 that established the euro, M. M. Austin and P. Vidal-Naquet write, "To strike coins with the badge of the city was to proclaim one's political independence."[16] Thus the development of coinage, which happened first around the Aegean, was in part a consequence of the development of the Greek *polis*. And the intimate and necessary interconnection between political identity and monetary identity was reinforced when the states discovered that they could make a profit out of issuing the coins society needed to lubricate its daily business and trade. They could monopolize the design they stamped on the coins, and this became the legal evidence of their value. They could then stamp that design on coins that had less precious-metal content than the design promised, a practice that worked best where traders had few practical alternatives to using the official coins, for example in the payment of taxes. This was perhaps an early version of what much later came to be called seigniorage, or the profit accruing to whoever has an exclusive right to issue money.

In passing we may note that Greece at this time established what has become one of the most consistent connections throughout economic history ever since, that between political sovereignty and currency areas. It worked both ways. States issued currencies because it was profitable and because it proclaimed their power and independence; and the existence of their own currencies liberated them to finance trade and defense to support their success and freedom.[17]

The same deep interconnection of political and economic forces helped silver to replace electrum and gold as the predominant monetary metal in Greece from the middle of the sixth century B.C.[18] To be sure, silver was convenient: It was more plentiful than electrum or gold; it was easier to value, simply by weighing, than an alloy of uncertain proportions; and it was long established as the main metal money in the Near East. But its spread also owed much to the political dominance of Athens as its trade, its central role in the Delian League (the confederation of city-states headed by Athens) and its eventual empire gave it the same sort of hegemonic position as the United States enjoyed after World War II. For the United States

- the Soviet threat played the role of the Persian Empire in presenting a common foe against which free men must unite
- the Bretton Woods institutions (the International Monetary Fund and the World Bank) played the role of the Delian League and its common treasury (in due course removed from the island of Delos to the imperial capital in Athens) in projecting American leadership under notionally multilateral rubrics
- the necessary political cover was provided, as for the Athenian empire, by the missions of spreading democracy and defending freedom, which persuaded many third parties, both in the ancient and in the modern case, to remain grateful and loyal to what was nonetheless an economically and militarily dominant central power
- the home currency became the reserve and trading currency for everyone

The mines at Laurium in Attica possessed a good slice of the area's available silver supplies, and by an early date the Athenian city-state had acquired these mines. This created the necessary monopoly for minting silver coins bearing what became the famous owl emblem. And so, by suitable adjustment of the face and content values of these coins, Athens began to earn (with the help of slave labor in the mines) the seigniorage profits that helped to finance the city's heavy public expenditure on the ships that enforced—and the public buildings that expressed—its power. At its zenith, over 150 states were paying tribute to Athens.[19]

As coins became more plentiful for these originally political reasons, so men discovered their more familiar economic uses, in settlement of transactions, as standards of value and as stores of wealth. In all these roles money, whether in coins or otherwise, facilitates and so increases the efficiency of the economic activities into which it enters. Once money has been invented, it is obvious to all that barter is a clumsy, slow and frequently impossible way of doing business.

It is less obvious, but far more important, that a system such as money (or a payments union or shared settlement account) that enables A to sell X to B, without B's being required to find some Y of equivalent value to A, revolutionizes the possibilities of trade. If there are a million As in the world wanting to sell X and there are a million Bs wanting to buy X at the going price, and if at the same time there are a million Cs wanting to sell Ys to a million Ds, all these transactions can take place given only a marketplace (or network of marketplaces) in which they can find one another and a neutral medium of exchange, such as money, to settle the transactions. And of course the chain of A, B, C and D and X, Y . . . can be indefinitely long, provided that the circle is eventually closed by A's wanting to buy something that Z wants to sell.

Without money none of these transactions can take place except to the extent that some of the Bs are in fact Cs and some of the Ds are As and that those precise B/Cs can find those precise D/As (and so on). Even then, the number of trades would be almost certainly an infinitesimally small fraction of the 2 million exchanges that are possible in our original A, B, C and D example using money. It is also fairly obvious, despite the apparently contrary practice of the Yap islanders in the western Pacific, who to this day use large, smooth and almost immovable boulders as money, that value cannot be efficiently stored in bulky, decaying or unprotectable forms.

Nor can value be measured and compared conveniently except in units that can be counted and exchanged for the thing to be valued. By minting coins the Greeks had created one of the fundamental building blocks of human economy. Its corollary in the gradual divorce of face value from content, or "intrinsic," value culminating in the development of paper money, whose value depends wholly on the fiat of the issuer and the confidence of the users, is a later story.

Although checks and bills of exchange were unknown in Athens, banking was conducted—commonly at tables set up in the agora, the marketplace below the Acropolis—in the form both of money changing and of accepting deposits that were then lent out at interest (usually 12 percent a year), the classic basis of banking profits almost ever since. But it would be wrong to read into Athenian practice the modern conception of banks as credit institutions supporting economic activity across the board. For the most part, Athenian bankers were closer to exchange offices and pawnbrokers and played little part in financing maritime trade, handicrafts or agriculture, although some of them, such as Pasion, a former slave who died in 370 B.C., did well enough to leave their names to posterity and useful fortunes to their heirs.

Maritime commercial loans, secured on ship and cargo, to finance risky voyages and loans secured on landed property (usually for noncommercial purposes) were nonetheless significant parts of a financial system that included important innovations in commercial law, such as the recognition of slaves and other noncitizens as legal persons and of foreigners as having equal legal status with citizens. Written agreements were recognized, and the idea that justice needed to be expeditious as well as fair found expression in a rule that commercial cases must be decided within a month so that traders could sail away in accordance with commercial necessity (an idea that the modern world appears to have mislaid).[20]

The dominating factor in the supply of money and credit to the ancient economy remained the minting of coins, which in turn depended on adequate supplies of precious metal and a credible sovereign state. The military and political successes of Philip II of Macedon (359–336 B.C.), who conquered Greece, and of his son Alexander the Great (336–323 B.C.), who defeated the Persian Empire itself and much else besides, were largely financed by their access to and control of the mines of Thrace.

The vast coinage that was produced from these mines (in gold, silver and bronze) paid the army, at least until the fabulous wealth of the Persian emperors fell as the spoils of war into Alexander's hands. The scale of this monetary wealth was of a different order of magnitude to anything previously known in the Greek world—even including the riches of King Croesus of Lydia—and was not seen again until the Roman Empire had conquered the entire Mediterranean. But the system of money embodied in coins, developed in Lydia and spread around the Aegean and the Mediterranean by the Greek city-states, remained the standard throughout the Hellenistic period of the ancient world (300–30 B.C.).[21]

The story of Rome starts with some superficial similarities. Rome was founded in the eighth century B.C. as a city in an agricultural zone, a small city-state. Early kings were displaced by an aristocracy that despite some democratic trappings came into periodic conflict with the people in a series of civil wars. A series of waltzlike figures was stepped out as economic advances were followed by political troubles and new, sometimes transient, settlements.

As with Athens, the defeat of a powerful invader from outside (Carthage, like Persia) and other external conquests increased the riches of Rome. But as economic opportunity increased, so, in accordance with the waltz motif we noted in the introduction, social tensions between landlords and peasants increased. There was no comparable Solon, Cleisthenes or Pericles to steer these pressures into a functioning democracy.

Civil war followed and then the inevitable tyranny, under Julius Caesar. Assassination and more civil war ended in the total triumph of Augustus, who established the empire. Augustus's greatest legacy was the doctrine that the empire should be confined within its existing natural frontiers of the Atlantic, the Rhine, the Danube, the Euphrates and the deserts of Arabia and Africa. As Edward Gibbon remarks dryly: "Happily for the repose of mankind, the moderate system recommended by the wisdom of Augustus, was adopted by the fears and vices of his immediate successors."[22]

This empire, unlike Pericles's, achieved two centuries of mostly peace and some prosperity before things began to go badly wrong—though even then with substantial interludes of stability and economic achievement. These first two centuries A.D. may present something of a puzzle to those who like to associate economic progress with political freedom and economic stultification with, among other evils, the dead hand of imperial bureaucracy, as indeed witnessed in some phases of the Mesopotamian and Egyptian civilizations examined in Chapter 1.

It is part of the thesis of this book that economic advance is a natural proclivity of mankind given, as it were, half a chance, though we also argue that that chance presupposes two things: (1) positive action to supply certain other favorable conditions, such as monetary stability, physical security and a predictable and accessible legal system that protects the person and his property, settles his disputes and upholds his agreements, and (2) abstention by political authority from the suppression of the freedoms and incentives that spur work, invention and investment.

The first 200-odd years of the Roman Empire (31 B.C.–A.D. 180) need to be examined to see how far they contradict this thesis; and some contemporary readers may find it illuminating, though others may not, to have in mind some of the modern debates about the relationship between political liberalization and economic success that are provoked by the seemingly rapid economic growth of China, before 1999, and the downward slide of Russia since their respective supposed conversions to market economics.

Is political freedom a condition of economic freedom and therefore of economic dynamism and success, eventually if not immediately? Or is political order a more pressing precondition of economic confidence and performance? Was Mikhail Gorbachev right, or was Deng Xiaoping? Should Augustus and the Antonines be added to the capitalist hall of fame with Solon, Cleisthenes and Pericles, with Jefferson, Locke, Peel and Gladstone, or consigned to the same monster-pit as Franco, Salazar, Suharto and Pinochet?

Our task is to chronicle and explain economic performance as we find it. It is too soon to offer a conclusion, but it may be useful to have in mind the questions that hang particularly heavily in the air as we enter (in the dating sense) the Christian era.

Keith Hopkins has argued, glossing the classic labors of Sir Moses Finley, that modest economic growth and an increasing economic surplus were achieved in the Mediterranean basin during the twelve centuries from 1000 B.C. to A.D. 200. He attributes this to political change and technical and social innovation. By political change he means mainly growing scale, and by technical and social change he has in mind for the most part less than revolutionary advances, such as iron instruments, screw presses, rotary mills and (slightly more radically) water mills, and the familiar wherewithal of ancient life, such as coins, money, taxes, chattel slavery, writing, schools, written contracts, commercial loans, technical handbooks, large sailing ships, shared risk investment and absentee landlordism.

Many of these did not originate in this period, but all contributed to consumption, production and trade. He gives seven reasons for believing that a growing surplus was produced throughout the main period of classical antiquity:

1. Farm output rose as the total area under arable cultivation increased, according at least to the limited evidence we have.

2. The population of the Roman world in the first two centuries A.D. was greater than it was one millennium earlier and half a millennium later.

3. The proportion of the population engaged in nonagricultural work increased, supported by the ever more elaborate division of labor visible in places such as Pompeii and Rome, for which we have concrete evidence.

4. Total nonagricultural output increased, as shown by the higher number of artifacts—coins, pots, lamps, iron tools, carved stones, ornaments.

5. Output per head of those engaged in farming and other production rose, which follows from the facts above that in the first two centuries A.D. proportionately fewer food producers were growing more food than ever before—chiefly because of intensifying exploitation of harder-pressed agricultural slaves and of ever more heavily taxed free peasants—for the benefit of more nonagricultural producers.

6. The total, measured both by value and by the proportion of output, exacted from primary producers in taxes and rent increased. In other words, as Hopkins puts it:

   > As the size and power of states increased in classical antiquity, the state exacted more for itself in order to support the superstructure of professional, regularly paid military defenders, an administrative infrastructure of paid officials and clerks, and an expensive imperial Court. In addition, the state permitted, indeed it supported, the extraction of a great surplus by rich landowners from tenants who paid rent. As a system of production, slavery set the benchmark for the degree of exploitation condoned. In that sense slavery dominated the ancient economy.[23]

7. Trade was promoted in the first two centuries A.D. as a direct con-

> sequence of the need to recycle the tax revenues the state was collecting throughout its territories and then spending along its frontiers and in Rome, where its military and administrative efforts were disproportionately concentrated.

Hopkins does not believe that this evidence of economic growth is enough to overthrow Sir Moses Finley's basic picture of an ancient economy that was primitive and, by later standards, static.[24] Still more modest is Peter Garnsey's reading of the Roman imperial economy as an underdeveloped economy enjoying little significant development, whether in the vital area of ship construction or in container design, commercial law (still reluctant to accept the concept of corporate identity) or banking law (where deposit taking was still seen mainly as an unrequited trust involving clear duties of repayment on demand rather than as a chargeable service).[25]

In this empire, as in the republic that preceded and created it, citizenship was the fundamental concept. It conferred upon those who had it rights and standing under the law that, though nothing could withstand the rapacity and iniquity of the most unscrupulous emperors, went a long way to establish a society in which (as in Athens) individuals were seen as sovereign constituents and sole ultimate beneficiaries of human economic affairs—even when the people had long forfeited the political rights and democratic powers that Athenians had briefly enjoyed. This ideal had not, of course, excluded important patron-client relationships in Roman society that sometimes left the ordinary citizen without redress against intimidation, assault and even illegal enslavement; and he was at times more vulnerable to the arbitrary exercise of power under the empire than under the republic.[26]

Roman citizenship, though never a universal right, spread from the original city to the whole of Italy and thence throughout the empire. By the time of the great age of the Antonines (the second century A.D.), Gibbon says, "the greater number of their subjects" enjoyed the very solid advantages of citizenship, including the benefit of Roman laws, especially of marriage, wills and inheritances, as well as a career open to both talent and favor. The system of civil law supported contracts in what North calls "the highly developed exchange economy which developed throughout the Mediterranean world in the first two centuries A.D."[27]

In the earlier time of Claudius (mid–first century A.D.), Gibbon estimates the population of the empire at about 120 million, more than the Europe of his day and "the most numerous society that has ever been united under the same system of government."[28] Modern estimates are not so very different. Rondo Cameron writes in 1997 that "estimates of the population of the empire at its height [around A.D. 180] range from 60 million to more than a hundred million, with the more recent estimates favouring the latter figure."[29] Both imply that much more than half the population of the empire was outside Europe, whose total population, including the Germanic and other tribes north of the Danube, peaked at less than 50 million in about A.D. 200 according to modern estimates.[30] This is possible given that the biggest cities after Rome itself included Alexandria and Carthage in Africa, Antioch and Apamea in Syria, and Pergamum and Ephesus in Asia Minor.[31]

Of his own estimate Gibbon says half (probably a large exaggeration) were slaves and half free, and two-thirds of the free were "provincials," not citizens. Fewer than 7 million adult males were counted in the census conducted during the reign of the Emperor Claudius (A.D. 41–54).

In practice both citizens and freedmen—and indeed some slaves, though not those in the mines and workshops or on the large landed estates—were relatively free to act as economic agents seeking their own gain and that of their families. They enjoyed some prospect of being able to retain the fruits of their efforts in a stable society where law and peace and freedom of movement gave added point and opportunity to those efforts.

Gradually, by colonization, assimilation, the deliberate propagation of the Latin language and the universal application of Roman law, the nations of the empire lost their political identity and became Roman in their own estimation, if not in that of their Roman masters, blending into a single people. To a degree there was a Roman dream driving a Roman melting pot.

The economic sinews of empire that linked the unprecedentedly large market it represented consisted of the Mediterranean Sea, whose ultimate limits could be reached from Ostia in seven to ten days with favorable winds, and, equally important, of superb roads on which a traveler could post 100 Roman miles a day (about 92 of our miles), connecting over nearly 5,000 miles from Scotland to Palestine. These arteries linked more than 3,000 "cities," from York to Antioch and Alexandria. All of this, combined with political and civil stability and the opportunities open to Roman citizens and other free agents, accomplished an economic advance—rising population, surplus and productivity—that confirms the place of the Roman Empire in our story.

This is already described, with liberal hyperbole, by the contemporary historian Pliny in A.D. 77 using concepts (social organization, law, technology and its transfer, good government and effective communication) that might have been taken from the pages of modern economic historians—with some rhetorical help from the architects of the European Union:

> They [the inhabitants of the empire] acknowledged that the true principles of social life, laws, agriculture and science, which had been first invented by the wisdom of Athens, were now firmly established by the power of Rome, under whose auspicious influence the fiercest barbarians were united by an equal government and common language. They affirm that with the improvement of arts, the human species was visibly multiplied. They celebrate the increasing splendour of the cities, the beautiful face of the country, cultivated and adorned like an immense garden; and the long festival of peace which was enjoyed by so many nations, forgetful of their ancient animosities, and delivered from the apprehension of future danger.

Beyond the empire, trade reached to the Baltic, Scythia, Babylon, equatorial Africa and even the Malabar coast, Ceylon and China. Rome imported 400,000 tons of grain a year from Egypt, Africa and Sicily and thereby generated a great deal of trade. Luxuries such as silk and spices were imported from further afield, and archaeological finds of Roman coinage, metal and glassware as well as coinage in Asia demonstrate the demand that existed for Roman exports.[32]

Nor was the profit of the empire mere plunder, though that frequently occurred when conquest made it possible. The freedom of exchange over these huge distances was the occasion for a comprehensive transfer of products, plants and industrial methods from the more advanced areas of the East to the western countries of Europe. Flowers, herbs, fruits, vines and olives were introduced, mainly northward and westward throughout much of the empire as knowledge and markets spread by sea and by road.

Once again the emphasis on citizenship, this time as a key factor in Rome's economic achievements, presupposes the idea that where men and women are free and have incentives to seek their own economic advantage they are likely thereby, given a suitable environment, to accomplish much. Rome, by its lawmaking and military achievements, progressively extended the economic and legal advantages associated with citizenship to the huge and formidably interconnected trading zone it created during the first two centuries A.D. This gave full scope to those basic forces of economic advancement.

Such statements must, however, be read in the context of the time, when technology was primitive and slow to change, when agriculture occupied most people and with limited opportunities for more than local exchange, when slavery excluded if not half then certainly many from the incentives and opportunities of a free economy and when women enjoyed negligible rights and opportunities outside the home.

Even so, *civis Romanus sum* (I am a Roman citizen) remains one of the most economically potent political ideas in the whole story of the wealth of man. Nonetheless, ideas are one thing and practice another. However potent the concept that Greece and Rome transmitted to later ages, the ancient world itself seemed to lose the plot, as Gibbon rightly sensed, from the end of the second century A.D., transiently splendid and impressive as were the periodic restorations of imperial order under Diocletian (A.D. 284–305) and Constantine (A.D. 306–337).

Insofar as the Roman story during the first two centuries of the empire may seem on balance to support the Deng Xiaoping priority for political *order* rather than political *freedom* as a condition of economic progress, the story thereafter tends to demonstrate how the abuse of absolute political power arising from a lack of public accountability can damage the economic health of the society over which it presides.

The populations of both Europe and the Roman Empire seem to have fallen markedly after about A.D. 200. The population of the empire probably peaked at the same time, and according to Livi-Bacci the population of Europe halved over the next 400 years.[33]

The causes of the decline appear to have been the usual suspects: disease, famine and war. Specifically, two episodes of devastating pestilence, probably measles and smallpox, afflicted the Mediterranean population in A.D. 165–180 and A.D. 251–266. From A.D. 235 civil disorder and barbarian invasions destroyed populations and undermined their economic foundations by increasing the cost of protection.

It appears that this double blow struck at the central mechanism of the earlier prosperity whereby economic surpluses generated in the central metropolitan areas of the empire were cycled through government taxes and military spending to the frontiers and then recycled back through trade, generating order and economically useful infrastructure in the process. As disease, invasion and civil disorder ravaged the urban population and disrupted production, the surpluses evaporated. This eroded the tax revenues and retarded the whole economic machine.[34]

There thus seem to have been at least three independent initiating causes of what became a self-extending decline in population, economic performance and political order:

1. There were two separate attacks from outside:

    - The Sassanian dynasty in Persia, having overthrown the Parthians, attacked the eastern empire through Mesopotamia in A.D. 253 and 260, actually capturing the emperor Valerian and taking him off in chains to Edessa, and later (A.D. 363) took Mesopotamia from the empire.

    - From beyond the Danube and the Rhine, the empire was attacked in the west from about A.D. 250 by Goths, Vandals, Alemani and Franks.

2. New diseases broke in upon a Mediterranean population with no immunity. They were probably brought back by soldiers returning from Mesopotamia (an early Gulf War syndrome), and they wrought the usual extraordinary havoc of new pathogens on a virgin population, killing perhaps a quarter to one-third of the population and putting Rome's many previous plagues and epidemics (from 387 B.C. to A.D. 65) into the shade.

3. The empire's system of government succumbed to its greatest constitutional weakness, namely, the lack of any effective provision for

> emperors, even successful ones, to be succeeded by those who both would and could rule wisely and well.

After describing the reigns of five consecutive emperors (A.D. 96–180: Nerva, Trajan, Hadrian, Antoninus Pius and Marcus Aurelius) as "the period in the history of the world, during which the condition of the human race was most happy" and the reign of the last two as "possibly the only period of history in which the happiness of a great people was the sole object of government," the great Gibbon observes

> The fatal moment was perhaps approaching when some licentious youth, or some jealous tyrant, would abuse, to the destruction, that absolute power which they [the predecessors] had exerted for the benefit of their people. . . . The monstrous vices of the son have cast a shade on the purity of the father's virtues. It has been objected to Marcus [Aurelius], that he sacrificed the happiness of millions to a fond partiality for a worthless boy [his son, Commodus, who succeeded him].[35]

Commodus's weaknesses, and in particular his ruinous extravagance, inaugurated a long though by no means steady decline in the quality of imperial government, aggravated at almost every turn by the needs of each emperor to buy at ever more inflated prices his election by bribes payable to the praetorian guard, unless indeed he could seize the purple by military force or by personal violence.

Citizenship was extended to virtually all free men in the empire in A.D. 212.[36] This was not, alas, intended as an extension of civil or democratic rights but rather as an attempt to extend the empire's tax base, recalling to a degree the way in which "European" citizenship, together with the European Union's laws and rules, is imposed willy-nilly by the Maastricht Treaty on almost all inhabitants of its member countries.

As the external pressures on the imperial budget intensified—with increased expenditure to repel the barbarians at the gate and decreased revenue resulting from the effects of plague and subsequent economic contraction—emperors were constrained to impose more irregular taxes and levies and to resort to the other great expedient of exigent governments, inflation fed by debasement of the currency, in this case by reducing the precious metal content of coins of given face value.

By A.D. 265 the silver content of the coin representing the chief unit of money, which had been solid silver since 212 B.C. but which had been diluted gradually from Nero's time (A.D. 54–68), had fallen almost to nil, a development only partially excused by the declining supplies of silver as mines in Spain were exhausted.[37] The nominal amount of soldiers' wages was inflated threefold—from about 600 denarii a year at the end of the second century A.D., not much more than twice what it had been in Julius Caesar's time 250 years earlier, to 1,800 denarii forty years later.[38]

Lack of sufficient revenue, even after the contribution of debased coinage, induced the government to impose levies in kind, in other words to heavy and unpredictable commandeering and requisitioning of food and other military supplies. These were eventually converted into a system of regular "contributions," all of which tended, even if they kept the imperial administration going a little longer, to dry up the wellsprings of economic activity.

Farmers fled their lands to seek protection from large landlords enjoying privileged tax exemptions. Trade contracted. Town and city populations, where they had not been devastated by disease, shrank from economic malnutrition. The vicious circle thus engendered drove desperate emperors to desperate attempts to override the forces of supply and demand by command. As Cameron observes, this all "subverted the very nature of the economic system of the empire. Production for the market declined."[39]

Diocletian (A.D. 284–305), whose political wisdom and military skills had restored the empire's external frontiers to the natural limits laid down by Augustus and who had mitigated its overdependence on a single overextended ruler by appointing a consort to rule in the western half of the empire, endeavored to manage the economic crisis with the same executive vigor. First he issued an imperial edict reforming and revaluing the currency.[40] Then he sought to fix wages and prices by another edict, at the same time reorganizing the empire's taxing and spending bureaucracy. The preamble to his edict expressed just the kind of frustration and indignation that has accompanied more modern attempts to suppress inflation by law or moral suasion:

> Who does not know that wherever the common safety requires our armies to be sent, the profiteers insolently and covertly attack the public welfare, not only in

> towns and villages, but on every road? They charge extortionate prices for merchandise, not just fourfold or eightfold, but on such a scale that human speech cannot find words to characterise their profit and their practices. Indeed, sometimes in a single retail sale a solder is stripped of his donative [a bounty] and pay. . . . Aroused justly and rightfully by all the facts set forth above . . . we have decided that maximum prices of articles for sale must be established.[41]

The same decree established a "capital" penalty for violators, which did not necessarily entail death but meant the loss of a citizen's rights. It soon failed, driving the government to the yet more drastic measure of compelling farmers and peasants to stay in their jobs and making all common occupations and offices hereditary, thereby obliging the sons of farmers, artisans, tradesmen and even local officials to follow the same trade as their fathers. This accentuated the downward spiral of the economy, pushing some rural life back to primitive subsistence while some towns and cities were deserted and big houses on landed estates often became fortified castles. Some areas remained prosperous in the fourth and fifth centuries. Desertion of the land was sporadic and regional, and the state frequently withdrew from direct supervision of production, leaving it in the hands of increasingly powerful large landholders.[42]

The consequences of this fell most heavily on the poorer part of the empire, the west, against which the hostility of the Germanic tribes across the Rhine and the Danube was anyway most freely directed. After the division of the empire into two and Constantine's removal of the main capital to the much less exposed Byzantium (renamed Constantinople), it was only human nature that the defense of the east became the first priority of the eastern emperors, whose resources remained more extensive than those of their western counterparts.

By the end of the fourth century, the empire in the west was fast becoming a shell ready to collapse under its own weight, and in A.D. 410 Rome was duly sacked by Alaric the Goth. In the east the empire continued for 1,000 years, at least in name, in its secure capital of Constantinople (secure from attacking Visigoths and Huns, though not from the bubonic plague in A.D. 542–543 that, along with comets and earthquakes, dreadfully afflicted the reign of Justinian). The empire's survival came thanks in part to the fiscal prudence of the emperor Anastasius (A.D.

491–518) and the martial and legislative talents of the emperor Justinian (A.D. 527–565).

As we take leave of this chapter, in about A.D. 700 the Dark Age was at its darkest hour, just before the dawn. To the west Europe was still in the grip of the Visigothic kingdom; to the east, as far as the Black Sea, it was a tangle of Vandals, Huns, Ostrogoths and other barbarians.

A decade into the next century the Muslim world, in the form of Arabs and Berbers crossing the Straits of Gibraltar from North Africa, irrupted into western Europe with profound long-term cultural and economic consequences. Twenty years later Charlemagne's great-grandfather and grandfather (Pepin II and Charles Martel), having put a stop to the Moorish advance at Poitiers in A.D. 732, founded the Carolingian dynasty (which pretended to be a restoration of the Roman Empire in the west) and devised the misleading but serviceable title of "holy Roman emperor," which survived for over 1,000 years. Under its rule, trade and towns in western Europe began to revive and a gradual process began that shifted the focus of economic life from the Mediterranean to the North Sea and the Atlantic coast. From this the prosperity of medieval Europe and the foundations of the modern age eventually emerged.[43]

In the east the baton of economic and cultural leadership in the central Eurasian region of the globe passed in due course to Islam, but by a different route. The first half of the sixth century saw the empire headquartered in Constantinople restored to economic and political health by the frugality of Anastasius and the prowess of Justinian, who by A.D. 554 had restored Roman control of the Mediterranean.

But new waves of barbarians (Avars from central Asia) crossed the Danube and provoked chaos in the Balkans and the capital, Constantinople, while the Persians continued to recover the strongholds in Mesopotamia. In A.D. 610 Heraclius, the son of the Roman governor in Africa, headed for Constantinople with an army, made himself emperor and established what came to be called the Byzantine Empire, with Greek as its official language. Abandoned forever were any dreams of restoring the realms of Augustus, the Antonines, Diocletian, Constantine and Justinian that had stretched from Spain to Mesopotamia. In A.D. 622 Heraclius set out on a campaign against the Persians, finally vanquishing them at Nineveh five years later, but only four years after that both the Avars and the Persians were briefly at the gates of Constantinople, failing, however, to link up thanks to the efforts of the Byzantine navy.

In that same year (A.D. 622) an Arabian ex-merchant named Muhammad fled from Mecca to Medina, both to the east of the Red Sea, claiming to be the last in a line of prophets from Adam via Moses to Jesus Christ, and founded the religion of Islam. We describe its economic consequences in a later chapter; it will suffice here to note that while Constantinople did not fall to Muhammadans for another 800 years, Arab conquests by the middle of the eighth century A.D. had established Islam in Spain, throughout North Africa and east as far as the Horn of Africa, throughout Arabia, the Near East and Mesopotamia and through Persia as far as the Indus and beyond Samarkand.[44]

It is from this time that the baton of economic pacemaking in the central Eurasian region may be said to have passed from the Byzantine Empire to Islam. The trajectory of economic and demographic rise and fall in the Mediterranean area that we have traced from the early part of the first millennium B.C. to the second half of the first millennium A.D. had run its course. New beginnings were stirring in the northwest and the southeast.

The story of the classical period cannot but be massively influenced—and to our eyes disfigured—by the huge fact of slavery in both Greece and Rome, under Athenian democracy, Roman imperial despotism and sundry other species of rule. Those who cherish historical ironies may seek an excuse for a wry smile in Cameron's theses that slavery was at the root of Rome's technological sterility and that this lack of dynamism was at the root of Rome's eventual economic failure, however much this may have been aggravated by barbarians, plagues and bad government.[45] If Cameron is right, the slaves had their revenge, though no consolation.

For the rest, the chief economic legacy of classical civilization may be found in the concept of citizenship, behind which lies the concept of a state, or polis, composed of people who (or at least the free adult males among whom) are in some ultimate sense the source of all legitimacy and whose well-being is the purpose of social and economic life. We find it in the rise of the Greek city-states, especially Athens, and in the concept of Roman citizenship during the republic. And we see first its abridgment by political despotism, however occasionally enlightened, and then more grossly its abnegation by rank tyranny and economic oppression under the empire, as decline and fall take hold.

And in all this we see repeated, both again and again in detail in short episodes and in a broader macrosense once through the whole chapter, the waltz motif: First, there is a surge of economic advance as new opportunities or new resolutions of old reverses are exploited. Then comes a sideways step or backward half-step as new wealth and success both attract predators and free riders from within and without the society and generate inequalities that may alienate large numbers of its members, in each case causing political and military strains that pose the question whether the society is willing and able to protect its gains against these challenges and defects. Finally, the resolution may lay the foundation for the next advance or, if unequal to the challenge, may lead to atrophy and a dark age.

CHAPTER THREE

Passing the Baton

THREE THOUSAND YEARS AGO THERE WERE ABOUT 40 MILLION people in the world, a quarter of whom dwelt in Europe. By A.D. 1500 the total was more than ten times larger, between 400 and 500 million, of whom about 80 million were in Europe, 100 million in China, 105 million in India, nearly 50 million in Africa, and 14 million in the Americas. If we treat Europe, North Africa, Egypt, and the Near East as a single theater of economic development, we can surmise very roughly that it contained about half the world's population in 1000 B.C., a third in 400 B.C., and a quarter in A.D. 1500.[1] But our attention at this stage in the story is now directed to that other half of the world's population, which over the next 2,500 years was to become first two-thirds and then three-quarters of the total. This huge canvas becomes even larger when we include in it, as we do in this chapter, the story of the Islamic Empire. Islam, though geographically centered in that single theater of economic development noted above and playing a large part in the economic and cultural life of North Africa and even Spain, owed so much of its economic impact to its presence on and across the Indian ocean that it would become artificial to treat it as part of a story principally centered on the Mediterranean.

The first recognizable Chinese state was established in the Yellow River basin when the Zhou dynasty replaced the Shang rulers just before 1000 B.C. During the following 750 years of their rule, the vast floodplain of the Yellow River was brought under cultivation by dikes and drains. This huge project transformed the northern Chinese economy forevermore, creating a fertile region that in modern times supported a population of hundreds of millions. Two other contributions of enduring importance to China's economic and social history were made during the Zhou dynasty. The first was the doctrine of the mandate of heaven, according to which the emperor was the son of heaven and ruled by divine authority but was also under an obligation to rule well. If he did not, his mandate and the moral basis of his authority could be withdrawn unless he reformed. Failing self-correction by the emperor or the ruling regime, the ultimate sanction of a revolt by the peasantry and the establishment of a new regime was available to restore the proper balance of good government.[2]

The second was the life and teaching of Confucius, who lived from 551 to 479 B.C. He legitimized the agrarian state by arguing that agriculture was the true basis of economic, political and moral well-being: "The greatest business of the people is agriculture. From agriculture, the millet which is used for sacrifice to God is produced; the density of population grows; the expense of the business is supplied; social harmony and peace arise; the multiplication of wealth begins; and the characters of honesty, great-mindedness, integrity and solidity become a general habit of the people." Confucianism also conferred higher status on the peasantry than on other workers or merchants, and the latter were placed at the bottom of the social hierarchy.

The twin beliefs in the conditionality of the emperor's authority and Confucian agrarianism were to underpin the Chinese state from 221 B.C., after the leadership of the Qin state had overthrown the Zhou rulers and finally created a truly unified Chinese empire, until its demise in the twentieth century A.D. The Qin introduced reforms of land and government that when combined with these underlying beliefs were to establish an extraordinarily durable and successful economic, social and political structure for over two millennia. By replacing the last vestiges of feudalism with private ownership of land and scrapping decentralized administration in favor of central government, the Qin created an independent peasantry and a centralized bureaucracy that became China's backbone and central nervous system.

Ideology, the landholding system and the state reinforced and interacted with one another. Individuals and society as a whole benefited from what Gang Deng has described as a self-regulating mechanism, a "trinary structure" that enabled the Chinese to expand their territory and perpetuate their empire and so assemble their remarkable record of relative stability.[3] Gang Deng's study of the Chinese "premodern" economy from 1500 B.C. to the early twentieth century is doubly interesting because it is written by a man who is at once a professional economic historian, lecturing at the London School of Economics and deploying all the appropriate quantitative and other techniques of academic economics, *and* a survivor of Mao Zedong's cultural revolution who at the age of fifteen was sentenced to a labor camp near the Sino-Soviet border. He served six years in the camp, was unsuccessfully brainwashed and, he claims, "developed a sense of reality, including an understanding how institutions worked and what ordinary day-to-day peasant life was like in China," before moving to the West.

To succeed, his thesis requires that the periodic invasions, peasant rebellions and overthrow of legal authority leading to the establishment of new dynasties be themselves regarded as part of the self-regulating mechanism. Earlier historians have seen such events as simply the failures of one system and the succession of another. For Deng, however, "a peasant rebellion would reset the clock for the structure . . . [and] the alien invasion and conquests of the nomads reinforced the structure. . . . [But] instead of gloating over the destruction of the trinary structure, the indigenous peasants and the alien nomads participated actively in its maintenance."

A homelier way of telling this tale might be that for most of 2,000 years China remained an immensely productive, heavily populated and socially conservative state under single political rule because landowning peasants were established as its ultimate beneficiaries and moral sovereigns and a form of government was evolved that either provided them with the protection and stability they needed or, if it did not, would correct itself either by moral pressure or the peasants' sanction of revolt. This also meant, as we shall see, that changes that threatened the ultimate ascendancy of the peasant society, land-based, landowning and farming, were successfully resisted by a combination of peasant opinion, moral doctrine and imperial bureaucracy implementing the resulting consensus.

What was missing, in comparison, for example, with the European Middle Ages, was the kind of pluralist political and economic setting in which new ideas and techniques could be hawked in the next town or market if they were suppressed by regulation in the first, thus opening the way for the Darwinian mechanism of survival to ensure that the most effective methods eventually prevailed. In global history, however, "eventually" is a long time, and the achievements of Chinese society during Deng's two millennia were formidable, in many ways unique. The mechanism's longevity is attributable not simply to its accommodation of revolt and calamity as part of the system but also to its success in generating recurrent eras of remarkable prosperity for between 40 and 100 million Chinese people from 200 B.C. to A.D. 1500 and beyond.

European myopia might seek to ascribe the durability of this Chinese system to China's geographical isolation, but this isolation is largely in the eye of the beholder. China was as much under pressure from the endlessly expanding nomadic tribes of central Asia as ever was the Roman Empire. From about 100 B.C. China was, moreover, as much in contact with western Asia and the Indian subcontinent through almost continuous caravan trade and the sea routes around Southeast Asia as they were with it; the flow of ideas and techniques meant that none of the civilizations of the Asian periphery or the Mediterranean basin could remain indefinitely in ignorance of developments in the others.

China held together its agrarian society so long because it had stumbled upon a classically durable structure that was strong, flexible and self-balancing. It accommodated the fundamental needs of its people to produce and to be protected. It absorbed shocks from without so that they were channeled into the further robustness of its own system, and it corrected, by less or more drastic means, serious deviations from the primary model of a sovereign mass of the people whose needs for good government were served by an imperial state bound equally by its mandate from heaven and by threat of revolt or invasion to perform, reform or depart.

Before passing on to note the early specifics of this extraordinary (and extraordinarily extended) episode in man's endless quest to fulfill his economic opportunities while managing the problems those opportunities present, we can see that the Chinese system we have described following Deng was a special case of the waltz motif we have seen at work in other periods and places. The potentials of the Yellow and Yangtze River basins, before and after the introduction of large-scale irrigation, represent in a massive way the first step of the figure, a straight enlargement of economic opportunity. The concentrated populations to which these gains in productivity led, as well as the covetous appetites of the warlike nomadic peoples to the north and west, represent the second step, the political antithesis to the economic thesis. Deng's trinary system becomes the third step, seeking to reconcile the contradictions between the first two in a new arrangement.

In the Chinese case, whether one regards the whole story from the agricultural revolution to the final collapse of the imperial system in the last (i.e., twentieth) century as one gigantic figure of the waltz motif or as an endless sequence of repetitions of the figure, it looks to have been more successful and less disastrously retrogressive than in some other cases we have examined. McNeill and McNeill point out that the Roman Empire suffered similarly calamitous incursions in the middle of the first millennium A.D. as did China.[4] But the Roman Empire never recovered as either an economic or a political system. When western Europe did achieve new economic momentum, it was less because of "good" government than because of a species of Darwinian competition between alternative governments, itself a different resolution of the waltz motif.

China's first major economic flowering occurred under the Han dynasty that replaced the Qin in 206 B.C. and lasted until A.D. 220, coinciding with the main rise of the Roman republic and the high period of the Roman Empire. China had been unified as a result of a series of campaigns between 230 and 221 B.C. by King Zheng of Qin, who then adopted the title *shi huangdi,* "first emperor." He replaced Chinese feudalism and its aristocracy by a centralized government and a nonhereditary bureaucracy, and he standardized weights and measures. But it was the Han, founded by Liu Bang, a commoner and Qin official, who converted this framework into a stable political and social order that encouraged economic prosperity. Taxes were reduced and other reforms made.

Agriculture, always the engine room of any Chinese economy, benefited from a redesigned plowshare and a newly invented seed-sowing machine, as well as from dikes and canals that irrigated farmland and controlled flooding.[5] McNeill and McNeill comment that this also facilitated centralized imperial government because canal boats could be used to bring tax revenue, paid in kind, to the capital (Chang'an) by a network of navigable waterways.[6]

Ironworking, under state monopoly, flourished in forty-nine foundries with large blast furnaces, supplying both weapons of war and civil manufactures for the home and the farm. Silk production and weaving and lacquerworking also flourished, providing suitable materials for export along the trade land routes, sometimes called the Silk Road, which were regularly used from 100 B.C. and reached as far as the Roman world. The affluence of the Han empire was, in accordance with our theme of the waltz motif, frequently put under strain by the military and political adventures of its rulers and of others who coveted their power. Rebellion, however, led to reform and restoration, as Gang Deng's thesis suggests, and by the end of the second century A.D. China was the world's largest economy, defined by ethnic and political unity, though the ethnically diverse Roman Empire in A.D. 180 contained at least 100 million people, far exceeding China's 50–60 million. China's essential socioeconomic system was also well established. But at this moment, about A.D. 185, the very moment from which Edward Gibbon dates the beginning of the decline of the Roman Empire after the death of Marcus Aurelius in A.D. 180, China's political system failed, weakened by the same defect as Rome: its inability to provide for the succession. A sequence of child emperors, weak and divided government, oppression of the peasantry and dislocation of agriculture led to the overthrow of the Han dynasty in A.D. 220. China broke into three separate kingdoms for over three and a half centuries.

The broadly simultaneous demise of the two great empires at the far eastern and far western extremes of the Eurasian land mass, though partly brought on by their own internal deficiencies, may have been aggravated by a common external circumstance. The endless pressure from the steppe people in the north to reach warmer and more fertile climes encountered an effective resistance in the central area east of the Caspian Sea. McNeill and McNeill see this as diverting pressures to the westerly and easterly theaters of barbarian expansion, across the Danube and the Rhine in the west and into northern China in the east.[7]

This resistance, according to William McNeill, provided a shield behind which Indian culture flowered for about three centuries, beginning in A.D. 300.[8] The key to this strategic defense was, he says, a Parthian warrior class who were paid sufficient rents by local villagers to enable them to armor and mount themselves as formidable cavalry impervious to the steppe people's arrows. But neither the dates nor the geography of this thesis appear fully convincing, since the Parthians only defended the approaches to Persia rather than the gateway to northern India through the Hindu Kush and the Indus valley, and since they were effective from the third century B.C., half a millennium before the barbarian pressure on Rome and China became overwhelming. And in any case many barbarian incursions through northwest India did occur in the fifth and sixth centuries A.D.

What is, however, clear is that from about the fourth century, when China was divided, Rome was coming under increasing strain and populations were falling in both of the world's two great former empires, India enjoyed a period of exceptional cultural and economic prosperity and can be said to have carried the baton of man's economic story. The population of the Indian subcontinent continued to rise throughout the whole of the first millennium A.D., from about 35 million at the start to almost 80 million in A.D. 1000, unlike Europe and China, whose populations fell from A.D. 200 to 600.[9]

Since we took our leave of this part of the world in Chapter 1 at about 1800 B.C., the Indus valley civilization had been displaced around 1500 B.C. by seminomadic Aryans from central Asia to the north. Over the next 1,000 years, the Hindu religion had formed itself as the dominant culture of India, whose economy by then included ironworking and rice farming, both in the Ganges plain. From 500 B.C. a dominant kingdom based in the Ganges valley had emerged, transformed in 321 B.C. into the Mauryan empire by Chandragupta Maurya, who also had seized the opportunity of Alexander the Great's departure from the Indus valley to enclose that area, too, in his empire.[10] This empire in turn had succumbed to a succession of internal and external pressures in the first centuries B.C. and A.D., and it had not been not until the rise of the Gupta empire under Chandragupta I in A.D. 320–335 that a new period of stability and prosperity could begin.

In the year in which Rome was sacked (A.D. 410), Chandragupta II presided over an empire at its peak, stretching in modern terms from Kabul to Madras and from Karachi to Calcutta.[11] The base was village-centered agriculture, rice in the Ganges valley and other crops and herding elsewhere. Ironworking continued from earlier times, and textile manufacturing was extensive, producing silk, muslin, calico, linen, wool and cotton that were traded in volume between north and south India and into the Roman Empire before its fall, thereafter into Southeast

Asia.[12] Other ways in which the relative political stability was exploited by the Indian version of man's recurrent urge to improve his material conditions, Adam Smith's "progress of opulence," included ivory work; stonecutting and -carving; copper- and leadworking; pearl fishing in the west; cutting, polishing and setting of precious stones; pottery; spice, perfume, sandalwood, indigo and herb trades; and transport by ox-drawn carts, pack animals, elephants, canal and riverboats and square-rigged, two-masted, canoe-hulled (sharp at both ends), oceangoing ships.[13]

The seagoing trade was supported by a lively interest in navigation, which in turn was supported by advances in numeracy that have left a decisive legacy to this day, namely, what we inaccurately call "Arabic" numerals, including the all-important, if null, zero. It is also to Indian mathematicians of this time that we owe the fact that we normally count in tens, or base ten (unless we are computers). In about A.D. 830 Muhammad ibn Musa al-Khwarizmi, a Muslim in Persia, translated from Sanskrit, the sacred language of ancient Hindu India, a book that three centuries later was translated into Latin under the title *Algoritmi de numero indorum* and became the channel by which "Arabic" numerals eventually reached Europe.[14] He also wrote a book on algebra that was used in the West as a textbook until the sixteenth century.[15]

Some have ranked these innovations with the wheel, the alphabet and the compass as among the most decisively enabling inventions of man's career upon earth.[16] Astronomy was recognized as a separate discipline. Aryabhata, the author of the oldest Indian text on mathematics (dated A.D. 499), who also calculated the value of π to within three-millionths of today's usual value (his Chinese predecessor Liu Hui had got even closer two centuries earlier), believed that the earth was a sphere rotating on its axis 1,000 years before Columbus sailed (as in fact did Columbus and most of his contemporaries).[17] The other cultural achievements of the Gupta era, which included rich philosophical debate between Brahmins and Buddhists, were a vast prose and poetic literature in Sanskrit and extremely refined life-styles for those able to afford them (a manual of agreeable daily—and nightly—life was set forth for them in the *Kamasutra*).

At a more inclusive level, Indian society had already embraced its characteristic caste system whereby societies were hierarchically structured into echelons to which individuals belonged by birth and, more spiritually, by the merit or otherwise of their own previous lives before reincarnation and by which individuals were customarily constrained to follow designated occupations. The number of castes and subcastes multiplied from the original four (priests, warriors/rulers, farmers/artisans/merchants and servants) and came to reflect the advancing division of labor and specialization in a growing economy, though to modern eyes it appears that it must also have been a barrier to social mobility and therefore to the efficient allocation of economic resources. It nonetheless survived into the twentieth century, not much less than the two millennia of China's trinary system. Like the trinary system, its tendency is likely to have been conservative, and like that system it appears to have had the strength and flexibility to continue through centuries of change and turbulence.

Whether it can claim to have contributed to the reconciliation of the needs, as we have seen in our discussions of the waltz motif, of Indian society for both economic change and political stability, allowing new economic opportunities to be seized while controlling the pressures they engender, is more difficult to say. Probably it survived and, up to a point, served the needs of Indian society—by ensuring a supply of skilled labor in certain essential economic functions and in transmitting, albeit by heredity, particular skills and knowledge—only by allowing itself to be overwhelmed by cruder economic forces when low castes became affluent or when affluent castes became poor. The resulting social mobility, reflecting the realities of population pressures and sundry catastrophes as well as new opportunities for wealth, occurred in practice, though sometimes at the price of ugly conflict. On balance, therefore, it is not plausible to claim for the caste system the same long-term role in supporting the stability of Indian society that the trinary system had in China.[18]

As was the case with the Roman Empire and the Han dynasty in China, conflict over the succession weakened the Gupta empire following the death of its ruler Skandagupta in A.D. 467. This political weakness left India divided among regional kingdoms and brief dynasties.[19] Kings who had paid tribute to the Guptas and previously conquered tribes became more independent, and the invading Huns established a kingdom in the northwest but were defeated in A.D. 528 by an Indian coalition. The Guptas, however, were only one element in the coalition, and although they ruled Magadha, comprising a large area of the Ganges basin around modern Patna, until A.D. 720, their imperial power had evaporated. During the first half of the seventh century, the states of the Ganges plain were reunited under Harsha of Kanauj, but no other Indian ruler emulated the Guptas until the thirteenth century.[20]

India's pluralistic system of states, however, was soon overshadowed by what McNeill and McNeill call "the explosive emergence of the realm of Islam."[21] In Arabia in A.D. 622 the Prophet Muhammad's flight (called the *hijrah,* or hegira) from his nomadic tribe at Mecca to the oasis town of Medina marked the beginning of Islam's rise to become a major world power, dominating the Middle East and extending at its height from the Iberian peninsula to South Asia and in the thirteenth century even to the islands of Southeast Asia. From A.D. 634 (when Umar became the second caliph—literally, "successor" to the Prophet—and launched the Arab expansion that overran Syria and Palestine, Mesopotamia, Alexandria and Persia), Muslims took over as the baton carriers of man's economic story for the next three centuries or so, becoming the linchpins of the commercial network that linked the whole of Eurasia from the Atlantic to the Pacific.

The people who made the Islamic empire and the economic civilization it encouraged were originally Arabs, but Arabs imbued with a new energy and self-confidence by their religious convictions based on the Quran and newly mobile thanks to their discovery of how to manage the camel. Like most early economic systems, it took its inception and its identity from the establishment of a political domain by military prowess. But in other ways it was significantly different from the preceding prototypes in Mesopotamia, Egypt, Rome, China and India. The engine room of all those economies was agriculture and the surplus that was generated and then invested in the creation of towns, cities and the further specialization of labor that urban life made possible.

The Arabs came out of the arid lands of the Arabian peninsula. Though they captured the two great fertile areas of the ancient world, Mesopotamia and the Nile valley, to say nothing of the former Roman granaries of northern Africa, these were not the sole or even perhaps the mainsprings of Islam's economic success. With the possible exception of Athenian Greece, Islam was the first economy to base a period of global leadership on commercial as much as on agrarian prowess, though the achievements of Islamic agriculture between A.D. 700 and 1100 have been called a "green revolution."[22]

This commercial preeminence had two main foundations: geography and ideology, which combined to make the Muslim Arabs of this period at once the best placed and the most apt of people to create and expand the sinews of trade from Spain to China and to develop and glorify the skills and techniques of business to quite new levels of sophistication.

The Islamic empire was centered in the Near East. Its first capital was Medina, then from A.D. 661 Damascus and from A.D. 763, despite some fragmentation of western Islam, Baghdad. It was thus strategically placed to exploit the great marine highways of the Eurasian world: the Mediterranean, the Red Sea, the Persian Gulf, the Indian Ocean, and the South and East China Seas. At the same time the western end of the Silk Road from China pivoted on Baghdad, linking into alternative routes up the Tigris and the Euphrates to Damascus and Constantinople.

From about A.D. 700 there was a Muslim colony in Ceylon. By the eighth century, Arab navigators had figured out the prevailing monsoon winds sufficiently to devise a reliable two-year return passage from Mesopotamia to China: down the Persian Gulf in September; a reach southeast across the Gulf of Arabia to the tip of India in the northeasterly monsoon of October–November; east across the Bay of Bengal running before the southwesterly monsoon in December; catching the southerly monsoon in the South China sea in the early months of the year for the northerly passage to Canton by April or May; remaining in port for the heavy winds of early summer before running south again and then west in the northerly monsoon in the autumn; catching the northeasterly monsoon for another reach back across the Gulf of Arabia in the winter; and returning to the Persian Gulf in the late spring.

They could scarcely have managed this without effective ways of both steering in a straight line when out of sight of land and knowing their positions and the direction of their intended destinations. This implies that in addition to known sailing routes that were described in contemporary works (*Relation of China and India,* written in A.D. 851, and the *Book of Roads and Provinces* by Ibn Khurdadhbih, A.D. 846–885), they must have had some method, presumably based on observing the sun and the polestar, of estimating at least their north-south positions.[23] This, combined with dead reckoning (figuring how long you have been going in what direction at what speed), may have enabled them, notwithstanding ocean currents, to plan landfalls on extended coastlines such as southern India and then feel their way to specific locations.

To avoid steering in circles, they must either have had some approximation to the compass—a magnetized needle free to float and seek the north magnetic pole—much earlier than has hitherto been supposed, or they must have used the wind, the swell and, when they could see them, the sun, moon and stars, which are highly approximate and anxious methods, especially in cloudy weather or when wind directions are fluky. The first recorded appearance of the compass was in the twelfth century.[24] But in the first century A.D. the great geomancers of the Chinese Han dynasty did have brass divining boards on whose polished surfaces a magnetized ladle or needle was allowed to align itself in a north-south direction, and it was from this that the first compasses evolved.[25]

It was not until the thirteenth century that Europeans began to use the compass, having acquired it from the Arabs, who seem to have had it from the Chinese or to have invented it independently.[26] In the annals of oceanic exploration, however, the achievements of Arabs, Chinese and Europeans pale by comparison with those of the Polynesian navigators, who started from Southeast Asia in about 1000 B.C. and colonized most of the Pacific Islands, including the Hawaiian group and Easter Island, by A.D. 500. They reached Madagascar in the first century A.D. and New Zealand (Aotearoa) in A.D. 1000.[27] Their mastery of ocean passages in outrigger canoes was based on their understanding, which we still only dimly share, of stars, weather, marine life, sea states and currents.

Navigators, of course, need ships, and Arab shipbuilders and riggers contributed notably to their development and capability for oceangoing trade. Almost as important as the ability to navigate for mariners is the ability to make progress in the intended direction, even when the wind is unfavorable. The greatest contribution before the invention of steam to this vital capability was the invention of the lateen sail, a triangular spread attached to a long rigid pole (or "yard") that is itself hoisted high on, and at 45° to, a short mast. The lateen can be trimmed so that the ship can catch the wind—and so make forward progress—even when the wind is coming from as much as 25° forward of the beam of the boat. Thus, by zigzagging (tacking), the vessel can make slow progress even to a destination directly upwind of its starting point, though this is not normally a preferred method of covering very long distances, as in the ocean trades.

Other lasting contributions by Islamic pioneers to economically important technological advance during the latter part of the first millennium A.D. reflected Islam's central geographical position in the Eurasian world as it then operated, for example:[28]

- They greatly improved the quality of textile fabrics and transmitted Persian inventions across the world, including introducing cotton production into the Near East, Sicily and Spain.
- They carried leather-working to new heights and established Morocco and Cordoba* as world-famous centers.
- They made the first tidal mill, exploiting the flood and ebb of the sea, in Basra in A.D. 1000.
- Windmills and waterwheels testified to their ability to adopt, modify and eventually transmit ideas they did not always originate, as with so-called Arabic numerals and possibly the compass, as well as sword-making using Indian steel.
- Papermaking was traditionally supposed to have been learned from Chinese prisoners captured in Samarkand in A.D. 753, leading to the first paper factory in Baghdad in A.D. 793. By A.D. 1000 the Islamic world had bound books, wrapping paper and paper napkins. Paper was not introduced to western Europe until the twelfth century.
- They learned sugar refining and confectionery techniques and later transmitted them westward.
- Asian fruits, cereals and vegetables brought to the West by Islam included sorghum and rice, hard durum wheat from which pasta is made, oranges, lemons, bananas, watermelons, asparagus, artichokes, spinach and eggplants.

*Hence "cordwainer" to mean a leather-worker or shoemaker, from "Cordovan" (in Andalusian, *Cordoban* or *Cordoves*).

- The two celebrated Muslim chemists Al Jabir and Al Razi (long known to Western students as Geber and Rhazes), wrote what became the standard textbooks for hundreds of years.[29]
- Recognizing that alchemy was doomed to failure, Muslims discovered alkalis, less glamorous but almost as economically important, and thus greatly improved the quality of glass and clay products.
- They produced naphtha, an inflammable petroleum product like kerosene.
- They developed much better perfumes and acids than were previously known.
- They "systematised and unified the field of medicine as never before."[30]
- They possessed a far more extensive pharmacological armory than Europe's at that time; they developed new surgical procedures, including the first use of animal gut for stitching wounds; and they improved the design of surgical tools, including scissors, syringes, various probes and exploratory devices and obstetric forceps.
- They developed the treatment of contagious diseases as a separate major branch of medicine.[31]

The second foundation of Islam's economic leadership and historic importance in this period was ideological. The Muslim religion embraced and encouraged a positive attitude to business, the Prophet himself having been a merchant in a wealthy family who had been successful in banking and the overland caravan trade in Arabia. Like Christianity, Islam forbade usury, and like Christianity it managed to forget this economically inconvenient doctrine when it needed to. Unlike Christianity, it did not commend a whole way of life indifferent and even hostile to the business life and material advancement. The Quran quite specifically set out to expound ethical commercial standards, not to overturn the tables of the money changers. Honestly made business profits were sanctioned in Islamic teaching as moral, and the business life was extolled as fully compatible with religious duties of prayer and pilgrimage.

In a more practical vein, Islamic law provided for several important kinds of business partnership, which offered flexible scope to mix risk, reward and liability according to the wishes of the parties and the nature of the business. Historians bewail the lack of surviving documentary evidence of business contracts in medieval Islam, but that does not mean that Muslims were any less sophisticated in business than their European contemporaries, simply that under their law proof of contract lay in the oral testimony of witnesses, not in written documents, which even where they existed were not officially preserved by public authorities as they were in the great European commercial centers such as Genoa and Champagne.[32]

Also important was the institution of the *wakil al-tujjar,* a kind of business ambassador who represented merchants from his own country in a foreign center and provided various other useful correspondent and allied business services. This absolved merchants from having to establish their own offices in every center and allowed trade to flow more smoothly. Similar functionaries came later to be widely used in medieval Europe, where the idea may have been independently reinvented to meet the same objective business need.[33]

Islamic business was supported in the latter part of the first millennium by a developed monetary and banking system. This provided commercial and private credit (despite the usury laws), suitably assayed and certified denominations of gold and silver coins for settlement purposes, deposit and money transmission mechanisms (including what amounted to checks and bills of exchange) and accounting systems that provided bank customers with what we would recognize as statements of their position. This legal and financial infrastructure supported—and was supported by—a well-developed real economy in which agriculture, trade and city-based industry all eventually (by early in the second millennium) thrived.

Islamic ideology also favored learning. Muslims were exhorted in the Quran to seek knowledge wherever they could find it, "even if they had to go to China."[34] From a European point of view, they were thus able to perform an all-important cultural function in receiving, preserving, enhancing and transmitting elements of classical Greek and Roman civilization following the decline of Rome, feeding them back into European centers as the Dark Age began to lift. They were, with the Chinese, the global baton carriers for science and philosophy from the seventh to the fifteenth centuries.

Our knowledge of many classical Greco-Roman authors depends entirely on surviving Arabic translations. Important medical texts that might have been lost were saved because they were translated into Arabic, and this heritage was eventually passed back to Europe, when Islamic medical works were subsequently translated into Latin.[35] All modern mathematics uses the numerals the Arabs passed on from their Indian inventors. The Muslim centers of learning in Cordoba and Granada were seedbeds in which the intellectual revival of western Europe in the eleventh and twelfth centuries was germinated.

Ibn Rushd (A.D. 1126–1198; known in Latin as Averroës), who had the greatest influence—Bertrand Russell acknowledges it as "very great"—of all Muslim philosophers on European thinking, was born in Cordoba and taught and studied theology, jurisprudence, medicine, mathematics and philosophy both there and in Seville before being exiled to Morocco for the heresy of supposing that truth could be discovered by unaided reason.[36] He expounded Aristotle in preference to Plato and denied personal immortality while acknowledging the existence of God, provable, he said, by reason alone. His influence spread rapidly both to professional philosophers and scholastics at the University of Paris and elsewhere and among private citizens who adopted his views on immortality and were called Averroists. Bertrand Russell nonetheless expresses the traditional European view that "Mohammedan civilisation in its great days was admirable in the arts and in many technical ways, but it showed no capacity for independent speculation in theoretical matters. Its importance, which must not be underrated, is as a transmitter."[37]

The positive part of this judgment is manifestly right, not only because of Islam's central geographical position in Eurasia at the turn of the millennium but also because of its chronological centrality between the classical and Indian civilizations that preceded it and the Chinese and European flowerings that followed. The negative part can make sense only if religion itself is excluded from the domain of "theoretical matters." Even then it may flatter European prejudices and do less than full justice to Abu-Nasr al-Farabi (A.D. 870–950), who deserves credit for keeping Islamic philosophy uncontaminated by Islamic religion and for his work on logic and political theory, or to Abu-Hamid al-Ghazali

(A.D. 1058–1111), who may have anticipated David Hume's doctrine of causal relationships—that we observe nothing but repeated coincidence.[38]

About A.D. 1000 the center of the Islamic world shifted from Baghdad to Egypt, specifically, to its chief inland port of Fustat on the Nile, just above the beginnings of its delta, and to the nearby royal center established by the new Fatimid dynasty from Tunis in what became Cairo. Fustat-Cairo became central Eurasia's greatest commercial hub, the place to go to make your fortune, the crossroads of world trade and "the glory of Islam."[39] The Fatimid rulers encouraged the business classes in Egypt, both Muslim and Jewish, and the state itself played an active role in the economy: It owned most of the land, was the main customer and agency for agricultural products and was much depended upon for protection of shipping in the Mediterranean trades against threatening Venetian fleets. But despite military reverses in the Mediterranean and in Egypt itself, when the Crusaders advanced and Saladin had to rescue Cairo, Islam clung to its monopoly access to the Red Sea and the Indian Ocean and so to the invaluable spice and other trades with the East—cloth, emeralds, silk, lead, porcelain, slaves and diamonds, to say nothing of banking and shipping—for another 300 years, until the appearance in the Indian Ocean of Vasco da Gama in A.D. 1498.

This Indian trade was the commercial foundation of the great period of the *Karimi* merchants—large-scale wholesale merchants or, as the name means, "big" businessmen—who seem to have started out in the eleventh century as Red Sea merchants, their trade protected from the usual piracy of that part of the world by armed ships belonging to the Fatimid and later Ayyubid ruling powers. Saladin himself supported them, getting four years' taxes paid in advance in return, and in A.D. 1182 he decisively repulsed the efforts of the Crusaders to break through into the Red Sea, leaving the *Karimi* in undisputed control of the eastern trade, chiefly spices, from their famous warehouse headquarters in Fustat.[40]

Egypt's and the Near East's commercial ascendancy was supported by agricultural and industrial success, above all textile manufacture based on flax and cotton and sugar production and refining, which were booming in the late thirteenth century. But gradually this era drew to a close as one blow after another weakened Egyptian prosperity and power.

Bad government played its part from the fourteenth century, with state monopolies and privileges, heavy taxation and forced labor. Forced purchases of state products, widespread corruption and poor management inhibited technological change, especially in sugar refining. Periodic military challenges from the Crusaders up to the middle of the fourteenth century and growing European economic competition thereafter, despite the cozy exclusive deals—northern slaves and European manufactures for eastern spices and Egyptian textiles—with first the Genoese and later the Venetians, put continuing pressure on the sultan's resources and so on the supporting economy, though never to the extent of breaching Egypt's and the *Karimi* merchants' control of the eastern trade.[41]

More serious was the impact of the Black Death in the middle and Tamerlane's conquests in the Levant at the end of the fourteenth century. Industrial production declined as more than a third of the population of Egypt and Syria, including 40 percent of the population of Cairo, was wiped out in a few years from the arrival in Alexandria in A.D. 1347 of the disease (pneumonic rather than bubonic, though imported directly from the Crimea, as was its bubonic version into Europe via Venice). Raw materials were sold directly to Europeans, unprocessed, leaving much of the final value to be added—and so rewarded—on the other side of the Mediterranean. Under this pressure the sultans became ever more oppressive in their search for revenue, accelerating the cycle of economic decline in much the manner of the Roman Empire in the west during parts of the third and fourth centuries A.D.

The final blow—a classic example of step two in the waltz motif—fell when Egypt's Indian trade was abruptly cut off by Portuguese naval action to close the Red Sea to Muslim shipping within five years of Vasco da Gama's first appearance in the Indian Ocean. Soon after this, in A.D. 1516, the Mamluk sultanate that had ruled Egypt since the middle of the thirteenth century succumbed to conquest by the Ottoman Turks.[42] Islamic Egypt had once been "a vanguard for the world system" at the heart of the interlocking economic network that linked northwestern Europe to China in the first half of the second millennium A.D.[43] Abu-Lughod sums up its final eclipse: "The weakened economy was severely debilitated by the effects of the Black Death, which left only the Indian trade as the primary surviving source of wealth. When the Portuguese took over that trade, Egypt was undone. It was less her lack of business acumen than her lack of fire power that caused her demotion from kingpin of the collapsing world system."[44]

But centuries before Vasco da Gama's end run, global leadership in economic affairs had passed from Islam to China. The Chinese Han empire had disintegrated into three rival states back in A.D. 220. After more than three and a half centuries, in A.D. 589, unity had finally been restored by Yang Jian, who founded the Sui empire as Emperor Wen. His land and state reforms had generated economic growth, which had been further enhanced by the construction between A.D. 606 and A.D. 609 of the Grand Canal from Yue on the eastern coast to Beijing in the north, linking the Yangtze and Yellow Rivers. As a result, the rice-growing Yangtze valley had been "economically acquired," in Mark Elvin's phrase.[45]

Although military transport canals had been built since the Qin dynasty (221–207 B.C.), the integrated national network had been constructed by conscripted labor in the early seventh century and had about 1,200 miles of main routes at a width of 40 paces. As Elvin has noted, "It was probably an engineering feat without parallel in the world of its time."[46] The Grand Canal had performed artificially for northern China what the Mediterranean had done naturally for the Byzantine Empire, providing the means to transport the surplus of the south (Egypt, the Yangtze valley) to a northern-based administration and army (Constantinople, Sui China). In addition, this major technological innovation had facilitated the colonization and economic development of the south, which provided the foundation for China's long-term economic expansion.

The prosperity created by Wen, however, had been squandered by his successor, Yang, whose ill-advised war against the Korean kingdom of Koguryo provoked peasant rebellion in the northeast. China had been saved in A.D. 617 when Li Yuan, a military governor, launched a coup and captured the Sui capital of Luoyang. After Yang's murder he had become (as Gaozong) the first emperor of the Tang dynasty in A.D. 618. His son, Taizong, having in turn deposed his father in A.D. 626, had proceeded to remodel China on traditional Han lines, giving pride of place to agriculture and the peasantry.

The foundations had been laid for China's economic revival and emergence as the world's most advanced and powerful preindustrial economy. Taizong had made the state bureaucracy more meritocratic while rewarding the peasantry with further land redistribution and less taxation. Agricultural output had been increased, internal trade had flourished, craft production had been stimulated and ceramics and silks had been widely exported.

In A.D. 750 the Tang capital of Chang'an had been the world's largest city, with over 1 million inhabitants (compare this with Cairo's half a million just before the Black Death).[47] But during the eighth century the Tang dynasty had fallen victim to the twin threats of external attack and internal unrest. The Arabs, the Thai kingdom of Nan Chao, Mongolian nomads and Tibetans all had inflicted damaging defeats, and the emperor's authority had been fatally undermined by peasant rebellions. The Tang dynasty had finally collapsed in A.D. 907, ushering in a further period of disunity, known as the Five Dynasties and Ten Kingdoms, that had lasted until the A.D. 960s.[48]

China had eventually been reunified between A.D. 963 and 979 by Song Taizu and his brother Song Taizong. But their catastrophic reforms of the bureaucracy and of landholding had led to the near collapse of administration and defense, increased nomadic invasions and the creation of a mass of landless peasants. The standing army that had been formed as a response to these crises had only exacerbated the state's economic problems.

Yet it was in the seemingly inauspicious circumstances of the Song dynasty's early years, known as the northern Song (A.D. 960–1126) because the capital was at Kaifeng, toward the Yellow River end of the Yangtze-Yellow River section of the Grand Canal, that China's remarkable economic resurgence had its origins. In its desperation for new sources of revenue, the Song government encouraged commerce and promoted maritime trade.[49] Less immediately happy were the consequences of the burdens imposed by the government on agriculture in the northern areas more nearly under its control. Heavy taxes and tight restrictions triggered a mass migration to southern China, as many peasants sought the lower taxes and greater freedom there.

This caused such population pressure on land in the south that the government was persuaded in about A.D. 1023 to seek a higher-yielding rice variety from Champa (now in Vietnam). The new variety succeeded beyond the wildest expectations of any official.[50] It became possible to grow two crops a year on the same land, thus greatly increasing agricultural productivity and indeed fueling further population growth.

As a result, the geographical distribution of China's population was eventually transformed. By A.D. 1380 the south had more than double the population of the north: 38 million compared with 15 million.[51] Labor-intensive wet-rice farming employed growing numbers, and this still yielded a sufficient agricultural surplus for the numbers working in nonagricultural sectors, including silk production and commerce, to increase at the same time.[52]

The Chinese notched up an impressive series of firsts with inventions that were in time to reach other economies and spur yet more economic growth and technological advance:

- They developed the use of paper during the second century A.D., an innovation that made possible the written examinations by which state officials were recruited.[53]

- Gunpowder was first put to military use in rockets in A.D. 969 during Song Taizu's campaign to reunite China.[54]

- They pioneered the use of coal and blast furnaces, following the deforestation of northern China and the resulting shortage of firewood during the Tang dynasty.

- In A.D. 806 China had been producing 13,500 tons of iron a year; by A.D. 1078 the revolution in iron production was yielding an annual output of 125,000 tons, a total that was not reached in Europe until well into the eighteenth century.[55]

- Iron and steel were used in the construction of bridges and even for the building of a cast-iron pagoda 70 feet high.

- In about A.D. 1000 they invented movable-type printing.[56]

- A water-driven mechanical clock was built for the Song court in A.D. 1090.[57]

- By A.D. 1130 paddle-wheel ships were in use.[58]

- By A.D. 1200 water-powered machinery was being used to manufacture textiles.[59]

- Chinese navigators were using the magnetic compass by A.D. 1150.[60]

- Chinese junks became more sophisticated, and foreign merchants increasingly chose to travel on them, a preference that is explained by Elvin's catalog of the junks' impressive features. Built with iron nails and waterproofed with the preservative oil of the tung tree, they were equipped with "watertight bulkheads, buoyancy chambers, bamboo fenders at the waterline, floating anchors to hold them steady during storms, axial rudders in place of steering oars, outrigger and leeboard devices, oars for use in calm weather, scoops for taking samples off the sea floor, sounding lines for determining the depth, compasses for navigation and small rockets propelled by gunpowder for self-defence."[61]

We now take for granted the use of banknotes as cash, but it was the Chinese who first achieved the major landmark of issuing paper money. The Song's encouragement of markets increased the demand for money in circulation. Various forms of private and official credit were developed. Hung Shih, a prefect of Hui-chou in what is now southern Anhwei, is quoted by Elvin as having observed during the twelfth century that if government transactions suddenly had to be made in ready cash, "the cash would all be used up within a year or six months and there would be no means to restore it to circulation."[62] With different and sometimes incompatible currencies also being used in different regions, notes of exchange came into greater use. The vouchers that merchants received as proof of payment of tolls for redemption at tea and salt warehouses also became a form of money. But these early types of paper money were privately issued remittance, credit or exchange notes with a date limitation.[63]

Paper money was first issued under government auspices in A.D. 1024 in Szechwan, a region with a different monetary system from the rest of China and one that otherwise faced imminent recession after the collapse through abuse of its privately issued paper money.[64] According to the British Museum's experts, however, "the first paper money as we know and use it today (i.e., officially issued exchange notes, with no date limitation) were the Exchange Certificates issued by the Yin in A.D. 1189."[65]

During Kublai Khan's rule, almost a century later, paper money was used exclusively (gold, silver and copper coins were not allowed in circulation), prompting Marco Polo, the legendary Venetian merchant, to pen his description of Chinese paper money:

> When these papers have been so long in circulation that they are growing torn and frayed, they are brought to the mint and changed for new and fresh ones at a discount of three per cent. If a man wants to buy gold or silver to make his service of plate or his belts or other finery, he goes to Khan's mint with some of these papers and gives them in payment for the gold and silver which he buys from the print-master. All the Khan's armies are paid with this sort of money.[66]

The loss of northern China in the early twelfth century to Jurchen Manchurians, or Tartar Yin, failed to stem the stream of innovation. The Song had previously bought off the threat from the nomadic Khitan Liao to the north for a heavy annual tribute. But in A.D. 1127 the more formidable Tartar Yin captured the Song capital of Kaifeng, forcing the Song to move their capital to Hangzhou in the south and thus inaugurating the southern Song dynasty (A.D. 1127–1279), which presided over a period of exceptional economic vigor.[67] Trade and manufacturing expanded. Towns and cities grew. Technology advanced.

But the southern Song, traditionally lauded in both Chinese and European histories, seem to have served the business classes and urbanized communities much better than the peasantry and the countryside. There was a massive population migration from south to north with the extraordinary consequence, according to Deng, that southern China's population fell by an estimated 46 percent between A.D. 1102 and A.D. 1159, while northern China's increased threefold by A.D. 1187.[68] The main reason for this upheaval appears to have been that the Tartar Yin regime was much friendlier to agrarian society, essentially upholding the traditional trinary structure of farming conservatism. Thus, the Chinese peasantry seem to have voted with their feet against the southern Song regime, for all its famed economic success. Indeed, part of the success, Deng suggests, was precisely that the departure of the half of the population with the lowest productivity hugely improved the ratio of resources to people and the productivity of the remaining southern labor force, thus delivering higher living standards.

The impact of this reverse migration, from the south back to the north, in the twelfth century was to intensify the southern Song's probusiness policies as the state sought to compensate for the loss of tax revenue from a reduced population. With the state more dependent than ever on trade to finance its existence, China could easily have made the mistakes that other regimes, earlier and later, made of increasing tax and other burdens on wealth-creating enterprises to the point where they were discouraged and even destroyed. But the southern Song had the wit not to damage their golden goose. Commercial undertakings were supported at the highest level. Merchants, who were treated as the basest of social classes through much of Chinese history, were favored.[69] Maritime trade and markets were encouraged. State officials became involved in making profits, notably in hotels and in the salt, tea and wine industries. The southern Song enjoyed for a while a trade-led economic boom.

By A.D. 1131 about half the state's income was derived from trade revenues, a proportion that had risen by A.D. 1300 to 70 percent, an astonishing figure for a premodern economy. Such was the size of the southern Song fleet that 2,050 ships had to be built annually simply to maintain its numbers. This commercial boom depended on the production of huge quantities of goods for trade, and the increased output of silk, ceramics, stationery and metalwares in turn triggered more economic growth.[70]

But although the Song promoted commercialization and urbanization, which entailed significant growth in the nationwide network of markets and manufacturing production, China did not industrialize. Just why not is one of the great questions of economic history. China seems to have been on the threshold of an industrial revolution over half a millennium before Europe, but it was Europe and not China that made the great leap forward.

It is tempting to blame this missed opportunity on the Mongols, who in the thirteenth century under first Genghis Khan and later Kublai Khan invaded and conquered China (to say nothing of central Asia, Persia, Mesopotamia and eastern Europe), establishing their own Chinese dynasty, the Yuan (A.D. 1271–1368). But deep internal forces in Chinese society, together with the physical disposition of its coal resources (see Chapter 6), probably had a more decisive impact. The Song's policies necessarily disadvantaged and offended rural society, especially the peasantry. Standards of living among ordinary citizens were squeezed by the priority given to business interests, government bureaucracy and national defense. Commercial growth and business prosperity were resented by the mass of Chinese who did not share in them. The Song's popularity was also undermined by the state's failure to prevent inflation, to provide adequate famine relief or water control or to defend its people against marauding invaders. It finally died, as Deng says, caught "in the crossfire between alien invasions and people's rebellions, armed or peaceful (in the form of tax-evading migrants)."[71] In the mid-fourteenth century, China was afflicted by plague and civil war as the Chinese rebelled against their Mongol rulers and eventually, in A.D. 1368, established a new dynasty, the Ming. According to McNeill, the plague was probably the biggest killer—it also spread to Europe, with devastating effect—and helps to explain why the Chinese population had by A.D. 1393 fallen to only 65 million, little more than half of the total in A.D. 1200 before the Mongol invasion.[72]

What does the Song saga tell us about economic development? In the last resort the Chinese peasantry and rural interests had it within their power to reject a strategy of commercial and industrial development that seemed to threaten the agrarian society. China had the science, technology, output surplus, urbanization and commercial infrastructure needed for industrialization. But it also had a central government, both under the southern Song and later under the Yuan, which could be forced to turn aside from developments that the peasantry rejected. In this sense institutions, socioeconomic structure, property rights, ideology and values coming together in China's conservative trinary system rejected industrialization far more decisively and lastingly than any Mongol horde.[73] None of this prevented the Chinese empire from having emerged under the Song, and then remaining under the Yuan and subsequently the Ming dynasty (A.D. 1368–1644), as the world's most advanced and powerful preindustrial economy, certainly for the first half of the last millennium and arguably for much longer.

During these three dynasties (A.D. 960–1433), until the great change of course, China's maritime trade flourished as never before.[74] Marco Polo describes China's chief port for foreign trade, Quanzhou (also Zaitun), in the late thirteenth century: "In this port there is such traffic of merchandise, precious stones and pearls, that it is a truly wonderful sight. From the harbour of this city all this is distributed over the whole province of Manji. And I assure you that for one shipload of pepper that goes to Alexandria or elsewhere to be taken to Christian lands, there are a hundred to this port of Zaitun."[75]

At that time Chinese ships mainly plied, in modern terms, the South China Sea and the Indonesian archipelago, touching at Malaya, Sumatra, Java, Timor and the Philippines. Passages were also made as far as India from the twelfth century.[76] But in the early fifteenth century there began one of those amazing manifestations of man's unpredictable capacities when occasion suits to behave as though he belonged naturally to a much later and completely different age and had been transplanted back in time for the occasion. The Ming emperor Yung Lo (born Zhu Di), having violently seized the throne, commissioned a giant treasure fleet to be constructed and put to sea, partly, at least, to search for his deposed and supposedly fleeing predecessor. He appointed in command his loyal lieutenant, the eunuch Ma He, renamed admiral Zheng He (Cheng Ho). Zheng He came from the substantial Muslim community in the port city of Quanzhou, and there is to this day a tablet on the hillside above the harbor commemorating the great man's visit in A.D. 1417 to the tombs of two Muslim "prophets" (probably Arab traders who married local women and stayed on).[77]

Over the next twenty-eight years (A.D. 1405–33) the admiral made seven cruises across the South China Sea, through the Spice Islands as far as the Timor Sea between Timor and Australia, to Java, through the Malacca Straits to Ceylon, to Chittagong in Bengal, to Cochin and Calicut in southwest India, to Hormuz at the mouth of the Persian Gulf, to Aden and to Jiddah halfway up the Red Sea and down the east African coast as far as the Mozambique channel.[78] His principal treasure ships were 400 feet long, nearly five times longer and as much as 100 times larger than Columbus's Santa Maria nearly a century later. His fleets increased from sixty to 300 ships, and his crews totaled nearly 30,000 men, the same as the Spanish armada more than a century and a half later and not exceeded in size until the world wars of the twentieth century.

The purpose of these astonishing manifestations is not wholly clear, though they certainly included the glorification of the emperor, who became more megalomaniac as his reign progressed toward its end in A.D.

1424. He insisted on moving China's capital from Nanjing to Beijing (which he named), in preparation for which he built the Forbidden City, a huge extravagance. The cruises produced spectacular tributes—including a giraffe from Kenya that was treated as the appearance of the celestial animal long foretold as a good omen and reputed to have been responsible for the pregnancy of Confucius's mother. Rulers along their routes were deemed by the Chinese to recognize the ultimate suzerainty of the son of heaven and were in certain cases removed if they had obstructed Chinese interests or disobliged Chinese representatives, though in no other practical sense did they appear to acknowledge the emperor's sovereignty over their lands. Some court officials complained that the expeditions produced too little hard profit.[79] But trade flowed in their wake, and China's standing was hugely enhanced wherever the fleet had touched.

In the year when Henry V of England was leading 6,000 men armed with bows and arrows into battle at Agincourt, Zheng He returned to Nanjing at the conclusion of his fourth cruise at the head of 28,560 men. With only moderate hyperbole Louise Levathes in *When China Ruled the Seas* has summed up China's naval superiority at that moment:

> Chinese influence abroad was at its peak, and all the important trading posts in the Indian Ocean basin and China seas—from Korea and Japan throughout the Malay archipelago and India to the east Africa coast—were at last nominally under Chinese authority and acknowledged the suzerainty of the dragon throne. From this lofty pinnacle China could have consolidated its position and become the dominant power in shaping the modern world. While Europe was still emerging from the Dark Ages, China, with her navy of giant junks, was poised to become the colonial power of the sixteenth century and tap the riches of the globe.... That moment at the pinnacle would last barely more than five years.[80]

Even so it is worth noting that when Vasco da Gama reached East Africa eighty years after Zheng He, he was greeted by natives in silks hats who shook their heads in derision at the petty nature of the ships in which the Portuguese had presumed to put to sea and scorned with laughter the shoddy goods he brought as trade. They had seen the real thing, though by then no one knew whence the white "ghosts" with large ships had come or whither they had gone.[81] Had Vasco da Gama and Zheng He met, one of the truly most decisive naval battles of world history might have resulted, though it is doubtful whether even victory in such an engagement would have persuaded the Chinese admiral to enter the Atlantic and colonize its shores, which were known to the Chinese, on the eastern side at least, to offer nothing more alluring than wool and wine, goods that were certainly not worth the passage.

As it was, Yung Lo's son ascended the throne and, in what might be entered into a competition for the falsest economy of all time, halted all further treasure ship voyages. He ordered all ships to return to harbor, all cargoes to be landed, all foreign envoys to return home and all shipbuilding and repair to cease. In reaction to his father's extravagance and out of a sincere desire to alleviate the burden of taxes on his people, he ordered that the capital should move back from Beijing to Nanking. Zheng He was given a military command on shore.

In short, the Confucian priority for agriculture had once again asserted itself. Land and the Great Wall, not the sea, should be the treasure and the safety of China, and in a centralized imperial bureaucracy it lay within the power of advisers to capture the mind of one ruler and change the course of the whole empire.[82] These counsels were reversed within two years by a new emperor, Schwan De, who dispatched Zheng He in command of his seventh and last expedition, in the course of which he reached halfway up the Red Sea, acquired all the latest Arab medicines the Chinese had read about in a book called *Hui yao fang* (Muslim pharmaceutical prescriptions) and acquired another giraffe. Even so, Chinese naval power was on the wane, doomed by the growing weakness and divisions of the central government and by what Chaudhuri calls "the problem of protecting the coastal provinces from the depredations of the ruthless sea bandits who infested the China Sea periodically."[83] In this case the waltz motif operated with exceptionally retrograde force: The wealth generated at the first step (Zheng He's expeditions) attracting ferocious predatory attack at the second step, which in turn is resolved at the third step by almost total withdrawal, at least for a time, from the initial opportunity.

Fairbank tells of the period immediately following:

> By mid-century Beijing also faced a revival of Mongol power and border raids. . . . After A.D. 1474 and during the sixteenth century the building of brick-and-stone-faced long walls with their many hundreds of watchtowers created today's Great Wall. It proved to be a futile military gesture but vividly expressed China's siege mentality. . . . The decline of Ming naval power, once shipbuilding

> was restricted to small-size vessels, opened the door to a growth of piracy on the South China coast ostensibly by Japanese but in fact mainly by Chinese. Instead of counterattacking, the Ming forced a costly Chinese withdrawal from the seacoast, vainly aimed at starving out the pirates. . . . In short, anticommercialism and xenophobia won out, and China retired from the world scene.[84]

Nonetheless, China consolidated its position as the world's preindustrial economic giant. The shift in emphasis of economic policy under the Ming from external trade to domestic self-sufficiency cannot be judged a disaster by any standards—other than possibly those of what might have happened if Admiral Zheng He's window on the world had been allowed to stay continuously open. Enjoying relative peace and stability from A.D. 1449, China's population more than doubled over the next 150 years, from 60 million to 130 million by A.D. 1580.

This expansion is a measure in itself of sustained economic growth. Although China remained a predominantly agrarian economy, and despite official antipathy to long-distance trade, large-scale manufacturing industries and extensive commercial activity expanded under the Ming, stimulated by initiatives such as the reconstruction of the transport system based on the Grand Canal and the introduction of an efficient nationwide courier service. The cities of the Yangtze delta became the center of the booming cotton textile industry, with raw cotton being shipped from the west by river and from the northern cotton fields, planted under the Mongols, by the Grand Canal.

Gradually as time went by even long-distance trade revived and prospered, extending over an area from Ceylon to Timor to Osaka. Cotton textiles, along with ceramics, silk and tea, were exported to Japan in exchange for metals and spices and to Southeast Asia, where they were reexported to Europe in return (from the sixteenth century) for silver from the New World.[85]

We have reached the eve of a dramatic transformation in man's economic story: the fundamental shift in the relative economic strength and wealth of the East and the West, to the latter's enormous gain, that culminated in the West's global hegemony. But in order to understand both how this upheaval occurred and how improbable it would have seemed in the medieval period, we must return to Europe and the period when we left it at the end of Chapter 2, about A.D. 700.

CHAPTER FOUR

Pluralism

THE POPULATION OF EUROPE (EXCLUDING TODAY'S RUSSIA) IN 700, having risen to around 40 million in 200 and collapsed to not much over 20 million by 600, was still below 25 million.[1] Before the Black Death in the mid-fourteenth century it peaked at about 75 million, fell to 50 million in 1400 and recovered to 67 million in 1500. So, in demographic terms the European part of man's economic story continues to be one of growth punctuated by periodic severe contractions. There had also been a huge redistribution of Europe's population between classical and late medieval times from the Mediterranean basin to the northwest. By 1300 the major concentrations of population—and of the political powers they supported—clustered around an axis from Italy to Belgium.[2]

In the aftermath of the disintegrating Roman administration, there had arisen in the fifth and sixth centuries A.D. in the heartlands of western Europe a kingdom (called Merovingian) based on the Frankish tribes in Gaul and the Rhine valley. Weak in itself it provided a platform from which in the early eighth century a high official, Charles Martel, was able to rally Europe's defenses against the advancing Saracen forces of Islam, whom he finally defeated in 732 at the battle variously called Tours or Poitiers.[3] Although the Muslims remained in parts of Spain for another 760 years, this was a historic turning point; never since has western Europe surrendered to an external power.

Charles Martel's son formally became the first Carolingian king in about 755; and his son, Charlemagne, crowned himself Roman emperor—the title that later became holy Roman emperor—on Christmas Day 800 in St. Peter's, Rome.[4] For a brief period, western Europe was unified, from the Pyrenees to almost exactly the line of the iron curtain after 1945, and from the North Sea to the Mediterranean. But this political framework broke down intermittently after Charlemagne's death in 814, undermined by the chronic problem of political power down the ages: succession. Barbarian attacks—Vikings from beyond the Baltic and Magyars from beyond the Carpathian mountains—continued to harass his heirs until the Saxon king Otto re-created the empire of the west.[5]

Otto the Great was crowned Roman emperor in Rome in 962 and established the Holy Roman Empire as an enduring feature of the political map of Europe for eight and a half centuries. Under Otto, whose personal control fell far short of absolute rule, power was shared among the emperor, the church, secular magnates and the whole network of negotiated embryonic feudal relationships that had grown up in the rural vacuum left by the collapse of Roman imperial power.[6] This compromise, which still encompassed a never-ending jostling competition and rivalry among the many different political authorities, nonetheless ended the preceding interval of disorder in central Europe and provided minimum orderly conditions in which Western civilization and economic prosperity could revive.

The true sun that illuminated the European dawn after 700 was economic rather than political. The backbone of the Roman Empire had been the army, and the foundation of political power had been the ability to pay the army. As the barbarian invasions increased in intensity in the fourth and fifth centuries, the burden of taxation grew heavier as the central authority struggled to meet an ever increasing defense budget.

Landlords and peasants progressively showed (in their behavior if not always in their conscious thoughts) that the supposed protection of the Roman Empire was no longer the best available deal. They switched their allegiance—where they found they had some effective choice—into the domain of the new states established in France and Spain by the invading Germanic tribes. These levied much lower taxes and financed their military exploits by rewarding their warriors with land. The landlords effectively chose a new money-for-protection deal, ceding some of their land and paying lower taxes to their new non-Roman rulers. Even within the empire the peasants had for a long time been trading in their land in exchange for lower taxes. They had done this by selling the land to those large landowners who enjoyed tax immunities because of past special services to the emperor. The peasants had then rented the land back. Now they extended this practice by gravitating toward those landlords who could offer lower tax bills because they had joined the Germanic states.[7]

The net result over the three centuries after the fall of Rome was a new political structure in the main rural areas of western Europe. At the grassroots level were fairly autonomous local communities in which peasants worked the land, supporting both themselves and a local lord in return for protection and order. This, it may be said, was not so different from the basic character of the social order under the empire. The peasants had indeed lost their former, at least notional, legal independence and property, and they were no longer in any strong sense "citizens." Slavery had diminished gradually, and in the Carolingian period what remained of it was drastically weakened. This to some extent created a social and economic space into which the formerly independent peasants settled in a condition somewhere between servility and freedom.

By the ninth century at the latest, the manorial system extended from the Loire to the Rhine and into northern Italy, and from there the Norman conquest reinforced its earlier development in England by the Anglo-Saxons, while it also spread to Spain, Portugal, Denmark and central Europe.[8] Although the decline of the Carolingian empire and the waves of invasions from the north and east prompted the abandonment of large areas of agrarian settlement, the manorial system remained the economic cornerstone when political stability was finally restored.[9] On this base there came to be erected a genuinely new kind of ruling superstructure within which lesser lords exchanged their support for the protection of greater lords and so on up to the king. In effect this so-called feudal system (from the feud, or fief, that a vassal held from his lord) was an informal social contract legitimized by the exchange of obligations for services (downward) and fealty (upward).

The economic bedrock was thus the local unit, the manor as it came to be called, within which was generated the agricultural surplus on which everything else depended. The essence of each manor was a largely self-sufficient economic and social unit, in which typically a village with a manor house, a church and certain facilities such as a smithy, a mill and a winepress accommodated peasants and the lord of the manor. The village would be surrounded by fields, commons and woodland, variously owned by the lord, held in strips by individual peasants or held in common. The land was both tilled and grazed, and the woodlands were exploited in accordance with the common rights of the peasantry and the special privileges of the lord. There were wide variations in the character, size and organization of manors, which continuously evolved and adapted to local and regional conditions.[10]

Within this unit there occurred crucial changes in farming methods that transformed the productivity of land in northwestern Europe, eventually supporting a long-term growth in population and production. The soils of northwestern Europe are heavy and moist, and though they contain enormous energy, they could not be cultivated by the light plows the Romans brought with them from the sandier soils of Italy. It was the invention of the heavy-wheeled plow, which dug deeper and broke and turned over heavier sods of clay and loam soils, that unlocked this energy for the benefit of its users. The heavy plow originated, it appears, with the Franks in Gaul from as early as the sixth century, but its use became widespread and its contribution to agricultural productivity significant only from the eighth century. The heavier soils required fewer fallow periods to replace their moisture than the light soils of the Mediterranean area. By making them cultivable, the heavy plow opened the way to three-course crop rotation—growing crops for two years out of three rather than every other year—thus raising productivity by a third. A field would typically rotate between fallow, winter crops and spring crops. Each year one field in three would lie fallow, providing grazing for animals who further fertilized it with their droppings.[11] This system also enabled the labor and farm tools of the manor to be used more efficiently and crop types to be varied, thereby raising the total gain in productivity from a third to a half. The implications of this, applied to half a continent, when the practice spread from northern France in the eighth century to most of northwestern Europe by the eleventh century, are evidently huge.

The heavy plow had initially to be pulled by a team of oxen, which represented a large capital investment for a peasant farmer and therefore contributed to the development of the cooperative principle in the manorial system, whereby one team served a whole community. Horses had long been used for military and transport purposes under the Roman Empire and indeed before; the invention of the stirrup at about the turn of the fifth century had established for centuries to come the ascendancy of cavalry over infantry. But certain problems had to be overcome before the horse, which could do the work of three or four oxen, could be economically used in agriculture. First, its hooves were vulnerable to damp, heavy soils. Second, any harness fitted round its neck to pull a plow or heavy wagon tended to pull on its windpipe and choke the beast. Third, a horse commonly eats three to four times as much as an ox, thus negating its apparently greater efficiency.

Solutions for all three problems became available toward the end of the first millennium. Greater use of iron, as ore and charcoal supplies were found to be more plentiful north of the Alps and as water power was applied to forges, gave farmers the horseshoe, as well as the sickle, the scythe and metal tips for wooden spades. Likewise, the invention by the ninth century of the breast strap and the padded horse collar enabled the horse to pull and breathe at the same time, which opened up the possibility of the heavy draft or cart horse that was thereupon bred for the purpose.[12] Finally, the three-course rotation offered an economical supply of oats to feed horses alongside wheat and barley for human consumption. This tilted the balance of efficiency increasingly in favor of the horse-drawn plow, especially in France, Flanders, England and parts of Germany, though oxen continued to be used in places for centuries.[13] The arrival of the horse as draft animal also gave a new lease on life to land transport by enabling heavy loads that had previously had to go by water or by slow oxcart to be hauled farther and faster by road.[14]

A fundamental part of man's economic story is his never-ending attempt to find substitutes for his own muscle power as a motive force in doing the work of the farm, the factory and the home. Animals were an important part of this story from early times. Another major power source of the pre-industrial world was water. Water is naturally transported from the world's oceans to higher places by condensation, wind and precipitation. It then finds its way back to the oceans by gravity. If man can harness this energy, he may save his own labor. The world's first water mills, which existed for this precise purpose, date back more than 2,000 years. Surprisingly, they were not widely used in the Roman Empire, perhaps because slavery took the edge off the incentive to develop and invest in labor-saving devices. They first became used as a general source of motive power in the early European Middle Ages from the seventh century A.D. Their main applications by the eleventh century were for grinding flour, cloth making, brewing, hammering, bellows driving, grinding cutlery, drawing wire and sawing.

The key advances, as so often in the story of technical progress, were not so much in the basic concept as in the engineering of the solution. It was the improvement of the gearing that made it possible to use both rapid- and slow-flowing streams, and efficient cams and cranks were used to convert the circular movement of the wheels into the back-and-forth motion needed for processes like hammering and crushing. The 1086 Doomsday Book tells us that there were 5,624 water mills in England, one for every fifty households.[15] These were supplying almost a third of the (nonhuman) energy, the rest provided by animal power.[16]

All these gains in productive potential—in total, per acre and per man—contributed to an economic space in which population could gradually rise and in which the growing agricultural surplus could support increased urban life and specialization of labor mediated through expanding trade and proliferating marketplaces.[17] Human settlements became more densely populated, and undeveloped lands were drawn into cultivation, some reclaimed from virgin forests or from flood lands in the Low Countries. Towns grew and prospered. Europe stood on the threshold of "a virtual explosion of urbanisation on the continent" in the eleventh and twelfth centuries.[18] European civilization itself expanded into new areas such as today's Poland, Czech and Slovak republics, Hungary, Romania and Lithuania. Scandinavia was incorporated into the European economy.[19]

At this point the reader may wonder how the waltz motif we introduced at the beginning of our story as a characteristic feature of our economic evolution was operating during the period of this chapter. Europe's Dark Age may itself be seen as the third step in the figure. It followed upon the failure of the political and social structures of the Roman Empire to cope with the external and internal pressures (barbarians at the gate and free-riding parasites of the Roman imperial establishment) at the second step. These in their turn had been attracted by the success of Rome at the first step.

As the Dark Age gives way to medieval Europe, the expansion in northwest Europe based on the successful exploitation of its heavy soils may be seen as the first step of another figure. This success obviously evoked the usual second-step threats from those who would prefer to live by force than by productive toil. The feudal system in its evolving guises, parallel to but different from the city-states in Italy, can thus be regarded as the third step, the political and social fix developed in order to contain and manage the pressures generated at the second step.

In contrast to the third step of the figure in the late Roman Empire this third step was to a degree successful, sustaining a gradual economic advance that became the first step of the next figure. That in turn ran into second-step challenges that preyed upon the growing population of Europe in a peculiarly devastating manner, the Black Death. But we anticipate.

For all its achievements in providing a form of social structure within which economic opportunities could be exploited, taking the place of the anarchy otherwise threatened by the breakdown of the Roman system, feudalism certainly was not an idyllic or ideal order. The legal wrangling it engendered and the curtailment of individual freedom promoted inefficiency and blunted incentives to innovation and enterprise. Norman Davies notes: "In reality, feudal society was built on a confused mass of conflicting dependencies and loyalties, riddled with exceptions and exemptions, where the once clear lines of service were fouled up by generations of contested privileges, disputed rights and half-forgotten obligations. It was certainly hierarchical, but it was anything but neat and regular."[20]

We have so far focused on the economic advances being made mainly in Europe north and west of the Alps through the exploitation under the manorial system of the huge reservoir of energy locked in its heavy soils, through the use of water power and through the growth of population, trade and production that these supported. A parallel but distinct evolution originated in Italy itself.

After the failure of the Roman Empire, rural northern Italy initially sought refuge from the threatened anarchy by expedients similar to those which led to the manorial system further north, namely, a retreat into small, localized and self-sufficient communities in which internal law and order and defense against external attack were provided from within the estate by lords or warriors who were in return supported by the produce of the estate. These naturally were developed on the foundations of the landed estates left over from Roman times.

But at the same time town life persisted, though much diminished, in the early Dark Age.[21] From the seventh century onward, cities like Venice, Genoa and Pisa began to be able to exploit Italy's geographical position between the Byzantine and Islamic empires to the east and southeast and the growing regions of northwestern Europe, which soon learned to offer timber and woolen cloth in exchange for the spices, silk cloth, brocades, porcelain and other luxuries from the East.[22] Thus Italian cities became middlemen between northwestern Europe and the Byzantine and Islamic empires, prospering by long-distance trade as well as by the normal functions of towns with rural agricultural hinterlands.

The independent prosperity of such cities, and their expanding exchange with the neighboring rural areas that fed them, progressively eroded the self-sufficiency and isolation of the rural estates, so altering the balance of forces in Italian society. Cities, towns and their merchant classes began to break free from feudal constraints, banding together to demand and win freedoms and privileges in business and rights of self-governance from the kings and feudal lords who had once claimed to rule them.[23] In 1035 Milan fought a battle to establish its freedom. In 1075 Pisa negotiated its own independent jurisdiction, and in 1176 a league of Lombard cities defeated the emperor Frederick Barbarossa. Indeed, the rivalry of emperors and popes for control of Italy from the eleventh century created opportunities for the cities. They were better placed than their more conservative opponents to exploit new military technologies and tactics, such as the crossbow, infantrymen armed with pikes and flanking cavalry, and thus to shift the balance of military power in their own favor.[24] By 1300 Milan had a population of 200,000, and Venice, Genoa and Florence were all over 100,000. Other parts of Europe witnessed the growth of towns and cities somewhat later—in the Low Countries, the Rhineland, northern France, Provence and Catalonia—though apart from Paris they were smaller and less politically independent than the Italian cities.

Just as the Mediterranean supported the Italian cities of Venice, Genoa and Pisa at the western end of the eastern trade, so the North Sea and later the Baltic and the rivers feeding those seas supported a spreading trade, eventually dominated by the 200 German cities and towns of the Hansa (or league) organized in 1367 to protect its members and regulate trade. German colonies in London, Bergen, Bruges and Novgorod were supplemented by entirely new German cities such as Riga, Memel and Danzig, planted as enclaves in foreign soil.

The two great sea-based trading systems, the Mediterranean and the North and Baltic Seas, needed to communicate with each other. After 1310 Venice and Genoa began to organize regular convoys on the Atlantic route that had previously been too difficult; the great markets of the Po valley in Milan and Verona were served by the busy passes over the Alps. The northern termini of this trade ranged from Vienna and Kraków to Lübeck, Hamburg and Bruges, with most of it flowing through Leipzig, Frankfurt and the four fair towns of Champagne.[25] Over time the periodic fairs became continuous, and their host towns developed into permanent regional markets, often in port cities.[26]

The evolution in Champagne and the neighboring county of Brie, an area roughly 100 miles square immediately southeast of Paris embracing the towns of Troyes, Provins, Lagny and Bar-sur-Aube, exemplified the importance of political pluralism in the economic developments of the time. The counts of Champagne, the feudal lords of the area, were sufficiently independent of their nominal overlords, the kings of France, to be able to disregard royal restrictions on trade and offer trading conditions, such as law and order and market infrastructure, that encouraged merchants to bring their business to Champagne, thus adding to the prosperity of the region and its tax base and so through extra tolls, leases, rents, licenses, fees and fines to the income of the counts.[27]

Other rulers began to draw the obvious moral, thereby propagating a business-friendly environment in medieval Europe more rapidly than would have been likely in a centralized bureaucratic empire in which there could be no such benign competition for economic activity. English kings had every incentive, after the revolt against King John that led to the Magna Carta and circumscribed some of the arbitrary powers he had seized, to look to new economic alliances to rebuild their strength. According to Britnell, this "compelled the monarchy to move in other directions to expand its income." And as Miller and Hatcher note, "Kings [of England] . . . were generally willing (especially when they could draw a profit from it) to act as patrons of urban development and emancipation, to license fairs and markets, and to offer protection to merchants, both alien and denizen."[28] It was a very different story in France. Indeed, when the king of France reasserted his control in Champagne and Brie in

1285, the four towns lost their attractions as business locations, and the Italian and Flemish merchants who were the protagonists in their markets transferred their activities to Bruges and Lyons, towns outside the French king's control.[29]

We have spoken so far of the rural developments in northwestern Europe and the Italian-led revival and expansion of medieval Europe's urban economy as mainly distinct phenomena. But in reality, of course, each reacted to the other in a single economic and demographic process. From the tenth century, at least, population in town and country was becoming denser as rural communities grew and new towns were established. There was a boom in the construction of churches, and other economic and cultural advances reflected the growth of population and the progress of the underlying agricultural surplus and division of labor. Between 1150 and 1280, eighty cathedrals were built in France; up to thirty cathedrals similar in scale and design to Westminster Abbey arose in England in the twelfth and thirteenth centuries.[30]

This period also saw the foundation of Europe's earliest universities, including Bologna in 1088, Paris in 1150, Oxford in 1167 and Cambridge in 1209.[31] Universities were modeled on the Islamic *madrasahs*, which Merson has aptly described as "the critical junction point in the transmission of knowledge from the ancient world of Greece and China to the west."[32] The *madrasah* was usually funded by merchants through a property trust, or *waqf.* Unlike Christian monasteries, however, the *madrasahs* aimed to provide religious education to the wider community and emphasized argument and debate.[33] By 1300, universities proliferated in Europe and were becoming the centers of intellectual life as the rediscovery of Greek philosophy and science—reimported into Europe via Islam—encouraged the use of argument, logic and investigation in human inquiry.[34] In the centuries ahead, this rational approach was to undermine the traditional foundations of religious faith and transform man's understanding of the world.[35] In the process, it paved the way for scientific and technical progress that is integral to the modern world.

The new economic vigor of western Europe's high medieval period was characterized by the application and development of a series of technological innovations. In power technology, the windmill combined the ideas of the water mill and the sail. Although windmills may have originated in central Asia, the use of gears and a horizontal axle in European mills suggests that they were an independent invention. The first European windmills that can be documented were in Yorkshire in 1185, and they were soon in use across the continent.[36] In hydraulic engineering, canal locks were developed in the Low Countries during the twelfth century and were widespread two centuries later.[37]

In manufacturing, the spinning wheel appeared in the wool industry in the twelfth century and marked the first application of a belt-driven transmission. An adaptation of the earlier flywheel that had been used only for grindstones, the spinning-wheel increased output compared with the traditional distaff-and-spindle method and boosted productivity in the Flemish cloth industry.[38] Adam Smith reckoned that the productivity of labor was doubled; more recent estimates suggest a threefold increase.[39] In weaving, the horizontal loom seems to have been first used in Troyes in the eleventh century, producing much longer cloths and stretching the warp more tightly. As a result, productivity increased by an estimated 325 percent.[40] Europeans mastered silk production in the thirteenth century; and Lucca's water-driven silk works, with their complex machinery, may well have been the first mechanized textile mills.[41] Water mills were also used in papermaking from the thirteenth century, when paper was finally introduced into Europe, having been invented by the Chinese before 100 and produced by the Arabs since the eighth century A.D.[42]

A diverse range of innovations improved people's lives. Skis, wheelbarrows, butter and the use of hops in brewing date from the early Middle Ages.[43] Clothes made of wool spread in England from the twelfth century, cakes of hard soap appeared at about the same time, and the button was developed in central Germany during the 1230s.[44] Many breakthroughs simultaneously ameliorated daily life and increased productivity. The invention of the fire grate and chimney, the use of coal and the introduction of window glass created greater indoor comfort, initially for the wealthy but spreading to the yeoman class by the sixteenth century. The world's oldest surviving chimney is probably the one from a Norman merchant's house in Southampton, and dates from the twelfth century, as do the earliest glass windows in northwest Europe at the church of St. Denis in Paris. Indoor comfort was not a matter of health and welfare alone. As E. L. Jones observes, "It offered a gain in productive efficiency for the mother and the housewife, the scribe and the worker in domestic industry."[45]

The invention of eyeglasses in Pisa toward the end of the thirteenth century more than doubled the working life of craftsmen, especially instrument and toolmakers, close weavers and metal workers. By the mid-fifteenth century, thousands of spectacles were being produced in Italian cities to correct both long- and shortsightedness. As David Landes has noted, the production of eyepieces was to fuel the development of precision engineering, although he regards the mechanical clock as even more important. Gravity replaced water as the driving principle around 1300, so that every city in Europe boasted at least one large, conspicuous and reliable clock.[46] By the mid-fourteenth century, clocks indicated not only the time but also every known astronomical motion. A century later, spring-driven clocks and watches appeared. It is difficult to underestimate the importance of accurate timekeeping in increasingly complex urban economies. In Landes's view, the very concept of productivity is itself a by-product of the clock.[47]

These developments and the growth of population, markets and towns all helped to erode the isolation and self-sufficiency of the original feudal unit, the manor, thus weakening its static ties of service and custom and offering rural labor new, market-driven opportunities as well as creating a wider market for urban products and services. This in turn accelerated economic and social change and supplied the main dynamic of the prosperity and growth of the High Middle Ages in thirteenth-century Europe.[48]

A corollary of this expansion was a growth in longer-distance trade and the development of regional specialization as a result of the operation of what economists now call "comparative advantage," which means (crudely paraphrased) that everyone and every place should do what they can do most economically and exchange their products for the most economical products of other people and other places. Longer-distance trade presupposes both that there is sufficient economic development for there to be products worth exchanging over long distances and that the goods can be transported safely and economically.

In the earliest stages of long-distance trade, the ideal tradable item was one produced only in a distant location, with a low weight-to-value ratio and the ability to travel well. Thus, exotic spices from the East had for millennia been the staple of trade between the Mediterranean basin and the shores of the Indian Ocean. But as economies grow more sophisticated, there come to be other products that, though they could be and probably have been produced in many locations, are so much more efficiently produced in one place rather than another that it becomes worthwhile to exchange them over great distances. This was happening in medieval Europe. Gascony, for example, became a leading wine-producing area, exporting its products to more northerly markets from the port of Bordeaux; wool was supplied from England and woolen products manufactured in Flanders; the shores of the Baltic became principal grain producers, feeding the dense urban populations of the Low Countries.[49]

Secure and economical carriage of this growing trade depended in the main on the same watercourses that the Romans had used, until the Atlantic route around Spain and France was opened up. Roman roads remained the basis of land transport, though these were now maintained and protected (to the extent that they were) by feudal lords who levied tolls to meet their costs. Boat technology advanced usefully when the cog, a seaworthy and efficient sailing cargo boat, was developed from primitive Celtic boats and came to dominate the seas of northern Europe by the twelfth century.[50] The one important change in the technology of land transport was, as we have seen, the development of the horse-drawn—and mule-drawn—heavy wagon as a result of the invention of the padded collar and breast strap and then the deliberate breeding of cart horses.

Trade cannot, however, flourish unless its commercial and financial infrastructure as well as its product and transport preconditions are present. An important aspect of the High Middle Age economic development of Europe lay in precisely this area. Europe's growing trade required the to us familiar building blocks of business: means of payment, credit, capital finance and control of risk.

The pure merchant of primitive trade, who owned, managed and traveled with the entire operation of export from and import back to his home city, supplied in his own person a daunting range of services: the capital to launch each venture (in the form of money to buy the initial stock of goods he would take with him to sell); the credit to finance his travels and the carriage of his goods (in the form of money to pay for transport and to feed and accommodate himself and his party); the transport management skills (in the form of his own direction of the caravan or the voyage he had to undertake); the banking services to arrange, finance, receive and convert payments by his customers (in the form of more finance and credit, money-changing services and secure homeward transmission of the realized cash); the underwriting of the entire risk to the limit of his personal resources, and even his personal security and the management of the whole operation.

This was too demanding and too risky to attract most people. At an early stage long-range trade became a specialized undertaking concentrated in particular families and ethnic minority groups, specifically Jews and other Levantines in the Mediterranean area from the tenth century, though these groups of course had as many other activities as any other. Families were the first and most natural form of business partnership, helping to spread the risk and labor of an enterprise while sharing the rewards.

We have already seen how many of these building blocks had already been developed and fostered in the Islamic world. The rich correspondence preserved in the Cairo *geniza* (a repository in the Ben Ezra synagogue in which Jews, forbidden to destroy any paper on which God's name was written, disposed of such documents, which survive to this day because of the dry air in the place) shows that Jewish and Muslim merchants who traded extensively in the Mediterranean and Indian Ocean during the eleventh and twelfth centuries formed business partnerships, employed agents to represent them abroad and made money transfers from one place to another without having to move large amounts of cash.[51] It was no accident that the Italians, who were Europe's foremost traders with the Islamic world, became the next ethnic group in the Mediterranean world to excel in the development of business methods and structures.

The family-based partnership, or *fraterna,* was used in Genoa and even longer in Venice as a mechanism for pooling capital and dividing the work, for instance, with one brother remaining at home to manage the supply of exports and the sale of imports while another traveled with the merchandise to conduct the distant business. In due course this model was adapted from the twelfth century for use outside family circles, under the names of the *commenda* or *colleganza,* with one partner supplying most of the capital and the other supplying a lesser part of the capital plus his own person to accompany the goods and manage the business.[52] The "true company," or *vera società*—combining several partners who supplied the capital and directed the business, employing others to do the work—arose later.

All this commercial activity stimulated the development of banking, often as a part of the activities of the same large companies who were coming to dominate European trade. Italian merchants and money-changers at the Champagne fairs gave us the word "bank," drawn from the bench, or *banco,* on which they placed their scales and coins and conducted their business.[53] And Italian banking houses in the thirteenth century pioneered new techniques in the financing of international trade and came to monopolize foreign money and credit business from Lombardy in northern Italy through Bruges in the Low Countries and on to London's Lombard Street.[54]

The bill of exchange, an IOU on paper whereby one party to an exchange promised to pay a specified sum on a particular date, became a convenient substitute for settlement in cash or bullion. The only cash was coins, which were widely minted by kings, dukes, counts, abbeys and cities. Apart from being issued in inconveniently small denominations, mostly pennies, they were, like bullion, heavy and risky to carry about. Their value in exchange for other coins also varied continuously from place to place and from time to time.

IOUs could be used to make payments at a distance, for example, by a purchaser in Bruges to a supplier in Milan. This of course presupposed that when the bill fell due, the purchaser would have access to funds in Milan with which to make the payment. This requirement further encouraged the development of international banking, so that the Bruges importer could deposit money with or arrange credit through the Bruges branch of a Milan bank.

The Italian bankers were thus performing two classic banking functions: providing security for money that could be deposited safely and no longer needed to be carried about the place in large quantities, and payment of bills by transferring money held in the name of one customer to the account of another customer in accordance with the written instructions of the payer. From this developed the form of instruction we know as the check.

To complete the picture, these early bankers also provided extensive credit to finance the trade by making commercial loans on a much larger scale than the Jewish moneylenders of the early medieval period.[55] Virtually all the business of the Champagne fairs, for example, was conducted by credit, and the letter of fair, a kind of bill of exchange, was used to carry over the balances owed at the end of one fair to the opening of business at the next, though this was more in order to avoid the risks and cost of carting around coin and bullion than for the purpose of raising credit to finance business.[56]

An alternative to credit, to running a tab in some convenient, internationally accepted unit of account (for example, Carolingian pounds, shillings and pence) as a way of overcoming the variability of the exchange value between different local coinages, even though the coins themselves often bore the same name, would have been some reliable international money in sufficiently large denominations to be able to pay for commercial quantities of goods. The need produced a solution in the second half of the thirteenth century, when Genoa, Pisa and Florence took over the gold trade with North Africa and were able for the first time to mint high-value gold coins.

Silver coins and bimetal silver-and-gold coins had never been entirely satisfactory in denomination or size. During 1251–1252 Genoa produced the gold *genovino* and Florence the gold florin, to be followed by the Venetian ducat in 1284.[57] This new practice, though highly successful for the issuers and popular with merchants, did not remove the cost and risk of physical transfers of large quantities of money. The banking innovations of the previous period survived and indeed prospered as part of what has even been called a "commercial revolution," but their main impact did not begin until the fifteenth century.[58] Even so, the largest business organizations in the world before the seventeenth century, such as the Bardi and the Peruzzi in Florence, flourished in the thirteenth and fourteenth centuries, until they unwisely lent large sums to cash-strapped kings, including England's Edward III, and went bankrupt in the 1340s.[59]

Less glamorous but arguably more important in the roots of modern economic systems was the evolution of double-entry bookkeeping in thirteenth- and fourteenth-century Italy.[60] Profitable business and trade had obviously predated this invention by many millennia, from at least Babylonian times.[61] But the precision and discipline of double-entry bookkeeping gave a definition and accuracy to a merchant's knowledge of how each part of his business was doing that transformed and forever afterward informed business management, opening the door to systematic profit maximization as the mainspring of privately run economic enterprises. To put it more crudely, as Werner Sombart (1863–1941), the great student of modern capitalism, commented: "One cannot imagine what capitalism would be without double-entry bookkeeping."[62]

By entering every transaction at least twice into his book of accounts, once as a change in real assets (e.g., the acquisition or sale of goods) and once as a change in financial position (e.g., disbursement or receipt of the money to pay for the goods), and then periodically reconciling the two systems, a merchant greatly reduced the danger of undetected clerical errors. Second, by reconciling running profit-and-loss accounts with end-period balance sheets, the merchant knew and could explain to himself and others how and why he was growing richer or poorer, thereby hugely improving his ability to focus his resources in the most worthwhile way.[63] The development of precise accounts in a standardized form also lent itself to the evolution of more complex and arms-length business relationships, including borrowing and other financing devices, because a more readily intelligible picture of a business and its affairs could be conveyed between strangers, though its accuracy of course still depended on the honesty of whoever prepared it.[64]

Sombart's view of the importance of double-entry bookkeeping to the development of capitalism is echoed by Rosenberg and Birdzell, who summarize the immense business potential of such a seemingly abstract and arid innovation:

> A bookkeeping system whose practical appeal lay in its ability to detect errors compelled the merchants and bookkeepers who used it to acquire the habit of thinking of the enterprise, either as a debtor to its owners or as itself the owner of its own net worth. Either way, it was an abstraction created by its own books of account.... [For] double-entry bookkeeping is an actualisation of the profit-seeking firm as a truly autonomous ... unit, the property of which is no longer mixed up with that of the family, the seignory, or other social units.[65]

A spur to this invention came from the arrival in Europe of so-called Arabic numerals, which had in fact, as we have seen, been invented in India. Their essence was the decimal positional number system. The Indians had long counted in tens, or decimally, like the Egyptians, the Greeks and the Romans but unlike the Babylonians, who counted in sixties, or sexagesimally, from which we get our sixty-minute hour, sixty-second minute and so on.

From the third century B.C., the Indians had used separate symbols (i.e., numerals) for the numbers from 1 to 9. To these were added in the sixth century A.D. the decisive breakthrough, the tenth numeral in the form of a round symbol for zero, thereby making possible a mature place-value system in which "10" represents ten times "1," "100" ten times "10" and so forth. Prior to this, basic calculations like addition and subtraction required an abacus—a board or tablet, later a counting frame—in which the place-values are symbolized by the rows and the "0" is represented by an empty column.[66] Such instruments were certainly used by the ancient Greeks and Romans, as well as in China from at least the second century A.D.[67]

For a while, a politico-mathematical struggle developed between defenders of the traditional Roman numerals (called "abacists") and advocates of al-Khwarizmi's "Arabic" numerals (called "algorists"). At one point, in 1299, the city of Florence banned the commercial use of the Hindu-Arabic numerals on the grounds that documents containing them could too easily be falsified, for example, by inserting a "0."[68]

But earlier in the thirteenth century Leonardo da Pisa (c. 1175–1250) had published his *Liber abbacci* that included a historic proposition as the first sentence of the first chapter: "These are the nine figures of the Indians: 9 8 7 6 5 4 3 2 1. With these nine figures, and with the sign 0 which in Arabic is called *zephirum*, any number can be written."[69] It soon became apparent that in addition to their advantages in pure mathematics, Arabic numerals including the "0" had advantages for practical arithmetic, in accounting, measuring and calculating. Elementary addition, subtraction, multiplication and division, as they have been taught in European schools for centuries, depend on the place-value system.

It is evident why accountancy should have seized upon the Arabic system and why such a system should have facilitated advances in accounting techniques. Mokyr observes fairly enough that it was "doubtless instrumental in the development of double-entry bookkeeping."[70] The first documentary evidence of this survives fully in the papers of a remarkable man known to history as "the merchant of Prato," Francesco di Marco Datini (d. 1410), whose voluminous account books and other papers record in extraordinary detail the operation of his Europe-wide business, all conducted under the motto "In the name of God and of Profit."[71]

About a century later these advances, together with other classical accounting principles, were codified in what may be seen as the first textbook of accountancy, *Summa de arithmetica, geometria proportioni et proportionalita* (1494) by Luca Pacioli (c. 1445–1514). Pacioli was a polymathic Franciscan friar who had had early experience of business in Venice, where he had been a tutor to the three sons of a successful merchant. He later joined the church and enjoyed the distinction of having his theological works illustrated by an even greater Renaissance man, Leonardo da Vinci. In expounding the principles of double-entry bookkeeping in their Venetian version, the *Summa de arithmetica* laid down homely rules, many of which echo down the centuries in every countinghouse, such as that "the books cannot be closed unless the debits equal the credits" and "he who does business without knowing all about it sees his money go like flies."[72]

There is ample evidence to suggest that the broad growth in the European population between 1000 and 1300 had reached a point where marginal lands (possibly hampered by adverse climatic changes) generated little or no surplus and marginal labor earned little or nothing more than subsistence incomes.[73] In the absence of a technological breakthrough, this implied a static or even declining agricultural surplus, which in turn constrained the possibilities of urban life and the division of labor therein. In other words, further economic growth, or indeed population growth, seemed difficult.

The events of the first half of the fourteenth century, especially in Britain, have provoked a fierce argument among economic historians as to whether or not this period illustrates the theory of the English economist Robert Malthus (1766–1834) that population naturally tends to grow geometrically (e.g., 2, 4, 8, 16 . . .) and will therefore sooner or later run into limits of essential supplies such as food, which can only grow arithmetically (e.g., 2, 4, 6, 8 . . .), unless war, disease or other calamity controls the numbers first.[74]

Indeed, Malthus argued that once all fertile land had been brought into production, yields would tend to diminish "from the nature of all soils." This famous theory of diminishing returns (not 2, 4, 6, 8 . . ., but 2, 4, 6, 7 . . .) was expounded later by another English economist, David Ricardo (1772–1823), who likewise predicted some kind of crisis from "a decreased rate of production while the power of population continues always the same."[75]

The opposite view—that population grows independently of food supply—has been most famously argued by Ester Boserup, who saw population growth as independently determined and capable of *causing* increased food production rather than dependent on it.[76] Detailed studies, for example, by Bruce Campbell and Mark Overton in Norfolk, England, suggest that although increased population pressure certainly increases the demand for food and may call forth increased production through higher yields from each acre of land, the increase in food supply may be less than proportionate to the increase in population, thereby still leading to shortages and malnutrition, if not famine.[77]

The whole economy did indeed stagnate and at times decline in Europe in the late thirteenth and early fourteenth centuries. There were periodic overt famines (e.g., the Great Famine of 1315–1317 that stretched from the Pyrenees to Russia and raised the death rate in Flanders, Europe's most populous region, ten-fold) and population growth leveled off.[78] Moreover, technological transformation was less likely where the marginal cost of labor was very low and the rewards for inventing and investing in substitutes for labor correspondingly slight or negative. Campbell and Overton state flatly that in Britain "with the exception of an increase in the draught-power available from livestock, there is no evidence of technical innovations that would have materially added to the efficiency of farm labour until the end of the eighteenth century."[79]

The economic weakness of labor, in the form of a feudal peasantry, left the conservative forces of the landowners and the ruling aristocracy unchallenged, thereby cementing traditional structures such as the manorial system against change. However precisely the interaction of population pressures, changes in the productivity of labor and land and resulting increases in food supplies are analyzed, it is hard to doubt that the population had greater difficulty in feeding itself adequately during most of the century up to the Black Death, that this contributed to a check to the previous growth rate of both population and economic production and that this was indeed the kind of danger that Malthus had in mind when he expounded his theory.

Whatever might have happened if Malthusian logic had been allowed to continue for another half century, there is no doubt at all what actually happened next. Europe was struck by a plague of extraordinary virulence, which may have been pneumonic as well as bubonic.[80] In its bubonic form the bacillus (*Yersinia pestis*) is spread by the bites of infected fleas that attack humans when their host rats die from the disease. It kills 60–80 percent of those infected after a distressing progress including "chest pains, coughing, vomiting of blood, breathing troubles, high fever and dark skin-blotches caused by internal bleeding (hence the name 'Black Death') as well as hard, painful, egg-sized swellings (buboes) in the lymph nodes in the arm-pit, groin, neck and behind the ears . . . restlessness, delirium and finally coma."[81] In its pneumonic form it is even more lethal, the infection being spread by droplets exhaled and inhaled.[82]

The great epidemics of the fourteenth century in Europe and Egypt originated in Asia, either in Burma and southwest China or in Mongolia and Manchuria. The plague attacked China, probably in 1331, spread west along the Silk Road and other caravan routes, invaded the Mongol khanate of the Golden Horde at Sarai on the lower Volga in the 1340s, and in 1343–1346 was injected into the Genoese colony of Kaffa (modern Theodosia) in the Crimea by the Mongol Khan Yannibeg: In an early use of germ warfare, he catapulted the bodies of plague victims over the city walls.[83] From there Genoese ships carried the fatal rats into the Mediterranean, reaching Constantinople, Cairo and Messina in 1347 and spreading from those centers to almost all of Europe, North Africa and the Near East.[84]

The plague advanced in waves until 1352, and there were renewed outbreaks, mainly regional, occasionally national, at irregular intervals throughout the next 300 years.[85] The first attack was unquestionably the worst. It killed something like 30 million people, about a third of the population of Europe, including nearly half the population of England.[86] Europe's population probably did not again reach its 1340 level until about 200 years later. Agricultural production and commercial life were devastated, especially in the economic heartlands around the north-south axis from Italy to the Low Countries and East Anglia. Total production and trade were lower in 1400 than they had been a century earlier.

In any economy people in general are both consumers and workers. When they are decimated—or indeed much more than decimated—both consumers and workers become scarce. The absence of consumers means that after the initial inflation caused by the physical dislocation of supply, the prices of the things they normally buy, including rent for land and houses, fall; the absence of workers means than the price of the thing they uniquely sell, labor, rises.

And so it was in Europe after the Black Death. By reversing the previous fundamental condition of labor surplus in relation to usable land, the Black Death turned on its head the incipient Malthusian crisis. This led in western Europe to widespread rural conflict (including the jacquerie wars in northern France in 1358 and the peasants' revolt in England in 1381). Prices of final goods, including food, eventually plunged, while wages began to rise. Authorities made conspicuous efforts, reminiscent of Diocletian's edict against inflation, to prohibit the operation of the law of supply and demand.[87] Lords tried to require their laborers to perform their traditional feudal duties, including on occasions the duties of their dead neighbors, and strove to restrict wages to their traditional level.

Cartels called guilds arose, permitted to limit supply in an attempt to keep prices up, but this provoked popular revolt and the erosion of the feudal system. The established order of things was unhinged by the inescapable facts that there was no one to do the work and no one to buy the merchandise. And so the balance of bargaining power shifted for a while decisively in favor of the peasantry, even where their revolts were brutally or cunningly suppressed.[88] Real wages, that is, money wages adjusted for what money would buy, were higher in England in 1460 than at any time previously or again until the nineteenth century.[89]

In eastern Europe, where the population was much thinner on the ground and where town life was virtually obliterated, the peasants were unable to exploit their new scarcity value because there was no functioning labor market to which they could take their services. Landlords were able to forbid them from moving, effectively making them slaves. They were forced into a more abject servitude than anything that had existed in western Europe since the time of Charlemagne.[90]

Everywhere else the long-run effects of the Black Death, which manifested themselves increasingly in the fifteenth century, reflected the restricted supply and higher price of labor. In 1363 an observer lamented the changing times in tones that, mutatis mutandis, became all too familiar in post–World War II Europe: "Serving girls and unskilled women with no experience in service and stable boys want at least 12 florins per year, and the most arrogant among them 18 or 24 florins per year, and so also nurses and minor artisans working with their hands want three times or nearly the usual pay, and labourers on the land all want oxen and all seed, and want to work the best lands, and to abandon all others."[91]

The effects of expensive labor were entirely predictable—people tried to do without it, and they invented and invested to that end. Land was switched from arable wheat-growing to pasture, cowherds and shepherds being able to service more acres than plowmen and harvesters. Oxen were bred and fertilizers spread. Urban artisans were equipped with more and better tools and machines. In 1421 Florence issued the first-known patent—for a canal boat equipped with cranes—thereby effecting, in the words of E. L. Jones, "an institutional change conducive to a high rate of technological change in the future."[92] About fifty years later, Venice enacted the first formal patent law. The formal recognition and statutory protection of inventors' rights in their inventions was an important step toward the eventual creation of a framework of incentives and property rights that encouraged experiment and innovation. It has its counterpart in late-twentieth-century assertions of intellectual property rights.

The mass production of books by battalions of scribes became expensive enough to encourage the search for a better solution, which involved key advances in metallurgy and culminated in Johann Gutenberg's invention of movable type in 1453. In less than thirty years there were 380 working presses, and by the turn of the century more volumes had been produced than in the previous millennium.[93]

Maritime travel and transport were revolutionized in ways we shall examine later in the context of the explosion of western European naval pioneers across, down and beyond the Atlantic Ocean at the end of the fifteenth century.[94] Even where inventions had been pioneered before the Black Death, its impact on the supply of labor stimulated the wider adoption of such new techniques.

In taking its toll on the clergy, the Black Death prompted a proliferation of new universities in order to train new clerics and reverse the decay in learning. New colleges were founded at Cambridge and Oxford, and the University of Florence was established in 1350. All the universities east of the Rhine and north of the Alps were established after the plague's outbreak, including Prague in 1348, Vienna and Kraków in 1364, Fünfkirchen in Hungary in 1367 and Heidelberg in 1385. Old centers of learning lost their dominance and the curriculum became less traditional.[95]

In medicine the crisis broke down professional distinctions, enhancing the status of surgeons, who cared directly for the sick, as opposed to the more theoretically minded physicians. It also led to a new emphasis on anatomical investigation.[96] As Roy Porter has noted, Milan and other Italian cities pioneered public health committees with powers to regulate markets, streets, hospitals and cemeteries and to control beggars, prostitutes and Jews. "Resentment was expressed about their cost and powers," Porter writes of the new bodies, "especially since economic disaster was almost inevitable once plague had been declared official, with commerce and travel suspended and markets closed."[97] It took more than a century before such reforms became standard practice in northern European towns.

But the most profound longer-term consequences of the Black Death in Europe were in its impact on the social structure. The feudal system had originated, as Roman imperial systems broke down, in a kind of informal social contract between peasants who needed protection and in some cases relief from oppressive taxes and local magnates who needed people to work their land and man their militias. As the centuries rolled by this basic deal had become overlaid by ever more complex and ossified customs, traditions, rights and laws that tended to curtail the economic freedom of the individual peasant and to constrain him more and more narrowly to the work and place of his forebears, thus stultifying economic change. The Black Death, by transforming the effective economic value and therefore bargaining power of laborers in the rural economy, except in eastern Europe, accelerated the breakdown of feudal constraints and so the gradual liberation of the lower feudal orders from these long-standing controls, a process that had started much earlier in towns where specialization, trade and markets tended to erode customary barriers. That in turn stimulated the substitution of cash payments for rent and other feudal obligations in lieu of services in kind, and this made the labor force more mobile and more independent.[98] Of its impact in England, Colin Platt has commented: "The greatest of all the poor's benefits were the choices they now enjoyed—of another lord, of another job, of whether to stay in the country or migrate to the towns, of how long to remain if they did go away, and of when to set up house and start a family. If winning freedom of choice is what revolutions are all about, I prefer to put my money on the Black Death."[99]

Important as were eventually both the technological and the social consequences of the Black Death, recovery from its impact on both population and production took a long time to get going, partly because of periodic further outbreaks of the plague. Europe's population did not clearly begin to rise until late in the fifteenth century, possibly not until the early sixteenth century.[100] And in England, at least, production, which fell less than proportionately to population because of greatly increased labor productivity after the first die-off from the plague, remained depressed in all economic sectors until at least the last quarter of the fifteenth century.

Employment, productivity and wages, however, were all held at a high level by the scarcity of labor, so that the fifteenth century as a whole contrived simultaneously to be a time of depressed output and of relatively high living standards, as well as incipient economic change.[101] It was also a century toward the end of which certain key events and trends laid the foundations of the modern age, as we shall see in Chapter 5.

CHAPTER FIVE

Globalization

ON THE EVE OF THE MODERN AGE, TOWARD THE END OF THE fifteenth century, about 400 million humans occupied the earth, more than half of them in Asia—chiefly India and China—and the rest spread mostly across Africa (70 million), Europe (60 million) and the Americas (40 million). Discrete concentrations of population, defined by distinct economic and social structures and linkages, were prominent in China, northern India, the Near and Middle East, and western Europe; smaller civilizations and societies were dispersed throughout the world's other regions, notably in central and southern America, Africa and Southeast Asia.

Some historians have wished to apply the concept of a "world system" to man's economy already at this time and even much earlier.[1] Andre Gunder Frank writes, "Contrary to widespread doubts and denials, there was a single global world economy with a worldwide division of labour and multilateral trade from 1500 onwards. This world economy had what can be identified as its own systemic character and dynamic, whose roots in Afro-Eurasia extended back for millennia."[2]

Other historians have thought that this alleged unity puts more weight on such linkages as there were between the main centers of economic life than is justified by their actual scale in relation to the total economic life of each regional economy.[3]

Links there undoubtedly were across the main Eurasian land mass in its most habitable northern latitudes from early times, reaching effectively from the Atlantic in the west to the Pacific in the east. The Mediterranean had linked western Europe to the Near East from Phoenician times (900–500 B.C.). Land routes had linked the eastern Mediterranean to the Persian Gulf and India from yet earlier times, long before Alexander the Great's march from the Aegean to the Indus. The first overland trade routes linking China to the Middle East, which later became the Silk Road, date back to 500 B.C. In the early centuries A.D., camels were carrying regular trade across the Sahara; by the fourth century A.D. West African gold was reaching the Mediterranean. Land routes over the Alpine passes linking to the northern European river systems had joined Italy at the center of the Mediterranean to northern and western Europe from at least the days of ancient Rome. Sea routes through the Straits of Gibraltar had also linked the Mediterranean to the Atlantic coasts of Europe by the fourteenth century A.D. The Indian Ocean had linked China, Southeast Asia, India, the Middle East and East Africa in active trade during the earliest centuries A.D.[4] By the fifteenth century Ibn Majid had compiled complete prose and verse works detailing the theory and practice of ocean navigation in, around and across the Indian Ocean, and the Chinese admiral Zheng He had conducted his huge fleet to all corners of that ocean, collecting tribute and showing the flag of his Ming emperor.[5]

The American continents were, however, not so connected, as far as we know, with any of the Eurasian centers. To the eye of common sense, dazzled in addition by the distortions of the Mercator projection of schoolroom maps, which exaggerates distances in far northern—and far southern—latitudes, the explanation is obvious: the huge expanse of the Atlantic and Pacific Oceans. The truth is a little more complex.

The Americas were originally settled from Eurasia by way of the Bering land bridge between Alaska and Siberia. Trans-Bering movements and exchanges continued intermittently by boat after the land bridge was last submerged at the end of the ice ages 14–12 kya and even included a brief contrasettlement by Inuit from Alaska onto the western side of the strait.[6] On the other side of the North American continent, contacts occurred from 1000 to 1350 by way of the natural stepping-stones: 400 miles from Norway to the Faeroes (reached in 800), 300 miles to Iceland (reached in 874), 700 miles to southern Greenland (reached in 986) and 600 miles to Labrador and Newfoundland (contact finally made in 1000).[7] As European incursions into the Americas, these failed, as Jared Diamond observes,

> because the source (Norway), the targets (Greenland and Newfoundland), and the time (984–1410) guaranteed that Europe's potential advantages of food production, technology and political organization could not be applied effectively. At latitudes too high for much production, the iron tools of a few Norse, weakly supported by one of Europe's poorer states, were no match for the stone, bone and wooden tools of Eskimo and Indian hunter-gatherers, the world's greatest masters of Arctic survival skills.[8]

For the rest, before Columbus we have no sure knowledge of any other Eurasian contact with the Americas and no reason to think that the main civilizations on either side of the Atlantic and the Pacific had any mutual influence at all.[9] The Americas were truly isolated over thousands of years from the other continents of the world, and vice versa.

The question remains whether it is helpful to see the rest of the world as belonging to a single economic system on the strength of the linkages we have noted. It is clear that knowledge, including key technologies, could and did pass between the main European and Asian centers all the way from western Europe to China during the first millennium A.D. and the first half of the second, including "Arabic" numerals, gunpowder, paper, printing and maybe the compass. It is equally clear that the different economies of the Eurasian world were separate enough to be able to operate at widely different levels of development for long periods, as we have seen. Had there been a truly unified Eurasian economy one would have expected knowledge and techniques to be much more rapidly diffused and equalized throughout the whole area. Marco Polo in 1275 and his like could hardly have been so astonished at what they found in China had they lived in an already globalized (or Eurasianized) economy.

And if the flows of knowledge were too meager a trickle to have established a pool of common technical development, the flows of actual trade fell even further short of the scale that would have been needed to knit the different economies into a single market or system. The available transport technologies before the fifteenth century—pack animals overland, riverboats and coastal shipping—did not favor long-distance movement of bulk cargoes, though the Greeks brought grain from the Black Sea, and the Roman Empire had evolved bulk-carrying craft and handling facilities to bring to Ostia the huge quantities of North African grain required by the capital. Most long-distance trade before 1500 consisted of high-value luxuries, with high value-to-weight ratios, the profit on which was sufficient to justify the heavy costs and multifarious risks of their carriage. This could never be a substantial aggregate in relation to the total output, spending and incomes of economies whose activity consisted overwhelmingly of agriculture and local trade. As Patrick O'Brien has noted of the European economy in the late fifteenth century, the impact of long-distance trade was marginal: "Meanwhile the growth of the European economy . . . continued to respond to endogenous forces of population growth, urbanisation, intra-regional trade within the continent and a modicum of organisational and technical progress in agriculture and industry."[10]

Broadly similar judgments can be made about the other main economic centers of the Eurasian world, notwithstanding the fuller development of Indian Ocean navigation by the Muslim Arabs and Chinese under the Sung dynasty—and indeed by their Roman, Greek and even Sumerian predecessors.[11] Bulk cargoes were carried between the Middle East, India and China, partly as ballast, and included eastbound dates, sugar, building materials and timber and westbound porcelain.[12] But the quantities involved were still tiny in relation to what we would now see as the gross domestic product (GDP) of the participating economies and far too small to justify any suggestion of a single Indian Ocean economy.

Quite simply, human economic activity before the dawn of the modern age was fragmented into essentially separate and independent spheres between which contact was marginal or, in the case of the Americas, negligible to the character and performance of each. As Rondo Cameron baldly states, "Before the sixteenth century [Europe] was only one of several more or less isolated regions."[13]

So what was it that from the fifteenth century began to change all this, knitting the world's economies into a single network, linking every ocean and so every port upon those oceans and every place with access to such ports? Two factors seem to have been directly important, both originating in western Europe: one was a growing ambition to bypass the Venetian and Arab control of the eastern trade by finding an alternative route to "the Indies"; the other was developments in naval architecture, navigation and gunnery.

The magnet of the Indies and the profitable supply of its good things—spices, silks, jewels, gold and silver—was by no means the sole incentive encouraging Europeans on the Atlantic seaboard to look for cheaper, better and different routes to those areas of the world known to lie beyond the Middle East and, presumably, beyond the western horizon as well.[14] The reconquest of southern Spain from its Muslim occupants since the eighth century, completed pregnantly enough in 1492, both opened a gateway through Cadiz to the Atlantic and developed a taste for engagement with Islam that drew Spanish and Portuguese adventurers into North Africa and down its west coast.[15] This military-religious motive, combined with the colonizing thrust of Genoa, Castile and Portugal into the near-Atlantic islands of Madeira (1418–1420), the Canaries (1402–1451), the Azores (1439) and eventually the Cape Verde Islands (1460s) and with the lure of the river of gold that was suspected to exist somewhere further south in West Africa, tempted Europeans to overcome (in 1434) their traditional inhibitions about passing beyond Cape Bojador, just south of the Canaries. The cape had long been considered the *ultima Thule* of prudent navigation, beyond which lay boiling seas, nameless terrors and—because of the prevailing northerlies—no safe return.[16]

Nonetheless, the frustration of European ambitions in the eastern Mediterranean, especially as a route to the East, was probably the biggest single factor in impelling the maritime eruption from Europe across, down and out of the Atlantic. Genoa, which was as important a naval center as any west of Venice, had long suffered from Venetian control of eastern Mediterranean trade and played a leading role in the western Mediterranean, not least in the seaports of southern Spain. Genoese merchants and navigators provided much of the enterprise that sent ships from Seville and Cadiz south and west, though at first in the fourteenth century they were not so much seeking a new route to the East as extrapolating the Mediterranean into the near-Atlantic.[17]

When in 1453 the fall of Constantinople to the Turks blocked Genoa's Black Sea trade in grain, fish and timber, its energies were further deflected to new horizons. When the city's most famous son, Christopher Columbus (c. 1446–1506), came to present his case first to the Portuguese king and later to the king of Spain for support of his great voyage to the west, he based it on the thesis (grossly underestimating the size of the globe and overestimating the easterly longitude of eastern Asia) that this would open a short route to the Orient, where ready access would be established to "incalculable gold, rhubarb and cinnamon, spices and cotton and slaves 'from among the idolators.'"[18]

But a completely different economic motive may have lured Europeans across the North Atlantic even before Columbus: cod. In a new study Mark Kurlansky presents a diverting speculation that first Basques before the fifteenth century and then in 1481 two Bristolians (one of them called John Jay) may have tried to break the Hanseatic League's monopoly by secretly visiting Newfoundland to catch cod on the Grand Banks.[19] But for them, unlike the later explorers—including John Cabot, who reached Newfoundland in the *Mathew* in 1497—secrecy was essential to success.[20] They did not want anyone else to know where they were getting their fish. Cabot, by contrast, was like Columbus looking for a route to Asia and had every reason to proclaim the newfound land and its rich fisheries and claim them in the name of the English king Henry VII. So history still insists that the chief economic motive for those European explorations of the Atlantic, north and south, was the wish for a more cost-effective access to the spices and other riches of southeast and eastern Asia. Whatever fishing boats may have achieved, the characteristic reticence of their owners and skippers will have precluded them from a glorious place in history.

Developments in maritime technology and navigation played a distinct and crucial part in enabling and to some extent propelling the European urge from the fifteenth century to push back the frontiers of nautical space beyond the seas bounding its known shores. To make the kind of voyages that Columbus, Vasco da Gama, Magellan and the other oceanic explorers made, it is necessary to be able to travel huge distances. This in turn requires that the navigator can find his way out and then home again without sighting land for weeks at a time and that he and his crew can survive at sea in all likely conditions for indefinite periods. Neither of these things had been possible for European mariners much before the fifteenth century, whatever intrepid feats Norsemen and maybe even Basque and Bristolian cod fishermen may have achieved by way of the Faeroes-Iceland-Greenland-Newfoundland stepping-stones.[21]

To make long ocean passages, sailors need ships that will be seaworthy in fair weather and foul; sail in whatever direction is required; carry sufficient food, water and merchandise to sustain the crew and finance the expedition and provide sufficient shelter for them to maintain their efforts week in and week out. Open boats are liable to be swamped by breaking seas coming inboard and offer little shelter for crew or cargo, though the fortitude of the Norsemen somehow overcame these perils and discomforts sufficiently to keep at sea for a week or so at a time. Square-rigged ships—ships with sails suitable only for running before the wind—were unable to travel upwind or even within much better than 90° of the wind. Oared ships—galleys—were limited to coastal work, being obliged to make short hops from port to port to enable the crew to rest, and though they were used in the Atlantic from the thirteenth to the sixteenth centuries by the Venetians and later the Florentines to reach England and France, they could never have made transoceanic passages.[22] This did not prevent one Genoese expedition in oared galleys from setting forth in 1291 down the West African coast, bound "for the regions of India by way of the ocean," never to be seen again.[23]

It was in about 1400 that the first really suitable ships for ocean work appeared in Europe.[24] One model was the fully rigged, three-masted carrack, or Portuguese *nau*, built by Portuguese yards, modifying the earlier cog from northern Europe and also drawing on Mediterranean shipbuilding know-how. It combined square sails (suitable for sailing downwind) with three-cornered lateen sails (suitable for maneuvering upwind) and was called "the great invention" because "it could do more than any of its predecessors and could do so with considerably less risk."[25] It was fully decked from bow to stern and provided sheltered accommodation for the crew as well as protected cargo space.

The carrack was complemented by the caravel, which was in general a smaller and more versatile craft, used in most of the early Portuguese explorations down the African coast. It is first mentioned as part of a voyage past Cape Bojador in 1440. But contrary to the happy legend that it was invented for the purposes of exploration by the Portuguese prince Henry (1394–1460), known as "the Navigator," it had existed, at least as a general term for a small coastal fishing boat, for two centuries or more, though Henry may have played a part in presenting its economic attractions to cash-strapped aristocratic investors as a vehicle for maritime enterprise.[26] The name was also easily confused with "carvel," the word for a type of hull construction that laid the exterior planking edge to edge rather than overlapping, as in the heavier clinker construction, and that was adopted from the Mediterranean on the European Atlantic coast in the fifteenth century.

The Portuguese caravels always used this carvel construction but took their name ultimately from the Arab *carib* or *caravo*, which was distinguished not by its hull but by its two or three triangular lateen sails. It could sail within 60–65° of the wind, and with its long, narrow, light and shallow hull, it made for a very fast and flexible vessel of about 65 tons, 65–115 feet long, 20–30 feet wide, with a crew of twenty plus. Its speeds on long reaches out into the Atlantic were not matched until the clipper ships in the nineteenth century.

In the fifteenth century Portuguese caravels grew larger, with more decking and in some cases a third mast. As voyage lengths increased beyond Cape Bojador and down to the Cape of Good Hope, ships needed more and more space to carry the water and supplies needed for each crew member, as much as 1 ton per man. Crew sizes had been reduced by giving up oared vessels, and larger vessels, made practical by the lighter carvel construction, offered a better ratio of carrying capacity to crew size, thus making oceanic voyages of exploration possible.

Carracks, which were larger, though less flexible in close work, may have been equally suitable for the requirements of long-distance exploration, mainly because their square sails were easier to handle when running before the wind.[27] Vasco da Gama took one caravel and three *naus*, each of which could have a capacity of about 500 tons, on his passage to India.[28] Columbus's *Nina* (55 feet overall) and *Pinta* (69 feet overall) were adapted "round" (or Andalusian) caravels. *Pinta* was, however, square-rigged, and *Nina* was rerigged on the outward passage in the Grand Canary with square as well as lateen sails. The *Santa Maria* (85 feet overall), the largest of the three and Columbus's flagship, was a *nau*.[29] The total crew of his fleet was still only about ninety "men and boys."[30]

Sailors cannot, however, succeed simply by having handy boats. They must find their way. To do so they must know three things: (1) where they are, (2) where they want to go, and (3) what course they are making, through the water and over the earth's surface. This all presupposes a picture—or chart—of the segment of the earth's surface on which the voyage is to be made. Knowledge of the first two things can be used to infer the desired direction of advance, which can then be combined with knowledge of the third to achieve—or approximate as nearly as may be possible to—the right course.

To achieve any course at all, the sailor has to avoid not sailing in circles. This may sound easy to lubbers who have never been out of sight of land or sailed in fog, but European sailors before the fifteenth century preferred whenever possible to cling to coastlines and to sail by day or when they could be sure of clear skies at night. Landmarks, coastlines, sun, moon and stars could prevent the danger of what the Norse called *hafvilla,* or losing all sense of direction. Wind and waves can sometimes perform the same role for short periods, if their constancy can be relied upon, but serious passages across oceans requires something better, and that is a compass.

The compass seems to have appeared in rudimentary form in Europe in the twelfth or thirteenth century, and by 1300 it had been fashioned into an integrated unit with a card depicting the main sixteen points. But it seems not to have been until the fifteenth century that seafarers, notoriously conservative types, embraced steering by compass.[31]

In 1409 the work on geography by the great Alexandrian mathematician and astronomer of the second century A.D. Claudius Ptolemy, was translated into Latin, and Europeans learned the system of latitude (degrees from 0° to 90° north or south of the equator) and longitude (degrees, in their modern form, from 0° to 180° east or west of a stipulated central line or meridian, e.g., Greenwich) for defining any point on the earth's surface.[32] Seafarers knew how to determine latitude at least three centuries before John Harrison's chronometer in 1762 solved the problem of fixing longitude.[33]

Latitude is much easier to determine because the earth revolves on a north-south axis. It follows that any heavenly body vertically above the North Pole (or the South Pole) will always appear to be at the same height above the horizon to a person situated on any given line of latitude. At the equator it will coincide with the horizon. At the pole it will be directly overhead, and in between its angle above the horizon will be that latitude, north or south. In the Northern Hemisphere the polestar, which is almost vertically above the North Pole, can be observed on any clear night all night.

Alternatively, latitude can be fixed by observing the height of the sun above the horizon at midday (defined as the moment when the sun reaches its highest point in the sky that day, when it will be due south, or due north in the Southern Hemisphere), provided that the navigator knows what adjustments to make for the tilt of the earth, which means that the sun is only directly above the equator at the spring and autumn equinoxes. The required correction at any other time is known as the sun's "declination," which is the amount north or south of the equator by which the sun's overhead track is displaced toward the tropic of Cancer (in the northern summer) or the tropic of Capricorn (in the northern winter).

Astronomers had long computed the necessary annual tables of the sun's declination (and that of other solar system bodies), and by the fifteenth century Arab and Jewish astronomers had provided mariners with tables suitable for navigational use.[34] These eased a problem familiar to sailors in equatorial and tropical latitudes. The North Star approaches so close to the horizon as ships get nearer the equator that it cannot in practice be used to establish latitude. The sun has to be used instead, and that became possible once declination tables were available.

Sailors remained essentially ignorant of their longitude, except in extremely crude terms, and compensated by placing themselves on the desired latitude and then sailing east or west until they found their goal. The great Arab navigator Ibn Majid, who was later credited—almost certainly wrongly—with piloting Vasco da Gama across the Indian Ocean, explained in one of his comprehensive navigational treatises that the typical sailor's claim to accurate knowledge of his longitude was doubly stupid, not only because he did not know but also because "he does not know that he does not know."[35]

To know your longitude you have to find some way of knowing, wherever you are, what time it is at some fixed reference point, for example, the Greenwich meridian. Then by observing the difference in time between the occurrence of a known astronomical event (e.g., the sun's reaching its highest point of the day) at the reference point (e.g., noon at Greenwich) and its occurrence where you are (e.g., at 3 p.m. Greenwich time), you can calculate that you are three hours' worth of the earth's rotation west of Greenwich, which is one-eighth of 360°, that is, 45° of longitude west of Greenwich.

Without an accurate clock that could keep time over many months of an ocean voyage, there was no practical way of establishing what time it was at the reference point. It was in theory possible, after Galileo (1564–1642) discovered Jupiter's moons, to deduce the time by observing the moment at which these moons appeared from behind the planet and then looking up in tables when this was due to occur measured in (for example) Greenwich time. The distance between the sun and the moon, when both were visible, was also used in later centuries by skilled observers to determine the true time. But most sailors before the second half of the eighteenth century simply used their own approximate estimate of their longitude based on guesstimates of the direction in which they had been sailing, the speed at which they had been sailing, the time for which they had been so sailing and any knowledge of currents they might have—the method known as dead reckoning. So long as they could be confident of their latitude, they could feel their way to a destination whose latitude they knew. This method, called "running down the latitude," was how Columbus returned from the West Indies, though Samuel Morison, perhaps the most nautically seasoned of historians, has argued that because the quadrant was so difficult to use at sea, Columbus relied in practice almost entirely on dead reckoning, which as a way of crossing the Atlantic is approximate to the point of guesswork.[36] Indeed, when he reached the Portuguese cliff-faced shore, he was of two minds about which way to turn to find Lisbon. He gambled on turning right—and won.[37]

Even to know your latitude, you need to be able to measure the height of the body you are observing above the horizon. Arab navigators used "fingers," that is, the number of widths of a finger held at arm's length, units that were standardized at 224 to the circle (about 1° or 36^1 each) by the time of Ibn Majid.[38] Europeans, following the Hellenistic tradition from the great Alexandrian astronomers, used degrees, and by the middle of the fifteenth century they had begun to use astrolabes and cross-staffs, and a little later quadrants, on board ship to measure altitudes above the horizon, though as Columbus found all were difficult to use in rough weather.[39]

Even when the mariner knew how to discover his latitude and guess his longitude and had suitable instruments and conditions to observe the heavens and to monitor the passage of time and his own course and speed, he still needed a chart on which this information could be plotted and related to the profiles of seas and shores through which he must pass.

Portolan charts, what today we would call "pilots," embodying both sketch maps and guidance notes for mariners, had been compiled by Italian navigators and admired by Portuguese monarchs anxious to promote Portuguese maritime enterprise.[40] But beyond the Mediterranean and the near-Atlantic, the Atlantic charts of the fifteenth century proved more successful as a spur to explorers' dreams than as a source of reliable information.[41] Men were tempted to discover what might be there rather than reassured by any knowledge of what exactly lay beyond—or even, in some cases, such as the discovery of the Azores and other Atlantic islands in the 1450s and 1460s, within—the limits of recent voyages. But at least it became possible to see the Atlantic as an identifiable space with certain known points of departure and certain other great unknowns (e.g., how far south the corner into the Indian Ocean was) and to plot return voyages in relation to those parameters.

One last piece of nautical knowledge was needed to facilitate the great ocean passages at the end of the fifteenth century that connected Europe to America and the Atlantic to its neighboring oceans: the prevailing wind patterns of the ocean on whose edge Europe stood. There was one great truth, twice repeated, that had to be learned before Columbus or Bartholomeu Dias could cross the ocean or exhaust its limits.

In the Atlantic, winds in the tropics flow toward the equator, but with a 45° slant to the west. These are the trade winds, and they have their similar counterparts in the Pacific and in the Indian Ocean south of the equator. Beyond these latitudes—and a calm belt of horse latitudes—lie strong westerlies, which merge into the roaring forties in the contiguous southern ocean.

In sailing ships that could not go to windward with any comfort for long distances, it was vital to find routes that kept the wind on or abaft the beam. Thus, the way to seek the Indies going west was to sail south from Europe as far as the bulge of Africa and then to pick up the northeasterly trade winds to waft one to what is in fact central America. Likewise the way to reach southern Africa was—and is—to sail southwest toward and beyond the tip of Brazil, before turning east around the latitude of Rio.

Columbus knew from his voyages down the African coast all about the wind patterns in the North Atlantic and took full advantage of them both, by sailing south to the Canaries and then west, outward bound, and north first and then east, returning home. This pattern, at least in the eastern part of the North Atlantic, had been known since the exploration of the Atlantic islands in the fourteenth and fifteenth centuries, though its extrapolation to the west Atlantic had to be a surmise.

The discovery of the mirror image counterclockwise pattern in the south Atlantic came much later. It is notable that Bartholomeu Dias in 1486–1488 bravely followed the African coast south and southeast, against the prevailing winds beyond the equator and through the inhospitable waters of the Gulf of Guinea and the west coast of southern Africa. But only a decade later Vasco da Gama kept due south from the Cape Verde islands and then deviated well to the southwest before turning south again and eventually east to reach the Cape of Good Hope. He, of course, had the great advantage over Dias of knowing from Dias's own report the latitude of that cape and was therefore able to make for it without hugging the coast. Two decades later Magellan needed only—in a manner of speaking—to let the prevailing northwesterly winds take him most of the way down the South American coast, until after a bitter winter in Patagonia with violent offshore storms, he found the entrance to "his" straits on 21 October 1520.[42]

So by the early sixteenth century ships and sailors were fashioned and equipped to undertake passages from the Atlantic seaboard of Europe that had previously been largely unthinkable and certainly unachieved. The lure of the East supplied a strong and persistent strategic motive for both monarchs and the explorers whom they sponsored to probe further and further south and west. We may speculate that even without the economic spur, the sheer possibility of such voyages would in the end have been sufficient to ensure that they were undertaken. As it is, it is hard to improve upon Rosenberg and Birdzell's summary of the forces that produced the explosion of European maritime enterprise over the length and breadth of the Atlantic Ocean at the end of the fifteenth century:

> The overseas voyages began in attempts to find all-water routes in which the new carracks and caravelles could be substituted for the difficult and costly overland trade routes with the Far East. They were thus attempts to exploit commercially a new shipbuilding technology by Western countries which had already learned, from trading with each other, the value of maritime trade and which had, again in trading with each other, already developed ships adequate to carrying substantial cargoes on long ocean voyages. Thus, to the extent that

> the carracks and caravelles originated in social and economic needs rather than in the general ebullience of the Renaissance, they were the effect of the earlier sizeable growth of intra-European trade, which was, in turn, a trade that grew with the growth of population, urbanisation and specialisation.[43]

We have so far examined the motives and the technical developments that contributed to the eruption of Europeans from the fifteenth century into, across, down and eventually beyond the Atlantic Ocean. But for these voyages to have had the consequences for global history that they did, it was necessary not just that European sailors could make immensely long oceanic passages but also that their arrival in, to them, new lands should not be easily or effectively resisted. However far you sail, you must eventually go ashore and engage in either military or economic—or both—enterprises in the lands you find, if your expeditions are to amount to anything more than a display of purely nautical virtuosity.

To explain why Europeans were, in the broadest sense, successful when they arrived as well as in reaching distant oceans and shores, one further technological factor has to be mentioned—gunnery. The invention of the gun, as a vessel for projecting a missile by the explosive force of gunpowder, appeared virtually simultaneously in Europe (1326) and China (1332), probably not by coincidence.[44] Gunpowder-based political empires were established or cemented in Muscovy, India, China and Japan between 1450 and 1600.[45] And before 1450 naval superiority—in shipbuilding, navigational techniques and fighting ability—looked if anything most likely to lie with the Chinese in the age of Zheng He, with the Muslim navies of the Ottoman Turks in the eastern Mediterranean and the Black Sea, and with the Arabs in the Red Sea and the Indian Ocean.[46]

Nor was it the case, when European ships appeared in the Indian Ocean and beyond, that the other gunpowder-using powers instantly collapsed in the way that the pre-Columbian American civilizations rapidly did (smitten by Europeans' germs as well as arms). Nonetheless, it is hard to quarrel with Paul Kennedy's broad judgment:

> Europe, fuelled by a flourishing arms trade, took a decisive lead over the other civilisations and power centres. Two consequences of this armaments spiral need be mentioned here. One ensured the political plurality of Europe, the other eventual maritime mastery. . . . The development of the long-range

> armed sailing ship heralded a fundamental advance in Europe's place in the world. With these vessels, the naval powers of the west were in a position to control the oceanic trade routes and to overawe all societies vulnerable to the workings of sea power.[47]

Both McNeill and Kennedy describe how political pluralism in Europe and the resulting market forces in the armaments industries of Europe provided, from the fourteenth century onward, far more powerful incentives to the development of more and more efficient cannons than existed in the other centers, where a single political authority had a monopoly of effective force.[48] Thus, the armaments first developed for intra-European wars were quickly and naturally adapted to naval gunnery. The new, more powerful bronze cannons—and later the cheaper iron versions—could find a safer and more stable platform in the midships areas of the beamy carracks and caravels, firing a potent broadside, than in the lighter, narrower galleys, dhows and junks of their principal seagoing opponents.[49]

Even so, despite the shattering impact, to judge from their own accounts, of Vasco da Gama's and Albuquerque's descents on the Arab fleets they encountered around the Indian Ocean, simply blasting them aside, European maritime rule was established gradually, was never absolute and only intermittently commanded the full attention and support of the governments in whose name it was proclaimed. East Asia never succumbed, partly because of its distance from Europe and because of the character and quantity of its peoples. Russia, too, remained relatively immune, comparatively inaccessible to ship-borne menaces. And of course the quest for maritime supremacy was a fertile source of competition and conflict among the various European powers, who for most of the three centuries after the Atlantic became a highway to the rest of the world, contended unceasingly for dominance and profit.

Trade follows the flag. And certainly with incipient naval supremacy allied to the powerful blessing of the pope's decision in 1493 to divide the globe by a line drawn from pole to pole 320 miles west of the Azores between Spanish (to the west) and Portuguese (to the east) spheres of exploitation, the non-Christian world was set up in Catholic minds to be ransacked, or otherwise converted, to the benefit, glory and sanctity of European monarchs.[50] Nonetheless, Spain and Portugal interpreted this opportunity very differently, and the French, the Dutch and the British came to have dissenting and discordant claims of their own.

An essay on the wealth of man does not need to chronicle every twist and turn in the struggle among European potentates for maximum political advantage. What is, however, important are the different ways in which their interpretation of their opportunities influenced the development of a world economic system built on the superhighway of transoceanic traffic and trade.

The standard cliché used by historians of the age of so-called discovery has been that the Spanish conquered and plundered whereas the Portuguese sought trade. Indeed, David Landes still writes, "As for objectives the Spanish aimed at treasure; the Portuguese, at profits from trade. Two views of empire."[51] Like most clichés, this one contains truth as well as oversimplification. The sixteenth-century Spaniards who followed in the wake of Columbus to Central America were the product of a society whose most recent formative experience had been the centuries-long reconquest of Spain from Islam—finally completed, neatly enough, in 1492. That project had engendered what John Elliott calls "a militant crusading tradition" that naturally projected itself first across the Straits of Gibraltar and in due course across the ocean to the west.[52] Moreover, long experience of endemic warfare had bred a concept of wealth as portable gold and booty, and of land as space ruled by a lord and peopled by vassals, slaves and converts.

The Portuguese experience was sufficiently similar for them to have developed comparable attitudes, which in both Iberian kingdoms coexisted with classic commercial profit-seeking in the great trading ports of Seville, Lisbon and the like. There is no convincing foundation in history for the suggestion that profound differences in national characteristics dictated the different outcomes of Spanish and Portuguese incursions into their demarcated spheres of exploitation.

The outcomes certainly were different. The Spanish in Central America, finding that there were no spices or similar commodities of the kind Columbus had prognosticated, quickly began to look for other ways of enriching themselves. Rumors of gold and silver drew the new arrivals on from the Caribbean islands to the Central American mainland and into its interior.[53] Within twenty-five years this brought them into contact with the first of the developed pre-Columbian civilizations that Europeans encountered, the Aztecs in what is now southern Mexico.

The result for the Aztecs, and over the ensuing decades for the Incas and other native American peoples, was catastrophic. Between 1519 and 1524 Hernán Cortés (1485–1547) and a few hundred men destroyed the Aztec empire by a combination of ignorance—the Aztec emperor Montezuma believed Cortés was a returning god and fatally admitted him to his capital Tenochtitlán—superior arms (steel weapons, horses and guns) and disease.[54] Smallpox, imported by the Europeans, reached the mainland in 1520, prostrated the Aztecs just when they were on the point of destroying Cortés's small band and killed Montezuma's successor and huge swathes of the Aztec population.[55]

Ten years later (1531–1535) in modern Peru, Francisco Pizarro (c. 1476–1541) destroyed the Inca empire by similar means, capturing the emperor Atahualpa in a simple trap and defeating armies of tens of thousands with troops of horsemen varying in number from thirty to 110.[56] He was also much assisted by the ravages of smallpox, which had arrived shortly before him, killing the previous emperor, Huayna Capac, and his heir, thereby provoking a civil war.[57]

It has been estimated that between 1519 and 1595 in central Mexico the native population was reduced by 55–96 percent mainly by epidemics (smallpox, measles, possibly typhus and influenza) acting on populations whose resistance had also been weakened by forced migration, enslavement, crushing levies and overwork.[58] Between 1532 and 1608, according to other estimates, the central Mexican native population fell from 16.9 million to 1 million.[59] In Peru, the evidence suggests, the Inca population was about halved between 1572 and 1620.[60]

Looking briefly at the bigger picture, one may note Jared Diamond's claim that smallpox, measles, influenza, typhus, bubonic plague and other European infectious diseases "played a decisive role in European conquests, by decimating people on other continents," a trade only slightly requited by the reverse transfer of syphilis from the new world to the old, supposedly on Columbus's return passage.[61] And Diamond estimates, "Throughout the Americas, diseases introduced with Europeans spread from tribe to tribe far in advance of the Europeans themselves, killing an estimated 95 percent of the pre-Columbian Native American population."[62]

History is not the place to seek ultimate judgments on this assault, however unintentional, on defenseless people and the resulting human calamity afflicting tens of millions of people in the Americas alone (whose population just before Columbus was about 40 million). But in an essay on the wealth of man it needs to be recorded as arguably among the greatest reverses suffered anywhere before the twentieth century A.D., quantitatively in at least a similar league to the impact of the Black Death in Europe and the simultaneous ravages of both Genghis Khan and the plague in China.[63]

Undeterred by such consequences, the Spanish conquerors took advantage of their opportunities. These were in the first instance to pillage the movable properties of the native Americans and then to exploit the resources of the Central and South American region systematically by shipping home as much wealth as their ships could bear. As Elliott summarizes it: "The seizure of the American mainland—the acquisition of an 'empire of the Indies'—came to be seen as justifying an investment of men, money and national energy on a scale that would have been unthinkable without the prospect not only of instant bonanzas, but also of continuing long-term yields."[64]

When gold artifacts for plunder soon ran out, rich silver deposits were discovered, as well as some gold, in modern Mexico and Bolivia in the 1540s and 1550s and mined with European techniques and forced native labor.[65] By the peak decade at the end of the sixteenth century, Spain was shipping home an annual average of 300 million grams of silver, as well as 1.9 million grams of gold, accounting for 95 percent by value of all Spain's imports from its colonies.[66] Trade scarcely featured because after the destruction of the Aztec and Inca civilizations there were few indigenous people sufficiently in control of their own property and produce to make any kind of meaningful bargain with their new masters. Where trade did develop, as in the Spanish islands of the Caribbean, it was with Spanish growers of sugar, cocoa and tobacco on the new colonial estates founded on the previous homes of the rapidly displaced and reduced aboriginal Caribs and Arawaks.[67]

On the mainland Spanish priorities in the sixteenth century were bullion and settlement by newly arriving Spanish adventurers in the fertile lands left by the political, military and demographic collapse of the native population with a view to wringing what they could out of the remaining native population by way of tribute and labor.[68] In the most basic sense, this was plunder, the seizure by force of wealth that had belonged to others and its transfer into the ownership of the plunderers. The driving force was the nature of the opportunities the Spanish, armed with their steel, their horses, their guns and their germs, found in a continent so long isolated from the rest of mankind's culture and diseases. Exploitation and expropriation were the obvious ways of enriching oneself in the circumstances in which the Spanish found themselves.

The Portuguese behaved differently, when they did, mainly because the opportunities they found proved different. But in the early stages (1430–1460) of the Portuguese push down the Atlantic coast of North Africa and into the near-Atlantic islands, they encountered the same opportunities and conditions as the Spanish, and they behaved similarly. In the latitudes that were hospitable to European settlement, colonies were established in the Canary Islands, Madeira and the Azores by both Spanish and Portuguese, as well as by other enterprising Genoese, Florentine and French venturers. Further south, in the uninhabited—and, to European minds, uninhabitable by European labor—Cape Verde Islands the Portuguese evolved from 1460 what became the model for European occupation of the Caribbean and Central and Southern America: sugar plantations owned and managed by Europeans and worked by imported African slaves, the supply of whom was conveniently close.[69] They thus reinvented, though with a different crop, the latifundia, the great, slave-based landed estates that had been the backbone of the rural economy of the Roman Empire more than 1,000 years earlier.

The Portuguese may have known of the existence of the land mass we now know as Brazil as early as 1494, when they persuaded the Spanish to agree to move the pope's 1493 demarcation line between Spanish and Portuguese interests 210 nautical miles west, just sufficient to include the hump of South America. Pedro de Cabral formally claimed Brazil for the Portuguese crown in 1500, and initially the new colony was exploited for its timber. Brazil's 3 million or so indigenous Indians—savannah and highland farmers—seem for a while to have resisted subjugation and exploitation more effectively than their counterparts in Mexico and Peru because they were scattered over a vast area and contact with the loggers was limited.[70]

Colonization began in the 1530s, and Brazil was transformed as the sugar plantations pioneered in the eastern Atlantic were introduced and thrived in the fertile conditions. But the coercion and enslavement of the Brazilian Indians to work the plantations made them more susceptible to European diseases, and the Portuguese increasingly resorted to importing African laborers. Although the Africans were more expensive to obtain, the first arrivals were already familiar with sugar production through their enslavement by the Portuguese in the eastern Atlantic. According to Stuart Schwartz, the historian of Brazilian slavery, African laborers "seemed to be more productive, less able to flee, and less susceptible to illness." During the next 300 years, until 1850, when the Brazilian slave trade was finally abolished, 3 million—and perhaps as many as 5 million—Africans were shipped to Brazil. No other American colony was to be as strongly influenced by slavery.[71]

It was when the Portuguese rounded the Cape of Good Hope and entered the Indian Ocean that they began to encounter radically different conditions from those of the Western Hemisphere and to respond differently to different opportunities. The basic economic opportunities were not, as in the New World, plunderable gold and silver and free space in the form of fertile land that was, or rapidly became, untenanted or at least undefended in the face of European arms and germs. The Indian Ocean already supported a network of trade from the East African coast, the Red Sea and the Persian Gulf to the Indian subcontinent, Ceylon and Southeast Asia, with China actively connected through the South China Sea (except when it chose at times during the fifteenth century to cut itself off). None of these populations was as vulnerable to the diseases that Europeans carried as were the pre-Columbian Americans, who had had no exposure to Eurasian germs for thousands of years.[72]

The Portuguese could not, as Cortés and Pizarro did, find the indigenous populations in their path simply melting away at their approach. Nor were the Arab, Indian and Chinese societies vulnerable to European steel, horses and gunpowder in the catastrophic way that precluded almost all effective resistance in America. They had all these things, though (as we have seen) their monolithic political cultures had not given the same spur to technological progress in the arms industry that Europe's multitude of competing rulers had encouraged. The one decisive advantage the Portuguese had was in naval warfare. Their ships, armed with bronze cannons firing broadsides from stable platforms, had an overwhelming advantage over the dhows and junks they confronted. The ferocity of the Portuguese onslaught on the maritime trade of the Indian ocean, traditionally conducted on broadly peaceable terms, astonished and stole a march on their opponents during an intense initial phase from 1500 to 1515, when Lisbon seized the most profitable ports in East Africa, the west coast of the Indian subcontinent (on the Malabar coast in the south and in Konkan further north), the Persian Gulf and the Malacca Strait.[73] In the next phase (1515–1560) the Portuguese established an oceanwide chain of fortified settlements, centered on Goa and backed by regular naval patrols, enforcing a valuable pepper monopoly and charging traditional merchants for protection and safe passage.[74]

This was at its maximum a trading empire, never a wholesale occupation and colonization of lands and resources. The profit would come from the trade and from the levies the Portuguese were able to impose on Asian merchants for continuing to ply upon the Indian Ocean. For the Portuguese crown, trade itself was the main economic prize, including pepper from the Malabar coast, cinnamon from Ceylon and luxury spices (cloves, nutmeg and mace) from the Moluccas and the Banda Islands between Borneo and New Guinea, although the protection effort in the long run cost more than it earned.[75] After the Portuguese established themselves in Macao, a third phase of the Portuguese presence in the Indian Ocean began. During this time the Asian traders started to recover some of their lost business, especially the pepper trade to the Red Sea and the Mediterranean, as they exploited weaknesses in Portugal's naval control and developed their own naval presence, reinforced by captured Portuguese cannons, for example, at the formidable port of Acheh under Sultan Ali Mughayat Shah on the northern tip of Sumatra.[76]

In sum, during the sixteenth century, while Spain was creating a land-based empire in America, albeit critically linked to the home country by huge convoys, Portugal was creating a sea empire around the Indian Ocean, only building bases on land to the extent necessary to supply and maintain its sea power and the trade that it protected. The difference was chiefly due to the different opportunities. The indigenous Americans could not withstand the European approach. The indigenous Asians around the Indian Ocean were vulnerable only insofar as they wished to put to sea and trade over long distances. The population of Asia in 1500 was about 250 million, including up to 100 million Indians and 30 million

Arabs and Persians in southwest Asia. Such societies could hardly be annihilated by a few score armed Europeans on horseback or by smallpox, influenza and other pestilences. The Portuguese, by violence and surprise, carved out a spectacular niche and an extraordinary profit, not least from intra-Asian trade that avoided the need to make the hazardous westbound passage back around the Cape of Good Hope.[77] But it was never more than a sea-based harassment of large, land-based economies in the Middle East, India and the Far East. These continued to determine their own fate, to support their own powerful political empires and to outproduce Europe in manufactured as well as agricultural products.[78]

Even so, the Atlantic had been connected to the Indian and Pacific Oceans, and to that extent there was by the middle of the sixteenth century a single network of ocean routes to and from all principal ports in the world. We should not, however, make false analogies with later traffic volumes. From 1500 to 1634 an average of only seven ships a year set forth from Portugal for the East, and only four ships a year actually completed the return journey from the Indian Ocean, numbers that contrast extraordinarily with the estimated 200 ships a year that entered Seville from the Spanish Main by 1600.[79]

Where the Spanish and Portuguese led, other European seafarers followed. News of where they had gone and what they had found spread fast, and it was inevitable that others should eventually relish the opportunities, even if it was not until the second half of the sixteenth century that really significant amounts of plunder and profit began to flow back into metropolitan coffers.[80] The Cabots sailed from Bristol for Newfoundland in 1494. In 1535 Jacques Cartier entered the St. Lawrence River and claimed for France what later became Canada. By mid-century, French, English and Dutch privateers were trading secretly with, if not directly plundering, Spanish and Portuguese colonies in the Caribbean and Brazil; and under Queen Elizabeth I of England (1558–1603) Francis Drake made a career out of raiding, sacking and otherwise harassing Spanish ships and settlements wherever he could find them, his motives apparently combining shameless treasure hunting with political service to his sovereign.[81]

After the Dutch had been excluded from Lisbon by the Spanish authorities in 1592 (the Dutch were fighting for independence from Spain, while Portugal was under the Spanish crown), they geared up for long-distance navigation and sent over fifty ships in less than a decade to the Indian Ocean.[82] The success of these early voyages encouraged the formation in 1602 of the Dutch East India Company to handle all trade between the Indies and the Netherlands. The English likewise rounded the Cape of Good Hope and entered the Indian Ocean from 1591 (Drake had crossed it from the east on his circumnavigation of 1577–1580), in due course persuading the political and commercial leadership in London to form the East India Company in 1600, building on the model of the Muscovy, Eastland (Baltic), Levant and first African chartered trading companies formed over the previous forty-five years.[83]

The impact on Europe of the opening of the new global ocean routes was stimulative, but in different ways. The flow of bullion into Spain, overwhelmingly the main direct effect of the "discoveries," expanded the money supply in Spain in particular and in Europe generally (monetary metals tripled in the sixteenth century). This in turn drove both real growth in commercial and manufacturing activity and inflation of prices (which quadrupled during the century), as more and more of the precious metals chased a supply of goods and services that was less than infinitely expandable in the medium term.[84]

But the reader in the twenty-first century needs to remember that the sixteenth century was not the modern world. The integration of economies had not proceeded more than a fraction of the way along the road to a world where such a high proportion of our daily expenditure is satisfied from sources all over the world. The vast majority of ordinary wants in sixteenth-century Europe were supplied locally and regionally; beyond certain special commodities like spices, international and intercontinental exchange represented a tiny fraction of economic life. Over time the opening of new routes, the servicing of them from key ports, the growth of financial and commercial communities and structures to exploit these opportunities and the development of new markets and new sources of supply had important consequences, political as well as economic. But they did not have an immediately transforming effect on the lives of most people, which were still dominated by the agricultural economy. The kind of dramatic and rapid effects to which we grew accustomed in the late twentieth century from globalized markets, information revolutions, astronomic financial flows and the internationalization of business simply had no counterpart half a millennium ago.

Growth rates, insofar as we can guess, remained slow by later postindustrial revolution standards, let alone by late-twentieth-century standards. Adam Smith had nonetheless good long-term reasons for writing, "The discovery of America, and that of a passage to the East Indies by the Cape of Good Hope, are the two greatest and most important events recorded in the history of mankind."[85]

That was because of the effects he saw and, even more importantly and presciently, expected from the creation of new markets and the enlargement of the whole global marketplace:

> By uniting, in some measure, the most distant parts of the world, by enabling them to relieve one another's wants, to increase one another's enjoyments, and to encourage one another's industry, their general tendency would seem to be beneficial. . . . Two new worlds have been opened to their [European commercial towns'] industry, each of them much greater and more extensive than the old one, and the market of one of them [America] growing still greater and greater every day.[86]

It was this uniting of distant parts of the world that beyond the sixteenth century, when bullion and specie dominated intercontinental trade, expanded the list of traded commodities to include exotic dyestuffs like indigo and cochineal, coffee from Africa, cocoa from America, silk and tea from Asia, cotton and sugar on a large scale, tobacco, tropical fruits and nuts, furs, hides, exotic woods, new fibers, potatoes, tomatoes, string beans, squash, red peppers, pumpkins and maize.[87]

Nor were the effects confined to Europe. Already in the sixteenth century the flow of bullion through Spain to Europe stimulated and financed increased purchases from Asia. Indeed, Frank has argued that Asia's larger and more flexible economies were better able to respond to the new demand and as a result grew more rapidly than the European economies.[88] This was most conspicuous in India, especially Bengal and Bihar, where in the late sixteenth century the Moghul empire had recently established itself, creating a stability that favored economic development. Similarly, in Ming China imported silver permitted a monetary expansion that encouraged economic growth until the Manchu invasions and other troubles of the mid-seventeenth century.[89]

Historians have generally agreed that Spain did not make the most of its opportunities after Columbus. The primary emphasis on extraction of bullion—plunder—did little to develop in the New World a market for Spanish products, and the bullion, when it arrived in Spain, was used more to enhance the power and magnificence of the ruling Castilians, engaged in endless wars with other European powers, than to prime commercial and productive investments. Kings Charles I (who became Emperor Charles V) and Philip II grossly overspent even their huge revenues, plunging themselves into crushing debt and imposing on their subjects the heaviest taxation in Europe. Spanish aristocrats, who enjoyed great privileges, frowned upon and discouraged the business classes, while religious intolerance at the hands of the Inquisition oppressed and drove into exile the Jews, nonconformists and other dissenters, many of whom had played and elsewhere continued to play a more than proportionate role in the commercial life of Europe.

Before they fell to the crown of Spain in 1580, the Portuguese had a better commercial policy, trade rather than plunder, but proved too small and inefficient to take full advantage of their head start over other European powers in the Indian Ocean and were almost equally blind to the advantages of religious tolerance. The natural reflex of political authorities everywhere to seek to convert their power into cash by granting valuable monopolies, privileges and immunities to favored groups of subjects weakened the Portuguese economy by adding to the burden of taxes imposed upon ordinary citizens and by delegating the government's regulatory powers to corrupt and incompetent agencies.[90]

In the sixteenth century the Spanish and the Portuguese had made global connections, established regular sea routes, created colonies and plantations and trading posts and brought home booty sufficiently to arouse both the envy and anxiety of other Europeans powers. In the seventeenth century new entrants to this seemingly attractive game challenged and eventually displaced the Iberian leaders. In the process they created new styles of economic empire building, new concepts of the role of economics in national political agenda and new interconnections between the key hubs of the global economy.

We saw in Chapter 4 how Europe's economic center of gravity had gradually shifted northward and westward from Italy and the Mediterranean, both as a consequence of the exploitation of the food-producing potential of the heavy soils of France, the Lowlands and Britain and as the commercial centers migrated from northern Italy to Champagne, Bruges and Antwerp. In 1551 Antwerp was a city of the Spanish Netherlands ruled by the Habsburg kings of Spain and holy Roman emperors. But in 1566 the Netherlands revolted, finally winning independence for the United Provinces of the Netherlands (as the seven northern Protestant provinces called themselves) in 1648 at the end of the Thirty Years' War. By 1600 Amsterdam, the chief Dutch city, had already taken over Antwerp's role as the commercial heart of northwest Europe, buoyed by the northward exodus from Spanish control of financiers and merchants, together with their expertise and liquid capital.[91]

The success of the Netherlands in the seventeenth century was rooted in several advantages: its geography, at the apex of its "mother trades" with the Baltic, the North Sea, the Bay of Biscay and the Mediterranean; its cultural legacy of tough, independent-minded burghers, merchants and skilled seafarers; its devolved political structure that minimized central power and fostered religious tolerance and economic freedom; its highly urbanized and growing population; its cheap energy from peat and its thriving brewing, refining, shipbuilding and textiles industries and its specialized agriculture and successful herring fisheries. It did not take long for these assets to enable the Dutch, as the people of the Netherlands have been collectively known in the English language, to become a lead country, operating near the technological frontier, and to make their presence felt on the global scene.[92]

From the late 1590s, Dutch merchants had every incentive to intervene in the Indian Ocean. The Dutch were excluded from the lucrative European trade in Asian commodities, since the contract for distributing Portugal's Asian goods was held by a syndicate that made Hamburg its main base. Pepper prices were also high, because Portuguese inefficiency meant that supply was insufficient to meet the growing European demand. But during 1595–1596 the Dutch were handed a detailed route map to the source of this lucrative trade when Jan van Linschoten, a Dutchman who had served the Portuguese in Asia, published his travel journals. These contained "sailing routes, winds, ports, and the Portuguese empire in Asia." If any further incentive were needed, the unity since 1580 of the Portuguese and Spanish empires under the Habsburg crown, against whom the Dutch were fighting for their independence, gave the Dutch added cause to ignore Iberian claims to monopoly rights in the New World and the Indies.[93]

Dutch inventiveness in shipbuilding, itself the result of growing demand for ships as the Netherlands became Europe's trade and commercial center, and their skills as sailors gave them a competitive edge at sea.[94] At the beginning of the seventeenth century, they had developed the *fluyt,* a refinement of the Iberian fully rigged *carveel,* a larger, longer, shallower, handier and more capacious version of the ships used by Spain and Portugal in the previous century.[95] At the same time the warship of choice became the galleon.[96] Such was the Dutch preeminence in shipping that by 1636 they had 1,750 seagoing merchant vessels active in Europe in addition to several hundred ships in the herring fleet.[97] The effective, albeit ungainly, *fluyt* was used mainly in the large Baltic trade, but ships sailing to Asia, the West Indies and the Mediterranean were more heavily constructed, with rows of gunports on their sides.[98] By 1659 the Dutch East Indies fleet totaled 119 ships, most of them sailing permanently in Asian seas and three or four times larger than the European *fluyt*s.[99]

Although building and operating costs were higher for the East Indies fleet than for other European ships, cost-saving in comparison with foreign competition was not the overriding concern in the Asian trade.[100] Voyages to the East were "uncertain and hazardous," as Russell Menard has noted, since they often lasted two years and were "troubled by disease, adverse weather, piracy, and warfare."[101] In these conditions the Dutch and other Europeans sought to corner the long-distance trade in Asian spices and other commodities for themselves and exclude their rivals by building networks of fortified bases and laying claim to trading rights.[102]

Of most importance to the Dutch success in what C. R. Boxer aptly described as the "first world war" in the Indian Ocean was the founding in 1602 of the Verenigde Oostindische Compagnie (United East India Company, or VOC).[103] By the early 1600s competing Dutch venturers in the Indian Ocean had already exposed Portugal's weakness and marginalized their British counterparts. These early Dutch gains, however, so boosted the supply of pepper in Europe as to send the price tumbling and threaten their financial backers with ruin. The Dutch government intervened to prevent financial disaster by merging the competing merchant groups into a new trading monopoly, the VOC, that was granted the exclusive right of trading and shipping east of the Cape of Good Hope and west of the Strait of Magellan.[104] The politicians, however, had an ulterior motive, as Jan de Vries and Ad van der Woude, emphasize: "It certainly did not escape the minds of the political leaders that a single, 'united' Dutch presence in Asia could pursue military objectives in the struggle against Spain and Portugal, something that competing merchant groups could never contemplate."[105]

Within forty years of the foundation of the VOC, the Dutch controlled much of the riches of the East for which the European voyages of discovery had been undertaken in the previous 150 years, including cloves, nutmeg, sandalwood, tea and Chinese products. Even before the VOC had won full control of the Moluccan spice islands, it expanded into the three large trading zones that spanned Asia. By 1612 the Dutch had replaced the Portuguese on India's Coromandel coast at Pulicat, where they established a fortified center of trade. This was significant because Indian cotton textiles were important in developing the spice trade. By the 1630s VOC influence extended to Bengal. In 1637 the Dutch secured the cinnamon trade after driving the Portuguese from their coastal defenses in Ceylon.[106]

The VOC had already expanded into the other two great Asian trading zones by the 1620s. In the Far East the Dutch established trading links with Japan from 1609 and overcame resistance from the Chinese, Spanish and Portuguese by attacking Chinese coastal shipping in 1624. From Fort Zeelandia on Taiwan, the Dutch were able to consolidate their Far Eastern trade. The most westerly trading zone, comprising India's Malabar coast, Persia and Arabia, was centered on Surat, where the VOC established a permanent settlement in 1616. From Surat the VOC's trading links extended to Mocha, at the entrance to the Red Sea.[107] By the 1640s the VOC had constructed "a remarkably comprehensive network of trading stations stretching from Persia to Japan."[108]

The Westindische Compagnie (West India Company, or WIC) was established in 1621 to complement the VOC's eastern trade in the Atlantic. The WIC promoted colonization and the fur trade in North America, developed sugar production in the Caribbean, extracted as much as possible (by fair means and foul) from the bullion-rich Spanish colonies and boosted the Atlantic slave trade. By the 1640s Dutch toeholds were to be found on the Gold Coast and in Angola in Africa; in Brazil and Venezuela in South America; in Curaçao, Tobago and Suriname in the Caribbean; and around the Hudson valley (New Netherland) in North America, where, in 1623, they had also founded New Amsterdam on an island called Manhattan.[109]

Within just two generations, the Dutch had established a global trading network that extended from the Netherlands to New Netherland and Curaçao in the west, to Formosa (Taiwan) and Deshima (Nagasaki) in the east, to Smeerenburg on Spitzbergen in the north and to Cape Town in the south.[110] But like the Portuguese and the Spanish before them, the Dutch now came under attack from other European powers, mainly the British and the French, who were anxious to muscle in and end the Dutch dominance of trade and shipping.

The first Anglo-Dutch War, beginning in 1652, heralded a quarter of a century of recurrent attacks. The Dutch lost their Brazilian and Angolan bases in 1654, Formosa in 1662 and New Amsterdam in 1664.[111] The loss of New Amsterdam was to prove a turning point in American and world history but seems to have been little mourned by the Dutch at the time. New Amsterdam was a small, poorly defended trading center with a population of about only 1,000 when the English captured it in 1664. The small English task force had been dispatched across the Atlantic on the orders of the duke of York, the future James II and brother of Charles II, in revenge for a Dutch assault on the spice island of Run and its nutmeg groves. When peace was made between the countries three years later, the English were allowed to keep New Amsterdam, which they renamed New York, and the Dutch kept Run.[112] It probably seemed a good deal to the Dutch at the time—they had never been as excited by beaver pelts as they were by spices—but the exchange of New York for Run must rank as one of the less visionary commercial deals in recorded history.[113]

Despite the steadily growing challenge from their larger European rivals, the Dutch republic's trade and shipping long remained, in the words of de Vries and van der Woude, "the single greatest concentration of international economic activity in Europe, and its entrepôt function long dominated international markets."[114] For our story, the most important legacies of Dutch international trading preeminence were the commercial and financial innovations that occurred in Amsterdam during the early 1600s, involving the VOC, the Bank of Amsterdam and the stock exchange. These institutions were themselves based on earlier innovations by European and Asian merchants, but their close proximity within Amsterdam and their development and increased sophistication by the Dutch enabled the city to be the leading international entrepôt throughout the seventeenth century. And eventually, albeit not in a neat progression, these organizations were to become the models for the building blocks of Western capitalism—the joint-stock, limited liability company, the public bank and the stock exchange.

As Jack Goody reminds us, if joint-stock companies were the forerunners of today's multinationals, "they were also the successors to the earlier forms of partnership, such as the *commenda,* that had existed for centuries throughout Eurasia."[115] Some of the early English chartered companies, including the Muscovy, Levant and East India companies, were set up as joint-stock companies, that is, the capital contributions of their members were pooled and put under common management. This was done because the sums and risks required for even a single voyage were substantially more than one or a few individuals were prepared to provide.[116] But whereas the English East India Company treated each voyage as a separate venture that might have different shareholders, its Dutch counterpart, the VOC, considered all its voyages part of a single, twenty-one-year venture. And since the VOC was also granted the power to build forts, maintain armies and negotiate treaties, an enormous amount of capital was inevitably required.[117]

The VOC's charter therefore provided that all investors would be responsible for the VOC's debts only to the extent of their investment, that is, what we now call a limited liability company. In addition, during the VOC's early years a series of ad hoc decisions established the principle that the capital invested would be permanent (that is, not subject to liquidation and distribution among the investors) and that investors who wished to liquidate their interest in the VOC could sell their share at the stock exchange. By the second decade of the seventeenth century, these practices were established and, as de Vries and van der Woude observe, "the VOC had become Europe's first effective joint-stock company."[118]

Banks had mostly been private affairs, but by founding the Bank of Amsterdam (Amsterdamsche Wisselbank) in 1609 as a municipal bank that provided a reliable means of payment, the city fathers created another vital ingredient of Dutch financial success. As with the VOC, the Bank of Amsterdam was modeled on a precedent—in its case the Venetian Banco della Piassa di Rialto, established in 1587. The Wisselbank was founded in response to the influx from 1585 of merchants and *kassiers* (money changers) from Antwerp, where the bill of exchange had been developed into a flexible instrument of short-term credit. The Amsterdam city fathers, however, were more concerned to uphold and increase the supply of stable, good-value coinage than to allow the proliferation of bills, and their new bank was designed to assert control over money changing and to curtail the lengthy chains of payment in bills of exchange. The Wisselbank took deposits, made transfers between accounts, and accepted (i.e., paid) bills of exchange. Merchants were effectively forced to open an account by the requirement that all bills of 600 guilders or more had to be made payable via the bank. De Vries and van der Woude encapsulate the bank's importance in the development of international trade:

> The Bank of Amsterdam succeeded instantly in attracting depositors, who became the envy of Europe for their access to deposit, transfer, and payment services that were trustworthy, safe, efficient, and virtually costless. It grew with the expansion of Amsterdam's commerce to become the clearinghouse of world trade, settling international debts and effecting transfers of capital. Moreover, it did this on a continuous basis rather than at long intervals, as had been the practice of the old fairs.[119]

Shipping, trade and financial services were brought together at the Amsterdam *beurs*, or exchange, which from the start of the seventeenth century superseded the exchanges at Bruges and Antwerp to become "the nerve centre of the entire international economy" until well into the eighteenth century.[120] The merchants and brokers who gathered in the arcades of the 1611 *beurs* building "traded in literally everything known to that society"; their deals included all manner of commodities, financial instruments (shares and government bonds), sea insurance, freighting, and foreign exchange. Within a stone's throw of the *beurs* were the Wisselbank and the VOC, enabling merchants to enjoy unrivaled business opportunities.[121]

Up-to-date information is vital for the efficient performance of any exchange, and Amsterdam enjoyed a comparative advantage. Although the flow of information was painfully slow by modern standards, merchants received more fresh news in Amsterdam than anywhere else. The city's location, its networks of merchants and commercial institutions, plus the republic's lack of censorship and toleration of religious groups (with their intelligence networks), all encouraged information to flow.[122] The Amsterdam *beurs* thus developed "the decision-making and capital-allocation functions" that are essential to the modern international economy and enabled the Dutch entrepôt "to become the nerve centre of *capitalism*, with its primary need for efficient access to information."[123]

This unsurpassed flow of information was vital to merchants, who were often trying to coordinate trade across different markets and were anxious to protect themselves against uncertainties such as epidemics, natural disasters, political upheavals, wars and weather. Information about the future inevitably fuels speculation. A form of futures trading was practiced by Amsterdam merchants as early as the 1550s when they wrote contracts for future delivery of grain and herring ahead of the harvest and the catch. With the growth in Dutch trade and the establishment of continuous markets at the *beurs*, modern-style futures trading was conducted in an array of commodities, including pepper, coffee, cacao, saltpeter, brandywine, whale oil and whalebone. Increasingly, neither buyer nor seller had any intention of exchanging physical goods.[124]

In Amsterdam's notorious tulip mania of 1636–1637, this form of speculation reached fever pitch. Speculation in the rare, multicolored flower patterns created by a virus that invades the mother bulb had been rising since 1634. From the summer of 1636, prices soared, reportedly because severe outbreaks of the plague "released inhibitions," and by early 1637 even ordinary citizens were gathering in their hundreds to gamble on the future price of tulip bulbs. But a decline in the price triggered a stampede to sell, and in the second week of February the price collapsed.[125] It was probably the first modern market mania, but it was certainly not the last.

The Dutch government repeatedly sought to prohibit futures trading, but by 1689 it relaxed its approach and relied instead on regulation and taxation. The politicians may have been persuaded that they were fighting a losing battle by the publication in 1688 of *Confusión de confusiones*, a book by a leading speculator on the Amsterdam *beurs*, Joseph Penso de la Vega, that gave detailed descriptions of "futures contracts, options (puts and calls), margin buying, bull and bear cabalas, and a form of stock index purchase known as ducat-actions, where small speculators could follow the market, winning or losing a ducat for every point or rise in the price of shares."[126]

The practices of speculators on the seventeenth-century *beurs* are familiar to us today. Indeed, De Vries and Van der Woude suggest that the Dutch republic should be called "the first modern economy."[127] It is certainly the case that the *beurs*, the VOC and the Wisselbank provided prototypes for the commercial and financial institutions that some two centuries later were to underpin the next great leap forward in the wealth of man—the industrial revolution. As K. N. Chaudhuri has argued:

> Was it a historical accident that when the Industrial Revolution changed the technological frontiers, the new system prospered as an economic force on capitalist lines, finding new strength in the evolution of impersonal business firms? The success of Western industrialists in utilising personal or institutional savings through share capital was founded on a type of money market and financial practice that was much older than the technological discoveries of the late eighteenth century. The capital market in Europe developed after 1600 almost in parallel with the growth of trade to Asia and the rising fortunes of the East India Companies.[128]

The Dutch remained Europe's most efficient economy until the late eighteenth century, and their financial sector continued to evolve. The government's decision in 1713 to divorce international finance from diplomatic considerations enabled Amsterdam to become a prime source of funding for governments, including most notably the English, and to emerge as the capital market for the whole of Europe.[129]

From the mid-seventeenth century, however, Dutch trading supremacy came under heavy attack in wars waged by the English (1652–1654, 1664–1667, 1672–1676) and the French and from protectionist policies. Jean-Baptiste Colbert, Louis XIV's principal minister (1661–1683), reckoned that all the trades of Europe were carried by 20,000 ships, more than three-quarters of which belonged to the Dutch, and acted on the belief that France could increase its share only by decreasing that of the Dutch.[130] The English Navigation Acts (1651, 1660 and at subsequent intervals) also targeted Dutch dominance of shipping.[131] Greater protectionism and the burden of fighting the French almost continuously during 1689–1713 brought about a shift in Dutch trading patterns, causing European trade to become relatively less important while colonial trade expanded much faster.[132]

The consequence of this shift in trade was that Amsterdam, "the entrepôt of the eighteenth century became increasingly an emporium of colonial goods."[133] The re-export of Asian goods, principally to the Baltic and Germany, developed into a key activity from the 1680s and enabled Dutch merchants to engage in other trades.

The monopoly privileges that had fueled the VOC's early expansion later disguised its weaknesses and sapped its vitality. From 1730, its profitability slumped as its share of inter-Asian trade shrank in the face of increased competition. The company was too centralized, corrupt and incompetent to respond. Whereas an original investor in the VOC who sold his shares in 1650 would have enjoyed an average annual total return of 27 percent, after 1650 the profits earned on the VOC's equity were modest and from 1730 became "vanishingly small."[134]

So much for any suggestion that the Dutch 150-year reign as "lead" country was sustained by vast profits from its empire.[135] But what part *does* foreign trade play in economic success? As de Vries and van der Woude argue: "Foreign trade rarely acts as the engine of growth of an economy. Even when the foreign trade is large relative to the size of the total economy—as it always was in the Netherlands and is to this day—*the dynamic role of foreign trade depends on the underlying capacity of the domestic economy to transform and to respond to new possibilities* of international specialisation and exchange."[136] The Dutch economic success "rested upon just such an interaction of domestic transformation and foreign trade expansion . . . that allowed Dutch merchants to dominate markets and encouraged Dutch producers to invest in increasing output."[137]

This positive interaction had ended by the late eighteenth century. Dutch shipping, trade and finance faced stiffer competition, and Dutch manufacturers failed to adapt to changing markets (Dutch food exporters were more successful). It cannot have helped Dutch manufacturers that by the end of the seventeenth century the country's supply of the peat that had provided cheap energy was running out, causing costs to rise. Importing coal, which was subject to export and import duties, put the Dutch at a disadvantage against the British, who could exploit accessible coal deposits.[138]

The British and Dutch faced strong competition for trade and empire from the French throughout most of the seventeenth and eighteenth centuries. France acquired extensive colonies in the Americas and Asia but failed to emulate its Protestant rivals in taking its place as Europe's lead economy. This was principally because the country's geography constrained French agriculture from becoming sufficiently productive to support the high degree of urbanization and industrialization that existed in the Netherlands and Britain. In addition, France's feudal political and legal system acted as a brake on change.[139] Indeed, France's longstanding failure to reform was to culminate in 1789 in bloody revolution.

In North America the French had established a base at Quebec (1609) and claimed the area around the Great Lakes as New France. Despite losing Newfoundland and Nova Scotia (previously French Arcadia) in the Treaty of Utrecht in 1713, the French vied for colonial supremacy with the British in the Americas and Asia for another fifty years.[140] They were finally ousted from Canada, India and most of the Caribbean during the Seven Years' War (1756–1763), largely as a result of the vision of William Pitt (Pitt the Elder, later the earl of Chatham, 1708–1778), the British prime minister, who saw the war as a global, not a European, conflict.

Pitt's strategy was based on foundations laid during the seventeenth century, when Britain's global trading network first took shape through the activities of the privileged trading companies (notably the East India in 1600; Guinea, 1618; Royal Adventurers into Africa, 1660; Hudson's Bay, 1670; Royal Africa, 1672) and the establishment of colonies in North America (including Virginia in 1607; New England, 1620; Massachusetts, 1630; Maryland, 1632; New Haven, 1637; Carolina, 1670; and Pennsylvania, 1681) and the Caribbean (notably St. Kitts in 1624; Barbados, 1627; Nevis, 1628; Montserrat and Antigua, 1632; and Jamaica, taken from Spain, 1655).[141] During the mid-eighteenth century, as markets expanded and the numbers of colonists increased, there was a huge shift in British trade from the Continent to the colonies. Whereas 80 percent of British exports went to continental Europe in 1720, by the 1780s this figure had fallen to 45 percent and colonial re-exports dominated. The colonies and Ireland became the primary markets for British products.[142]

By the late eighteenth century, the British were enjoying a similar positive interaction between their domestic economy and foreign trade to the one experienced by the Dutch over the previous 150 years. Just how important the role of foreign, and especially colonial, trade was in boosting the British economy has been the subject of heated debate among historians. Foreign and colonial trade certainly became increasingly significant. About 8 percent of national output was exported at the end of the seventeenth century, but during the reign of George III (1760–1820), the share peaked at about 16 percent.[143] About half the increase in manufactured output during 1700–1760 went abroad.[144] As Patrick O'Brien notes: "The figures and contemporary commentaries validate the point that the growth of British industry from the Restoration [1660] onwards was promoted by an increasing involvement with the international economy in general and with an 'Imperial' system in particular."[145]

But after reviewing the evidence, O'Brien eschews a simple cause-and-effect relationship between colonial trade and economic expansion. Instead, he emphasizes the "inseparable and favourable connections" among Britain's economy, its highly effective fiscal system, its expanding empire and its trade.[146] In Britain during the eighteenth century "benign natural endowments, the early industrialisation of the workforce, the prior and steady accumulation of the mercantile and financial skills required to manage global commerce, strong and consistent support from an effective fiscal state, dominated by perceptive aristocrats, are among the structural preconditions that emerge decade after decade, war after war."[147]

Britain's specialized agriculture, which was able to support a growing population; its urbanized, highly skilled workforce and the availability of cheap energy from accessible coal deposits were important, and we say more about them in the next chapter, when we look at the industrial revolution. As regards the expansion of foreign trade, English merchants, like their Dutch counterparts, played a crucial role, especially after 1688, when Parliament became less inclined to renew trade monopolies. Corporate bodies such as the East India, Hudson's Bay, Royal African, Levant and South Sea companies became even more of an exception, and instead "merchants operated in partnerships, kin groups and a variety of associations, [and] formed and reformed for particular voyages and ventures."[148] The merchants who pioneered the coordination and financing of trade were the antecedents of London's international bankers.

In our story, however, Britain's experience is illuminating because it demonstrates the importance of the interaction between the economy and government. The Glorious Revolution of 1688–1689, in which James II was replaced by his daughter and son-in-law, Mary and William of Orange (the Dutch *stadtholder*) as constitutional monarchs within a parliamentary system, heralded a financial revolution. The state played the key role by introducing a series of institutional reforms, largely modeled on the Dutch financial system, that provided the financial foundations on which Britain simultaneously waged European wars, built a worldwide empire and expanded its economy. The key measures were the institution of a national debt that was the responsibility of Parliament rather than the monarch, the development of an effective tax system, the establishment in 1694 of the Bank of England and the emergence of an organized market for public as well as private securities.[149]

The concepts of the virtuous and the vicious circle have been used more than once in describing the success and failure of successive European states from the sixteenth century onward. It is important to see how these metaphors are supposed to work. Both imply a continuing two-way interaction between the domestic economy and foreign trade. In the first case the interaction is benign and mutually reinforcing, in the second the reverse. Likewise, the interaction between political and economic performance can also trigger either a vicious or a virtuous circle. The crux in this latter instance appears to lie in whether or not political performance and organization are of a kind to encourage strengthening economic performance, in which case economic growth generates an expanding tax base and production base that can be used in the next round to support the goals and activities of government, which in turn can support growing opportunities for and facilitation of further economic success.

Indeed, these interactions are but another way of regarding the final step of the waltz figure with which we have interpreted the alternations of economic history and their intimate connection with political and social arrangements. It is at this point, at the third step, that the shape of the next figure is determined, either as a new surge forward or as a relapse. For it is then that the political and social response to the predatory threats at the second step to the new economic opportunities opened up at the first step either succeeds or fails in reconciling the requirements of continued prosperity with the demands of the predators.

The events of this chapter as a whole comprehend a whole series of waltz figures at global, regional, and local levels. For some, notably the pre-Columbian peoples of the Americas, the outcome is catastrophe. Their wealth and lands attract predators whose challenge—and that of the diseases they carry—is uncontained; and the new political and social order that emerges at the third step is, from the point of view of the pre-Columbians, simply subjection, impoverishment and destruction.

For others, notably the expanding Europeans, the figure looks very different. Their arrival in the Americas—a second-step predatory threat to the indigenous Americans—is for the Europeans a first-step new opportunity on a scale unprecedented since the original agricultural revolution. In due course it too attracts its threats and generates its political and social solutions, not least the creation of the United States of America, which in turn support the first steps in subsequent figures.

But it is worth noting that at the global level this chapter also witnesses the first step in the biggest and most dramatic of all the waltz figures in this book: the global unification that flowed from the opening of long sea routes between all the world's oceans and most of their surrounding coasts and rivers. This unleashed a blizzard of new economic opportunities, reactive predatory threats and searches for political and social accommodations of these conflicting forces that shaped much of the rest of human history. In that sense Columbus and his like had opened the ball with a figure that was to whirl in an accelerating crescendo down to our own time and beyond, spawning in its frenzy thousands upon thousands of figures conforming to the original motif. Johann Strauss, it seems, has written the theme tune for the film of our story.

The particular historical interest of the British performance from 1688 lies in the creation of a financial and economic structure that contained the key ingredients of what is considered, as we enter the third millennium, to be the classical recipe for economic success. The first of these is macroeconomic stability, based on sound money underwritten by an independent reserve bank and on fiscal balance supported by moderate spending, a buoyant tax base and a cost-effective mechanism for government borrowing. The second is a liberal economic structure in which individuals can seek their own advantage in competitive market conditions.

Neither the Tories nor the Whigs who contended for power in eighteenth-century Britain thought in these terms, but it is clear in hindsight that the outcome was a political settlement under which executive power was shared among the main propertied interests in the society, allied to an economic and financial structure that nurtured the industrial revolution. The sharing of political power with those who would mainly supply the money for government activities imposed a restraint on the kind of fiscal excesses that in other places, for example Bourbon France, overburdened and stunted economic enterprise. Such power was not, of course, shared with the American colonists, with famous consequences.

The establishment of a sound form of money, together with forms of government borrowing in which a widening circle of private institutions and individuals could confidently invest, created an environment of financial stability, relatively free of the kind of shocks, crises and hyperinflations that destroy and discourage economic enterprise in unstable centers. Despite the South Sea bubble, to which we come later, these broad ingredients of public stability and private opportunity were the preconditions of British economic success from the middle of the eighteenth century and of the political and naval successes that interacted with it, and they were the source of the conventional architecture of sound political economy still dominant three centuries later.

The Bank of England was formed as a private joint-stock company with a royal charter in 1694 in response to King William III's borrowing needs for his war with France.[150] The successful precedent of the Bank of Amsterdam and the preference of London's merchants for lending to a private institution rather than directly to the monarch explained its form. It enjoyed initially a monopoly of note issue in London, as well as a franchise to circulate exchequer and other bills, as a result of which it became the government's bank and chief adviser on financing and managing the government's debts. Its eventual evolution into what today we call a reserve or central bank managing the nation's currency, in conjunction with or independent of the government, was a gradual process. But within twenty years it was already acting as a lender of last resort and discounting good-quality bills from favored customers—both major functions of any central banker through which control of the money supply is frequently exercised.[151]

Simultaneous with but distinct from the formation of the Bank of England was the fixing of the value of the pound sterling and the subsequent evolution of the gold standard. No comparable pair of linked economic events can have had such illustrious progenitors as this one. The philosopher John Locke (1632–1704), the intellectual godfather of Britain's Glorious Revolution, and the mathematician Isaac Newton (1642–1727), the discoverer of gravity, played the key roles. In 1695 Locke argued against the secretary of the treasury that there was an overriding moral duty to maintain in any new coinage, as then proposed, the true value of money as represented by a certain weight of gold or silver. This, Locke said, required that a pound sterling retain in its sterling silver content its "ancient right standard of England" rather than the lesser amount that rising silver prices had recently implied. This ancient standard, he said, amounted to 3 ounces, 17 pennyweight, 10 grains (a pennyweight defined as 24 grains, or one-twentieth of an ounce troy). By parity of reasoning, he said, an ounce of gold should be worth £3 17s. 10 1/2 d. His view, supported by Isaac Newton, who the next year became warden of the mint, prevailed, and Parliament so decided. As with the similarly purist decision to return the pound to the gold standard in 1925, when Winston Churchill was chancellor of the exchequer, this led to financial deflation, political unrest and even an insurrection of miners. Unlike Churchill's measure, Locke's fixing of the gold price of the pound lasted for more than two centuries. Both exercises ended when the gold standard was abandoned in August 1931.[152]

Locke's double gold-and-silver standards came under pressure as the value of gold relative to silver fluctuated. Isaac Newton was once again called upon, this time to define the money value of the principal gold coin of the time, the guinea, which through the greater availability of gold was threatening to drive out the silver coinage. In order to protect the silver coinage, Newton recommended in 1717 that the value of the guinea should be capped at 21 shillings, which was the equivalent of Locke's sterling price for an ounce of gold. As time went by and the guinea became more and more widely used while no further formal changes were made, the implied gold value of the pound at just over a quarter of an ounce of gold became accepted as the primary standard of the pound's value. This became the gold standard, silently established in England by what Lord Liverpool called "the disposition of the people" and eventually used in the latter part of the nineteenth century as a pillar of the first truly global economy.[153]

If monetary stabilization was one component of the greater macroeconomic stability that the mid-eighteenth century witnessed in Britain, fiscal efficiency was another. It cannot exactly be claimed that government spending or the tax burden, however measured, were moderate or stable. Successive wars (the Nine Years' War in 1689–1698, the War of the Spanish Succession in 1701–1713, the War of the Austrian Succession in 1740–1747, the Seven Years' War in 1756–1763 and the American War of Independence in 1775–1883) raised Britain's national debt from a few million to more than £240 million, increased annual tax revenues from £2 million to £12 million and raised the tax burden (revenues as a percentage of national income) from 3.5 percent to 11–12 percent.[154] Indeed, British taxation ratios were anything up to double those in France, despite the much inferior fiscal reputation of the ancien régime and its far more spectacular political consequences.[155]

In the face of such figures, talk of fiscal efficiency may seem misplaced, except perhaps in an ironic sense implying that the British crown was remarkably successful at extracting large amounts of revenue from its subjects. But if that had been all there was to the British story, adverse economic consequences on a strategic scale could have been expected. In fact the three main indicators of fiscal excess—rising interest rates, political upheaval and economic decline—are conspicuously absent.

The solution to this puzzle (a sharply rising tax burden without adverse consequences for the economy) appears to lie in the skillful development of financing mechanisms that made it easier and more attractive for those with money to lend to the government, less burdensome for the government to borrow and easier for tax revenues to be enhanced without insupportable resistance or unacceptable disincentive effects. British taxes seem to have been less resented and less oppressive than their French equivalents, partly because they were less arbitrarily and offensively collected and partly because they were less visible. British incomes also were somewhat higher, perhaps making a higher tax burden more supportable. The relatively light burden of direct tax (such as land taxes), however inequitable it appears to social philosophers, may as in more modern times have greatly reduced the general unpopularity of any given weight of tax. It probably did leave individuals more keen to enhance their incomes by whatever opportunities were open to them; more willing to save, invest and lend to the state; and more ready to be plucked when in time the true national emergency of the Napoleonic Wars required the first income tax to be introduced.[156]

But as Paul Kennedy has pointed out, and Bishop Berkeley before him, it was the British government's economic and reliable access to credit that gave it a decisive advantage over its much larger French neighbor.[157] The cost of borrowing, anywhere at any time, includes an element for having the use of the other fellow's money (the true "real" rate of interest), an element for expected inflation and an element, or "premium," for the risk that the lender may not get his money back. The British financial revolution and its sequel served to reduce the second and third of these elements: the first as an eventual consequence of the fixing of the precious metal value of the pound, and the second as a result of a number of institutional and structural developments that gave lenders greatly increased confidence that their money would be repaid. The creation of the Bank of England as an intermediary for short-term lenders, the underwriting of the crown's borrowing by Parliament and therefore by its taxing power—including the allocation of the revenues of specific taxes to the servicing of particular debts, the development of secondary markets trading in government paper (which meant that one lender who found he wanted his money back could sell his claim to another lender without having to go to the government), and the evolution of more transparent systems of public accounts under parliamentary scrutiny, at least by the standards of the times—all made lenders more willing to lend and to lend much longer-term, and therefore made borrowing cheaper and more secure for the government.[158]

Among those willing lenders were, very importantly, the Dutch financial community of Amsterdam, which supplied a large and steady flow of funds well beyond the period of this chapter. The consequence of all this up to 1750 was—and this was the acid test—that interest rates in London fell, despite heavy and increased borrowing.[159] The money was needed mainly for the conduct of wars that up to the end of the Seven Years' War (which "gave" Britain Canada and India) may on balance be judged to have paid off as economic speculations. This mobilization of capital was impressive, but it was not trouble-free.

In 1720 the first international, speculative mania and subsequent crash rocked Europe's financial markets.[160] The huge cost of the War of the Spanish Succession, which ended in 1713, had caused state indebtedness to soar, especially in Britain and France. Because the capacity to fund vast military spending was as vital in early-eighteenth-century Europe as it was during the cold war in the twentieth century, the British and French were susceptible to fears that their rivals were stealing a march on them financially as well as militarily. At the same time, the euphoria that swept the markets after almost twenty-five years of continuous warfare was likely to encourage innovation and speculation.

In England kingly borrowing before the development of properly funded longer-term debt described above had left a large number of past individual lenders in possession of expensive annuities that the government had no option to redeem. The cost of this debt was considered insupportable, so plans were laid to convert the debt into lower-cost redeemable securities. These would be issued by the three great joint-stock companies of the day (which were the South Sea Company, the Bank of England and the East India Company), and to them would be added a one-off cash inducement as compensation to the annuitants for forgoing their higher rates of return and irredeemable status.[161]

The British innovation, which today would be called "debt-for-equity swaps," inspired John Law (1671–1729), who further developed it as part of a grandiose scheme to transform the French financial and monetary system. Law, a Scottish beau and a gambler who had fled London for the Continent after being sentenced to death for murder during a duel in 1694, was something of a financial genius. His work on the link between supply and demand and prices predated Adam Smith. By showing how inflation would follow if the supply of money exceeded the demand for money, Law foreshadowed by 250 years the Chicago-based monetarist Milton Friedman. In other respects, he was a precursor of John Maynard Keynes, since he believed that increasing the money supply in the depressed Scottish economy would stimulate production. Moreover, Law's realization that there was no need for the monetary system to be linked to gold or silver was finally given practical effect in 1971, when the last vestiges of the gold standard were removed from the international monetary system.[162] But Law had what Karl Marx was later to describe as "the nicely mixed character of swindler and prophet," and it would have been better for all concerned if he had stuck to theorizing instead of policymaking.[163]

In 1716 Law persuaded the French regent, Philippe, duc d'Orléans, to allow him to form a bank, the Banque Générale (subsequently the Banque Royale). Such was its success that in 1717 he founded the Compagnie des Indes (commonly known as the Mississippi Company), with trading rights and control over French Louisiana (an area covering about half of the lower forty-eight states of the modern United States).[164] The Mississippi Company rapidly took control of all colonial trading, tax collecting and the mint. In 1719 the company issued large numbers of shares to assume the French national debt. An enormous issue of banknotes supported the conversion and was intended by Law to rid the monetary system of specie, thereby ending its link with the value of gold and silver.[165] By January 1720, when Law was appointed controller general (the equivalent of prime minister), shares in the Mississippi Company that had been worth 160 francs in 1717 had soared to more than 10,000 francs.[166]

The public imagination had been captured by the prospect of the profits that were to be made from joint-stock companies with government-backed monopolies, a point that was later well understood by both the political and the financial architects of the 1980s "privatization" program of Margaret Thatcher's government in Britain. As enthusiasm spread, promoters floated new companies and lured investors with promises of lavish profits. During 1720 over twenty joint-stock companies were created in the Dutch republic.[167] British enthusiasm for similar measures to reduce the national debt was heightened by the prospect of France's becoming the greatest financial power in Europe.[168] For the first time, according to de Vries and van der Woude, "short-term international capital flowed in large volumes" between Paris (where Law's system created enormous liquidity), London and Amsterdam.[169]

In London the South Sea Company decided to bid for the whole debt-reducing operation that had been proposed, in accordance with its strategy of challenging the Bank of England's lucrative role as manager of the government's debt. With Law's Mississippi Company seeming to be a dazzling success, Parliament by an act of 1720 permitted the South Sea Company to offer its own stock as an alternative to the cash inducement. By immediately doing just this, the company rendered the whole scheme dependent on the perceived value of its shares. The price of South Sea shares was talked up, not least by government representatives, up to and including the king, from £128 to £1,050 in the first six months of 1720, and 85 percent of the annuitants (by value) surrendered their claims in exchange for these shares.[170] They were also frantically speculated in by other investors, in a manner later emulated by those romantic souls who have recently bought Internet company shares in the belief not merely that they will be able to sell them to others even more romantic than themselves but also that before too long those companies will earn profits beyond the wildest dreams of avarice.[171]

The bubble burst over the summer of 1720 beginning in France, when Law sought to damp down speculation and lost the public's confidence. The collapse of both the Mississippi and South Sea companies triggered Europe's first big stock market crashes. The usual grief, anger, partial rescue operations and hunts for the guilty followed. Law was forced to flee from France in December 1720, and the French set their face against financial innovation, with ultimately disastrous consequences.[172]

In Britain it was found that the duchess of Marlborough had made a fortune by selling at the right time and that Isaac Newton had lost one—by selling at the right time but then buying again at just the wrong time. The government was forever disembarrassed of expensive debt (the annual charge of terminable annuities to public expenditure was cut from £1.87 million in 1717 to £0.21 million in 1722), and the City of London was a sadder and a wiser place for nearly 100 years. Perhaps the most economically damaging consequence was the passage of the 1720 Bubble Act, which banned the formation of joint-stock companies without the express authorization of Parliament.[173] The impact of this prohibition, which lasted for more than a century, has been much debated. Although it restricted British entrepreneurs and industrialists to forming partnerships or proprietorships and denied them the greater security and readier access to capital enjoyed by limited liability companies, it did not prevent Britain from becoming Europe's lead economy.

In the immediate aftermath of the 1720 crash, short-term international capital sought a safe haven and moved to Amsterdam. The Dutch republic's governments had not felt the need to convert their debts into company shares, and debt-for-equity swaps were banned in Amsterdam and several other Dutch cities. As to Europe's two other financial centers at the time, Paris was seen as unstable but London recovered because of its strong banking system. Indeed, according to Peter Dickson, author of the great study of the financial revolution: "Despite all the defects in the handling of English public finance, for the rest of the century it remained more honest, as well as more efficient, than that of any other country in Europe."[174]

Together with Amsterdam, London became a center of the emerging international financial system in which new short-term (or "spot") bills (intended purely for financial transfers) complemented the longer-term commercial bills of exchange.[175] In short, by the completion of the "financial revolution" in England (1694–1713) a stable financial framework had been established in London that enabled it to survive the South Sea bubble. It then supported a growing and integrated national and imperial capital market that in turn supported the creation of a politico-commercial empire and, linked to it, an industrial revolution.[176]

We consider more fully in the following chapter Britain's eventual emergence as the first industrial nation and the leading imperial power. We shall examine as well the specific roles in this process that Britain's cotton textiles industry and its Atlantic-based slave trade played, since they spanned the eighteenth and early nineteenth centuries. Nonetheless, it would be misleading to conclude the present chapter on the emergence of the first international trading network and the rise of the European merchant empires without understanding the continuing strength of the Asian economies and their role by the mid-eighteenth century.

The Indian and Chinese economies remained stronger than their European counterparts for much longer than has often been appreciated. In other words, "the rise of the West" to global preeminence occurred much later than is sometimes realized and only followed the comparatively recent (in terms of world history) economic decline of the Asian economic giants. Indeed, India remained a major economic power until well into the eighteenth century, and China continued to be an economic powerhouse until the nineteenth century.[177]

In India the political background to the three centuries leading up to Robert Clive's Indian conquests of the 1750s was the rise and decline of a great empire, that of the Moghuls, descendants of the fourteenth-century Mongol ruler Timur the Lame (Marlowe's Tamburlaine). From the second half of the sixteenth century, political stability under the Moghul emperor Akbar initially fostered efficient agriculture and an extensive internal market in which cash crops such as indigo, cotton, sugar, opium, pepper and later tobacco throve. Over the following two centuries, cheap labor fed the world's largest textile industry and an iron industry to challenge the best steel and cannons in Europe.[178]

The date when India's economic decline began is much debated, but it seems that political changes played a crucial part. Andre Gunder Frank, in his review of the extensive literature on the subject, notes that the simultaneous weakening at the beginning of the eighteenth century of the Moghuls in India, the Safavids in Persia and the Ottomans in the Near East prompted the decline of the trading centers of Surat on the west coast and Musalipatam and other Coromandel coastal centers and their hinterlands.[179] "Only when their Indian counterparts were drastically weakened," argues P. J. Marshall, the historian of the British in India, "did the English influence on western Indian trade begin to grow."[180]

During the 1730s and 1740s, India's economic difficulties grew worse as even competitively strong regions such as Bengal were affected. This raises the question of the impact of European colonialism and the intense rivalry between Europeans in India. Frank concludes: "There is substantial evidence that economic decline in India and in particular in the Bengali textile industry had already begun before the Battle of Plassey in 1757. The accompanying political disarray of the Mughals [Moghuls] and others rendered Asians vulnerable to predatory European merchant, naval and ultimately political power."[181] During the mid-eighteenth century, Europeans captured the carrying trade in Indian waters. In Frank's judgment, "India was the first Asian political economic power to begin the 'fall' to European hegemony."[182]

China's continuing economic strength from 1450 to 1750 was based on exceptional political stability, the high productivity of Chinese agriculture based on rice and major river basins, as well as a high degree of manufacturing and regional specialization. There was another factor, to which it is hard to give any other name than "Smithian growth," that is, what Adam Smith himself called the "natural progress of opulence."[183] This occurs when man's appetite for material betterment and his cunning in devising better methods combine in the absence of any specific contrary influence to increase output. After the initial fit of isolationism in the fifteenth century under the Ming dynasty, and apart from the brief but massive disruption with the rise of the Qing dynasty during 1627–1644, China's trade extended in the seventeenth and eighteenth centuries to Southeast Asia, India and Europe. The Chinese imported mainly silver and raw materials in exchange for their valuable manufactures such as cotton fabrics, ironware, porcelain and silk, as well as tea. In Europe these exports often became fashionable items. In 1793 Emperor Qianlong, writing to King George III via the British ambassador, famously commented: "As your ambassador can see for himself, we possess all things. I set no value on objects strange or ingenious, and we have no use for your country's manufactures. . . . There is therefore no need to import the manufactures of outside barbarians in exchange for our own produce."[184]

It is helpful to conclude with a clear summary of the pattern and scale of international trade as it had developed by the first half of the eighteenth century, on the eve of the industrial revolution. Writing of the period 1700–1750, K. N. Chaudhuri has observed, "Amsterdam and London became leading emporia in the West, and the task of re-exporting the imported goods from Asia or the New World was assumed by a secondary group of wholesale merchants drawn from all parts of Europe. The great trading regions of the Indian Ocean—India, China, and South East Asia—were drawn into a system of interdependent economic relations, though their internal economies continued to follow an autonomous rhythm of activity."[185]

It was only after the industrial revolution and the subsequent revolution in mass transportation during the middle decades of the nineteenth century that a truly global economy was first created. It is to the story of this next great transformation in the wealth of man that we turn in the next chapter.

CHAPTER SIX

Inventions and Surpluses

BY 1750, THE WORLD'S POPULATION WAS 771 MILLION, AND ALTHOUGH this was double the total in 1400 after the Black Death, even the wealthiest agrarian societies had not entirely escaped the ever-present danger that the number of mouths to be fed might exceed the resources available to feed them.[1] Recurrent bouts of disease, famine, unrest, and war, were fearful reminders of the overriding constraints on population. Adam Smith, whom we now regard as the founder of modern, free-market economics, nonetheless assumed in *The Wealth of Nations*, published in 1776, that food production could not increase indefinitely; or to put it in today's vernacular, that there were limits to growth.[2] But from the late eighteenth century, the constraints that held population in check seemed to be swept away.

The sequence of events from about 1760 that we know as the "industrial revolution" has attracted as much interest among economic historians—and correspondingly baffled them—as almost the whole of the rest of the story of the wealth of man.* The scale of the change in average living standards in the areas most affected by the development of industrial economies was extraordinary, eclipsing all previous advance. But its cause or causes are exceedingly hard to pin down.

We are at the brink of the largest and the most puzzling event in our

*The term "industrial revolution" was first used in 1837 by the French revolutionary Louis-Auguste Blanqui, but it was established in general British usage by Arnold Toynbee (1852–1883), who delivered a course of lectures on the subject at the University of Oxford in 1880–1881.

story. In 1930 John Maynard Keynes, contemplating the impact of technical change (we would say technological change today) since 1700 and projecting its influence a further century into the future, remarks:

> From the earliest times of which we have record—back, say to two thousand years before Christ—down to the beginning of the eighteenth century, there was no very great change in the standard of life of the average man living in the civilised centres of the earth. Ups and downs certainly. Visitations of plague, famine, and war. Golden intervals. But no progressive, violent change. Some periods perhaps 50 percent better than others—at the utmost 100 percent better—in the four thousand years which ended (say) in A.D. 1700. . . . What is the result [of the next two centuries]? In spite of an enormous growth in the population of the world, which it has been necessary to equip with houses and machines, the average standard of life in Europe and the United States has been raised, I think, about fourfold. . . . I would predict that the standard of life in progressive countries one hundred years hence will be between four and eight times as high as it is today.[3]

This stark contrast between pre- and post-eighteenth-century growth in industrializing economies is broadly confirmed by modern scholars. D. N. McCloskey writes, "The heart of the matter is twelve. Twelve is the factor by which real income per head nowadays exceeds that around 1780, in Britain and other countries that have experienced modern economic growth."[4]

If economics, applied to history, is to have any claim to validity and relevance, it should above all else be able to explain what is arguably the greatest event in economic history. How and why did incomes begin to rise in the unprecedented way that Keynes expressed so pithily in 1930? We have seen that "real" (i.e., adjusted to exclude the effects of inflation on monetary values) incomes per head in countries experiencing modern economic growth rose roughly twelvefold since 1780. Other measures of economic change capture the scale of the transformation that began, or accelerated, in Britain from about 1760: Male employment in agriculture fell from 53 percent to 29 percent by 1840; male employment in industry rose from 24 percent to 47 percent; and the proportion of the population living in towns and cities rose from 21 percent to 48 percent.[5]

Verbal testimony to the scale and importance of what was happening reinforces the numbers. Eric Hobsbawm writes in his celebrated 1969 study *Industry and Empire*, "No change in human life since the invention of agriculture, metallurgy, and towns in the New Stone Age has been so profound as the coming of industrialisation."[6] The timing of the acceleration of the growth of total economic output (gross domestic product) in Britain has been more controversial. Forty years ago historians reported annual growth rates as high as 2 and even 3 percent in the fifty years following 1780.[7] Those figures have recently been lowered to a more modest 1.5 to 2 percent, accelerating to a 3.5 percent peak after 1820.[8] The buildup of the industrial revolution may have been slower and more gradual than once thought. Indeed, Crafts concludes, "It is likely that the growth of income per head only moved significantly above the long-run pre-industrial average in the second quarter of the nineteenth century." Crafts, unlike Keynes in 1930, appears to accept a steady rate of positive economic growth before the industrial revolution.

The timing of the fullest effects of the industrial revolution, however, does not tell us about the timing—or therefore the identity—of its prime causes. In a telling passage about the logic of historical causality, McCloskey cites Crafts's warning that

> the timing of the beginnings of modern economic growth should not anyway be the thing to be studied because . . . if the onset of modern economic growth fed on itself, then its start could be a trivial accident. Yet one might wonder why then it did not happen before. "Sensitive dependence on initial conditions" is the technical term for some "non-linear" models—a piece of so-called "chaos theory". But history under such circumstance becomes untellable.[9]

In order for history to remain tellable, we must heed McCloskey's observation (quoting Mokyr) that

> rummaging among the possible acorns from which the great oak of the industrial revolution grew "is a bit like studying the history of Jewish dissenters between 50 B.C. and 50 A.D. What we are looking for is the inception of something which was at first insignificant and even bizarre," though "destined to change the life of every man and women in the west." What is destined or not destined to change our lives will look rather different to each of us . . . and is therefore not well explained by a dice throw: the industrial revolution was not one event but

> a set of loosely related events, a trick in steam engines here, a new dock there. Something more widespread than mere chance was going on.[10]

In other words, the accelerating growth of the nineteenth century in Britain may have been triggered by small events in the eighteenth century, but those small events may still not be beyond the discernment of the careful historian. There is nothing new in saying that great events, as judged with hindsight, may be beyond the discernment of even the highest-caliber contemporary observers. No one who has read it can ever forget Gibbon's discussion of this tendency, though his irony may have had other targets than the fallibility of even the greatest thinkers:

> How shall we excuse the supine inattention of the Pagan and philosophic world to those evidences [of Christian truth] which were presented by the hand of Omnipotence, not to their reason, but to their senses? During the age of Christ, of his apostles, and of their first disciples, the doctrine which they preached was confirmed by innumerable prodigies. The lame walked, the blind saw, the sick were healed, the dead were raised, dæmons were expelled, and the laws of Nature were frequently suspended for the benefit of the church. But the sages of Greece and Rome turned aside . . . unconscious of any alterations in the moral or physical government of the world. Under the reign of Tiberius, the whole earth, or at least a celebrated province of the Roman empire, was involved in a preternatural darkness of three hours. Even this miraculous event, which ought to have excited the wonder, the curiosity, and the devotion of mankind, passed without notice in an age of science and history. It happened during the lifetime of Seneca and the elder Pliny. . . . Both the one and the other have omitted to mention the greatest phenomenon to which the mortal eye has been witness since the creation of the globe.[11]

Neither Adam Smith nor David Hume nor Robert Malthus nor David Ricardo nor John Stuart Mill (1806–1873) recognized, in McCloskey's words, "the factor of twelve as it was happening. . . . They did not notice that the change to be explained, 1780 to 1860, was not 10 percent but 100 percent, on its way to 1100 percent. Only recently has the enquiry into the nature and causes of the wealth of nations begun to recognise this astonishing oversight."[12]

Even the great Alfred Marshall, writing a century ago, barely perceived the overriding importance of the growth of output and incomes per head during the 100 years before he wrote. He acknowledged that England's

> powers of production have been immensely increased; free trade and the growth of steam communication have enabled a largely increased population to obtain sufficient supplies of food on easy terms . . . and [that] the nation has grown in wealth, in health, in education and in morality; and we are no longer compelled to subordinate almost every other consideration to the need of increasing the total produce of industry.[13]

But his whole interest is in the sociological consequences of the change in production from agrarian to industrial and from small firm to large factory "undertaker" (we would say "entrepreneur" or "capitalist boss"). "Free enterprise grew fast and fiercely," writes the man whose more technical writings have made him in many ways the father of Chicago-school "free market" economics, but he ends the sentence with the very un-Chicago emphasis that "it was one-sided in its action and cruel to the poor."[14]

When he looks for explanations of the whole event, he starts with ethnicity, climate and geography (crediting Britain with "the strongest members of the strongest races of northern Europe," who live in the best-adapted climate in a country of "no high hills, and no part . . . more than twenty miles from navigable water"). He continues by invoking the capitalist organization of agriculture carried over into the factory system and the natural selection of the most efficient methods and managers under conditions of free competition.

When he finally comes to "the progress of mechanical invention," his interest, despite a memorable footnote epitomizing the key events of the industrial revolution's technological advances, is purely that "they caused the workers to be gathered more and more into small factories . . . then into larger factories in great towns."[15] The new organization, he said, "added vastly to the efficiency of production. . . . But it brought with it great evils."[16]

Inventions, Inventions . . .

In the two centuries after 1750, "daily life changed more than it had in the 7,000 years before."[17] Joel Mokyr identifies technology as the "de-stabilising agent in this dizzying tale." He argues that although "technological progress did not start in 1750, and the difference between the period after 1750 and the period before it was one of degree," nonetheless "degree was everything." In short, "the effects of the gains in productivity allowed Europe to expand its population many-fold in blatant defiance of Malthusian constraints."[18]

The following inventions (and inventors, all in Great Britain, unless otherwise noted) contributed to the productivity gains that created the industrial revolution:[19]

1698 steam pump for draining mines (Thomas Savery)
1700s seed drill in farming (Jethro Tull)
1708 porcelain (in Europe; already developed in China) (J. F. Boetger, Saxony)
1709 coke used for iron smelting (Abraham Darby)
1712 "atmospheric" steam engine for draining coal mines (Thomas Newcomen)
1717 silk-throwing works (Thomas Lombe)
1720 salt-glaze earthenware, substitute for porcelain (John Astbury)
1720s silk loom, for weaving patterns into fabric (Basile Bouchon and Jean Baptiste Falcon, France)
1738 flying shuttle for weaving textiles (John Kay)
rollers for spinning cotton (Lewis Paul)
1740 crucible technique for casting steel (Benjamin Huntsman)
glass-chamber process for production of sulfuric acid (vitriol), for use in bleaching and metallurgy (Joshua Ward)
1742 carding machine, for cotton manufacturing (Lewis Paul)
lead-chamber process for production of sulfuric acid (John Roebuck)
1750s breast waterwheel (John Smeaton)
improved road building with smooth, convex surface and ditches below road level for drainage (John Metcalfe)
attachment to knitting frame for ribbed fabrics in hosiery industry (Jedediah Strutt)
pottery factory using steam engines, division of labor and sophisticated marketing (Josiah Wedgwood)
1760s water-powered blowing cylinders to replace bellows in ironmaking (John Smeaton)
duke of Bridgewater's canal, for coal transport (James Brindley)
dividing machine for accurate graduation of circles for navigational and surveying instruments (Jesse Ramsden)

1760s *(cont.)*
spinning jenny, for cotton manufacturing (James Hargreaves)
efficient steam engine with separate condenser; not patented until 1769 and not in use until 1775 (James Watt)
discovery of hydrogen, a gas lighter than air (Henry Cavendish)

1767 Liverpool to Manchester canal (James Brindley)

1769 water frame, or throstle, for cotton spinning (Richard Arkwright)

1772 Staffordshire and Worcestershire canal (James Brindley)
drill for more accurate boring of cylinders, precursor of machine tools (John Wilkinson)

1775 improved carding machine, for textile manufacturing (Richard Arkwright)
winnowing machine (James Sharp)
Grand Trunk (Trent and Mersey) canal (James Brindley)
spinning mule, for spinning cotton yarn (Samuel Crompton)
first cast-iron bridge with 100-foot single span across river Severn, Coalbrookdale (Abraham Darby III and John Wilkinson)

1780s sliding hatch waterwheel (John Rennie)
recognition of use of gas as a source of light (J. G. Pickel, Germany; Jean-Pierre Minkelers, France)
gas lamp (Aimé Argand, France)
roads repaired and built with good drainage (John McAdam)
metal cylinders for printing patterns on cloth (Thomas Bell)
hot-air ballooning (Montgolfier brothers, France)

1784 puddling and rolling process for wrought iron (Henry Cort)
chlorine bleaching of finished cotton yarn (Claude L. Berthollet, France)
threshing machine (Andrew Meikle)
power loom; not fully effective until 1815 (Edmund Cartwright)

1787 soda from sea salt (Nicholas Leblanc)

1790s cotton gin (Eli Whitney, United States)
idea for preserving food by vacuum sealing in glassware after cooking (Nicolas Appert, France)
vaccination against smallpox (Edward Jenner)
screw-cutting lathe (Henry Maudslay)
coal gas to provide light (William Murdock)
machine to produce continuous sheets of paper patented (Nicholas

Louis Robert, France); leads to Fourdrinier papermaking machine (Bryan Donkin)

1799 bleaching powder from chlorine and lime, for finished cotton yarn (Charles Tennant)

thermolamp using wood-derived gas (Philippe Lebon, France)

block-making machines to produce wooden gears and pulleys for the navy (Henry Maudslay and Marc Brunel)

improved loom for silk weaving (Joseph-Marie Jacquard, France)

successful high-pressure steam engine (Richard Trevithick)

Shrewsbury-Holyhead (present A5 in England) road built on "Roman" principles with solid, stone foundations (Thomas Telford)

"compound" steam engine; not practical till 1845 (Robert Woolf)

steam locomotive specifically for railway (Richard Trevithick)

first documented assembly-line production, biscuit factory, Deptford, England

1805 dandy loom, moving the cloth beam automatically for weaving (Thomas Johnson)

steamboat (Robert Fulton, United States)

gas lamps in Manchester cotton mills and London's Pall Mall; gas distributed from central production site (Samuel Clegg)

1808 demonstration of lighting properties of electricity (Humphrey Davy)

wet-spinning process for linen (Philippe de Girard, France)

demonstration of capabilities of electric telegraph (S. T. von Soemmering, Germany)

idea of using tin-plated cans for preserving food (Peter Durand)

beet sugar refinement process; not a threat to cane sugar until 1840s (Benjamin Delesert, France)

cylindrical impression and inking for newspaper and book printing (Friedrich Koenig, German immigrant in London)

1814 supply of tinned meats and soups to navy (Bryan Donkin)

1815 mining safety lamp (Humphrey Davy)

screw gill for flax/wool fibers

gas metering for each customer (John Malam)

Savannah, first steamship to cross the Atlantic

1820s power looms for worsteds

electric motor, but was 20 percent more expensive than steam engines and dependent on batteries (Michael Faraday)

1820s *(cont.)*

spinners' strike, prompting research into automatic self-acting mule, which took six years to develop (see below, 1830)

Stockton-Darlington (England) 27-mile iron railway (Edward Pease) and steam locomotive, the *Locomotion* (George Stephenson)

linen wet-spinning, prompting mechanization of linen spinning

Menai suspension bridge (Thomas Telford)

1826 gas lighting of Berlin streets (William Lampadus)

1827 combing machines for wool in worsted industry

victory of *Rocket* in the competition between steam locomotives on the Rainhill level of the Liverpool-Manchester railway (George and Robert Stephenson)

hot-blast smelting (James Nielson)

completion of Liverpool and Manchester railway

self-acting cotton mule (Richard Roberts)

steam-driven fans in coal mines to reduce risk of explosion

1830s power looms to weave finer cotton yarns

start of mechanization in preparation of flax

sewing machine (Barthélemy Thimonnier, France)

permanent photographic pictures (Joseph N. Niépce and Louis Daguerre, France

electric dynamo (Michael Faraday)

start of development of electric telegraph (Samuel Morse, United States)

mechanical reaper (Cyrus McCormick, United States)

Royal William steamship transatlantic crossing, Quebec-Gravesend, largely by steam power[20]

1837 water turbine engine (Benoît Fourneyron, France)

London-Birmingham railway linking London to industrial heartlands

1839 patenting of five-needle system to send messages by electric telegraph (William Cooke)

vulcanization process of rubber, making industrial use of rubber possible (Charles Goodyear, United States)

J. G. Bodmer's machine tool workshop being run as an assembly line

1840s mechanization of woolen and hosiery industries

patent for taking photographs on paper (W. H. Fox Talbot)

1843 superphosphates factory, for agriculture (John Bennet Lawes)

Morse code, making single-needle system feasible for electric telegraph (Samuel Morse, United States)
compound steam engine became practical (John McNaught)
successful combing machine for wool (Josué Heilmann, France)
rotary printing press (Robert Hoe, United States)
lock stitch, a step toward sewing machine (Elias Howe, United States)
tea clippers sailing at speeds of up to 15 knots (Britain and United States)
1850s milk powder (Gail Borden, United States)
sewing machine with foot treadle (Isaac Merritt Singer, United States)
Crystal Palace exhibition at which machine-toolmaker Joseph Whitworth has twenty-three exhibits
laying of submarine cable, Dover-Calais (Thomas Crampton)

Keynes understood the entirely new scale of change that resulted from growth at compound interest. This had been taking place since the eighteenth century and he understood also the potential of its continuance into the future, though his attention was exclusively fixed on "the civilised centres of the earth" and he romantically imagined that most people would cash in their increasing productivity in increased leisure. When it came to explanations, Keynes thought the answer was obvious, remarking merely that the slow growth before 1700 was

> due to two reasons—to the remarkable absence of important technical improvements and to the failure of capital to accumulate. The absence of important technical inventions between the prehistoric age and comparatively modern times is truly remarkable. Almost everything which really matters and which the world possessed at the commencement of the modern age was already known to man at the dawn of history. Language, fire, the same domestic animals which we have today, wheat, barley, the vine and the olive, the plough, the wheel, the oar, the sail, leather, linen and cloth, bricks and pots, gold and silver, copper, tin, and lead—and iron was added to the list before 1000 B.C.—banking, statecraft, mathematics, astronomy and religion.[21]

This fine flight of Keynesian prose needs perhaps to be balanced by a passage from McCloskey—equally comprehensive but wholly contrary in sense:

> From an explosion of ingenuity down to 1500 we got in addition [to the horse collar, the stirrup and the mold-board plow in the ninth and tenth centuries] the blast furnace, cake of soap, cam, canal lock, carrack ship, cast-iron pot, chimney, coal-fuelled fire, cog boat, compass, crank, cross-shaft, eyeglass, fly-wheel, glass window, grindstone, hops in beer, marine chart, nailed horseshoe, overshoot water wheel, printing press, ribbed ship, shingle, ski, spinning wheel, suction pump, spring watch, treadle loom, water-driven bellows, weight-driven clock, whisky, wheelbarrow, whippletree . . . and the windmill.[22]

Keynes notes that "at some epoch before the dawn of history . . . there must have been an era of progress and invention comparable to that in which we live today. But through the greater part of recorded history there was nothing of the kind."[23] The era he surmises was in part the subject of Chapter 1 of this book, but the important point here is that Keynes takes it as axiomatic that the cause of the great leap forward in living standards after 1700 was technological improvement allied to capital accumulation in tune with the laws of compound interest, which greatly fascinated him.[24] Keynes was not blind to McCloskey's later point that "an idea without financing is just an idea" (or as Edward de Bono said at an international forum in the 1970s when asked where we would get the ideas of the future: "in the bankruptcy files.")[25]

Modern scholars have been anything but certain that the industrial revolution should be ascribed to technological progress and inventions. As McCloskey has shown with wit and style, English economic historians have seemingly come close to proving that absolutely nothing caused the industrial revolution, or at least that none of the candidates did. McCloskey demonstrates, teasingly, that no specific cause could ever explain the macro-outcome because of Harberger's law, which holds that if one takes a gain amounting to some fraction and multiplies it by the weight in the whole economy of the sector to which it belongs, itself a fraction of the whole economy, the result must be a yet smaller fraction (e.g., $0.99 \times 0.99 = 0.98$). This smaller number will, McCloskey shows, always be dwarfed by the 1,100 percent rise in incomes between 1780 and now, which is the thing to be explained.[26] This neat reductio ad absurdum liberates the speculative mind from the bonds of dry econometric calculations to exercise the historian's normal and necessary intelligence, though not with reckless disregard for quantities, about what did cause the twelvefold increase in incomes in industrialized countries following the industrial revolution.

Nick Crafts offers a masterly survey of the data on the sources of economic growth, including the high savings and investment potential of the English economy based on high and unequal incomes (which, however, was not exploited until technological progress raised the payoff to investment) and the failure of normal economic explanations (such as scarcity of wood, water power and labor) to account adequately for the spurt in inventiveness in the late eighteenth century.[27] He then turns his attention to the underlying mechanisms of growth and structural change. Before 1750 any population growth above 0.5 percent a year tended to reduce living standards, in accordance with the standard hypothesis of the Malthusian trap, that a rising level of real income per head generates sufficiently faster population growth to reverse the initial gains in living standards.[28] In the industrial revolution population growth accelerated to 0.9 percent and eventually 1.5 percent per year by 1816. This coincided with rising living standards, an impressive result that seems critically to have depended on the kind of demographic self-restraint in the form of social and cultural restraints on marriage and thus fertility.

A second "underlying mechanism" has to be the right structure of incentives, so that self-interest, Adam Smith's "natural progress of opulence," may operate undeterred by governmental excesses and inhibitions. As Crafts notes, Douglass North with Weingast has put primary emphasis on the Glorious Revolution of 1688 and the resulting balance of power between king and Parliament, which discouraged excessive taxation and other executive abuses destructive of economic incentives.[29] Indeed, North has argued that the macroeconomic stability engendered by the establishment of the Bank of England and the fixing of the value of the pound were fundamental explanations of England's economic progress over the next two centuries. He writes: "The security of property rights and the development of the public and private capital markets were instrumental factors not only in England's subsequent rapid economic development, but in its political hegemony and ultimate dominance of the world."[30]

Taxes in Britain were kept within a range of 8.7–11.7 percent of national income between 1700 and 1780.[31] Government legislation—the Enclosure Acts, which made it easier to transfer common land into private ownership at whatever cost to its poorer and weaker users, and the Navigation Acts and the invention of turnpike trusts, which boosted infrastructural investment in roads and river transport—actually contributed to the greater efficiency of the economy and better integration of markets. As Crafts says, the toll road was "a (second best) solution to a well-recognised problem of market failure, the inadequate provision of 'public goods', otherwise known as the 'free-rider' problem, with which the previous 'parish repair' system had failed adequately to deal and which had led to sub-optimal provision of high-class roads."[32]

The final underlying mechanism that the industrial revolution had to operate successfully was the transfer of labor on a huge scale out of agriculture while continuing to feed a rising population with rising incomes. There is no doubt that agricultural productivity in England outpaced productivity elsewhere in the economy between 1700 and 1760. Indeed, over the whole three centuries to 1800 England was far more successful than other leading economies such as France in being able to release labor from farming to support the division of labor and the development of other occupations on which all progress beyond subsistence necessarily depends. By 1850 British agricultural productivity was much the highest in Europe.[33]

But even that is only part of the story. If exceptionally rapid increase in the productivity of farmworkers had been the whole story, this would have tended to slow industrialization down by boosting the value of those workers in their current occupation, so raising what economists call the opportunity cost of releasing them into new occupations. As it was, Britain was able to import food from abroad, its net balance in wheat and wheaten flour swinging from net exports of 0.6 million quarters in 1750 to net imports of 2.6 million quarters in 1840, still before the repeal of the Corn Laws.* To the lay reader it may seem a paradox, much echoed in the rhetoric of more recent debates about the European Union's Common Agricultural Policy, that an economy with productivity that is high, rising and higher than others should change rapidly from exporting to importing food. This was indeed a classic example of the operation of the economic principle of "comparative advantage," suitably expounded by Ricardo in 1817:

*A quarter is a grain measure equivalent to 64 gallons.

> A country possessing very considerable advantages in machinery and skill and which may therefore be enabled to manufacture commodities with much less labour than her neighbours, may in return for such commodities, import a portion of the corn required for its consumption, even if its land were more fertile, and corn could be grown with less labour than in the country from which it was imported.[34]

It is here that we come to the heart of the matter. Britain in the late eighteenth and early nineteenth centuries acquired as a result of technological change (invention and application) a competitive advantage through higher productivity in tradable manufactures that was even greater than its advantage in farm products. Cotton textiles were the panzers of this onslaught and opened the way to the structural changes in the British economy that we know as the industrial revolution.[35]

We are entitled to conclude that this technological change was indeed a vital link in the chain of cause and effect that produced that revolution. It only remains to decide whether that chain can be traced further back to the environmental conditions—political, fiscal, legal, geographical, climatic, spiritual and so on—that sundry historians have urged as the true sources of the great transformation. Crafts has concluded:

> Although the search for improvements was doubtless encouraged by prospects of profit, the success of such a search was highly uncertain. It may be wrong to look for something special about the mid-eighteenth century economy which marked it out beforehand as more likely to embark upon rapid industrialisation than the economy of, say, fifty years earlier—there was an element of randomness in the timing of particular inventions. Indeed Crouzet [who had earlier been the chief exponent of the argument that "the inventions were designed to make possible the replacement of relatively scarce and expensive resources . . . by others that were relatively plentiful and cheap, such as coal, steam power and capital"[36]] concluded that the factor scarcity hypothesis could not sustain the weight he and others had put on it and that the search for the origins of the spurt in inventiveness had been inconclusive. Perhaps it is appropriate still to think of exogenous technical shocks raising rates of return and economic growth. . . . In other words technological change provoked a serious switch in direction from the course which was inherent in the type of growth experienced up to that time and the outcome can be regarded as truly revolutionary.[37]

This would, of course, excuse in some degree the failure of so many of the great economists who were around at the time to understand what was going on under their noses. Nonetheless, it was a profound error. As McCloskey has expressed it: "At the moment that Adam Smith and John Stuart Mill came to understand an economy in equilibrium the economy grew away from their equilibrium. It was as though an engineer had satisfied himself of the statics that kept a jumbo jet from collapsing as it sat humming on the tarmac, but did not notice when the whole thing proceeded to launch into dynamic flight."[38]

When we come in the final chapter to the view in the year 2000, we shall do well to remember those who erred through undue pessimism 200 years ago and those like Keynes who came much closer to getting the big picture right, even at the price of carrying optimism to the point of seemingly terminal euphoria. Especially high marks should be awarded to the historian Thomas Babington Macaulay, who wrote in 1830, exactly 100 years before Keynes made his own 100-year forecast:

> If we were to prophesy that in the year 1930 a population of fifty millions, better fed, clad and lodged than the English of our time, will cover these islands, that Sussex and Huntingdonshire will be wealthier than the wealthiest parts of the West Riding of Yorkshire now are . . . that machines constructed on principles yet undiscovered will be in every house . . . many people would think us insane.[39]

And Marshall, preoccupied as he was by what he saw as the evil social consequences of the untrammeled fulfillment of the free enterprise principle, of which he was himself the supreme prophet and interpreter, still deserves credit for his insight a century ago:

> The system of large business controlled by the specialised ability of capitalist undertakers [entrepreneurs] . . . would have worked itself out very much as it has done even if there had been no factories: and it will go on working itself out even if the retail distribution of force [power] by electric or other agencies should cause part of the work that is now done in factories to be taken to the home of the workers.[40]

Teleworking and the IT revolution in a nutshell!

But we are still left with a question. If Crafts is right that the wave of inventions that marked and sparked the rising payoff to investment and the resulting takeoff into self-sustaining industrial growth was, in economists' jargon "exogenous" (i.e., not predictable from the preexisting circumstances), can we say anything useful about why the growth happened when and where it did?

The argument has been made that Britain was an exceptionally affluent, bustling and inventive society from the beginning of the eighteenth century, and that by midcentury this generated not merely a form of so-called protoindustrialization but also the conditions that naturally, perhaps inevitably, called forth the final explosion of technological innovation that later historians recognized as an industrial revolution.[41] As Crafts sums it up: "The long period of industrial growth in the centuries before the industrial revolution did lead to a build-up of expertise. At a time when improvements in productivity were often achieved by trial and error methods and through continuing incremental advances based on experience of using inventions, Britain had a major advantage in realising the potential gains when technological change materialised."[42]

Daniel Defoe certainly provides us with a marvelous description of the busy Britain he observed during his 1724–1726 tour of the country:

> From Blackstone Edge to Hallifax is eight Miles.... The nearer we came to Hallifax, we found the Houses thicker and the Villages greater in every Bottom; ... the sides of the Hills, which were very steep every way, were spread with Houses, and that very thick; ... the land being divided into small Enclosures ... this Division of the Land into small pieces ... was occasioned by and done for the Convenience of the Business which the People were generally employed in.... This whole Country ... is yet infinitely full of People; these People all full of Business; not a Beggar, not an idle Person to be seen, except here and there an Alms-House where People ancient, decrepid and past Labour might perhaps be found; ... nor is the Health of the People lessen'd, but help'd and establish'd by their being constantly employ'd and, as well call it, their working hard; so that they find a double Advantage by their being always in Business. This Business is the Clothing Trade.... Such has been the Bounty of Nature to this otherwise frightful Country that two Things essentials to the Business, as well as to the Ease of the People, are found here.... I mean Coals and running Water upon the Tops of the highest Hills. This seems to have been directed by the wise Hand

> of Providence for the very purpose which is now served by it, namely the Manufactures. . . . Neither indeed could one fifth part of the Inhabitants be supported without them, for the Land could not maintain them.[43]

McCloskey follows Kirzner's different suggestion that alertness, a sort of general on-the-ballness lying somewhere on a spectrum between hard work and dumb luck, is the true source of an entrepreneur's profit, and he supposes that alertness may explain European and British ingenuity and inventiveness at this time.[44] But for alertness to work it requires persuasion. The inventor must persuade someone with the financial means or some other ability to put his invention into effect. That requires the speculative impulse to take wing:

> At the root of technological progress is . . . a rhetorical environment that makes it possible for inventors to be heard. . . . Such a hypothesis . . . would suggest that free speech and an openness to persuasion leads to riches. . . . When the Europeans, or at any rate some of them, stopped torturing, beheading and burning each other, the economy grew. No wonder that the nations where speech was free by contemporary standards were the first to grow rich: Holland, Scotland, England, Belgium and the United States.[45]

For our own more prosaic purposes, it must suffice to say that the inventions occurred, that they were the first link of which we can be sure in the chain of cause and effect that led by way of the industrial revolution—in Britain and then spreading throughout northwestern Europe and North America—to a twelvefold rise in incomes, and that we cannot confidently identify any one sufficient condition to explain why, when and where they happened. A number of conditions were favorable, perhaps even necessary, but each one had been present at other places and at other times without generating such a wave of gadgets.

If this is a case for chaos theory, where very small differences in the starting conditions have massive consequences, then we may never trace the true cause of the industrial revolution. But like sensible and appropriately humble historians, we may continue to be fascinated by the story, to seek fuller understanding and more knowledge and to believe that it was like most things in life: a matter of the right place, the right time and the right luck. The combination of man's perpetual quest to better himself with circumstances that permitted and rewarded individual enterprise, and where capital could be mobilized in support of promising ideas, looks likely to have been a helpful background. But after Keynes's forty centuries of "no very great change in the standard of living of the average man," you would hardly have bet at short odds on a twelvefold rise in the next two on the basis of a pro-enterprise culture not seemingly so different from that enjoyed from time to time by ancient Greece and Rome, medieval Europe, China ancient and modern, Muslim Arabia, Moghul India and several others.

Such parallels are indeed picked up by Pomeranz, who notes "a rough comparability between the more advanced portions of eighteenth century China and the more advanced portions of eighteenth century Europe."[46] He rejects the conventional view that Europe and China were already locked into completely different paths, arguing instead that the subsequent divergence—between Europe's industrialization and China's stagnation—stemmed from new departures in Europe that cannot be explained simply in terms of the preexisting conditions.

The kind of "natural progress of opulence" through division of labor and more efficient allocation of resources under market pressures that Adam Smith identified as the causes of the wealth of nations—sometimes called "Smithian growth"—operated equally in eighteenth-century China as in western Europe. What distinguished Europe, or at least Britain, and seems to have been crucial to its escape from the serious resource constraints that Smith, Malthus and others in the eighteenth century believed to place close limits on growth, were what we know as the inventions, plus coal, the resources of the New World and certain other lucky circumstances. The argument of de Vries that the industrial revolution was one aspect of a wider and longer "industrious revolution" in Europe generally, which took the form of people working longer and more efficiently from a time well before the famous inventions, describes an important antecedent of industrialization.[47] But it applies equally well to eighteenth-century China up to the point where it did *not* produce industrial takeoff. Wrigley emphasizes "the staggering dimensions" and importance of the coal bonanza in Britain:

> In 1800 the output of coal in Britain had reached about 15 million tons a year, at a time when the combined production of the whole of continental Europe

> probably did not exceed 3 million tons. In 1700, when British output was probably between 2.5 and 3 million tons, it has been estimated that it was five times as large as the output of the whole of the rest of the world. . . . An annual production of, say, 1 million tons of coal provided as much heat as could have been obtained from 1 million acres of forested land. . . . The transition to a partial dependence upon inorganic [sic] * *stocks* of energy rather than upon organic energy *flows* played an important role in allowing the English economy to expand without debilitating pressure on the land in the early modern period. Already, therefore, well before the date normally assigned to the industrial revolution, the dependence of the English economy on organic raw materials had been significantly reduced, and as a result the constraints on growth were eased. Of the four necessaries of life which Malthus had listed one, firing [Malthus's word for "fire"], gradually ceased to entail competition with the other three as the use of coal spread.[48]

Pomeranz explains that though China also had coal, it was in the wrong place, Shaanxi, and difficult to mine. As he says: "Imagine Europe's coal in an equivalent place, say under the Carpathian mountains, and it becomes a lot harder to imagine a smooth transition from proto-industrialisation to industrialisation and an escape from the limits of an organic economy."[49]

Second to coal was the supply of cotton as the raw material of the cotton textile industry, which had received its original impulse in Britain from the highly protectionist Calico Acts of 1700 and 1721 prohibiting the import and even wearing of East Indian prints and dyestuffs. Though cotton was Asia's main fiber source, its production in Asia displaced large quantities of food production from the land.[50] Britain was able to supply its raw cotton needs without displacing food production because it could rely on the cotton-producing areas of the southern United States. And other key commodities, such as sugar (calories that would have required about a million acres of best farming land to produce in England), became available from the new lands across the Atlantic, thus further relieving the burden on domestic land and resources and relaxing Malthu-

*Strictly speaking, coal in an organic source of energy. In mineralogy and geology, inorganic chemical elements and compounds are those that have been formed through inorganic processes. Petroleum and coal, which are formed by the decomposition of organic matter, are not minerals in the strict sense.

sian limits to growth. Long-distance trade was a crucial escape valve that eased the pressure on local resources that would otherwise have constricted output growth at compound rates of interest. Posing the question "Why wasn't England the Yangzi delta?"—where such limits did apply—Pomeranz concludes:

> But for certain important and sharp discontinuities, based on both fossil fuels and access to New World resources, which together obviated the need to manage land intensively, Europe, too, could have wound up on an "East Asian", labour-intensive path.... The new technologies of the 1750–1850 period do not seem sufficient by themselves to relax the land constraint enough to create self-sustaining growth; moreover, without the land-saving (but not very labour-using) windfalls from coal and the New World, one can imagine the focus of inventive efforts themselves being very different.[51]

Such an emphasis on cotton, sugar and New World land necessarily raises the old question whether and to what degree slavery caused or contributed to the industrial revolution, either by the output it produced or by the profits the slave traders made. Between 1662 and 1807, when British slave-carrying was legally abolished, over 3.4 million slaves were taken by British ships from Africa to the New World. This was about 3.5 percent of the population of Africa and was a much higher proportion of the West African communities between the Senegal and Orange Rivers (stretching from modern Senegal to modern Angola) from which the slaves were taken.[52] The number was three to four times the total of voluntary white settlers who landed in British America, including the West Indies, during this period. The long-term disruptive effect on those African communities of this hijacking of sizable fractions of their able-bodied labor force (two-thirds of the slaves who reached British colonies in British ships were male, most aged fifteen to thirty) is the subject of a growing literature on the economic history of Africa.[53] About 450,000, or 13 percent, died before arriving at destinations others had chosen for them. The traffic peaked in the very decades when the industrial revolution was starting, 1763–1793, at over 40,000 a year.[54] Non-British slavers brought the total carried up to 5.8 million in the eighteenth century, with a height of 75,000 a year in the 1780s.[55] As O'Brien has summed it up: "Almost the whole of the *increment* to non-bullion trade between western Europe and the New World from 1600 to 1800 depended directly and indirectly on the exchange of tropical foodstuffs, tobacco and industrial raw materials, cultivated basically with slave labour and exchanged for manufactured goods and commercial services produced by Europeans."[56]

Eric Williams, before he became prime minister of Trinidad and Tobago, pioneered the argument that slave trade profits financed an important part of the industrial revolution: "There is hardly a town in England which was not in some way connected with the triangular or direct colonial trade. The profits obtained provided one of the main streams of that accumulation of capital in England which financed the industrial revolution."[57] But this neat and poignant thought is not well supported by the numbers. Slaving voyages probably yielded about £150,000 a year in profits at the end of the eighteenth century, and if a third of this had been invested in new enterprises, it would have been under 1 percent of total domestic investment in Britain at the time, hardly enough to spark an industrial revolution or an economic miracle.[58] This does not, however, rule out the possibility that, as Pomeranz suggests, the supply of the things on which the slaves labored had a dynamic and strategic importance beyond the value of the profits earned. Britain's trading empire in America indubitably rested, as Malachy Postlethwayt had pointed out in 1745, on an "African foundation."[59] In short, while commercial and political elites in West and Central Africa creamed off a healthy slice of the available profit to be made on the American demand for slave labor, there seems no compelling reason for rejecting the prompting of common sense that the involuntary and, subsistence apart, unrecompensed toil of millions of able-bodied workers and their descendants contributed hugely to the supplies, comfort and wealth not only of their owners but also of the societies and metropolitan powers who enslaved them. How far this was or was not significant in enabling, if not sparking, the industrial revolution depends on how much weight can be put on Pomeranz's finding that New World supplies were critical in enabling Britain to escape the constraints on self-perpetuating growth that normally placed economies like China experienced.

Pomeranz's conclusion that coal and New World lands were at least part of the explanation why England and Europe did not go down the same nonindustrial path as China is not formally incompatible with Crafts's conclusion about the basically "exogenous" role of the inventions. The two may coexist. Maybe the inventions explain better than anything else the sudden change of gear of British and in due course European economic growth in the early nineteenth century. But maybe also that change of gear would not have been indefinitely sustainable if the usual feedback effects of rising incomes, consumption and output had operated as they did in the lower Yangtze and as they might well have done in Europe but for the extra scope provided by coal and the New World.

What we do now know, which eighteenth-century man had not conceived, is that finite amounts of capital investment every year allied to a supply of technological innovation that does not dry up can eventually relax almost any supply constraint and so support seemingly perpetual economic growth at compound interest. Further, the consequences of such growth, even at modest rates per annum, are spectacular when stretched over centuries. There may still be, as we shall consider in the final chapter, limits to growth, as the eighteenth-century economists supposed, though of a different kind and at a much higher level of production, in total and per person. But these limits did not bite much in the nineteenth or twentieth centuries.

Once this instrument—compound growth driven by technological change and continuing investment—had fallen into the hands of men in Britain and northwestern Europe, it was not thereafter a mystery that its consequences were so vast. The laws of compound interest took care of that, so long as men did not, as they frequently threatened to do, derail the whole process by ceaseless political and military conflicts over the division of the spoils and other matters.

To that we turn in the next chapter. First we must inquire into the human and social effects of all this accelerated growth. The nineteenth century, after all, produced in Britain and Europe an unprecedented outpouring of lamentations and protest at the allegedly deteriorating and inequitable condition of man, or at least large classes of men and women, and the most important political movements of the next century or so received their greatest impetus from such ideas. The 1840s produced an exceptional concentration of economic, social and intellectual drama, including a business slump—one of the first of this new post-industrial species; an agricultural depression; the potato famine in Ireland; Friedrich Engels's (1820–1895) *Condition of the Working Class in England in 1844;* Karl Marx and Friedrich Engels's *Communist Manifesto;* John Stuart Mill's *Principles of Political Economy;* the repeal of the Corn Laws and the Chartists' (rather lame) march on Parliament.[60] And all this against a background of revolutionary rising in 1848 that overthrew nearly all the despotic governments in Europe, if only briefly.[61] In the same year 53,000 died of cholera in Britain; a year later a similar number died in France.[62]

The most vivid summary of the physical and social charge sheet against rampant industrialization and urbanization is probably still to be found in Charles Dickens's *Hard Times,* a work informed by a personal visit to Preston in Lancashire, which appears in the novel as Coketown:

> It was a town of red brick, or of brick that would have been red if the smoke and ashes had allowed it; but as matters stood it was a town of unnatural red and black like the painted face of a savage. It was a town of machinery and tall chimneys, out of which interminable serpents of smoke trailed themselves for ever and ever, and never got uncoiled. It had a black canal in it, and a river that ran purple with ill-smelling dye, and vast piles of buildings full of windows where there was a rattling and a trembling all day long, and where the piston of the steam-engine worked monotonously up and down like the head of an elephant in a state of melancholy madness. It contained several large streets all very like one another, and many small streets still more like one another, inhabited by people equally like one another, who all went in and out at the same hours, with the same sound upon the same pavements, to do the same work, and to whom every day was the same as yesterday and tomorrow, and every year the counterpart of the last. . . .
>
> In the hardest working part of Coketown; in the innermost fortifications of that ugly citadel, where Nature was as strongly bricked out as killing airs and gases were bricked in; at the heart of the labyrinth of narrow courts upon courts, and close streets upon streets, which had come into existence piecemeal, every piece in a violent hurry for some one man's purpose, and the whole an unnatural family, shouldering, and trampling, and pressing one another to death; in the last close nook of this great exhausted receiver, where the chimneys, for want of air to make a draught, were built in an immense variety of stunted and crooked shapes as though every house put out a sign of the kind people who might be expected to be born in it; among the multitude of Coketown, generally called "the Hands",—a race who would have found more favour

> with some people, if Providence had seen fit to make them only hands, or, like the lower creatures of the sea-shore, only hands and stomachs—lived a certain Stephen Blackpool, forty years of age.[63]

Whether the "hands" actually felt like this about their own condition and whether their migration from country to town horrified them as much as it wrenched the guts of middle-class observers who wrote about it is more difficult to be sure about. Modern research seems to suggest that although infant mortality and life expectancy data for Britain in the mid-nineteenth century compare poorly with the rest of Europe because of the speed of urbanization and despite clear evidence that public spending and intervention could have done much to improve public health and even to earn good returns on such investment, British quality of life at that time compares favorably with that of other European countries, whether narrow "income" or wider "living standard" indicators (such as body heights, literacy, schooling and civil and political rights) are used.[64] The working classes may well as a result have been better off than if industrialization had not occurred.[65]

It may also have been true, however, that such gains occurred almost entirely after 1820.[66] And there are still historians who argue that if sufficient weight is given to the plight of women and children, then the date by which a long era of deterioration finally ends may be as late as 1870, and that undeniable improvement begins only as late as the 1870s and 1880s.[67]

CHAPTER SEVEN

International Economy and Economic Nationalism

AFTER THE APPARENT EASING OF MALTHUSIAN CONSTRAINTS ON population growth that we observed in the last chapter, Europe's rapid population increase continued and even accelerated after 1850. During just sixty-four years to 1914, Europe's population soared from 266 million to 450 million, an increase of 184 million people, almost 70 percent.[1] Such an explosion in numbers was unprecedented. During the 10,000 years between the agricultural and industrial revolutions, the world's population had doubled roughly every 1,000 years, but in the nineteenth century Europe's population doubled in less than one hundred years.[2] But even these figures understate the scale of the population explosion. Europe's population in 1914 would have been 500 million, or about 50 million greater than it was, had it not been for mass emigration to the New World.[3]

The Americas were transformed as the continent's population rocketed from 59 million in 1850 to about 150 million in 1914. The Americas' share of world population almost doubled from 5 percent to 9 percent.[4] Neither Africa nor Asia could match Europe's prodigious rate of population growth during the late 1800s and the first decade of the twentieth century. Africa's population rose from 81 million in 1850 to about 115 million by 1914.[5] The slave trade was finally brought to an end, but the continent was colonized by the European powers and although the number of white settlers was tiny compared with America, by 1900 about 50 million Africans (roughly half the continent's population) had become subjects of Queen Victoria and another ten million were subjects of the Kaiser.[6]

Asia remained the most populous continent, increasing from 795 million in 1850 to about 1 billion in 1914, but this represented a slower increase than Africa and reflected the passing of the baton as the world's economic pacesetter to Europe and North America.[7] The Asian slowdown was largely due to China's troubles, as political problems and external aggression, notably by the British and the Russians, contributed to its demise as the world's most powerful economy.[8]

The high period of British Victorian economic expansion is traditionally dated from the repeal of the Corn Laws in 1846, which undoubtedly inaugurated an era of British free trade lasting until World War I. The event was a political trauma for the Conservative Party in Britain, which did not recover its majority for twenty-eight years.[9]

The Corn Laws dated back at least to the seventeenth century, when agriculture was the overwhelmingly dominant industry of the country and was more than proportionately represented in the nation's decision-making. Corn Bounty Acts established export subsidies in response to the usual doom-mongering of farm interests that they—and therefore of course the nation—were threatened with extinction by the specter of plenty. England remained a net exporter of grain until the 1770s under a system that both subsidized exports and imposed duties on imports in accordance with a sliding scale that reduced the subsidies and the duties alike as home prices rose. Farmers gained; consumers paid.

During the Napoleonic Wars the Corn Laws (which had been amended in 1773 and 1791) were usually a dead letter, since wartime demand raised grain prices well above the levels at which protection operated. But the end of the wars produced a new and unprecedented pressure for protection. It was feared that peacetime conditions would lead to a flood of imports from the Continent. Economists were, as ever, divided. In a pamphlet of 1815, Robert Malthus argued that the national economic interest required the prosperity of farming because a third or more of national income and spending came from agriculture.[10] But David Ricardo believed that new inventions and more efficient industries could and should be allowed to replace agriculture.

By a familiar rhetorical device of protectionists down the ages, the farm interests managed to argue that the effects of past protection and export subsidy had been to encourage so much investment and cultivation of marginal lands that even greater protection was now needed in order to keep those investments profitable. As Chambers and Mingay sum it up: "Eighty shillings a quarter, a famine price back in the halcyon 1780s, was everywhere put forward as the reasonable level for the prohibition of imports. It was pointed out that during the wars enormous amounts of capital had been devoted to expanding cultivation and improving production, while since 1795 the costs of cultivation had doubled and the landlords' share of the gross proceeds had fallen."[11]

In 1815 Parliament duly prohibited sales of imported wheat whenever the price fell below 80 shillings a quarter, with equivalent thresholds for other grains. This produced such instability in the market, as imports were switched on and off, and such an overproduction of corn on unsuitable lands that in 1828 the system was replaced by a sliding scale that began when wheat was under 73 shillings a quarter.[12] These laws were regarded by the landed interests as the cornerstone of their way of life but were increasingly rejected by industrialists, who saw the advantages of free trade, and were bitterly resented by the middle and working classes, whose food bills were inflated by the system.

By the early 1840s the Conservative prime minister Robert Peel had become personally convinced that the Corn Laws must go. They were unnecessary to the prosperity of agriculture in an economy that was expanding through industrialization, and a tax for the benefit of the rich on the food of the poor, causing as it did such distress among the industrial working class, was politically and morally insufferable.[13] His party, deeply rooted in the countryside, would have none of it, until the Irish famine in 1845 coinciding with a blighted harvest in England forced the repeal of the Corn Laws on pain of mass starvation. Temporary suspension was not a realistic option, and when the Whigs (the greatest landowners of all) and Liberals refused an invitation to form a government to carry through the repeal (known as the "grand refusal"), Peel forced it through with opposition support. Later the same day Peel fell forever from power and office, defeated, as G. M. Trevelyan puts it, by "a coalition between the Whigs seeking office and the protectionists seeking revenge."[14] What is remembered by economic historians as a high point of economic enlightenment remained in the list of all-time Conservative low points.

The story after 1846 is certainly one of trade liberalization by the British Parliament and of the massive transformation of the British economy away from agriculture. The greatest impact on British agriculture of the repeal of the Corn Laws was slow in coming, because for the first thirty years British farmers continued to enjoy partial de facto protection from the full force of free trade in grain. Wars and transport difficulties cushioned for a while the impact of the rapidly increasing supplies potentially available from America, Russia and elsewhere. Only in the last quarter of the century, after the American Civil War and the coming of age of the railway and the steamship, did British consumers begin to gain economic access to the great breadbaskets of the world: the American prairies, the Ukraine and central Asia. Between the 1870s and the end of the century, for example, the cost of carrying grain from Chicago to Liverpool fell by nearly three-quarters. By the end of the century, farming, which had accounted for 40 percent of national output and a third of the labor force in 1800, accounted for less than 10 percent of both. Home production, which had supplied four-fifths of food consumption as late as 1868, was by the early 1900s supplying less than half.[15]

As a precedent, the repeal of the Corn Laws had a more rapid effect on British legislators. In 1849 the Navigation Acts, an ark of the former mercantilist covenant that broadly restricted the carriage of British and British colonial trade to British subjects, also obliging the British colonies to trade through British ports, were repealed.[16] In 1860 Chancellor of the Exchequer William Gladstone's budget and the linked Cobden-Chevalier treaty between Britain and France, which paved the way to a series of commercial agreements granting antidiscriminatory most-favored-nation treatment between European states, removed duties on some 400 articles, effectively abolishing the old system of protection, leaving duties mainly on sugar, tea, coffee, tobacco, spirits and wine.[17] Import duties, which in 1841 had amounted to 35 percent of the value of imports, fell by 1881 to a mere 6 percent (the identical figure to that quoted as the average level of tariffs in the world at the conclusion of the Kennedy round of the General Agreement on Tariffs and Trade tariff reduction talks in 1967).[18] This liberalization was made easier as the government's finances between 1841 and 1881 became less dependent on high tariffs, partly because liberalization itself helped to increase imports from 12 percent to 30 percent of national income and partly because government expenditure fell from 9 percent to 6 percent of national income.[19]

Britain thus stood at the center of an emerging international economy, well summed up by Foreman-Peck:

> Europe dominated world trade and income, but not world population. Europe accounted for somewhere between one-sixth and one-quarter of the world's population, but for almost 70 percent of world trade at mid-century. One "guesstimate" gives north-western Europe almost one-third of world income earned by little over one-tenth of the people on the earth. Within Europe, Britain achieved the highest national income per head with one-third of total fixed steam power installed in the world's factories. Britain also disproportionately engaged in international trade. Perhaps one-fifth of this trade . . . originated in, was destined for, or passed through Britain, even though those islands were occupied by less than two percent of the world's population in the middle of the nineteenth century.[20]

Britain's dominant position at the center of this new international economy, deriving both from its nautico-commercial successes in the eighteenth century and from the transforming effects of the industrial revolution, neither rested on nor contributed to any military ascendancy on land in Europe after 1815. The whole ideology of British nineteenth-century liberalism rejected the idea of the economy as a means to the higher end of the nation's political and military glory, at least until the brief splutter of high Victorian imperialism at the end of the century.[21]

As in the United States a century later, the nation's convenience and success were secured under banners of supposedly immutable and universal principles: peace, government economy and low taxes, liberal trade and individuals' freedom to do as they wished with their private property. These principles were somehow reconciled in Victorian minds with British political dominion over a rapidly increasing colonial empire—at about 100,000 square miles annually from 1815 to 1865—which was formidably strengthened by the Royal Navy's unchallenged control of the seas for most of a century after the victory at Trafalgar (1805).[22]

Nonetheless, a conspicuous and probably crucial aspect of British global ascendancy in the mid-nineteenth century was its low cost to the taxpayer, as well as its high profitability to British investors. A government budget of barely a tenth of gross national product (GNP) and a military budget of a mere 2–3 percent meant that the classic burdens of overcommitment that have afflicted hegemonic powers down the ages were avoided so long as the world's other potential powers were prepared to play the international game by similar rules, at least in regard to peace, trade and limited national ambitions. The navy's continued rule of the waves, international waters though they may legally have been, on such a shoestring seems to have rested partly on past reputation, partly on the halfhearted nature of other nations' naval aspirations and partly on high confidence after Waterloo (1815) that a large British land army in Europe was unnecessary in order to maintain the continental balance of power, which remained the keystone of British security policy.

Economy was further much assisted by the insistence that the costs of the governance and policing of the empire should be borne by the dominions so ruled, especially India. And as we shall see later in this chapter, Britain's central position in the emerging financial mechanisms of the international economy that developed in the nineteenth century gave it a profit that contributed significantly to its national income and to its external solvency.

The physical sinews of this emerging global economy, centered on Britain, Europe and their links to the Americas, were the famous triad of steamships, railways and the telegraph. The first passenger railway service, between Liverpool and Manchester, was opened in 1830 in the presence of the supreme representative of the horse-drawn age that was departing, the victor of Waterloo and prime minister of the day, the duke of Wellington. He might have been almost as surprised to learn that the site of his great victory would live in popular fame nearly two centuries later as the name of a great railway terminus linking London, Brussels and Paris as he was shocked by the death that day of his former cabinet colleague and arch advocate of free trade, William Huskisson, run over by the inaugural service of *Rocket.**

By 1840 Britain had almost 1,500 miles of railway open, the United

*Michael Bailey, past president of the Newcomen Society, to which serious steam engine buffs belong, in conversation with the author. The *Dictionary of National Biography* names *Dart* as the killer locomotive, but other contemporary sources all name *Rocket,* George Stevenson's winning design for the best locomotive.

States nearly twice that much and continental Europe, including Russia, less than 900. By 1870 the numbers were respectively 13,400, 52,600 and 44,000, and in 1914 they were 20,300, 255,000 and 252,000.[23] In the United States the freight carried rose from 39,000 million ton-miles in 1866 to 142,000 ton-miles in 1900.[24]

The railways' first advantage was speed, which led to a huge initial growth of passenger traffic, notably in Britain, far exceeding the expectations of the railway pioneers, who had expected mainly to haul freight. It took decades for freight revenues to catch up with passenger revenues in Britain. Second, railways extended the coverage of long-distance overseas trade to areas and commodities that had previously been confined to local markets. Before railways, bulk cargoes could be carried only by water—by sea, river, lake and canal. Markets for such commodities that were not linked in that way were separate, and different prices prevailed. The railways integrated many such markets, and insofar as some of them were already connected with others by ocean shipping, all the markets that the railways joined became integrated with other markets all over the world, bringing nearer a single global market in a far wider range of commodities than the previously narrow list of high-value, low-bulk items such as silks and spices.

Travel also became possible for people over distances and terrain that had previously seemed impassable, prohibitively dangerous and/or expensive. From 1869 a single rail ticket would get you across the American continent in a matter of days—this only sixty years after it had taken Thomas Jefferson's pioneers, Meriwether Lewis and William Clark, a year and a half to go from St. Louis on the Mississippi to the Pacific.[25]

In Europe the extent and implications of the railway revolution were greater than they could ever be in insular Britain. Alfred Chandler has compared the British, German and American experiences in detail:

> The coming of the railroad (and its handmaiden, the telegraph) had a much greater impact on Germany than it did on Britain. In Germany distances were greater, the terrain was much more rugged, and the area available to coastal, canal, and other water traffic was smaller. The transportation revolution heavily influenced Germany's economic growth and the accompanying institutional changes. As in the United States, but not in Britain, the rapid growth of the railroad network was an integral part of the initial industrialisation as well as the

> continuing industrial growth of the nation. J. H. Clapham makes this point effectively by citing an earlier eminent historian: "The railways, as [Heinrich von] Treitschke said, first dragged the nation from its economic stagnation—and with astonishing abruptness". . . . By the 1880s German industrialists, like those in the United States, enjoyed the benefits of a new transportation system that permitted the movement of materials and goods and messages with unprecedented regularity and speed over a continental area—the essential precondition for achieving the cost advantages of the economies of scale and scope inherent in capital-intensive, high-volume technologies of production. The Continental railroad network . . . gave German entrepreneurs a readier access to the industrial markets of Europe than British or even French manufacturers had. The Continental network thus hastened the transformation of Germany's export trade from consumer to industrial products.[26]

Steamships used, of course, the same principle as the railways, steam power, but their displacement of earlier methods of navigation was more gradual.[27] Robert Fulton's *Clermont,* which is usually acknowledged to have been the first steam-powered boat, made its first run on the Hudson River, New York, in 1807. But it was not until 1845 that I. K. Brunel's *Great Britain* made the first propeller-driven Atlantic crossing, which with the subsequent development of the efficient "compound" steam engine (1854) and steel hulls (1860s) heralded the mature age of maritime steam transport.[28] The Suez Canal was opened in 1869, halving the sailing distance between Liverpool and Bombay, and by the eve of World War I return journeys between Britain and India, which at the beginning of the nineteenth century had taken up to two years, could be completed within a month.[29] Freight costs by sea fell by nearly 1 percent a year in the first half of the century, a rate that accelerated to 1.5 percent in the second half, despite rising labor costs.[30] Exports from Europe grew much faster than the European economies in the 1860s and 1870s, thus extending the openness of those economies and intensifying market competition within them, though most of this expansion was due to intra-European trade carried by the new railways and by internal waterways, as well as by traditional transport.[31]

The nineteenth century also produced a revolution in long-distance communication, using the principles of electricity and radio. The first chemical battery was produced in 1800 by Alessandro Volta. The economic potential of electricity was apprehended from the first decade when Humphrey Davy demonstrated an electric arc light in 1808.[32] In 1810 S. T. von Soemmering showed what the telegraph might do.[33] In 1820 Hans Christian Oersted, a Danish physicist, observed the phenomenon known as electromagnetism, the detectable electrical field generated by a current flowing through wires. In 1821 Michael Faraday made an electric motor, and in 1831 he made the first dynamo.[34] Later that decade William Cooke and Charles Wheatstone in Britain and Samuel Morse, working separately in the United States, created the electromagnetic telegraph, essentially a very long wire down which could be sent electric impulses in a pattern (e.g., the Morse code), which could convey an intelligible human message at close to the speed of light.[35]

In 1845 it took eight weeks to carry news to England by sea or overland from Cape Town, six weeks from Rio, four weeks from New York and a week from Berlin.[36] The telegraph cable transformed all that. It spread fastest in the United States, starting with Morse's experimental 40-mile link from Baltimore to Washington in 1846. Within six years working lines covered 23,000 miles, with another 10,000 under construction.[37] Britain's first line ran along the Great Western Railway tracks from Paddington to West Drayton and later to Slough; they were used in August 1844 to announce the birth, at Windsor, of Queen Victoria's second son. In less than an hour of the birth the *Times* had the news on the streets.[38] By 1850 Britain had over 2,000 miles of telegraph lines, and two years later the system grew explosively in many parts of the world, including a network based on Berlin, lines in Austria, Canada, Italy, southern Germany, Spain, Russia, the Netherlands, Australia, Cuba and Chile.[39]

The first submarine telegraph cable was laid under the English Channel in 1851, and the first successful transatlantic cable was laid in 1866, though Queen Victoria of England had achieved an exchange of messages with President James Buchanan of the United States in 1858 on a cable that failed shortly thereafter.[40] San Francisco was linked to New York by the first transcontinental cable in 1864.[41] In the same year Britain was linked to India by land and coastal cables; the link by submarine cables, via Gibraltar, the Mediterranean, the Red Sea and the Indian Ocean, followed six years later.[42]

By 1874 there were over 650,000 miles of wire and 30,000 miles of submarine cable. A total of 20,000 towns and villages were so wired, and messages could be telegraphed from London to Bombay and back in as little as four minutes. Standage writes, "'Time itself is telegraphed out of existence', declared the *Daily Telegraph,* a newspaper whose very name was chosen to give the impression of rapid, up-to-date delivery of news. The world would shrink further and faster than it ever had before.... By 1880 there were almost 100,000 miles of undersea cable."[43]

In 1876 Alexander Graham Bell patented the telephone, enabling voice communication to be carried by wire, initially over short distances until Thomas Edison's improved system could be introduced.[44] The telephone's success was even greater and faster than that of the telegraph. Within a year of Bell's patent and within a month of the first advertisement, there were 230 telephones in use in the United States and two months later more than five times as many. By 1886 over a quarter of a million telephones were being used throughout the world; five years later one in ten American homes had a telephone.

In 1865 James Clerk Maxwell had proposed the theory of electromagnetic waves, and in 1888 Heinrich Hertz showed they existed.[45] In 1895 Guglielmo Marconi took this knowledge to invent wireless telegraphy using radio waves, and in 1901 a radio message was transmitted across the Atlantic.[46] In 1906 Lee DeForest and R. A. Fessenden showed that sound waves as well as Morse signals could be sent by radio, an important step toward voice telecommunications.[47]

Nothing has contributed more to the shrinkage of the globe or to the acceleration of international economic and financial activity than instant communications, which depend to this day on the physical speed of electricity. Mokyr and Foreman-Peck have summed up the economic impact of the telegraph: According to Mokyr, "The telegraph had an enormous impact on nineteenth century society—possibly as great as that of the railroads. Its military and political value was vast, as was its effect in coordinating international financial and commodity markets."[48] And as Foreman-Peck describes it, "By introducing greater certainty into international transactions, the telegraph cut stock levels and allowed the money markets to finance the inventories previously held by great merchants. The level of raw cotton stocks held in British ports and mills was much lower after the spread of the telegraph than in the 1840s, despite the far greater volume of business."[49]

Between 1850 and 1870 the liberalization of trade that had received its greatest legislative boost with the repeal of the Corn Laws in 1846 spread across Europe. Restrictions and levies on the use of international waterways in Europe were relaxed. The multiplication of local currencies—almost one for each political sovereignty in Europe, in line with both long historical practice and evident political logic—was reversed and simplified in favor of the thaler throughout the German union, the florin throughout Austria and the Latin monetary agreement in 1865 among France, Belgium, Italy and Switzerland. Tariffs were reduced in a spate of bilateral treaties among Britain, France, Belgium, Prussia and the German *Zollverein* (the commercial forerunner of the German state).[50] David Landes comments with raised eyebrows: "It was as though the very expansiveness of the economy, the general euphoria of growth and prosperity, had persuaded nations and people to let their guard down, to trade control for freedom, parochialism for universalism, tradition for change, the safety of exclusiveness for the danger yet potential profit of the open world."[51]

Nor was the explosion in trade confined to international exchanges. Business won new freedoms at home as well. Indeed, business in Europe in the mid-nineteenth century was as resentful of and as sensitive to the opportunities for fruitful political lobbying against red tape as it is today. Arguably the biggest breakthrough ever achieved in business regulation was limited liability. This became available by an act of 1856 in Britain at no greater cost to the owners than registration as a company. The shareholders and directors thereby escaped responsibility to creditors and others for the (nonfraudulent) failure and debts of the business, however mismanaged. This immense privilege, which has been the foundation stone of corporate enterprise ever since, was extended by stages to France and the constituent jurisdictions of Germany by 1870.[52] Nor were these the only ways in which the load of regulation on business was lightened. The laws on usury, foreign businesses, checks, the penalties for debt and bankruptcy, patents and general business relations were repealed, relaxed and/or simplified in Britain and northern Europe.[53]

In the mid-nineteenth century, tariffs imposed by the United States were low, mainly because of the political influence of the cotton and tobacco interests who were exporters rather than importers and accordingly sensitive to the opinion of nations to which they sold, like Britain. But in general the federal government was more dependent on tariff income than, for example, Britain, and when expenditures rose massively during the Civil War, duties were increased alongside huge borrowing. The result of the war reduced the influence of the southern cotton and tobacco lobbyists. Manufacturers and wool producers won substantial protection (35–40 percent tariffs), which stimulated a rapid expansion of manufacturing production; iron and steel interests won even higher protection. But a desire to maximize government revenues by keeping the general level of taxes low, as advocated by economic liberals on both sides of the Atlantic, explains the broadly moderate level of U.S. tariffs in the third quarter of the century at least as well as the influence of lobbyists.[54]

The greater capacity and speed of the physical sinews of the developing world economy in the second half of the nineteenth century, as well as expanding trade and extending the integration of separate economies, created bigger opportunities and increased incentives for capital and labor to move, either away from areas of low opportunity and return or to areas of high opportunity and return.

In the case of labor, this may not necessarily imply a benefit to the owners of the labor, the laborers themselves. If they are effectively forced to move by enslavement or deteriorating economic opportunities, they may well find themselves worse off at the end of the process than at the beginning, either because their material conditions are actually worse or because the loss of the intangible benefits of home outweigh any material improvement that they achieve.

This factor was undoubtedly present in the huge migrations of European labor to North America in the nineteenth century—the greatest, when combined with simultaneous Indian and Chinese movements to work on plantations around the world, that had ever occurred. But there was a counterbalancing positive factor, which was the huge gain in wealth and welfare available to the new settlers in North America as result of its huge endowment of natural resources, essentially land. Of course, it can be argued that their gain was a loss to the indigenous natives who previously owned or otherwise had the use of these resources. Nonetheless, the population and living standards sustained by that land rose immeasurably after the displacement of those native Americans because of the way in which the new settlers used it. As a result the economic yield available to global mankind increased hugely, both in total and per head.

This is in no way nor is it meant to be a justification for the wrong that was manifestly done to the native Americans. But it helps to explain why an economic audit almost inevitably identifies the combination of very large numbers of European immigrants with the natural resources of North—and to a lesser extent South—America as a primary source of global economic growth and rising living standards during the century from 1850 to 1950. This is an important part of the reason why, despite notable limitations and qualifications to the general doctrine that opening trade opportunities will necessarily raise incomes for all, there is not much doubt that, as Foreman-Peck puts it, "the extension of international economic relations allowed Europe and the regions of recent European settlement to support larger populations with longer life expectations."[55]

Capital flows, like labor migration, also reached unprecedented levels in this period, and the developing American economy, together with the lesser European satellites in South America, Australia and Asia, was a big part of the story. American direct investment abroad—investment whose use was directly controlled by the investor (as, for example, when a large company creates a plant in a foreign country)—dominated all such investment, chiefly because that type of big industrial business with multiple sites was first developed in the United States. Indeed, the growth of the physical sinews already described was a crucial factor in making the management and control of such firms possible. Large-scale firms likewise developed in the late nineteenth century in Britain, Germany and France, and their spread received an additional spur from the growing economic nationalism of governments, which were reluctant to place orders with foreign firms unless they had a manufacturing presence in the host economy. As a result, already by 1914 large multinational manufacturing businesses were supplying world markets increasingly by direct investment as well as by exports, partly in response to the ordinary economics of investment (combining capital as profitably as possible with the most cost-effective labor and locations), but partly also as a way of circumventing informal barriers, especially nontariff barriers, to traditional trade.

The story of portfolio investment, where the investor buys shares in a foreign company but does not seek to manage the business, is different. The big flows reflected mainly the relative maturity of the financial institutions of the Old World. These efficiently mobilized savings for lending to foreign governments and businesses and to feed the capital hunger of the overseas European settlements in America and elsewhere, which required huge infrastructure investments to exploit their vast endowments of resources. Although those economies also contained a disproportionately large young adult population at the stage of their life cycles in which savings are naturally most heavily concentrated, this was not enough to satisfy the gross scale of investment required. In any case this demographic advantage was offset by the tendency of pioneers in countries like America, where land was plentiful and labor was scarce, to have large families, thereby consuming the earnings that might otherwise have been saved.[56]

Before 1914 by far the biggest overseas investor, mostly in portfolio form, was Britain. The long peace after 1815, the growing sophistication of banks and capital markets and high incomes relative to other European countries all encouraged savers both to save and to invest their savings overseas. This habit has been blamed by some economists for Britain's relative economic decline after the first surge of the industrial revolution. But recent studies have shown that British-based businesses had no special difficulty in raising the capital they wanted, though British investment was low and in general British investors may have been rather less willing to risk their money in domestic business (about which very little information was at that time available to shareholders) than American and German banks who actively directed funds into newer industries using high technologies.[57] British overseas investment rose from £6 million a year just after the Napoleonic Wars to more than £30 million a year by 1850 and to £75 million after 1870.[58] By the eve of World War I, Britain was drawing a tenth of its national income from the fruits of past foreign investments, a war chest that was used, and largely used up, for just that purpose—financing wars—over the next thirty-odd years. In 1914 British foreign investments were over two-fifths of the world total, more than double those of Germany or France and five times those of the United States, despite the Americans' dominant position in foreign direct investment.[59]

We have described so far a rapidly emerging international economy in which the old European nations, especially Britain, and the European settlements in "new" lands, especially North America, are playing the key roles. Asia continues to account for over half the world's population but barely a fifth of its income.[60] The big driving forces of the new order include the appearance of the physical and the institutional framework of an increasingly integrated single international economy. Trade flows exploded after 1830, soaring at 30 percent in the decade to 1840 and then at over 50 percent a decade until 1880.[61]

This new framework was based both on steam and electrical power harnessed to ships, railways and the telegraph and on relatively liberal regimes governing trade, capital flows and migration in a world where, after 1815, general war between large nations was the exception rather than the rule. The big driving forces also include the massive consequences of combining the huge resources of the Americas, as well as Australia and New Zealand, with Europe's population and culture. They include as well the industrial revolution itself and its second wave, the industrialization of America, Japan and the rest of Europe apart from Britain. In this second industrial revolution, science and mass production are systematically applied for the first time as key industrial principles. And finally, they include the growing politicization of economic growth and industrial development as nations and their leaders become increasingly self-conscious about their economic success or failure and its effects on their political and military strength.

But before addressing these latter driving forces of the world economy in the late nineteenth century, we must put in place one further building block of its international framework—the monetary system. At the end of the Napoleonic Wars, world monetary arrangements were, as in the last resort they are always likely to be, a patchwork reflecting the pattern of political authority in the world. Money, as we commonly understand it, is a fiat of the competent political authority in the area in question, tempered by the willingness or otherwise of the user to credit it, more or less, with the value asserted by authority.

In practice the economically advanced world was divided among those countries which sought to give credibility to their currencies by affirming a parity with a certain weight of silver, those which preferred gold and those which acknowledged both (bimetallism). We have seen how John Locke and Isaac Newton had by 1717 established bimetallic values for the British currency that gave the guinea (equivalent to £1.05 sterling) a gold value such that an ounce of gold was worth £3 17s. 10 1/2 d.[62] The implied price of silver in terms of gold weight, based on Locke's reaffirmation of the "ancient right standard of England," namely, the pound sterling as worth 3 ounces, 17 pennyweight, 10 grains of sterling silver, was too low to attract people to the use of silver coins.[63] It paid them to melt the coins down or sell them for their intrinsic silver value. As a result, the silver coinage disappeared from circulation. Britain was effectively on a gold standard, as was acknowledged in 1774 when silver's legal-tender status was abolished for transactions above £25 and in 1821 when it was abolished for all transactions.[64]

In fact Britain's formal gold standard had been suspended during the Napoleonic Wars, demonstrating for the nth time that when the chips are down currency values depend on political say-so and that any general claim to the contrary is a polite peacetime fiction that, with luck, will last as long as the peace. In this case it was restored in 1819 and lasted until 1914, briefly and catastrophically to be restored again, in a triumph of nostalgia over reality, from 1925 to 1931.

Although France and other countries struggled hard to keep their silver and/or bimetallic standards alive late into the nineteenth century, Britain's dominant position in the world economy led one country after another to accommodate itself to the gold standard, in accordance with what economists infelicitously call "the model of network externalities" (i.e., the advantages of doing whatever your economic neighbors are doing). Germany went onto a gold standard in 1871, immediately after its empire-founding triumph over France at the battle of Sedan in 1870. Denmark, the Netherlands, Norway and Sweden and the countries of the Latin monetary union (France, Belgium, Italy and Switzerland) soon fell into line, as in 1879 effectively did the United States.[65] In 1897 Russia and Japan embraced gold standards, followed immediately by India, Ceylon and Siam, and even in the silver-producing stronghold of Latin America one nation after another—Argentina, Mexico, Peru and Uruguay—officially guaranteed convertibility of their currencies into gold.[66]

The effect of all this was to offer the international businessman a currency, or standard of value, in which he could conduct his business with limited and known exchange-rate risk. Costs and prices became more easily comparable in global terms, and market forces and information were thereby more powerfully transmitted around the world to the greater efficiency of the global economy and the greater satisfaction of consumers.

These were the classic microeconomic or supply-side effects of the heyday of the gold standard, which was also the world's first fixed-exchange-rate system, from 1875 to 1914. There were also macroeconomic effects, which were less ideal. For a start, if national currencies are linked to gold at a fixed price, then broadly the behavior of prices in general, especially the international prices of widely traded items, will follow the ebbs and flows of the world supply of gold, which contracted from 1873 to 1896 and then expanded.[67] The corresponding fall and then rise in international prices could come about only, as basic monetary theory requires that they should, through the effects of changing gold supply and monetary conditions on real economic activity. A gold shortage tightens monetary conditions, pushes up interest rates, discourages borrowing and investment and slows down spending and production, with the result that prices fall; gold plenty has the reverse effects. This means that the constancy of the relationship of prices to gold supply is purchased at the price of fluctuations, sometimes painful and disruptive, in the real economy and so in the economic lives of real people.

There was another consequence of this paramountcy of nominal stability (of prices in relation to the quantity of gold and so of national currency) over the stability of the real economy. Countries could find their currencies to be overvalued at the fixed gold parity, as, for example, when silver fell in value relative to gold and so devalued those currencies fixed to silver. This gave the economies that used them a competitive advantage against the economies whose currencies were based on gold. Then the gold standard countries could restore equilibrium only by driving down their own prices and wages or by living with permanently high unemployment, rather as France has done in modern times as a consequence of its *franc fort* (strong franc) policy since 1983.[68]

Profound economic fluctuations indubitably marred the performance of the new international economy in the second half of the nineteenth century. Britain in particular suffered slumps in 1878, 1882–1883 and 1907, chiefly as a result of gold outflows from the Bank of England caused by various economic and financial crises elsewhere, for example, in Germany, France and North and South America.[69]

The depression of the international economy that began in 1873 was indeed the longest and deepest the world experienced, until the Great Depression of the 1930s.[70] It seems to have been triggered by a financial crisis in Germany (the ironic result of receiving a gigantic reparations payment from France in consequence of the German victory over France at the battle of Sedan in 1870) and spread quickly around Europe to the United States, where unemployment exceeded one million and a fifth of the railways were bankrupt or teetering on the edge of bankruptcy, and to Brazil and Argentina, where banks stopped lending and property values fell by a third.[71]

This experience later became a powerful stimulant to studies of the trade cycle and the causes of booms and slumps, which have since come to be known, by a kind of mealymouthed progression in euphemism, as "depressions," "recessions," "rolling readjustments," "growth recessions" and "slowdowns." It seems indisputable that investor and consumer psychology play a crucial role in magnifying initial influences into exaggerated stampedes, whether buying or selling, rather as shallow water turns moderate waves into monstrous breakers.

It is clear, too, that monetary policies and exchange-rate systems greatly influence the transmission of the boom-or-bust waves around the world, with fixed exchange rates, as under the gold standard, speeding the transmission, and floating exchange rates making it easier for individual economies to escape the shocks. But what starts the process, the first flake in the avalanche, is harder to identify.

It may be that the seemingly inescapable tendency (despite even Alan Greenspan's remarkable defiance of the normal laws of economic gravity as chairman of the U.S. Federal Reserve in the 1990s) to rhythm—stop and go—in every developed economy since the industrial revolution is rooted in some feature of group psychology that requires that optimism become euphoria until broken by its own hideous consequences and that concern become despair until relieved by the very opportunities that it creates. If this is true, even a perfectly conducted monetary policy could not forever keep euphoria and despair at bay. Indeed, the longer it succeeded in appearing to do so, the greater would be the eventual euphoria and, later, despair. Greenspan, the Bank of England's Monetary Policy Committee and the European Central Bank all please note.

Or it may be, as Foreman-Peck argues of the depression of the 1870s, that such events have "real" causes.[72] Examples would be the opening of the Suez Canal in 1869 and the spread of railways. These caused large and unexpected declines in agricultural and raw material prices as a result of easier and cheaper transport. This in turn discouraged capital flows into emerging markets and provoked financial crises similar to those suffered by such places in the 1990s. These triggers then set off sympathetic panics and contraction by the usual processes of financial psychology and monetary transmission.

Or, third, the whole tendency of national economies—and, when integrated by fixed exchange rates, the single international economy—to hunt from boom to slump may have a purely monetary explanation rooted in the unevenness of the supply of whatever is used for money, at times rising too fast, so sparking boom and inflation, at times too slow, so causing depression and deflation. If that is so, then at least in theory really skillful money managers, or central banks, could iron out the fluctuations and get it just right. Greenspan's miracle might then be possible after all.

Economic historians will not settle this question, at least not until well into the third millennium. What they can and do notice, however, is that the great depression of the 1870s did more than stimulate the study of the trade cycle. It began a process that altered the perceptions of statesmen (and those who influence them) with far more profound consequences than any purely academic vista could offer. Foreman-Peck spots the new trend:

> A belief that the international market would not raise or preserve living standards adequately became more widespread. Instead, governments or other corporate forms of organisation such as trade unions and cartels were increasingly expected to take remedial or positive action in the face of market forces. Even in Britain the verities of free trade seemed less than eternal. . . . Britain no longer occupied the same dominant position in the international economy that it had in the 1850s. In the new era that was beginning, the industrial capacities of the leading nations were more equal, trade was less free and the international economy was increasingly used to achieve objectives of foreign policy.[73]

We have so far in this chapter examined the emergence of an international economy in the sense of a world in which trade, capital and labor moved on an unprecedented scale and with unprecedented freedom between different markets, thanks both to improved means of transport and communication and to relatively liberal rules. It would be a mistake, however, to construe this as implying that there was one single, homogenized global economy undifferentiated into distinct regional and national economies. Indeed, that would be an exaggeration even today, when global economic integration has proceeded immensely much further than was possible or contemplated in the second half of the nineteenth century.

In terms of economic development, growth and industrialization, a new consciousness of national progress, both absolutely and relative to others, had begun to emerge. The national economy became a more prominent concept, as the spectacle of the industrial revolution in Britain and its seeming contribution to the potency and standing of that nation impressed a widening circle of onlookers in other key countries. It is not necessary to believe that governments in fact played a decisive role in spurring economic development and industrial catch-up in those countries—especially Germany, the United States and Japan—in order to believe that economic and industrial realities played an increasing part on the agenda of governments and that this contributed to a sense of national competition, rivalry and eventually conflict that displaced the liberal ideology from the dominance it enjoyed until late in the century.

It was above all industrialization—in essence the use of the steam engine to deliver fantastic quantities of usable power from coal—that transformed the countries and the people who profited from it and set them on a path of seemingly endless compound growth. It also set them apart from all previous generations of mankind as well, perhaps for centuries, as from those who did not have it or only began to have it in the twentieth century. It even seemed to set them free from the Malthusian trap, enabling societies to supply, by ever advancing productivity based on ever advancing technical development, ever growing populations without the multiplication of the mouths catching up with the multiplication of the output. Coal in Britain in 1870 supplied the energy that would have fed a population almost thirty times greater than actually existed. Steam engines, which needed no food, delivered as much power as a labor force that exceeded the whole population of Britain at the time by some 10 million and that would have consumed three times the country's annual wheat production.[74] Kennedy quotes Ashton's pithy comparison in 1947 with the fate of the great nonindustrializing Asian economies: "There are today on the plains of India and China men and women, plague-ridden and hungry, living lives little better, to outward appearance, than those of the cattle that toil with them by day and share their places of sleep by night. . . . Such unmechanized horrors are the lot of those who increase their numbers without first passing through an industrial revolution."[75]

This indeed is all part of D. N. McCloskey's "heart of the matter," the twelvefold increase in living standards since 1780 in modern industrialized economies.[76] Kennedy quotes telling, though not undisputed, calculations by Bairoch showing the different progress of industrialization in different national economies and the extreme contrast between the industrializers and the rest.[77] Using as an index the number 100 to represent the level of industrialization per head of population in Britain in 1900, these estimates show

- in 1860 Britain scored 64, the United States 21, France 20, Germany 15, Europe as a whole 16, Japan 7 and India and China 3 or 4
- in 1900 (with Britain at 100) the United States scored 69, Germany 52, France 39, Europe as a whole 35, Japan 12 and India and China 1 to 3

The United States, Europe and incipiently Japan were catching up. China and conspicuously India were falling further behind. The Great Exhibition "of the Works of Industry of All Nations" at the newly built Crystal Palace in Hyde Park, London, in 1851 became both an expression of British national pride and a spur to others who were tempted to see international competition in such nationalistic terms, however much economic theorists might deprecate such concepts. Charles Kingsley, the English novelist, could rhapsodize, like so many others temporarily blessed by good fortune, that one's own triumph demonstrated divine favor: "The spinning jenny and the railroad, Cunard's liners and the electric telegraphs, are to me . . . signs that we are on some points at least, in harmony with the universe; that there is a mighty spirit working among us . . . the Ordering and Creating God."[78]

Within twenty years of that exhibition, other national economies were competing with a will in the game. They were less advanced or "mature" than Britain, but they had the knowledge and the means to compete. They were free to exploit the prerogative of all followers to choose the best successes and avoid the mistakes of the leader, and they had at least an equal capacity to grow.[79] It was not necessary for Britain to "fail," as

Crafts has shown, for Britain's industrial lead to cease to grow and in due course to disappear.[80] It was only necessary for others to follow the same path and to improve upon it, as they did, though as others, like Cameron, have alleged, there may also have been failures (for example, entrepreneurial failure).[81]

We need not trace in comparable detail to the story of the original industrial revolution the story of the second industrial revolution, as the progress of industrialization in the second half of the nineteenth century, especially in Germany, the United States and Japan, has been called. What is mainly of interest to the historian are certain specific features that characterized it and enabled it to achieve higher levels of industrialization, productivity and output than the first industrial revolution, as well as its consequences for the rivalry of nations.

Railways opened up the continental interiors of Europe and America and played the role of the textile industry in the first industrial revolution in spearheading the general advance, absorbing the lion's share of capital and becoming the biggest new user of both labor and capital goods. These effects multiplied and reverberated through the rest of the economy.

The discovery and exploitation of coal in France, Germany and America made possible the kind of escape from the biological constraints of human and animal power already discussed. The rapid spread after 1850 of retail banking networks in France, Germany, Belgium and America mobilized the savings and ready cash of a huge financial hinterland for the use of the central money markets, greatly increasing the capacity of the main capital markets to support industrial development. Investment banks and corporate finance companies also helped to channel investment into industry across the European continent.

Technology advanced piecemeal on many fronts, such as textiles and iron smelting, especially in the replacement of scarce charcoal by more plentiful coke. But more strategic advances in the second half of the nineteenth century included the Bessemer process, invented in England in 1856, for making steel from molten iron without the difficult and expensive puddling process. When this was combined with new open-hearth furnaces and the Thomas-Gilchrist "basic" processes for neutralizing the excessive amounts of acid in the most plentiful, phosphorus-bearing forms of iron ore, world production of steel soared more than a hundredfold in the half-century before World War I. The strength, durability and cheapness of this newly available material transformed the industries that characterized the second industrial revolution—railways, shipping and shipbuilding and civil engineering construction (bridges, skyscrapers).[82]

Electricity, or at least its manifestations, had been noticed since man was first astonished by thunder and lightning; but its general use as a power source for industry and in the home had to wait for the invention of the steam turbine to generate large quantities of electricity from coal. Its early uses were mainly for lighting, though its capacity to generate heat combined with its convenience made it a potential substitute for traditional power sources throughout manufacturing industry. The electric motor and, as we have seen, the electric telegraph, both based on the fuller understanding of electromagnetisim, opened yet more vistas of limitless opportunity for economic development.[83]

Indeed, the deliberate application of science to industry was a new characteristic of the second industrial revolution, not shared by the first. This applied after 1870 not only to electricity but also to the use of the sciences of optics and chemistry in the growing industries using glass, metals and farm products.[84] Andrew Carnegie (1835–1919), who built the American steel industry and supplied the exploding American railway system, had seen his father in Scotland lose his livelihood as a weaver because of the invention of the steam-powered weaving loom. He was determined never to be caught behind the curve of technological advance, and he was one of the first great industrialists to employ scientists in-house in his businesses.

Carnegie was also a pioneer of two special characteristics of the second industrial revolution, scale and concentration. Huge plants covering many acres and the single ownership of all the stages of production back to the raw material were shown, given a large enough market, to offer economies of scale, as well as sheer business muscle and monopolistic opportunities. They spawned the giant corporations of this era, such as Standard Oil in the United States (the basis of the Rockefeller fortune, still judged to be the largest ever relative to the economic scale of its time) and Bayer, Hoechst and BASF in Germany.

This in time gave rise to the ideology of maturity, still much favored in the rhetoric of capital markets and their attendant "analysts." This ideology holds that an industry is mature only when an initial proliferation of competing entrepreneurs, gladdening as they are to the hearts of classically reared economists, are replaced by a handful of mighty oligopolistic corporations, which, as a consequence of the advantages of scale or by the operation of some other law of the financial jungle, are able to prevent competition from the new entrants who should appear according to the romantic convictions of the pure economists.

Chandler, however, still sees competition as firmly enshrined in American law and practice and as contributing to a distinctive American brand of corporation-based capitalism that he distinguishes from the British and German varieties:

> In the United States the structure of the new industries had become, with rare exceptions, oligopolistic, not monopolistic. This was partly because of the size of the market place and partly because of the antitrust legislation that reflected the commitment of Americans to competition as well as their suspicion of concentrated power. In these oligopolies the new managerial enterprises continued to compete functionally and strategically for market share and profit. By World War I the system of competitive managerial capitalism in capital-intensive industries in the United States was already different from the continuing personal or family capitalism practiced in Britain and the cooperative or organized capitalism developing in Germany.[85]

We have already suggested that economic success, defined primarily in industrial terms, came increasingly to dominate the political agendas of those nations that looked with covetous eyes upon the first industrial revolution and what it seemed to have done for Britain's place in the world. But in this perhaps natural reflection lay the seeds of an attitude violently at odds with the open and liberal creed of the mid-nineteenth-century international economy, which had anyway received a nasty knock from the great depression of the 1870s, as we have seen.

If the nation and its industrial muscle come to be considered some kind of collective or corporate entity, whose splendor and performance in competition with the rival entities of other nations become ends in themselves, higher than and separate from the humdrum and prosaic business of satisfying consumer wants, then the basic prescriptions of classical economics—markets, competition, consumer sovereignty, the price mechanism, profit maximization, limited government—will be quickly displaced by grander state goals. These may include military capability, public buildings and monuments, accumulation of monetary reserves (seen, for example, by the Bank of France in the 1880s as a form of war chest) and the growth of great corporations to act as national champions in a global struggle for ascendancy.[86] This is not the economist's concept of competition in which all or most can be winners, but the geopolitician's—or indeed the sportsman's—concept of championship, in which all but at most one must be losers.

It is important to see how such economic nationalism came gradually to infect the thinking of leading governments in the final decades before World War I. Kennedy has traced this half-conscious revolution in thought, which finally affected Britain as well as Germany, America and Japan. He notes that in 1885 opinion formers and ordinary politicians in Europe "talked and wrote in terms of a vulgar Darwinistic world of struggle, success and failure, of growth and decline."[87] They worried that the century that would begin in 1900 would be dominated by American economic might alongside sheer Russian military weight. Mercantilism—the belief that the goal of a nation's trade is to maximize a surplus of exports over imports by whatever means and that for every winner there must therefore be a loser—was making a comeback against the free trade principles of midcentury. This was quickly and easily linked in men's minds with the idea that such economical struggle was but one facet of the greater political struggle for survival among the powers. Size and population were seen to give America and Russia, as it were, a buy into the coming twentieth-century round.

In Britain the radical politician Joseph Chamberlain and the Cambridge historian J. R. Seeley expounded the idea of the British Empire as a third candidate. On the Continent Otto von Bismarck, the architect of German union in 1870, who had reportedly stated that the great decisions of the day would be decided by "blood and iron" and who was still German chancellor in 1879, was converted to the need for agricultural and industrial protection.[88] He was influenced partly by crude political pressures but partly also by arguments of industrial strategy: A protected "soft" home market where easy profits could be earned was supposedly needed in order to support a huge expansion of barely profitable exports, as required by the mercantilist concept of the national interest. Admiral Alfred von Tirpitz told the kaiser that a big German navy was necessary in order to place Germany among the four world powers, with America, Russia and England. French commentators made similar arguments for securing a place at the top table by engineering the essential economic progress. As Kennedy has summed it up: "There existed in governing elites, military circles and imperialist organisations a prevailing view of the world order which stressed struggle, change, competition, the use of force and the organisation of national resources to enhance state power."[89]

The British imperialist Leo Amery, who in 1940 was to speak the words that dismissed Neville Chamberlain as British prime minister and brought Winston Churchill to 10 Downing Street, expressed the essence of the creed of economic nationalism in 1904 when he wrote, "The successful powers will be those who have the greatest industrial base. . . . [They] will be able to defeat all others."*[90]

Economic nationalism never infected the United States in quite the virulent form that gripped Europe. But protectionism, social and political Darwinism and, at least in the Western Hemisphere, a species of imperialism clearly linked the progress of American economic performance to the country's ability and need to become an active world power. As already noted, American manufacturing had been dependent on tariff protection in the mid-nineteenth century, even if the main motive for setting tariffs had been different, namely, the need for revenue.[91] They were raised in 1890 (the McKinley Tariff), 1897 and (on imported manufactures) 1909.[92]

For a fuller discussion of the origins of American imperialism, seen as the logical alternative to an isolationism that was no longer either practical or worthy of the nation the United States was becoming, readers are directed to Warren Zimmermann's forthcoming study, the relevant chapter of which he has kindly allowed me to see in draft.[93] The key figure in this change in American thinking was Captain Alfred Thayer Mahan of the U.S. Navy. His classic study, *The Influence of Sea Power Upon History 1660–1783*,[94] advocated a forward American strategy of global sea-power supported by fleets, heavy warships and suitably located and defended bases. He was much encouraged by and had great influence upon the thinking of the young Theodore Roosevelt.

Mahan rested his thesis on that familiar combination of American na-

*During a speech in the House of Commons, Amery turned on Chamberlain and quoted the words that Oliver Cromwell had used in 1657, "In the name of God, go!"

tional interest and high moral purpose that has so frequently marked the presentation of U.S. foreign policy. And it seemed logical enough in a world which, toward the end of the nineteenth century, was coming to be dominated, not by the globalized international marketplace, which appeared to be opening up at mid-century, but by the competition and rivalry of great nations, in strategic as much as in commercial and economic matters. Mahan wrote:

> Let us start from the fundamental truth, warranted by history, that the control of the seas, and especially along the great lines drawn by national interest or national commerce, is the chief among the merely material elements in the power and prosperity of nations. It is so because the sea is the world's great medium of circulation. From this necessarily follows the principle that, as subsidiary to such control, it is imperative to take possession, when it can be done righteously, of such maritime positions as contribute to secure command.[95]

Exactly when the United States became the world's largest economy is of more interest to statisticians than historians, but some time in the second half of the nineteenth century, certainly by about 1890, it had surpassed all rivals in industrial production, though its population was barely half that of Russia and less than a fifth that of China.[96] In the thirty-five years before World War I, the United States increased its gross national product roughly fivefold, compared with three and a half times in Germany and just over double in Britain. Thus even output per head, at a time of very rapid population growth in the United States, through immigration as well as natural increase, rose faster (at 2.4 times) than in industrializing Germany (double) or industrialized Britain (1.5 times).[97]

A trumped-up war with Spain in 1898 gave the United States new colonies in the Philippines, Puerto Rico and Guam, as well as full economic access to a newly independent Cuba. A year later President William McKinley's secretary of state, John Hay, declared the "open-door" policy—demanding equal access to China's markets for all nations—in order to establish the Americans as an at least equal imperialist power to the Europeans in the scramble for Asia.[98] Their "arrival" in this dubious company was ratified by the ultimate effusion from Rudyard Kipling, aiming to recruit America to his version of the Anglo-Saxon mission in an uncivilized world:

> Take up the White Man's burden—
> Send forth the best ye breed—
> Go bind your sons to exile
> To serve your captives' need; . . .
> Take up the White Man's burden—
> Have done with childish days—
> The lightly proffered laurel,
> The easy, ungrudged praise.
> Comes now, to search your manhood
> Through all the thankless years,
> Cold-edged with dear-bought wisdom,
> The judgment of your peers![99]

These words may yet have a resonance for Americans after the vicissitudes of U.S. foreign involvement since the Korean War.

American nationalism was thus different from its European counterpart: less statist and less purposely economic, but nonetheless assertive and more powerfully sustained by industrial transformation. Even so, nothing could have been more vividly an act of government in support of economic goals than the arrival in 1853 in Tokyo Bay of U.S. commodore Matthew Perry with a message from President Franklin Pierce demanding the opening of Japan to foreign commerce and diplomatic relations on pain of immediate bombardment of the capital.[100]

This painful apparition provoked a conscious, deliberate and government-led reengineering of the Japanese economy; over the next half century Japan was converted from an isolated commercial and agricultural society into an industrializing power with extensive foreign trade.[101] The aforementioned calculations by Bairoch show that after 1860 Japan began to lift off from the low and flat level of industrial capacity per head of population that it had experienced during the previous 100 years.[102] The shock of Commodore Perry's unanswerable threats—he had the ships, including steamships, and he had the guns, while Japan had no navy—persuaded the ruling Tokugawa shogunate, which had kept Japan secluded from the outside world for two and a half centuries, that the time had come to open up and catch up, not least in military methods and industrial technology.[103] Their efforts were soon overtaken by the undermining effects of the implied confession of previous mismanagement.

The last shogun was overthrown by a combination of opponents, the most focused of whom—the hereditary bureaucrats drawn from the traditional samurai warrior class—were determined to reverse Japan's backwardness and to restore its honor.[104]

To this end in 1868 they restored the Meiji emperor, whose role had degenerated under the shoguns into impotent ceremonial, and used his authority to modernize the economy as an adjunct to creating a new and highly centralized nation. Specifically, their reforms in the first decade of the Meiji restoration aped the results of the European revolutions of the previous 100 years in emancipating the middle classes, though in Japan the bourgeoisie had little hand in imposing the change.[105] The chief instrument of Japan's economic transformation, an early forerunner of the Ministry of International Trade and Industry to which such supernal powers were widely attributed during the years of Japan's economic miracle after World War II, was from 1870 to 1885 the Kôbushô, or Ministry of Industry (or Engineering or Construction, depending on the translator's taste). Its head summed up its mission: "[to] make good Japan's deficiencies by swiftly seizing upon the strengths of the western industrial arts; to construct within Japan all kinds of mechanical equipment on the western model, including ship-building, railways, telegraph, mines and buildings; and thus with one great leap to introduce to Japan the concepts of enlightenment."[106]

All of this was begun, although as always Western observers can never be wholly sure how far the Japanese simulacra of American and European prototypes are indeed the real thing—firms, markets, private property, enterprise, trade unions, governments—and how far they are just some ghostly parody of their Western counterparts, twitching to some entirely different and uniquely Japanese dynamic. Do they ape the form only to deny the spirit of the original institutions, born in chaotic, pluralistic, democratic, entrepreneurial, individualistic and nonconformist societies and grafted by official surgeons onto a designed, centralized, bureaucratic, corporatist and conforming body? This stereotype of an oriental charade is too glib to be profound. We are probably wise to content ourselves instead with the conclusion that although a number of peculiarly Japanese circumstances, including Commodore Perry's irruption, determined when and why and how Japan began to tread the same path of industrialization and modernization that directed the ambitions of the world's other main powers in the latter part of the nineteenth century, the results of these trends and the impetus of the energies released by the greater scope afforded to market forces and private initiative were not so different in an Asian society from what they are anywhere human beings are free to seek better conditions. Nor was the growing identification of national success with economic advancement all that different in its hold on the minds of those who influenced opinion and moved the levers of power. What may have been different, especially from the American model, was the degree—still hotly debated—to which such thinking actually delivered measurable results, with change really being brought about by central orchestration as much as by the "invisible hand" of private appetites.[107]

So by 1910 Japan had for several decades been growing as fast as any European economy, and its developing manufacturing sector, now accounting for a fifth of national output, was growing at a rapid catch-up rate of 5 percent a year, never falling even in a recession year.[108] Railways and the telegraph extended across the country in a national network. Japan had a large merchant navy, and its military forces were the strongest in Asia. Nearly a million workers were employed in tens of thousands of factories of varying size using over 5,000 steam engines and nearly 3,000 electrical machines.[109]

It had wielded this new power in wars against China in 1894–1895 (victorious, though not fulfilling the objective of taking Korea), against Russia in 1904–1905 (victorious) and in 1910 annexing Korea.[110] It was not a global power, and some of its military success came with imported ships and guns that it had great difficulty affording.[111] But its regional ascendancy was established and seemed to those who cared about national pride to vindicate the economic and cultural transformation brought about under the restored Meiji emperor.[112] The new century would test this logic to destruction, not because of any imaginable limits (at least until its last decade) to Japan's economic potential but because of the nemesis that follows when nationalism is vaunted beyond prudence.

Russia, too, had been modernizing since 1855, under Czars Alexander II and III. Serfdom was abolished in 1861, and government policy actively encouraged industrialization in the last two decades of the century. Factories, mines and banks became the spearheads of a recognizably capitalist development. The output of manufacturing and extraction industries rose at 8 percent a year in the 1890s and at 6 percent during the seven years leading up to World War I. Over 30,000 miles of railways reached from the Baltic to the Pacific.[113] And of course Russia's population, at 175 million, exceeded those of the next two largest powers, the United States and Germany, combined.[114] That was not an unqualified advantage, since this huge population had to feed itself, a task that occupied most of its labor not very successfully. The miraculous empowerment and consequent liberation brought by coal, iron and steam had only scratched the surface of Russia's potential, producing in 1913 a tenth as much coal as Britain and less than half as much iron and steel.[115] Protective tariffs from 1891 and other incentives to industrialization raised Russia's production tenfold in the half century to 1910, more than the world's and Germany's sixfold increases, but from a very low base. Income per head (which was less than a quarter of Britain's in 1913 and about a third of Germany's) grew slowly because slow-growing agriculture dominated the Russian economy and because population rose very fast, illustrating yet again Ashton's point about "the lot of those who increase their numbers without first passing through an industrial revolution."[116] In sum, on the eve of World War I Russia was a great power, despite its humiliation by Japan ten years earlier, because of the absolute size of its population and territory. Economic nationalism had infected it only as far as successive czars tried to emulate the industrial development they saw in western Europe through tariffs and other direct encouragements. But the defeat by Japan combined with the new political forces released by modernization to shake the throne of Nicholas II.[117] Imperial Russia's energies were turned more inward than outward and were comparatively innocent of the aggressive nationalism and imperialism that were exciting so many of its contemporaries.

The focus of this chapter has been first on the emergence in the middle of the nineteenth century of a more truly international economy than the world had seen before, or indeed was to see for thirty, arguably even seventy, years after 1914. We then turned to growth of forms of economic nationalism as the dash for industrialization became a conscious priority of governments as well as a natural business response to opportunity. In consequence the affairs of Britain, as the epicenter of that international economy, and of continental Europe, the United States and Japan have successively occupied center stage, and we have seen Russia's belated attempts at modernization. But this account does not exhaust world economic history between 1850 and 1910.

China, as noted in Chapter 6, did not industrialize when Britain did. But after 1870 a process of modernization that included some industrialization consciously adopted from European models was encouraged by the Qing emperors and officials.[118] Railways, steamships, heavy and light industries all appeared, and some general prosperity was reflected in healthy and buoyant government revenues.[119] But from the 1890s disastrous external interventions, based on the superior military strength of Japan, Britain and others and imposing huge indemnity payments on Beijing, wrecked the 2,000-year-old imperial regime and changed China from a power into a carcass to be carved up by others, not least foreign banks who virtually ran the economy in the early twentieth century.[120] In 1800 China had produced one-third of the world's industrial output; by 1900 that had fallen to 6 percent.[121] The ordinary Chinese peasants were still locked into the basic agrarian trap described by Keynes in the passage quoted in Chapter 6: "From the earliest times of which we have record—back, say, to two thousand years before Christ—down to the beginning of the eighteenth century, there was no very great change in the standard of life of the average man living in the civilised centres of the earth."[122] But for them it was the beginning not of the eighteenth but of the twentieth century.

India, after the great rebellion in 1857 that the British tendentiously called "the mutiny" but that Indians today, equally intent on getting the right spin, call "the first war of independence," was brought under the direct rule of the British crown.[123] Railways were built from 1853, with enough track by 1900 to reach around the world. They may have been built for mainly military and imperial reasons, but they also had large commercial and economic consequences, integrating Indian markets, mobilizing raw materials for world use and distributing manufactured imports, especially from Britain. Steamships and, after 1869, the Suez Canal linked India ever more closely into the international economy centered on the North Atlantic. But no effort was made to develop India's industrial base. Indeed, India's textile industry suffered from British competition based on the steam-powered loom; the country was a net importer of cloth from Britain by 1853.[124]

By the end of the century, India's share of world manufacturing output had fallen from one-fifth to one-fiftieth, chiefly because of the explosive increase in the world total led by Europe and North America.[125] Indian peasants, never mind the occasional famines that punctuated British rule, languished in the same static agrarian poverty as their Chinese counterparts. The great industrial liftoff of nineteenth-century Europe and America passed them largely by, generating what later became known as un- or less-developed economies. Commercial classes, landowners and educated professionals did better, tasting the fruits of the European enlightenment as a consequence of Macaulay's educational reforms in the 1830s—based on his expressed conviction that there was more wisdom to be found in a single shelf of books in any good European library than in all the wisdom of the East—and exploiting the opportunities of a law-abiding, if intermittently restive, society under the raj. India may or may not have been an asset to, as well as the ornament it undoubtedly was of, the British Empire, which thought itself—and seemed superficially to be—at the height of its power at the time of the King-Emperor George V's durbar in 1911. But India was not a pacemaker in world economic development, nor a great power, nor a source of prosperity to its more than 300 million inhabitants.

The economics of empire were dubious indeed when applied to the imperial possessions acquired in the late nineteenth century, conspicuously in the scramble for Africa as ratified by the Berlin Conference of 1884–1885. This conclave established the doctrine of "effective occupation," whereby occupying European powers justified their claim to the hinterlands associated with their coastal possessions.[126] By 1914 almost all Africa was so parceled out.[127]

Many economic theories have been propounded to explain, to justify and to condemn colonialism and imperialism, including the civilizing mission much beloved of late Victorian imperialists and the economic determinism of Lenin. The loot—or near loot that comes from exchange on absurdly unequal terms—of early European intervention in Africa in search of slaves, gold and anything else that might enrich the merchant venturer along the coasts of the Dark Continent has a simple economic logic that all can understand. High levels of risk may have seemed to justify the large profit margins enjoyed by the successful in their own eyes, if not in the eyes of those who were enslaved, robbed and diddled of their birthrights. Indeed, for both Europeans and Africans it may often have been a negative-sum game, impoverishing both Africa and the colonial power, where dominion was imposed in areas of low economic potential and high social vulnerability.

The mineral wealth of South Africa after 1871 was, however, a clear case of real gains being available, though the human price that was paid by Africans who were forced off their land and into quasi-slavery to quarry the gold and diamonds for European investors must strike a modern observer as beyond calculation. This human price was indeed high, however low was the opportunity cost for a tribesman whose only other employment was as a simple farmer or herdsman, and even if the cash sums sometimes remitted to his village raised standards for other family members.

For the colonial power, the cost of administration often was a financial drain, as France experienced at the end of the century when colonial expenditures massively exceeded receipts. Germany's outgoings on its colonies, not counting defense, were greater in the twenty years before World War I than the whole of the value of its colonial trade. Even Britain had growing difficulties in making colonial ends meet, and recent studies suggest that the value of the empire as a whole to Britain at this time was less than sometimes thought.[128] The low volume of trade with the colonies acquired in the scramble of the 1880s contradicts any idea that they were acquired as critically necessary outlets for overproductive European capitalism.[129]

If theories and principles are needed in order to condemn imperialism and colonialism, it should be sufficient to invoke the principle that no people should be ruled against their will. Between 1800 and 1914 the territory under European occupation or control rose from one-third to more than four-fifths of the world's land areas.[130] The economic pluses and minuses were probably too modest and inadequate to have explained such a large and general rush as actually occurred in the decades before World War I.

The true explanation lies in the same growing beliefs of governments and of the men who influenced them that the nations of the world, or at least those which aspired to be significant independent players in the next century, were locked in a mortal competition that required all contestants to bid as strongly for global territorial reach as for domestic industrial strength. The same devil of nationalism, conforming almost to the sterile norms of a sporting competition in which every contest and every winner required a loser, distorted and derailed the open and international economy of the mid-nineteenth century in favor of a clashing cacophony of rival economic champions. It impelled national statesmen to strive for a strategic edge in the matter of colonies and—they may in their frenzy have believed—of markets for their new industries.

Had they studied their economic textbooks more carefully, they might have understood better that their true advantage lay in playing positive-sum games with their partners—as when economic exchange is free and competitive rather than controlled and rivalrous—and in playing them under conditions of global peace and stability. But in 1910 such wisdom was running low, even if time itself was not strictly running out. War was not inevitable, but there were many who believed that Darwinian struggle between survival-seeking nations might make it so. And if it came, there were many in the mood to wage it, believing, too, that their new industrial strength gave them the means to prevail.

CHAPTER EIGHT

Cul-de-Sac, 1910–1945

BETWEEN 1900 AND 1950 THE WORLD'S POPULATION ROSE BY MORE than half, from 1.6 billion to 2.5 billion.[1] World economic output rose much faster, by somewhere between doubling and quadrupling (by 160 percent and 270 percent[2]). Accordingly world production per head of population rose by between two thirds and one-and-a-half fold.[3]

The difference between the higher and the lower figure depends on how much credit is given to the development of new products, which have extended our choice and better met our needs, so enhancing the living standards commanded by incomes of supposedly equal purchasing power to those of, say, a century ago.

To the hyper-casual empiricist from outer space this record may appear to be one of impressive advance. To the historian, and indeed to most people who were alive and taking notice, the third of a century from 1910 must rank as one of the direst retrogressions in the whole human economic story.

It encompassed the only two "world wars" man has yet perpetrated upon himself. They inflicted a scale of damage on people and property that, while not perhaps quite exceeding all natural calamities from flood, famine, and disease, certainly exceeded that of any other man-made harm.

It also provided the most starkly contrasting figures of the waltz motif. The industrial revolution, like the earlier agricultural revolution, had been a huge first-step leap forward in human economic opportunity. It provoked strong appetites among those who observed but did not originally enjoy the opportunity, and those appetites bred conflicts between the haves and the have-nots. These conflicts, aggravated by other causes, produced their most extreme manifestations in war and massive destruction of people and property—the second step. The unsuccessful search for a third step that would resolve the conflicts of the second step and establish the conditions for the fullest enjoyment of the opportunities of the first step is the story of the inter-war years. The second step was repeated in World War II, and the search for the third step was postponed until after 1945.

A single chapter in a history of mankind cannot present a comprehensive chronicle of the events of any period, least of all of so recent a period as 1910–1945, for which our records are so extensive and the literature so vast. Those who want to read the full story and study the full range of issues posed by recent and contemporary scholars of the period must go to works that focus exclusively on those tasks.

Our aim here is different: to look at the events in the context of the story of the wealth of man, seen as a never-ending, though frequently failing, search by mankind individually and collectively to ameliorate his material conditions and to manage the horrendous conflicts to which this search gives rise. We have already described the extraordinary leap forward of the industrial revolution, the dawning of an unprecedented prosperity in a newly integrated international economy for those in the right place to enjoy it in the mid-nineteenth century, and the corruption of this order by a new and virulent nationalism, including economic nationalism, in many of the leading powers in the Northern Hemisphere as the new century began.

We now aim to tell the tale, in similarly broad and thematic terms, of the culminating disaster of this false turn on the road and of the failed attempts between the two world wars to get human economic affairs back onto a healthier path. The key events in this sequence are:

- World War I and the damage it inflicted
- the Russian revolution and its descent into Stalin's tyranny
- the terms of the peace treaty at Versailles, which attempted to define

the rules of the postwar world, as well as to make Germany pay for the ravages of war

- attempts to establish a stable international monetary order, including the return by Britain and other nations to the prewar gold standard and the direct consequences thereof
- the boom, bubble and crash of the U.S. stock market in the late 1920s and the subsequent Great Depression
- the rise of Hitler leading to World War II

The human destruction of War World I was horrific: About 8 million were killed in the fighting and perhaps as many as another 20 million civilians were casualties during the war and its immediate aftermath.[4] The damage to property and infrastructure was equally great, if mercifully less awful.

Calibrating the wreckage by putting a dollar rule against it is an exercise of limited value and scarcely aids the imagination to comprehend what four years of such a war does to a continent. But for what it is worth, the war appears to have cost the governments who conducted it as much as $260 billion, six and a half times more than the national debt accumulated by all countries in the world between 1800 and 1914.[5] Other estimates, which include the cost of physical damage to property and social capital, range as high as $380 billion (at 1914 prices).[6]

A better conception of what the war meant can be gleaned from other partial evidence. For example, after the war worldwide farm production was a third below the prewar level, and manufacturing was down by over a fifth in Europe and seven-eighths in Russia, though well up in the United States and the rest of the world.[7] The long rise in European total output was put back about eight years and that of the world by nearly five years.[8] Houses, farms, livestock, ships, roads, railways, bridges, telegraph lines, factories, mines, countryside and buildings of all kinds were laid waste with all the heedless fury of war. And though the speed with which such investments can be replaced once growth resumes is an endless source of wonder to those who contemplate the initial devastation, this was mayhem on a scale never previously accomplished by man.

Nonetheless, if we ask what it was about the events of 1914–1918 that made those years such a supreme symbol of the failure and follies of human societies and such an ultimate definition of the experience to be avoided above all others and at whatever cost, the answer does not lie in the economic cost. Seen in the long perspective of output growth, it was a blip, in no way comparable with the Black Death or even the Great Depression in Europe from 1873 to 1896. It was the loss of life—and the vivid, violent and futile way in which so many such young lives were lost—that scarred the consciousness of a generation and a continent so deeply. It seemed that it would be a crime and a disgrace rather than just an unaffordable economic price that any part of mankind should ever live through such a thing again.

There were two main lasting economic effects of the war. First was the relative, as well as absolute, advance of the United States. Its manufacturing output rose by almost a half between 1913 and 1925, while that of Europe (despite the immediate postwar-dip) was virtually unchanged.[9] Its share of world trade rose from a fifth to a third.[10] It was mostly spared the financial and physical ravages of war, and it continued apace to exploit the formidable potential of its growing population, wide-open spaces, technical can-do and entrepreneurial energy to grow ever bigger. By 1929 its manufacturing production was 80 percent above its 1913 level, whereas that in Germany was up only 17 percent and Britain's, in its best year before 1935, not at all. By contrast, Russia/USSR and Italy both also posted 80 percent increases, from low starting levels, and Japan had more than tripled its output.

The second lasting effect was the final disruption of the whole open-trading, gold-standard-based, international economy of the nineteenth century. The system had been losing ground to the advancing economic nationalism and protectionism of important new powers, including the United States, Germany and Japan, for more than a decade. But it took the world war to force the suspension of the gold standard even in Britain, to shatter the verities of macroeconomic stability, otherwise revered as Gladstonian finance, as government after government reached for the solvent of deficit finance and to disrupt forever the trade patterns that Britain's version of free trade had laid down seventy years earlier.[11]

Before the war was over, the first of several botched attempts to find a better way forward—or back, to the supposed golden age of the mid-nineteenth-century international economy—began. In November 1917

(October by the local, unreformed calendar) the Russian revolution violently transferred power from the absolutist Romanov dynasty, with a brief seven-month interlude of quasi-parliamentary government, to the upstart Bolshevik Party.[12]

The inspirations for this event included unusually, in addition to all the usual motives for the overthrow of an oppressive—albeit reformist—regime, an elaborate body of theory justifying and giving form to its proposed transformation of the economy and society through the agency of revolution followed by a so-called dictatorship of the proletariat, reinforced by a "Red terror." Its principal authors were, of course, Karl Marx (1818–1883), Friedrich Engels (1820–1895) and V. I. Ulyanov (Lenin, 1870–1924).

The final result of the required transformation would be communism, a state of society in which each would be supplied "according to his needs" and each would contribute "according to his ability," in which all property would be owned in common and in which all would be equal in a classless society.[13] This state of society was seen as remedying the injustices and contradictions of its predecessor, bourgeois capitalism, which necessarily derives all value from the labor used to create it while rewarding the laborer with less than the true value of his work. Indeed, according to the "scientific" history the Marxists offered, rooting all explanations in economic causation, especially in the basic modes of production (e.g., feudalism or capitalism), the eventual collapse of capitalism was inevitable. This did not, however, remove the need to strive to the uttermost to "make the revolution."[14]

Because of the powerful interests arrayed against the full achievement of communist justice, extreme ruthlessness was required during the transition between the overthrow of capitalism and the final establishment of communism. This ruthlessness had to be exercised by the state, controlled by the party, until as communism dawned the state would wither away.

Communism—and the socialist society that would pave the way to it according to the Marxist view of socialism—would be morally superior to capitalism because it would be fair, not depriving workers of the true value of their labor. Marx and Engels, it should be noted, had begun their collaboration in Paris as far back as 1844 and were much influenced by the social distress that industrialism had by then generated in Britain.[15]

But communism and the socialist road to it would also be more efficient, lacking the contradictions of capitalism, of which the trade cycle, periodic "overproduction" and diminishing returns to investment—forcing capitalists to look wider and wider afield to find suitable outlets for the reinvestment of their ever accumulating profits and so drawing them along the path of colonialism, imperialism and war—were thought to be examples. The Russian revolutionaries and those who for a while admired them from afar believed that in both moral and practical terms they had the key to a better economic system than that which had, they thought, just convulsed the world in war, sucking in imperial Russia until the new rulers abruptly withdrew from the conflict by the Treaty of Brest-Litovsk in early 1918.

The subsequent history of Russian communism can be examined under four main headings: Stalin's tyranny, interwar economic performance, the great patriotic war and the era of the cold war. The last belongs in the next chapter. The first three can be quickly summarized for the purposes of our present inquiry.

The revolution immediately ran into immense difficulties. The Russian economy and society were by 1917 in a state of near collapse under the pressures of war. The czarist regime's grip on affairs had been slipping for a decade since the humiliating military and naval defeats by Japan at the battle of Mukden and in the Tsushima Strait in 1905, as Nicholas II struggled alternately to modernize and liberalize his country and then to reimpose his crumbling authority.[16] The war itself, on Germany's eastern front, had strained Russia's transport system to near breakdown, diverted the capacity of its nascent industries to war production, cut it off from imported products and caused acute food shortages, raging inflation and waves of strikes.[17]

The Bolsheviks' early struggles to manage the situation by nationalizing large factories and all the banks, centralizing foreign trade under government control and canceling all previous government debts produced further chaos in both agriculture and industry.[18] The Treaty of Brest-Litovsk obliged the new Soviet government to abandon two-fifths of the country's industrial capacity and crucial grain-producing areas located in the forfeited territories of Ukraine, Belorussia and the Baltic region.[19] Russia was immediately plunged into a bitter civil war as the new regime fought "white" counterrevolutionary armies, who were supported by foreign forces sent to crush the revolution. In all, 10 million people died, far more than the total number of combatants killed in World War I.[20]

By the end of 1920, Russia's economy had collapsed. Industrial output was one-eighth of its 1913 level. Food production and distribution were utterly disrupted. The harvest was two-fifths lower than the average in the five years before the war. Famine afflicted the towns. Transport and communications parodied their names. Peasant revolt threatened on a scale unseen for more than a century.[21]

Lenin decided that the time had come for a tactical retreat. Decrees, requisitions, commands and the energies of the proliferating secret police could no longer stand against the macrothreat of economic and social implosion. In early 1921 the party embraced what became known as the "new economic policy," which increased the space allowed for market forces and private enterprise at the local level in both industry and the countryside. This, though profoundly controversial among the communists, at least enabled the economy to function sufficiently for the new regime to avoid final catastrophe and retain power. In fact farm production got back to its 1913 level by 1926, as did industrial output two years later.[22]

But by then an even more fateful change had occurred. Lenin had been struck down by a series of strokes, and he died in January 1924. Effective political power remained concentrated in the central organs of the party, especially the Politburo. But already in 1922 the newly appointed general secretary of the party, a Georgian called Josef Dzhugashvili (1879–1953), who had worked his way up the party hierarchy by stealth rather than ideological brilliance, understood that ultimately power lay with whoever could deliver the votes in the Politburo and other key party forums and that the way to achieve this was to place your own creatures in such positions.[23]

This the general secretary, by that time known as Stalin, set about doing, and by 1928 he had cemented his own absolute tyranny of the party, having discredited, displaced and sooner or later killed all his rivals. He extended this tyranny to the Soviet Union itself over the next decade as he developed political policing to levels of ruthlessness and scales of deployment seldom if ever before contemplated.

It is possible to argue that some aspects of this extreme centralization of political control and abnegation of all personal rights, even the right to life itself, were impelled by the extraordinary requirements of the crash modernization of a preindustrial society and, later, by the exigencies of the life-or-death struggle with the Nazis. But it is hard not to conclude from the wealth of information increasingly available about the egregious life and conduct of this monster among men that the primary driving force of his odious career was anything other than the lust for absolute power, in one with such severe personality defects that he would almost certainly have been recognized for and rejected as a dangerous lunatic in any society less deeply disturbed than Russia after 1917.[24]

It remains an important question how far the economic performance of the Soviet Union in its first twenty years warrants any of the claims that were made for the greater efficiency, even if not for any greater fairness, of the Russian brand of centralized economic planning and state ownership. A quagmire of statistical uncertainty awaits anyone eager to draw up a sharp-edged account of Soviet economic growth in this period. Methodological traps and ideological lies compete to lead historians astray. It is clear that the figures issued by communist officialdom at the time and subsequently hugely exaggerate the achievements. But it is also clear that there were extraordinary accomplishments, horrifying though many of their human consequences were.

An economy seeking rapid development from a low level normally requires large injections of capital from outside. These were denied to the Soviet Union both by its own and by its neighbors' attitudes to the Soviet economic system. The only alternative source of the required savings was to increase the gap between its own citizens' earnings and their consumption by forcing that consumption down to even lower levels than they were already suffering. This, it seems, was actually achieved, with consumption falling from the 80 percent of national income that is customary in most modern societies to little over half, something that would be possible only under extreme totalitarian rule.[25]

As a result large resources were available for industrial development as well as military expenditure, and a huge proliferation of industrial plants, in themselves also huge, occurred in many parts of the Soviet Union. Manufacturing output may have been as much as eight times as high in 1938 as it was in 1913, whereas in the United States and Germany it was about one-half higher, in Britain it was only one-seventh higher, and in Japan it was five and a half times higher, though all except Japan had started from much higher base levels.[26] Industrial output in the USSR probably surpassed that of Britain, the pioneer of the industrial revolution, by the late 1930s.[27] Russia was not just population and space and snow and ice. It was an economy that could outbuild and outsupply Germany in tanks, ammunition and aircraft in the mortal struggle that began in 1941.

None of this definitively proves anything about the growth potential of the Soviet economic system, any more than the circumstances of Mikhail Gorbachev's voluntary partial withdrawal from command economics in the 1980s definitively proves the contrary. It has long been evident that extraordinary economic production can be stimulated by nationally concerted efforts for a time, when exceptional pressures seem to warrant it. The Dunkirk spirit, the Apollo space program, the success of Japan's Ministry of International Trade and Industry in the heyday of Japanese postwar economic recovery attest in different ways to the prodigious response governments can sometimes command or evoke.

It has long also been clear that governments are at their least effective when they have to operate year in and year out in the dark, cut off from the signals and information that markets give of changing consumer choices, changing technologies, changing efficiency and changing opportunities. Governments find it exceedingly difficult, however great their police powers, to replicate the incentives markets naturally set to encourage suppliers to satisfy consumers as efficiently as possible, though they can be very effective in providing incentives—positive and negative—for compliant political behavior.

It is also clear that to the extent that governments can force savings upon their population—whether by taxes, inflation or rationing—increased investment, at least in name, becomes possible. And if such investment is achieved, this may dramatically increase capacity, especially if that capacity is easy to specify—another steel factory of the same type as the last—and if it is measured physically. It all becomes much more difficult, however, when the secondary effects of such suasion are taken into account.

Deprived of a reasonable opportunity to consume, people may simply prefer not to work, seeing no point in earning what they cannot spend, and if the deprivation denies them food, then malnutrition may make them unable to work. The syndrome summed up in the quip "They pretend to pay us, and we pretend to work" lies at the heart of the probable eventual failure of economic systems that rely on centrally set strategic goals and administrative hierarchies. It also becomes increasingly difficult in the absence of market information to specify just how much and what type of investment ought to be made; huge resources may be wasted investing in obsolete or surplus facilities.

But these are long-term problems and need not show up as potentially fatal weaknesses for a generation or more, especially if competitor systems appear at the same time to be suffering from rather more drastic and immediate flaws of their own. Measured physically and by the short-to-medium timescale of the industrial modernization desired at the moment, the quantitative accomplishments of the Soviet Union up to 1938 were, even after the fullest discounting for propaganda exaggeration, formidable and in many ways astonishing. The feet may have been of clay, albeit slow-moving clay, but on them stood for several decades an indubitable giant, unhappily dependent on a diet of human beings and animated by the mind of a fiend.

In 1941 all the giant's strength and all the fiend's purpose were suddenly required to face a new challenge from another fiend-directed giant, the Third German Reich. The scale and human consequences of that ordeal were without precedent. At its end the Soviet people had suffered death and destruction as probably no such population had ever suffered before, certainly outside China. They were still waiting, as in 1914 and 1917, for that better way forward—or backward—to a world in which one country's or one system's advance need not be seen as a defeat for its neighbors. They were still waiting for a world in which mankind could play a positive-sum game and so share in the general interest—not of rival nations and ideologies, but of each person—in becoming less poor.

The third key event in the sequence of botched attempts to get human economic affairs back onto a healthier path than the economic nationalism of the beginning of the century was the Peace of Paris, including the Treaty of Versailles, which was negotiated between the Allies and Germany in the half year after the armistice at the end of World War I.[28]

The confusion of Allied aims, the incompatibility of the protagonists and the degrading effects of the compromises made in the process of negotiation are memorably summed up by Keynes in his best-seller, *The*

Economic Consequences of the Peace: "These were the personalities of Paris . . . : Clemenceau, aesthetically the noblest; the President [Woodrow Wilson], morally the most admirable; Lloyd George, intellectually the subtlest. Out of their disparities and weaknesses the Treaty was born, child of the least worthy attributes of each of its parents, without nobility, without morality and without intellect."[29]

The treaty (and the other treaties with successor powers of the other defeated enemies of the Allies: Austria, Hungary, Bulgaria and Turkey) was founded on no coherent or agreed analysis of the forces that had led to war and on no consistent realistic purpose of building a better world in which such calamities would be unlikely to recur. The dream of a better world—free of war and consisting of free democratic states—certainly illuminated President Wilson's mind, and his Fourteen Points were supposed to embody the building blocks of such a better world. But they were mainly abstract, idealistic and formalistic. They did little to create the conditions of a true prosperity based on effective cooperation. Yet that was what was needed to lead mankind, especially European mankind, away from the temptations of nationalism and war.

The League of Nations was to discipline nations that misbehaved, but its powers were weak, especially after the United States refused to join, and its agenda of political disputes was not matched by any effective machinery for promoting constructive economic and monetary behavior. The roots of the next war lay not in any simple failure of the league to play the international policeman. They lay in the massive economic malfunctions of the 1920s and 1930s, which primed whole populations for the desperate doctrines that made war the solution rather than the problem.

A contributory cause of this economic hole in the design of the postwar order may well have been the absence of what economists have come to call a "hegemonic" power imposing structure on others and itself bearing at least some of the costs, as well as enjoying hegemonic privileges. According to this view, Britain had played such a role in the mid-nineteenth century as the guarantor of the international economy built around the openness of a unified global trading environment and the monetary stability of the gold standard. After 1918 Britain was no longer strong enough, and the United States was not yet convinced of the need for it to take on such a role. So the role was unfilled, except collectively and imperfectly in a series of ad hoc grand economic conferences organized by the league and in a widely shared faith that the real answer was to restore the gold standard.[30]

In modern terms we would say that there was no sufficient recognition of the concept of macroeconomic stability or of the rules and cooperation required for its achievement. There was no mechanism nudging the world back toward free and open trade of the kind that had been disrupted both by prewar nationalism and wartime controls. Nor was there a monetary framework to ensure adequate liquidity and appropriate balance-of-payments adjustment, let alone domestic price stability.

These deficiencies in the design of the postwar world were hugely aggravated by the disastrous direct effects of other parts of the peace. Article 231 of the Treaty of Versailles made Germany and its allies directly responsible for "causing all the loss and damage . . . as a consequence of the war."[31] On this foundation of "war guilt" was erected a huge structure of reparations—compensation and indemnity payments Germany was to make to the victors.[32]

Although there were ample precedents for such payments in the terms imposed upon France after its defeats in 1815 and again in 1870, there was insufficient appreciation of the economic implications of requiring transfers on such a scale as were now demanded.[33] The war had left Britain and France owing more to the United States, from whom they had borrowed, than they could pay unless they got the money from Germany. The United States refused to cancel these debts on the simple grounds that it was entitled to its money.[34]

Lloyd George's proposal to cancel all war debts and reparations foundered on this rock, and in the end France was able to impose on Germany the maximum amount of reparations it believed it could extract, $33 billion, equivalent to about twice Germany's annual national income.[35] To pay this by transferring real resources to the recipients, Germany would need to run an equivalent surplus in its balance of payments in order to earn the gold necessary to make the payments. The German population would need to work to produce the exports while consuming the far smaller quantity of imports that could be afforded, consistent with the necessary surplus. This implied such a huge gap between the incomes Germans would be earning and the much lower living standards they could be permitted that taxes would have to preempt nearly half the German national income, according to Keynes's calculations at the time.[36] This, he believed, was a political impossibility as well as economic nonsense, which would cause either the scheme or the German political economy or both to break down.

What actually happened was that real resources were never transferred from Germany to the Allies on anything approaching the scale envisaged by the Reparations Commission. The German population was unwilling to make the necessary sacrifices, and the receiving nations were not at all happy to find jobs at home obliterated by a massive inflow of cheap imports from Germany. Instead, the payments were made out of private capital inflows into Germany caused, before 1924, by the mistaken belief of foreigners that the mark must soon recover some of the huge depreciation it had suffered and, after 1924, by U.S. investments following the Dawes Plan of that year for stabilizing the German economy.

In this way a purely financial circle was completed, with funds flowing from Germany to France, Britain and the United States and then back to Germany. As a result the economic nonsense of reparations—impossibly large net transfers of real goods and services—never happened on the ground and so cannot be blamed for subsequent economic failures in Europe. But the political consequences of the reparations and the Allied war debts problem were a different matter. The normally clinical Foreman-Peck lets himself go to the extent of a large conclusion: "The war debts and reparation issue caused political instability and government deflation throughout the 1920s, culminating in the German deflationary policies of the early 1930s that helped Hitler to power, and which perhaps contributed to the crucial failure in 1931 of the Austrian Credit-Anstalt bank."[37]

The sequence of this causality was that Germany's initial attempts to meet its obligations by real transfers of resources failed, as we have seen, because the postwar Weimar government was too weak to impose the required sacrifices on the German people and because the postwar British and French economies were too weak to withstand the impact on their unemployment of a flood of German exports. The foreign exchange markets realized that Germany would be paying out as reparations gold that it had not earned by any true balance-of-payments surplus or by any balancing private capital inflow. They therefore speculated against the mark, whose value fell precipitously.[38] Although this generated the short-term capital inflow intended to take advantage of an expected bounce-back of the mark, it also provoked the German government at the end of 1922 to cease all payments.[39]

France and Belgium took this as sufficient justification for occupying the Ruhr, in January 1923, in an attempt to extract coal in lieu of the overdue payments.[40] German workers resisted passively by sabotaging output and distribution, and the German government found itself obliged to square the circle, on pain of social breakdown, by providing the money to pay wages to nonproducing workers as well as compensation to dispossessed owners.[41] (It has, however, also been suspected of deliberately taking this action in order to prove that it could not pay reparations.)[42]

Whatever the reason, the German government created huge quantities of paper money simply by printing it, with the inevitable result that its purchasing power collapsed or—which is the same thing—prices soared, not just by double or triple or even ten- or a hundredfold, but by more than 500-billion-fold in one year.[43] In other words, a 500-mark note, worth in 1922 about $1, had a purchasing power a year later of about $0.000000001, or one-billionth of a dollar, not merely less than the paper it was written on but effectively nothing. All wealth held or recorded in nominal money values had been obliterated.

The effect of such hyperinflation is to compress into months, weeks and even days the changes in relative wealth and social status that normally occur over decades and generations. The human and political rage this generates can easily be imagined; German society, already scarred by war and a humiliating peace, now also had to endure the random redistribution overnight of its most basic structures and expectations.

A solid burgher became a pauper. A hopeless debtor could at one bound be free of all encumbrances and a chancy speculator become a man of property. Workers were in the main better protected, seeing in the final stages of the crisis their wages adjusted daily, but a boss who failed to adjust his prices fast enough could quickly become an unemployed hand.

All this occurred before any of them knew what was happening, let alone why. Conspiracy and paranoia filled the air, and the scene was set for the ruthless exploitation of extreme fears and hatreds by any demagogue with a plausible tale to tell. Almost any tale seemed plausible; the only wonder is that German democratic society survived this shock for another decade.[44]

As so often in human affairs, one awful experience distorted perceptions and behavior for a long time after: the phenomenon familiarly known as "fighting the last war." Inflation aversion became an overriding preoccupation of those who had lived through the German nightmare of 1923. It impaired their ability to understand, prevent or manage the opposite evil, depression, when it came.[45] Indeed, it was not only the Germans who had suffered from inflation during and after the war; all combatant nations had in practice suspended the convertibility link between their currencies and gold during the hostilities. The surge in government spending only partially financed by taxes (for example, a mere quarter in Britain in 1915–1916) that war commonly causes hugely boosted the pressure of demand on available resources, with the natural result that prices tended to rise.[46] Immediately after the war a short boom, driven by plentiful, pent-up cash supplies and the general wish to rebuild war losses and damage, sent prices soaring.[47] Runaway inflation did not become universal, but Austria, Hungary, Poland, Bulgaria and Greece were all ravaged by price explosions (by 14,000-fold in Austria compared with prewar, 23,000-fold in Hungary and 2.5-million-fold in Poland), reducing the value of their currencies also virtually to nil.[48]

The whole experience, war and immediate postwar, was less inflationary in the United States than in Europe both because the war affected the United States less, though it had the strongest postwar boom, and because its still huge stock of only partially tapped resources of land, manpower and materials could and did respond more elastically to the surge in demand than in continental Europe.[49] In the United States the short, sharp boom quickly turned into the classic postwar slump familiar throughout history as governments demobilize their forces, stop buying armaments and try to retrench their budgets.[50] Two years (1921–1922) of business depression with sharply falling prices and wages spread to Britain and most parts of the world other than continental Europe, where inflation continued.[51]

By 1924 the scene was thus set for the fourth key event of this chapter, the first attempt to restore stability to a world economy racked by violent cyclical swings in both prices and economic activity. The return to the gold standard, though already accomplished by the United States immediately after the war, was seen as the panacea.

Earlier attempts at conferences in Brussels (1920), Genoa (1922) and elsewhere to stabilize world currencies had mobilized large loans and promoted currency reorganizations in various countries. But it was the Dawes Plan of 1924, negotiated by the first director of the U.S. Budget Bureau, Charles Dawes (1865–1951), that set the world on a new course back to the gold standard.[52] A new German currency, called the reichsmark, was successfully stabilized by a large international loan, budget retrenchment and the restoration of the prewar gold parity, which meant that the new marks replaced the old, depreciated marks at the rate of one reichsmark for 1 trillion old marks.[53]

The Dawes Plan also rescheduled Germany's reparations payments in what was supposed to be a more realistic way, though as we have seen it was the return of confidence in Germany and the resulting inflow of U.S. capital that actually enabled payments to be made. (They continued until confidence collapsed again at the end of the 1920s, the inflow stopped and the repayments were halted forever, being formally abandoned in 1932.)[54]

Other currencies swiftly returned to the gold standard. By 1929 virtually every European country, as well as many others outside Europe, had adopted a gold parity. Some, like Britain in 1925 and Sweden, the Netherlands, Switzerland, Denmark and Norway, returned to their prewar values. Others, like France, Italy and Belgium, accepted a more realistic depreciation of between 70 and 85 percent, reflecting the rise in retail prices since 1913. Still others, like Germany and most of the Central and East European countries, as well as Portugal, effectively launched new currencies whose units were worth a negligible fraction of their prewar equivalents, reflecting their hyperinflation in the early 1920s.[55]

The general return to the gold standard and its actual or alleged consequences are among the grand topics of economic history, pitting theories and methods and evidence against one another in a huge debate that admits of no unanimity or even consensus. There was and is a purist case for the gold standard, essentially that it contributes to the efficiency and success of the real economy (the world of production and jobs and living standards) by promoting the efficiency of money as a supporting mechanism of real economic activity.

This it is supposed to do by making it difficult or impossible for unscrupulous statesmen to abuse the money-creating functions of government and by so breeding confidence that any currency based on the gold standard will hold its value. That confidence promotes the efficient use of that currency as a store and standard of value and as a means of settlement. It also discourages inefficient economic behavior driven by speculation on changes in purely nominal or monetary values and thereby constrains the main players in the economy to focus on the profits to be earned by real economic advances based on investment, judgment of consumer preferences and control of costs.

The basic tenet is, "Make money honest and market forces will do the rest." Like all such maxims, it has just enough of truth about it, memorably and compellingly expounded by David Hume (1711–1776), the Scottish philosopher and economist, to divert attention from its deficiencies.[56] It is easy as well as fascinating to see that in very broad terms prices, in any given money, must ultimately reflect some basic relationship between the amount of money and the amount of stuff—or real value—on which it can be spent. This is the bedrock of the quantity theory of money.

So, argued the gold standard devotees, especially those in the mid-1920s who had been scarred by the great inflations, tie the amount of money to something whose supply is relatively fixed and beyond human or political manipulation and prices will be stable, or at least will fluctuate either side of some reliable mean. Gold was the obvious and traditional candidate, given the gradual eclipse of silver during the nineteenth century.

The objectors to this great nineteenth-century symbol of British monetary integrity and economic magnificence complained that its mechanisms were crude, wasteful and wrongly gave priority to nominal, that is price, stability over real stability, that is of spending, output and jobs. Prices were only forced to revert to their earlier levels by slumps and/or booms.

Moreover, the supply of gold, or, more specifically, of gold available for monetary purposes, was not reliably stable, sometimes increasing or decreasing rapidly and sometimes just too plentiful or too scarce. It was precisely this last phenomenon that inspired the American bimetallists at the end of the nineteenth century to argue that silver as well as gold must be included in the backing for the U.S. dollar so that there could be sufficient money in circulation to support an adequate flow of spending in the American economy.

This was the heart of arguably the most eloquent expression of an economic thesis, when William Jennings Bryan (1860–1925), four times unsuccessful candidate for president of the United States as well as prosecutor in the notorious anti-Darwin "monkey trial" of 1925 in Dayton, Tennessee, declared:

> If they say bi-metallism is good, but we cannot have it until other nations help us, we reply, that instead of having a gold standard because England has, we will restore bi-metallism, and then let England have bi-metallism because the United States has it. If they dare to come out in the open field and defend the gold standard as a good thing, we will fight them to the uttermost. Having behind us the producing masses of this nation and the world, supported by the commercial interests, the labouring interests and the toilers everywhere, we will answer their demand for a gold standard by saying to them: You shall not press down upon the brow of labour this crown of thorns, you shall not crucify mankind upon a cross of gold.[57]

That, despite a better relationship between American prosperity and the gold value of the dollar in the immediately ensuing decade, was in the opinion of a broadening coalition in Britain, from John Maynard Keynes to the Trades Union Congress, precisely what Winston Churchill was doing as British chancellor of the exchequer in 1925 when he nailed the pound back to its old prewar gold standard value (£3, 17 shillings, 10 1/2 pence to an ounce of gold, which made £1 worth $4.86).[58] The crux of the matter has been well analyzed by Charles P. Kindleberger. In true gold standard theory, there can be no unemployment because the unemployed will always be willing to work for less than the employed, thus driving wages down to a level where everyone can work. But, says Kindleberger, after the sharp fall in wages (38 percent in Britain in 1921–1922) in the postwar slump: "For the first time on any substantial scale, the economic system developed an asymmetry: with expansion from full employment one encountered price and wage increases in the manufacturing sector; with contraction, there was stubborn resistance of prices and wages and unemployment."[59]

Keynes explains the reasons in another eloquent passage, which happens also to go to the very heart of many subsequent and furious arguments between "sound money" men and latter-day "Keynesians" and between those who do and do not believe that immutably fixed exchange rates and very large currency areas (e.g., Euroland) are compatible with high employment evenly spread:

> If miners were free to transfer to other industries, if a collier out of work or underpaid could offer himself as a baker, a bricklayer, or a railway porter at a lower wage than is now current in these industries, it would be another matter. But notoriously they are not so free. Like other victims of economic transition in past times, the miners are to be offered the choice between starvation and submission, the fruits of their submission to accrue to the benefit of other classes. But in view of the disappearance of an effective mobility of labour and of a competitive wage level between different industries, I am not sure that they are not worse placed in some ways than their grandfathers were. . . . They are the victims of the economic juggernaut. They represent in the flesh the "fundamental adjustment" engineered by the Treasury and the Bank of England to satisfy the impatience of the City fathers to bridge the "moderate gap" between $4.40 [the realistic value of £1 at the time] and $4.86 [the gold standard value]. *They* (and others to follow) are the "moderate sacrifice" still necessary to ensure the gold standard. The plight of the coal miners is the first, but not—unless we are very lucky—the last of the economic consequences of Mr Churchill."[60]

By 1931 almost fifty of the world's sovereign states, which then was most of them, including all the large ones except the Soviet Union, China and Spain, had been marched up the hill of the gold standard and had duly embraced its rigors. But by September of that year Britain had marched down again, followed by dozens of others over the next year or so, culminating in the newly inaugurated U.S. president Franklin Roosevelt's decision to abandon the gold link for the dollar in April 1933.[61] By 1934 fewer than ten countries clung to gold; by 1937 there were none.[62]

How was it that such a deeply believed and widely supported principle of national and international economic policy was both raised to an almost universal law and dashed to smithereens within barely a decade, despite its apparent success for more than two centuries before World

War I? The short answer is the Great Depression. At worst the gold standard was blamed as the cause; at best it was judged incompatible with efforts to mitigate the slump.

But to give a fuller answer we must now pick up the threads of our story following Churchill's decision to restore the gold standard in Britain in 1925. The pound was overvalued, probably by between 5 and 10 percent.[63] British labor could be competitive, where it was employed making internationally traded goods, only if its money wages could be reduced by that amount. "What wonder that our export trades are in trouble," snaps Keynes.[64]

Within a year Britain was in the grip of its first—and as it turned out only—general strike, as the resistance of the miners to attempts to cut their wages in line with the logic of the gold standard value of the pound spread to a general collision between the government and the organized working classes. The overvaluation of the pound, coming on top of the setbacks Britain had suffered both before and as a consequence of World War I in its competitiveness with other, more recently industrializing nations, meant that the country was almost wholly excluded from the boom enjoyed both in the United States and on continental Europe in the second half of the 1920s. Iron and steel, coal mining, shipbuilding and textiles, the historic backbone of Britain's post–industrial revolution economy, were flat on their backs, producing less in 1929 than in 1913.[65]

The countries of continental Europe benefited from adopting much more realistic gold values for their currencies when they returned to the gold standard after the great inflations. And the United States, though restoring the full pre-1914 parity for the dollar, was much less dependent than Britain on international trade for its internal economic vigor and had suffered less inflationary wage and price increases during the war. The 1920s in the United States saw the full flowering of the great new home markets, lubricated by new "buy now, pay later" consumer credit schemes. Cars and their accessories; electrical appliances like radios, vacuum cleaners and refrigerators and the cinema all came of age in a great American boom from 1926 to 1929, propelled by high postwar confidence, technological dynamism and—always indispensable to a boom—easy money.[66] Indeed, American national output grew at the extraordinarily rapid rate of 5.5 percent a year from 1922 to 1929, and unemployment crashed from 11 percent in 1921 to 3.5 percent in the second half of the decade.[67]

The boom in the American economy was act 1 of what we called the fifth key event during the period covered in this chapter, namely, the boom, bubble and crash of the American stock market in the latter 1920s and the subsequent Great Depression. The confidence generated by America's economic expansion during the 1920s and the expectation that the profits associated with this growth would continue—or in the end just a blind faith that stock market prices must rise forever and probably at an accelerating rate—fueled an unprecedented boom on Wall Street.[68]

Stock market prices rose on average by 18 percent a year, more than doubling between March 1926 and October 1929.[69] In an increasingly frenetic atmosphere, daily turnover reached new peaks of 6.9 million shares in November 1928 and 8.2 million shares in March 1929.[70] The illusion that the good times would last indefinitely was strengthened when two brief falls in the stock market were quickly reversed.

But like all speculative bubbles, it burst. On Thursday, 24 October 1929, the date traditionally treated as the beginning of the crash, shares plunged in the morning by as much as 40 Dow Jones points (from 312.76 to 272.32), or 13 percent. On Tuesday the 29th—"Black Tuesday," as it became known—the index slumped by a further 40 points before ending the day at 230.

The Great Crash may be popularly dated to 1929, but what really shattered American self-confidence was the remorseless continuing slide over most of the next three years. On 8 July 1932, the Dow, which had peaked at 386.10 on 3 September 1929, had collapsed to a low of just 40.56.[71] America's big industrial companies had lost all but 90 percent of their stock market value in less than three years. Although John Kenneth Galbraith in his immortal study of the crash seemed to demonstrate that the suicide rate in the United States at this time never deviated from its normal trend, the gallows humor of the period had the check-in clerks in New York hotels asking new arrivals whether they required a room for sleeping or for jumping.

Few issues in economic history have attracted more attention or stimulated more argument than that of the true causal relationship between the antecedent boom (both of the economy and of the stock market), the crash of the stock market and the depression of the economy. The learned Christopher Dow, in his magisterial study of large recessions since 1925, observes dryly: "Economists have gone on arguing about the Great Depression because it was uniquely large, and in the circumstances there can be no 'normal' ways of explaining it. There seem to have been no identifiable exogenous shocks of the size necessary to account for it; and economies are not normally subject to endogenously generated fluctuations of that sort."[72]

After thinking about it for a decade or more at the end of a lifetime of meticulous study of the boom-bust, stop-go cycles in developed economies, he concluded that the main factor was "a swing from high to low consumer and business confidence." He rejected more mechanistic explanations based on mainly monetary mismanagement, either flowing from America's return to the gold standard a decade earlier or caused by the Federal Reserve's handling of interest rates and the money supply. Specifically, he attributes the beginning of the depression to the excessive preceding boom itself, to the Wall Street crash and to sundry aggravating external influences, such as a recession in Germany and weak demand in primary producing countries. He attributes its continuation and depth mainly to the widespread bank closures—he even uses the word "meltdown"—which resulted both from the natural bursting of the preceding bubble of financial overconfidence and "the fragility of a banking structure organised locally and out of reach of any system of central bank support."[73]

Common sense can be a false guide in economics, especially macroeconomics and especially where the possibility of the fallacy of composition (believing that the big picture is the vignette blown up) lurks. Indeed, Milton Friedman has wisely observed that "it's generally correct that what's true for the individual is the opposite of what's true for the society," an aspect of his teaching that appears to have eluded Margaret (later Baroness) Thatcher, British Prime Minister (1979–1990).[74] Nonetheless, it is almost impossible to immerse oneself in study of the buildup to the 1929 boom on Wall Street without coming to the conclusion that it was in itself a sufficient condition of the crash.

When prices reach and are sustained at extreme heights largely by a belief that they will continue to rise as they have in the recent past without any detectable counterpart in those things—company profits—which give value to shares in the long run, it becomes a certainty that the falsity of this belief must sooner or later dawn and that, when it dawns, prices will collapse. The higher they have risen and the greater and longer the suspense of reality that accompanies the rise, the harder and further will be the fall. Such a truism manifestly applied by the middle months of 1929, as indeed it did again seventy years later—with an aftermath not yet revealed to the author at the time of writing, though the reader may be better informed.

Even if the crash is sufficiently explained by the nature of the boom that begat it, it did not come out of clear blue economic sky. The real economy—the world of production, jobs, incomes and spending—began to turn down in the United States in the summer of 1929. Car production peaked in March.[75] Industrial production fell from June. Personal incomes and prices fell sharply from August to October. Farm incomes had been stagnant since 1925 because of world conditions, and farm prices in the United States began a plunge of 50 percent from 1929 to 1932.[76]

This evidence that the real economy turned down before the crash has persuaded some economists that the crash was merely a financial epiphenomenon of the real business cycle and that though it was caused by the economic change of trend, it exerted little causal influence back onto the real economy. This view is too mechanistic. Certainly, the first straws of a colder economic wind may have been among the sharp points that finally pricked the bubble in October. But given its stretched vulnerability by then, almost anything could be blamed as the final cause.

More important, it beggars historical belief to suppose that so huge a financial shock as the Wall Street collapse did not profoundly influence economic behavior, directly and indirectly, both by its effects on men's minds—what is called "confidence"—and by its effects on the solvency of many key players, large and not so large, in the industrial and commercial life of the United States. As Kindleberger puts it: "The crash led to a scramble for liquidity on the part of both lenders to the call market and owners of stocks. In the process orders were cancelled and loans called. . . . The deflation [was] communicated to fragile commodity markets and durable goods industries. The stock market crash [started] a process that took on a dynamic of its own."[77]

How far the crash worked its way through into the rash of bank failures, which by almost universal consent appears to have been a vital link in the causal chain leading to severe depression, is hard to pin down. Banks fail when public confidence in them declines and when they have inadequate reserves or size or central bank support to ride the storm. Banks had been failing in the United States from 1925 in the Midwest after the downturn in farm incomes and prices, but such failures did not become a spectacular part of the general economic scene until late 1930, when the collapse of Caldwell and Company in Tennessee and the Bank of the United States in New York sparked a wider panic.[78] Failure was not the only way in which banks transmitted the loss of financial confidence back into the real economy. They also reduced their lending and called in existing loans as their confidence in their customers' ability to repay declined.

The best way, therefore, of looking at this complex of mutually interacting events—real economy, stock market, business and consumer confidence and banking behavior—is to see it as exactly that, a complex, with each component being acted upon by and acting back upon the others in what became a ferocious downward spiral. But even spirals require explanations of what sets them off and what brings them to an end. Milton Friedman and Anna Schwartz offer such an explanation, namely, the failure of the authorities (the Federal Reserve and/or the U.S. Treasury) to ensure that the stock of money did not decline.[79]

This has been challenged on the grounds both that the money stock did not decline until November 1930—and only slightly until March 1931—and that the Federal Reserve could not have forced unwilling banks to increase their loans and so boost the money supply even if it had been their policy to attempt this.[80] To an extent the argument is semantic in that it is almost always possible to see mismanagement by those in charge as the cause of any untoward event, since it would not have happened if those authorities had taken sufficiently effective action to prevent it.

To the historian, however, the question depends more on how far such preventive action would at the time have been regarded as part of the normal order of things and therefore on how far the failure to take it sticks out as an exceptional event explaining the consequences. The Federal Reserve can certainly be represented as complicit in the buildup of the boom—as Galbraith effectively shows, pinpointing the extreme anxiety of the authorities not to be blamed for sparking off the crash that they feared might follow from any cooling action they might take.[81] But it was not part of the general intellectual currency of the late 1920s that the relatively recently formed Federal Reserve (established in 1913) could or should iron out large fluctuations in the economy by stabilizing the total stock of money through its control of interest rates and its influence on bank reserves and so on bank behavior.

It seems more consonant with the historian's normal way of thinking to see the exceptional influences that produced the unique severity of the Great Depression as lying in the extreme euphoria of the boom at its peak (though booms and bubbles are a recurring pattern in modern financial history) and in the exceptional vulnerability of the banking system to a general loss of confidence. The crash was the natural, perhaps inevitable consequence of the first and played a significant part in converting the second into a widespread pattern of contraction and closure that ensured that New York's loss of nerve reached throughout the entire American continent, not just as sensational news but as a direct assault on the wealth, liquidity, incomes and spending of American entrepreneurs, consumers and workers generally.

The Great Depression, however precisely caused, was a uniquely severe experience in the United States by the standards of the trade and business cycles since the early nineteenth century. Between 1929 and 1932 the national output of the United States fell by 10 percent a year, a total decline of 32 percent, with industrial production falling by close to half, a contraction without precedent in the industrial world.[82] Measured relative to where output would have been if it had continued along the line of its historic trend, the actual level of output in 1932 was down 46 percent, overwhelmingly the most drastic setback suffered by any mature nation's peacetime output at any time in modern history—until that suffered by the Soviet Union and its successor states between 1989 and 1998, when the decline was 45 percent absolute, never mind relative to rising trends (see the next chapter).[83] Unemployment soared from 3.1 percent in 1929 to 23.6 percent in 1932, also a peacetime record before or since.[84]

In other parts of the world, the contraction was less acute. German output in 1932 was 15.8 percent below 1929 levels, and for Europe as a whole the shortfall below the historic trend was a mere 12 percent.[85] Britain's experience, judged by national aggregates, was much milder, though starting from a position in 1929 that was conspicuously boom-free. The fall in output in 1931 was less than in most other developed economies apart from Italy, and the 1929 peak was recouped more rapidly.[86]

None of this has prevented the 1930s from going down in British folk memory as the decade of mass unemployment and great social misery. Unemployment actually fell, from 15.6 percent in 1932 to 8 percent in 1937.[87] The latter level (give or take changed statistical definitions) was not again exceeded until 1981.[88] The former was not reached even at the trough of the 1980s recession (11.2 percent in 1986).

The year 1933 was the hinge of the interwar period. Franklin Delano Roosevelt replaced Herbert Hoover as president of the United States and launched the New Deal. The United States went off gold. World trade and the depression in the United States touched their low points, having done so in Britain and Germany in 1932.[89] In January 1933 Adolf Hitler became the head of the German government; later, the day after Roosevelt's inauguration on 4 March, Hitler won "full powers," to govern by decree.

Roosevelt's diagnosis of the collapse of American confidence was memorably psychological:

> This great nation will endure as it has endured, will revive and will prosper. So first of all let me assert my firm belief that the only thing we have to fear is fear itself—nameless, unreasoning, unjustified terror which paralyses needed efforts to convert retreat into advance. . . . The people of the United States have not failed. In their need they have registered a mandate that they want direct, vigorous action. They have asked for discipline and direction under leadership.[90]

Hitler, broadcasting a month earlier, blamed political conspiracy, but like Roosevelt he diagnosed a mood of despair and predicated revival on strong action: "If Germany is to experience political and economic revival, a decisive act is required: We must overcome the demoralisation of Germany by the Communists."[91]

Full recovery from the depression came only when these two leaders were at war nine years later, but the long, slow climb out of the pit began in 1933.[92] Demand and output in the United States began to rise about twice as fast as the long-term trend rate of growth, thereby taking up slack, reducing the depression and bringing down unemployment. The recovery was uneven—there was a hiccup in 1938, and even in 1939 unemployment was still over 11 percent, compared with 3 percent in 1929—but it was real.[93]

The key explanations for the recovery need to include a certain natural tendency for economies to return to trend rates of growth after exceptional shocks have disturbed them for a while. But the U.S. recovery did more than just return to trend, and the most compelling explanations for this center on the policy actions of the Roosevelt administration, including the abandonment of the gold standard, greatly increased government expenditure under the New Deal, lower interest rates and the stabilization of the banking system through the introduction of deposit insurance. But another factor, perhaps equally important, was a change of mood, as the activism and style of Roosevelt's leadership seemed to demonstrate the truth of his inaugural analysis of America's problem.[94] Confidence returned, if only gradually.

In Europe the recovery came too late to remedy the sins of omission and commission of the postwar settlement in Paris. The challenge was to get the world economy back onto a healthy footing, prosperous and purged of nationalist rivalries, open to the enterprise of individuals and businesses, blind to the distractions of national status symbols and competition. That was the way to retrace its steps out of the cul-de-sac that led to war.

We have already seen that the follies of reparations and war debt, the inattention to the need for a benign monetary and trading order and the bungled return to the gold standard had contributed to, without being the sole causes of, the European hyperinflations and the subsequent reaction into hyperorthodoxy and depression.[95] Deflationary policies forced world trade into a downward spiral, declining 60 percent in value and 35 percent in volume between 1929 and 1932.[96] And although America alone accounted for perhaps 80 percent of the global depression, industrial production in Europe fell by over a quarter between 1929 and 1932. Growing protectionism, including the Smoot-Hawley tariffs of 1930 in the United States, were a classic reaction to hard times, and they added their torque to the beggar-my-neighbor screw of national policies that sought to pass their unemployment problems on to their trading partners.

It is hard not to conclude that the lamentable state of economic affairs in Europe that developed from 1928 to 1932 was appreciably a consequence of mismanagement at an international level. It was, of course, not the responsibility of any specific country or agency to govern at the world level or to ensure stable and open monetary and trading structures, still less to manage demand so as to eliminate booms and busts. No power was both able and disposed to play the role of the single hegemon imposing order on the rest. But that does not remove the historian's right to see this gap in economic governance at the global level, whatever the virtuous aspirations of the League of Nations, as a reason for what went wrong.

By the time that recovery started, the mischief had been done. And so we come to our sixth and last key event of this chapter, the rise of Hitler leading to World War II. By 1933 Hitler had been able to persuade a sufficient number of Germans that their sufferings were the consequence of an unjust peace and that their salvation was to be found in his brand of extreme nationalism. As Charles Feinstein and his coauthors say, "The evils of the Nazi regime must be accounted among the worst effects of the Great Depression."[97]

This is not in any way to diminish the historical responsibility of Hitler and the other Nazi leaders for what they said and did. But it is hard to conceive that they could have succeeded had postwar Germany under the Weimar constitution enjoyed the kind of prosperity and stability that West Germany enjoyed in the 1950s and 1960s. In this sense the arguments among historians about how much credit the Nazis should be given for economic recovery in Germany in the 1930s are beside the point. Once they were in power with the objectives they had, unclear though these were to many contemporary observers, the eventual outcome was probable, however successful or unsuccessful Hitler might be in rebuilding the economy. Some have likened not merely his language but also his deeds to those of Roosevelt, as a proactive administration launching public works and willy-nilly giving a sort of Keynesian boost through increased government spending.[98] But his purpose was entirely different; any economic effects of his policies were incidental to his plans for Germany's final triumph over its enemies. Putting people back to work, or at least removing the appearance and the costs of their unemployment, was certainly an early objective, and it achieved substantial statistical results. But the real aim of successive four-year plans was to prepare for war by favoring heavy industries, airplane manufacture and armaments, as well as strategic infrastructural improvements like the autobahn. Private consumption received a shrinking share of national output; military and militarily useful investment preempted a growing share.[99]

This is not the place to pursue the arguments about whether the Nazis could have been stopped if other world leaders had been willing to recognize the truth about Hitler's aims earlier and to act more resolutely to stop him. Perhaps they could have succeeded, perhaps not. But the historian can only be sure that they did not, and that what Hitler did he did and was able to do because the economic system of the world after Versailles, especially in Germany, functioned badly enough for rampant nationalism to command sufficient assent. That was the essential failure of the interwar period, and it brought Europe and the wider world back in 1939 to where it had been in 1914.

CHAPTER NINE

False Dawns? 1945–1999

DURING THE FINAL FIFTY YEARS OF THE SECOND MILLENNIUM A.D., the human species grew as never before. Total population more than doubled from 2.5 billion in 1950 to 6 billion in October 1999.[1] It took only thirty-nine years from 1960 for the number of people on the planet to double, and only twelve years from 1987 to increase by one billion.[2] The sheer scale of this explosion in numbers appears to show that the world was following north-western Europe's example in the late eighteenth and early nineteenth centuries and escaping the Malthusian constraints of famine, disease, and war on population growth by rapid and seemingly limitless economic growth.

Over the same fifty years, the wealth of man increased even faster than the global population. The world's economy more than quintupled in size, and average income per head increased by 2.6 times to reach U.S. $5,000 a year.[3] One aspect of higher living standards was the seventeen-fold increase in the number of motor vehicles on the world's roads, from about 40 million in 1945 to 680 million by 1997.[4] Improved health care led to a dramatic increase in life expectancy, from thirty-five years to fifty-eight years, itself a principal reason for the population explosion.[5]

Although these impressive global figures for the wealth of man testify to real improvements in many people's lives, they also mask great and increasing inequalities. Between 1960 and 1995, the ratio of income between the richest and poorest 20 percent of the world rose from 30:1 to more than 80:1.[6] An estimated 1.3 billion people—about a quarter of humanity—were living on less than U.S. $1 per day in the 1990s, in a world whose average income was U.S. $14 a day and whose more affluent economies averaged over $50 per day.[7]

Underlying the West's economic success story was the "never again" impulse that developed during World War II. This conviction held that the errors and failures that led to two world wars, especially the more recent failures of the 1920s and 1930s, must never again be allowed to happen.

The world at war, 1939–1945, was divided between its two sides: on the one side Adolf Hitler's German Reich, the other Axis power, Benito Mussolini's Italy, and their Asian ally, Japan; on the other the Soviet Union and the English-speaking Allies, with whatever moral and practical support was intermittently available from the nationalist and communist Chinese and from sundry European resistance movements. Upon the unconditional surrender of the losing side, the opportunity formally presented itself to construct a new order. To the extent of establishing the United Nations, whose constitution recognized the role of the victors (the Soviet Union, the United States and Britain) and their special friends (nationalist-not-yet-communist China and France), this was accomplished for the sphere of international relations and collective security against the kind of unilateral aggression Hitler had launched against his western and eastern neighbors, insanely also declaring war on the United States.

But very soon the deep ideological hostility between the United States and the Soviet Union overcame any feelings of solidarity they had briefly affected as they raced to Berlin in the closing months of the war. The West already had an agenda for reconstructing the world to avoid the blunders of the first half of the century. Joseph Stalin, having prevailed largely alone in the greatest and overwhelmingly most costly war any nation had ever fought, was determined above all to ensure that Germany would never again threaten the mother country, and to extend Soviet power and influence wherever opportunity offered. Very rapidly this led to conflict between the former Allies over Berlin, culminating in 1948–1949 in Stalin's attempt to starve the western sector of the city into submission and the Allied response in the form of the Berlin airlift. From that moment the cold war, initially threatening to become hot, was engaged. The North Atlantic Treaty was made on 4 April 1949 in response to the perceived threat of communist westward expansion beyond the line where the two sides had met at the end of the war, already stigmatized by Winston Churchill the "iron curtain."[8]

The Western agenda for a better world had first been sketched, in what was arguably the most extraordinary feat of forward-looking statesmanship the world witnessed at any time in the twentieth century, by Churchill and Franklin Roosevelt meeting on the British battleship *Prince of Wales* and other ships in Placentia Bay, Newfoundland, in August 1941. At that moment Britain had been driven off the European continent, narrowly escaping annihilation at Dunkirk, and had only survived the looming threat of German invasion and final defeat by a lucky and plucky combination of Nazi errors and aerial valor in the Battle of Britain. British ground forces were on their back foot in North Africa, and convoys from America were being successfully harried by German U-boats and menaced by German battleships. Britain had no active allies outside its own commonwealth and empire. As Churchill wrote in his memoirs, "We were alone, with victorious Germany and Italy engaged in mortal attack upon us, with Soviet Russia a hostile neutral actively aiding Hitler, and Japan an unknowable menace."[9] No reasonable person could have confidently expected survival, let alone victory. As for the United States, opinion was still overwhelmingly opposed to intervention in this European war, and there was therefore no prospect of the nation's becoming a combatant, let alone a victor.

Despite all this, these two extraordinary men found time to meet in a remote recess of the North Atlantic and set down in what they called the "Atlantic Charter," the principles on which the world should be better reconstructed after the war was won.[10] Churchill's first objective was, of course, to secure as soon as possible American assistance in the war, preferably the United States' full engagement as a combatant. The American side's agenda certainly included a strong wish to avoid what was seen as the error of 1918, when the fourteen principles on which the postwar order was to be constructed had to be retrospectively invented and negotiated by Woodrow Wilson. The United States was also historically hostile to Britain's Empire, though not to Britain, and particularly disliked the system of imperial preference in trade that had been embodied in the Ottawa Agreement between Britain and its self-governing dominions in 1932, establishing general tariff preference in favor of commonwealth imports.[11]

Nonetheless, the fundamentally liberal tradition of English-language economics from the time of Adam Smith and David Hume contributed to the common ground that was found in Placentia Bay, galling as it was to British imperialists and, on the left, dirigistes.[12] In addition to general political principles outlawing territorial or other aggrandizement, affirming the right of national self-determination and aspiring to an eventual abandonment by all nations of the use of force, the British and U.S. leaders embraced multilateralism as the informing idea for postwar reconstruction.[13] Expressed in very general terms, this avowed the ideal of free, nondiscriminatory trade and pledged cooperation between all nations in the economic field to raise living standards, promote development and provide social security.

These general principles were further defined in the mutual aid agreement of February 1942, after Pearl Harbor and Hitler's declaration of war on the United States, which had made the country a fighting ally. Article 7 of the agreement established the basis of all subsequent postwar economic planning. It was consciously inspired by a wish to avoid the mistakes of Versailles, such as reparations and war debts; and it laid down economic expansion and liberal trade as the shared goals of a postwar regime, to be held open to all other countries of like mind.[14]

We need not here trace in detail the negotiations over the next five years that led first to the conference and agreement at Bretton Woods, New Hampshire, in the summer of 1944, establishing the International Monetary Fund (IMF) and the International Bank for Reconstruction and Development (the World Bank) and then to the further UN conference at Geneva in 1947, which produced the General Agreement on Tariffs and Trade.[15] The important point for this history is that their authors, many and passionate as were some of their disagreements, were driven by a shared and overriding desire to create a monetary and economic architecture for the postwar world that by emphasizing economic expansion, monetary stability and liberal trade principles would prevent any repetition of the errors and disasters of the interwar period.

The institutions and agreements that emerged reflected both the superior economic leverage of the United States and a large admixture of fudge and compromise. Pure principles jostled with acute national anxieties, especially in Europe, about postwar solvency and employment. But one way and another a new order was born that progressively defined itself as liberal, multilateral and expansionist.[16] This was critically helped by the Marshall Plan, which made huge quantities of dollars (over $11 billion between 1948 and 1951) available to western Europe (the Soviet Union and eastern Europe declined the United States' offer), thereby enabling western Europe to finance its dependence on dollar imports during the period of recovery and reconstruction. Substantial currency realignments in 1949, including the 30 percent devaluation of the British pound, overcame the undervaluation of the U.S. dollar, and the 1950s dawned for the First World as a decade of high employment, price stability and, in war-ravaged Europe and Japan, extremely rapid economic growth, notwithstanding some instability caused by the Korean War boom and subsequent relapse of military spending.

In many, though by no means all, of these developments contemporaries recognized the influence and frequently the hand of John Maynard Keynes, the British economist who had most eloquently denounced the economic follies of Versailles and Churchill's return to the gold standard in 1925. In 1936 Keynes had produced the book that economists for thirty years afterward saw as having explained the Great Depression and shown how to prevent its repetition by manipulating government spending and taxes so as to ensure a sufficient level of demand to employ the full resources of an economy.[17] He joined the British Treasury as an unpaid adviser in 1940, and though he was not at Placentia Bay, he was the main British negotiator with the Americans over lend-lease and the Bretton Woods agreement.

Keynes failed to secure many of his objectives, including his plan at Bretton Woods for a postwar world currency and quasi-autonomous supranational central bank and for an international monetary system that would semiautomatically have obliged surplus and deficit countries equally to seek adjustment rather than putting most of the burden on deficit countries to deflate. Nevertheless, his personal reputation and intellectual prowess gained for his country and his point of view concessions that might not otherwise have been made, as well as helping to convince his own ministers that no better terms could be obtained than those which were on offer. And because the postwar world believed Keynes had found the key to full employment, he was regarded as the architect of an era.

In one form or another, the governments of the United States, Britain and the rest of Western Europe embraced commitments to full employment that were understood to be at least partly underwritten by the Keynesian notion that large-scale unemployment was caused by demand deficiency and that it lay within the power of governments to remedy, indeed forestall, such deficiencies either by increasing their own spending or by remitting taxes so that the private sector would increase its spending. The role of monetary policy and interest rates was regarded as subsidiary and indeed ineffective against a depression. In the European version of this strategy, a welfare state with universal social security and a substantial public sector including nationalized utilities and other key industries were seen as equally necessary parts of a mixed economy that could deliver the social conditions that would deny sustenance to the extreme political ideas that had flourished between the wars.

The British coalition government embraced a high-employment strategy, though with many caveats and weasel words, in the white paper *Employment Policy* in 1944. The U.S. Congress in 1946 passed the Employment Act, which, with many circumlocutions and qualifications, committed the government to "foster and promote . . . conditions under which there will be afforded useful employment for those able, willing, and seeking to work." The act came to be regarded thereafter, especially by Democrats, as at least a weak form of Keynesian strategy.

Continental Europe, where, after all, the interwar disasters had been most fully consummated, gave at least equal priority to achieving and maintaining full employment. But traditions other than Anglo-Saxon liberalism and Keynesian demand-management ideas exerted a strong influence. The intense European preoccupation with questions of ownership, Marxist and anti-Marxist, dominated the formal political divisions in France and Italy. West Germany was divided between the Social Democrats, who favored a mixed and planned economy, and the Christian Democrats, who preferred a social market economy. As time went by this ideological distinction grew blurred, with the success of Ludwig Erhard's "German economic miracle" carrying the day in practice for the mainly market economy even when the Social Democrats finally won power under former Berlin mayor Willy Brandt in 1969.

In France the political culture of a centralized society that had been dominated by its capital and by its proficient governing elite for centuries was less sympathetic to market forces and offered an ideal theater for economic planning. Such planning was successfully launched with high institutional grandeur in the form of the Monnet Plan in 1946, the planners reporting directly to the prime minister.[18] Whatever its technical weaknesses, this gave France a sense of top-down technocratic purpose and confidence that may well have been salutary after the humiliations of war and in the face of the formal instability of the Fourth Republic, where governments came and went with bewildering rapidity. A French economic miracle, whether based on the Monnet Plan or rather more probably on the animal spirits of French entrepreneurs energized by a de facto competitiveness strategy of "devalue early and devalue often," exceeded even the German paradigm in its annual gains in output, at least until 1957, when Charles de Gaulle, as president under the new Fifth Republic, brought the party to a shuddering halt with his decision that a weak franc was prejudicial to French amour propre.

Italy, too, drew on its own political culture to produce a version of the mixed economy under which a species of state capitalism displayed conspicuous vigor alongside some classically private capitalism in the northern part of the country. Planning was mainly implemented through the large agencies of the public sector, such as the Istituto per la Ricostruzione Industriale (Institute for Industrial Reconstruction, or IRI) and the Ente Nazionale Idrocarburi (National Hydrocarbons Association, or ENI).[19]

It is, however, unlikely that the passionate political arguments about institutions, ideology and ownership in Europe were nearly as important as the fundamental macroeconomic environment in procuring the spectacular success of the First World's economic performance in the first two decades after World War II, especially when compared with 1918–1938. High employment and rapid reconstruction and recovery owed much more to the return of peacetime conditions accompanied by expansionist economic policies—geared to high employment in the United States and Britain and accompanied by American tolerance of highly competitive exchange rates for the continental European and Japanese currencies—than they did to any particular ideology in individual countries. Germany, France, Italy and Japan performed outstandingly in part because as wartime losers they had suffered the most devastation and therefore had the most ground to make up and in part because, with widely differing ideological tilts, they all enjoyed export-led economic growth unconstrained by the kind of balance-of-payments difficulties that afflicted those like Britain who relied upon home demand to provide the motor of expansion and employment.

The story thereafter falls conveniently into two parts, pre- and post-1975. Fundamental to the early period, as we have seen, was the belief, known in shorthand as "Keynesian," that the supreme economic failure of the interwar period was mass unemployment and that the goal of full, or high, employment must and could be the overriding aim of policy in the new postwar world. That premise dictated much of what followed the peace in the United States, Britain, continental Europe and the international framework that was created. Postwar reconstruction, Marshall Plan aid, the fiscal and monetary policies of both American and European regimes, the faith placed in various schemes for directly influencing price and pay independently of normal market forces, the role of the public sector as employer and paymaster and the elaborate apparatus of international economic cooperation were all predicated on the almost unchallenged convictions that employment should be stabilized at a high level and that failure to do so would incur an unacceptable risk of rerunning the nightmare of the 1930s and its supposed corollaries of virulent nationalism and war.

Three results stand out from the general performance of the main First World economies in the quarter of a century or so after World War II:

- They enjoyed exceptionally rapid growth compared to both previous and subsequent performance.
- They enjoyed exceptionally stable economic conditions, that is, mild business cycles.
- They experienced exceptionally low levels (for peacetime) of unemployment.

Growth in the United States, strongly influenced in all periods by population growth, averaged 4.3 percent a year in the four and half decades before World War I, 2.9 percent between the wars and 3.0 percent in the 1970s. In the 1950s and 1960s, it averaged 3.2 and 4.3 percent. For Britain, the corresponding figures were 2.2, 1.7 and 1.8 percent before and after the postwar decades and 2.7 and 2.8 percent during the 1950s and 1960s.

Elsewhere the comparisons are even more spectacular. In West Germany the figures were 2.9, 1.2 and 2.8 percent, compared to 7.8 and 4.8 percent; in France 1.6, 0.7 and 3.7 percent, compared to 4.6 and 5.8 percent; in Japan 2.4, 1.8 and 4.9 percent, compared to 9.5 and 10.5 percent; and in Italy 1.4, 1.3 and 3.2 percent, compared to 5.8 and 5.7 percent. It is obvious why the 1950s and 1960s have sometimes been described as a "golden age."[20]

Stability was equally remarkable. In the United States boom-bust shocks, measured by percentage declines from peak to trough in either GNP or (where stated) industrial production (IP), topped 8 percent before World War I, 28 percent between the wars and 9 percent (IP) in the 1970s, compared to less than 2 percent in the 1950s and 1960s. In Britain shocks of over 4 and over 13 percent in the early periods and 5 percent (IP) in the 1970s contrasted with 0.5 percent in the 1950s and 1960s. For West Germany, shocks of over 4, 16 and 5 (IP) percent contrasted with 0.2 percent in the golden age; and for France shocks of over 19 and 8 (IP) percent in the interwar era and 1970s contrasted with literally nil (0.0) from 1948 to 1970. Japan and Italy, too, suffered nil shocks in the golden age compared to nearly 3 percent in the decade to 1938 and almost 10 percent (IP) in the 1970s (Japan) and over 5 percent in both the pre–World War I and the interwar periods and over 9 percent (IP) in the 1970s (Italy).[21]

Unemployment in the United States averaged 18 percent of the labor force in 1930–1938 and 6.3 percent in the 1970s, compared to less than 5 percent in the 1950s and 1960s. For western Europe, averages of over 7 and over 4 percent compared to under 3 and 1.5 percent in the golden decades. For Japan, the prewar numbers are not available, though there has been a clear increase from an exceedingly low level, less than 1.5 percent, before 1973 to 1.9 percent in the next six years. The United States averaged 7.2 percent in the 1980s and 6.4 percent in the first half of the 1990s and less since. Western Europe has averaged close to 9 percent in both periods; Japan has risen to 2.5 percent.[22]

The exact explanation for this outstanding performance has divided economists, though not quite as drastically as the causes of the Great Depression. For our purposes, it is sufficient to rely on:

- the strength of the "never again" determination of the postwar world—that the mistakes that led to both world wars must never be allowed to happen again

- the memories of the dire distress and high unemployment of the interwar years
- the timely appearance of Keynes's ideas, duly simplified for political consumption, which appeared to offer mechanisms for securing the desired full employment that could be stomached by almost all shades of ideological opinion
- the scope for rapid reconstruction of war-ravaged countries
- U.S. willingness to be the enlightened hegemon and "play the sucker" so that Europe and Japan could enjoy payments surpluses while running their economies at high levels of demand
- the powerful hold of "money illusion" (the belief that inflation is not something one needs to worry about in making economic decisions) after the deflationary 1930s, which meant that all players were slow to exploit fully the strong bargaining position of suppliers in a general seller's market. (This was especially true in the labor markets, where the trade unions failed to realize their bargaining power as monopolistic suppliers of labor.)

In the early 1970s, if not sooner, it became apparent that there was nonetheless a flaw. The flaw was that a high-employment strategy appeared to have an unforeseen and unacceptable side effect, namely, accelerating inflation. It had long been supposed that some level of very high—or "overfull"—employment would cause inflation. It had been thought possible as well as necessary to avoid this zone without diluting the goal of full employment unduly. What began to appear as the 1960s wore on and gave way to the 1970s was that every time the economy went round its roughly four-year business cycle, the peak levels of both unemployment and inflation seemed to get higher. This suggested that it was becoming harder to achieve the supposed golden mean between these two perils, perhaps even that there was no such middle ground, however narrow, whether or not nurtured by various species of price controls and incomes policies.

These problems afflicted some more than others. High growth rates in continental Europe and Japan, as the ravages of war were repaired and as these economies began to catch up toward leading-edge productivity levels, masked for a while the threat to employment implied by the inflationary potential of managing demand according to a full employment standard. But in the late 1960s France and Germany suffered wage explosions that shook even their confidence.

Japan was able to rely on extremely rapid export-led growth to support social and rural systems that disguised almost any potential unemployment in an immensely overmanned "third sector." But this, even more than continental Europe's postwar recovery, was predicated on the United States' willingness to play the sucker and absorb Japan's export surpluses into a matching American deficit.

Despite the inflation at the end of the 1960s, by 1971 the impact of the resulting overvaluation of the U.S. dollar on American business and jobs reached a point where the hegemonic responsibilities of the United States for the success of the world economic order were too costly even for the world's strongest economy. To restore competitiveness to U.S. products, the dollar needed to be devalued in relation to the other leading currencies. Notwithstanding a European rearguard action to protect their competitive advantage, this was achieved by the Smithsonian Agreement of December 1971 between the members of the Group of Ten—the U.S., the UK, Japan, Canada, West Germany, France, Italy, the Netherlands, Belgium and Luxembourg—for the realignment of their mutual exchange rates.

The agreement effectively destroyed the indispensable premise of the Bretton Woods system, namely, that the Americans would run a sufficient balance-of-payments deficit to accommodate the surplus that every other government felt it needed. By the following summer most major exchange rates were floating, ending at a stroke the general atmosphere of impending currency crisis that had needlessly dominated events in the previous decade. But it also removed what had been regarded as the postwar world's best anchor against inflation.

One more turn of the inflationary screw was necessary before the recognition became general among governments that high employment could no longer be underwritten by expansionary fiscal and monetary policies without an unacceptable consequence for prices. Interpretation was, as so often, complicated by a coincidental shock: The Organization of Petroleum Exporting Countries (OPEC) in November 1973 increased by fourfold its posted prices for oil, and some observers tried to lay the whole or the main blame for the inflationary breakdown of the high-employment strategy in the mid-1970s on the cartel's actions.

But the evidence was and remains too strong that that fatal weakness had been building up for the previous two decades, as "money illusion" was eroded and that OPEC did little more than simulate the tax increase on consumers that Western governments would anyway have had to impose in order to control the boom that was beginning to build in 1973 as a result of reflationary actions taken, especially in the United States and Britain, over the previous year or two. This of course does not invalidate Christopher Dow's finding that the two oil shocks of 1973–1974 and 1978–1980 were the main causes of the recessions that followed each.[23]

But the era of the high-employment standard was effectively dead from the moment when a British prime minister declared in September 1976 that the option no longer existed, if it ever had, to spend one's way out of a recession and increase employment by cutting taxes and boosting government spending. Three years later President Jimmy Carter appointed Paul Volcker chairman of the U.S. Federal Reserve with a mission to stabilize prices by monetary policy.

From then on a new orthodoxy came to prevail, though sometimes confused with the purely political quirks and preferences of strongly conservative leaders like Ronald Reagan and Margaret Thatcher, who in truth had little interest in macroeconomics and for whom even microeconomics was more a matter of ideology than efficiency. The new orthodoxy held that price stability must be pursued as an overriding goal and that no trade-off could or should be made with employment or other economic goals. Price stability was the sole and proper goal of monetary policy, and that monetary policy was the sole and proper instrument of that strategy, later stigmatized as "one club golf." The function of fiscal policy was to contribute to macroeconomic stability by balancing the budget and possibly also to support strategies of shrinking the public sector and extending those sectors of the economy in which market forces allocated resources.

The most apparent first consequence of this change of strategy was a marked increase in average unemployment levels, accompanied by slower growth in those countries—Japan and continental Europe—which had enjoyed rapid postwar recovery. There is some less conclusive evidence that economic volatility also increased from the mid-1970s, certainly in Britain. Dow treats 1945–1973 as a "long interval without major recessions."[24] Recessions involving absolute falls in output from year to year, commonly for two years, resumed in 1973–1975 and recurred with increasing depth and duration (in Britain, at least) in 1979–1982 and the early 1990s.[25] Dow finds that all main industrial countries shared in the pattern of slow-fast-slow growth in the three periods (1920–1938, 1950–1973 and 1973–1990) and in a similar high-low-high pattern for unemployment.[26] For almost all countries, the first postwar period was also a time of steady growth without major fluctuations. After 1973, however, only in Britain did the recessions become deeper toward the end, though other countries had recessions at about the same time.

Elsewhere in the world, notably in the Soviet Union, eastern Europe and much of South America, Asia and Africa, people invested an extraordinary amount of confidence in state planning as a motor of economic change in the aftermath of World War II. Likewise, it was almost universally believed that economic development in the Third World could be financed by a combination of domestic savings and international aid, and that as a result developing countries could and would gradually close the economic gap with the developed world.

These beliefs proved at least as flawed as the First World's reliance on the full-employment standard as its principal guide to routine economic management. In one of the supreme ironies of twentieth-century economic history, the division of the victorious alliance against Hitler into rival economic blocs coldly contesting the planet for dominance was precipitated by the British embassy in Washington, the base from which what became the Marshall Plan was being concerted between British and U.S. postwar planners in order to overcome a threatened economic collapse in western Europe. From the desk of the acting head of chancery, the day-to-day political director of any embassy, went a cable, not to the British Foreign Office or the U.S. State Department or any other normal outlet for such communications, but to Moscow for the general secretary of the Communist Party of the Soviet Union, Joseph Stalin.

At this moment in 1947, shortly after General George C. Marshall had launched his plan in his famous speech at Harvard on 5 June, the Soviet foreign minister, Vyacheslav Molotov, was in Paris with instructions to cooperate with the Western Allies in implementing the Marshall Plan, which offered funds to the Soviet Union and eastern Europe as well as to

Western Europe. The cable from Washington, whose author, Donald Maclean, was later revealed as a Soviet spy, convinced Stalin that Marshall Plan aid was a hostile plot to replace German reparations, on which the Soviet Union heavily depended for postwar reconstruction, with U.S. aid whose use would be under international, not Russian, control. Stalin issued orders to Molotov, who duly walked out of the Paris talks.

From then on, without Marshall Plan aid and wholly dependent on resources whose supply was tightly controlled from Moscow, the eastern European states had no alternative to a Soviet future. Six months later multiparty rule came to an end in eastern Europe, and the Soviet bloc was established. It remained the controlling economic regime for over forty years.[27]

Had Molotov proceeded with his original instructions, it is still possible that the threat allegedly implied by Marshall aid to Moscow's control of eastern Europe would have become apparent and would still have wrecked the intended cooperation. The Berlin crisis of 1948 began because the West reacted to Soviet rejection of the Marshall plan by unilaterally extending it to West Berlin.[28] So it is also possible that but for Maclean's intervention, eastern Europe and even the Soviet Union itself would have been drawn into a more prosperous and less antagonistic relationship with the West, with profound consequences for the history of the next four decades.

The story of the Soviet bloc as an economic protagonist looks different in retrospect from how it was seen during most of its active life. Between 1948 and 1989, when Mikhail Gorbachev—with the whole world listening told East Germany's ruler, Erich Honecker, that no tanks would be sent to underwrite Honecker's regime and that therefore Moscow abdicated the whole postwar settlement based on the Red Army's guarantee of a divided Germany and a divided Europe, most people thought of the communist world as representing one of two alternative systems on which economic life could be based and into which the world was mainly divided. It was certainly thought to be less agreeable than the other "free" alternative, as well as philosophically "wrong," because of its unpleasant dependence on aggressive political policing. But the secondary question, whether it was more or less economically efficient, was for most of that era regarded as uncertain, with some suspicion that its achievements in terms of growth, price stability, full employment, cyclical fluctuation, technical progress and industrial investment were superior precisely because they were less susceptible to the vagaries of the free market. Soviet premier Nikita Khrushchev could claim that communism would bury capitalism, which he also described as like "a dead herring in the moonlight, shining brilliantly as it rotted," without being thought guilty of more than moderate hyperbole.[29] In a well-received polemic on the British economy in 1961, Michael Shanks, the journalist, author and adviser to government on industrial policy, could write without any apparent absurdity that economic growth rates in the Soviet economies far exceeded those in the West, that the date when Soviet output per head in Russia would overtake "ours" could be foreseen and that in order to avert this we must run our economic system more efficiently. To this end he waxed almost lyrical about purpose and planning, adding that his book had been conceived at the end of a visit to Bulgaria, where "Life . . . as in other Communist states is dominated by the concept of the Plan. All aspects of public life have to be dovetailed into it. . . . In this disciplining of society to the attainment of particular social and economic goals, there is . . . something decent, honest and inspiring. Whatever else it lacks this society contains within itself a sense of purpose. This, *vis-à-vis* the West, is its great strength."[30]

Shanks was no fellow traveler, and he was far from alone in his conviction that the West's struggle for survival in competition with the ruthlessly efficient and purposeful East was akin to glorious, self-indulgent Athens' doomed contest with single-minded Sparta. Shanks was shocked—"like a man seeing his face in the morning mirror after a night of debauch"—on reaching Vienna to find Western newspapers "full of the conflicts of society: take-over bids, labour disputes, murders, sex crimes, political scandal" in contrast with Bulgaria, where "all efforts were being concentrated 'on building socialism'" and where the average official turned out to be not the devilish fiend of our "childhood image" of a communist but "a prosaic figure, of limited intelligence and imagination, for the most part strictly honest and of an almost puritan morality."[31]

The truth was different. Soviet communism, as practiced by Stalin and, slightly less bloodily, by his successors suffered from fatal deficiencies that should have been expected to, and did, rule out long-term success and long-term sustainability. However prodigious, Stakhanovite or other were the efforts made in the short term to lift the Soviet economy by its bootstraps, not least during and immediately after World War II, the problems of the four Is—information, incentives, investment and innovation—were insuperable and eventually fatal. But this truth was hard to demonstrate, except a priori, because of a number of obstacles to vision. First and foremost, the weaknesses were long-term, gradual and progressive and were easily overlaid by short-term, one-shot achievements. Second, most statistical information about the Soviet economy was straightforwardly false, though the scale of this lie was not fully recognized until very late in the day. Third, huge amounts of political wishful thinking added to the difficulty of interpreting such information as there was.

In the first aftermath of the war, the Soviet Union did what it was best at, returning to previous levels of production of heavy industrial products that it already knew how to make, as under the New Economic Policy after 1921. As military expenditure and employment ran down, the output of heavy industry doubled between 1945 and 1950.[32] And the feel-good sense of achievement, at least among the rulers, extended through the 1950s and into the early 1960s. At a time when a British prime minister, Harold Macmillan, had been reported as telling his voters that they had "never had it so good" and a new, young U.S. president, John Kennedy, was talking incessantly about "getting the economy moving again," Khrushchev could side firmly with Macmillan.[33] He could take pride in the material improvements in the living standards of Soviet people—high-rise apartment blocks in all cities; improved diet, with meat consumption rising by over half in seven years; refrigerators, televisions and even washing machines; hospital and education services free and available to everyone; low rents and other home charges; zero unemployment; rising wages and so on. This perhaps explained the outbreak of euphoria that overtook the Kremlin in 1961, well summarized by Robert Service:

> The Party Programme . . . described the USSR as an "all-people's state" which no longer needed to use dictatorial methods. . . . By the end of the 1960s, according to the Programme's prediction, the per capita output of the USA would be overtaken; by 1980 the "material-technical basis" of a communist society would have been laid down. Full communism would be in prospect. . . . The Soviet Union would enter an age of unparalleled human happiness.[34]

But gradually and inexorably a more somber reality was asserting itself. Despite the brief morale boost flowing from Khrushchev's relaxation of the viler and madder excesses of Stalin's political and economic tyranny, Soviet agriculture increasingly failed to supply the food needed by people and animals, and Soviet industry failed altogether to match what was happening in the developed market economies of the free world, and it may indeed have achieved little or no net growth since the revolution.

By the end of the 1970s, Soviet industry was staring at a prospect of absolute long-term decline. Thanks to OPEC's two oil price hikes in the 1970s, the products of the Soviet oil and natural gas industries could be sold successfully abroad, thus giving the budget and payments balance a much-needed boost. But the net result was that the Soviet economy was as dependent on exporting its natural resources as czarist Russia had been, and by now it could not even generate a grain surplus to send to its European neighbors.[35]

This degree of failure was as yet not generally visible to the outside world. Official statistics still spoke of industrial output rising at over 4 percent a year in the late 1970s, though this lie was an anemic boast compared to the growth at double that rate claimed a decade earlier. Even within the Soviet Union, the truth could be disguised. Workers' living standards had probably never been so high, as Leonid Brezhnev took care to ensure that consumer goods got sufficient priority in official investment plans to enable conditions to improve gradually. Things like refrigerators and television sets were to be found in three-quarters or more of Soviet homes by 1980, and shop prices for basics like food, clothing, housing and heating were kept at nearly prewar levels. Indeed, this Brezhnev era came later to be looked back upon by many as a golden age compared to the privations that followed the fall of communism.

But the fundamental and progressive failure of the Soviet economic system in all sectors except military technology was apparent enough to those with eyes to see, which included the next generation's Mikhail Gorbachev. By the time he came to power in 1985, Gorbachev had few illusions about the Soviet Union's economic performance, either absolutely or relatively to Western capitalism. The technological gap between East and West was widening and reaching proportions for which even the

KGB's best efforts at industrial espionage could not indefinitely compensate.

Soviet finances depended more and more heavily on selling off oil and gas, which by 1984 accounted for more than half of all exports, and on sales of vodka in oceanic quantities to a vulnerable population.[36] Forty percent of imports, costing hard currency, was food for animals, leaving much less for the capital goods and high-technology equipment that were so urgently needed. Over the next five years, the Soviet economy fell into overt and total crisis, partly as Gorbachev's policies of perestroika permitted the underlying rottenness to become more apparent and partly as his efforts at reform, including many misguided expedients, were overwhelmed by the implosion of the whole system of governance and control that was the Soviet Union and its European empire.

The anatomy of that final collapse—of how far it was or was not expedited by the active hostility and challenge of the West after it had been antagonized by the Soviet incursion into Afghanistan and of how far Gorbachev should be seen, as Robert Service sees him, as a "holy fool" blundering unintentionally into the disintegration of a system he merely intended to modernize or instead as a historic pragmatist like Franklin Roosevelt whose ability to see what did not work impelled him into ever more radical experiments—these questions need not be settled here. What is certain is that the four Is had finally caught up with the Soviet system. For perhaps the first time in history, a huge totalitarian empire was swiftly dismantled with almost none of the bloody death throes that such an event might normally be expected to cause, and it seems hard to deny Gorbachev credit for repeatedly refusing to reach for the Stalinist option.

The four Is are intimately linked. A properly functioning market economy generates information about consumer preferences and about the comparative costs of different ways of satisfying them. It allows all the subtle gradations of those preferences and those production solutions to be sifted so as to produce "optimum" combinations, at least within the limitations of the income distribution operating in such an economy. This information—showing up as prices and spending decisions—is transmitted in a form that there and then creates an incentive and supplies the means to heed it. My dollar spent on a purchase becomes to the supplier his profit and his means of meeting the costs of supplying me.

This information and this incentive guide and also finance his investment. Over time they also spur, guide and select innovations that will better satisfy the desire of consumers for better value for their money. And so the whole juggernaut of an economy—quivering jelly may be a better metaphor—is continually constrained to respond, through millions of decisions being made by millions of people all day every day, to the sovereign consumer.

Of course, this idealized sketch is a gross oversimplification of a reality that is full of imperfections, abuses and inefficiencies, to say nothing of some problems, such as environmental "externalities," of which it may take no account at all. But at least it creates a momentum in the direction of the efficient provision of things people mainly want, and it does not saddle any administrative or political apparatus with the impossible burden of discovering a priori what people want and then of requiring them to provide it for each other by a series of commands, unsupported by proportionate incentives and seemingly in conflict with the inclinations and interests of those required to produce and distribute what is needed.

The end of that road lies (and in the Soviet Union lay) in the old joke worth repeating: "They pretend to pay us, and we pretend to work." Less and less work for less and less pay becomes an inevitable vicious circle when information about consumer preferences and production economies are not being signaled through prices set by supply and demand; when such information as does exist is not automatically translated into incentives to act; when investment is determined blindly and by crude political dogmas or administrative simplicities riding roughshod over the myriad gradations of possible choice and when innovation is only reluctantly tolerated by an exhausted and superannuated ruling clique when news of it penetrates belatedly and despite all barriers to its diffusion from a remote and distrusted outside world. One does not need to be starry-eyed about market economics or blind to the ethical and practical shortcomings of laissez-faire capitalism (e.g., inequality, instability and monopolistic exploitation) to understand that any system that depends in the long run on a central command structure to determine the general pattern and detailed composition of production, investment and rewards will tend to grow more and more out of touch with what people want and how best to provide it; and more and more dependent on monitoring an outside world that is supposedly inferior; more and more unable to find and motivate the people who are supposed to fulfill the superhuman task of omniscient central management. It just cannot be done, not even by an army of wise saints, let alone by normal people exposed to the normal pressures and temptations of official power.

In the early postwar period, as we have seen, the eastern European countries, those across whose territory the iron grip of the Red Army lay, had no choice after Stalin had rejected Marshall Plan aid for himself and for the states the Soviet Union had newly liberated from the Nazis' "Greater Germany" but to become satellites of Moscow, parts of a new Soviet empire from the iron curtain to the Pacific. As such, their economic development was constrained by the Kremlin's overriding political priorities of control in eastern Europe and reconstruction at home.

Economic freedoms were suppressed almost as thoroughly as political freedoms. By the early 1960s state ownership and control of all mining, agriculture, industry, transport, trading and financial activities accounted for 95 percent of national income from the public sector in Bulgaria, Czechoslovakia, East Germany, Hungary and Romania. Farming remained largely private in Poland and Yugoslavia, which kept the public sector down to about 75 percent of the whole economy.[37] Central planning laid down the shares of investment and consumption in national claims on resources and their deployment between sectors and branches. Heavy industry received priority, and the strategy of boosting growth and industrialization simply by allocating huge amounts of capital to goals the central planners recognized meant that these resources were used with little regard to efficiency or changing needs.

As in the Soviet Union itself, the best performances in eastern Europe probably came at the beginning, when the industrial priorities were obvious and the ruthless priority given to investment over consumption produced palpable results. Up until the 1970s, indeed, some of the eastern European economies achieved impressive figures for output, employment and productivity. The available figures credit the bloc with a 7 percent annual growth rate through the 1950s and 1960s, compared with less than 5 percent in the West, and a nearly 6 percent growth in per capita output, compared with less than 4 percent in the West.[38]

There remains, in hindsight, a question how far we should believe these figures. They may have been correct as to physical quantities while becoming more and more misleading as to value. That, at least, is consistent with the notion that centralized economic planning can be quite effective at marshaling an exceptional physical effort in pursuit of readily ascertainable goals, while such command economics is almost completely defeated by the longer-term problem of change and innovation. The physical output of established categories of production—power, dwelling units, machines of given design, basic consumer items—may well have raced ahead in the first decades after the war, but this performance would have grown more and more wasteful and irrelevant when compared to the West, where free markets could price the available goods according to the true preferences of consumers and the true costs of production.

The defects of the system became more telling as time went by and change in targets and techniques became harder and harder to manage because of that same lack of information and incentives to guide and spur investment and innovation. The Eastern bloc grew ever more imitative of Western projects even as it sought to demonstrate the superiority of its rival ideology. Marshall Plan aid in the West was implemented mainly through the new Organisation for European Economic Cooperation, which seems to have stimulated the Council for Mutual Economic Assistance (COMECON) in the East. COMECON's achievements were modest, perhaps taking the edge off the more extreme search for individual self-sufficiency in each Eastern bloc country and promoting some grudging recognition of mutual dependency and comparative advantage in the plans and labor use of the communist family. But by cutting the eastern European economies off completely from any normal exchange with the outside world, it progressively inhibited the changes that would have been needed to enable them to match western European economic development.

In addition, the narrow convenience of the USSR, as the hegemonic power of the bloc, obliged satellite economies to supply the Soviet Union's priority needs and to accept its available supplies in return. This distorted the trade and impeded the growth of economies like East Germany and Czechoslovakia that might well have performed more successfully without such an incubus.

Rude reminders of Soviet political control were periodically delivered, most notoriously at the time of the Hungarian uprising of 1956—lamentably downgraded in the news by the simultaneous Anglo-French invasion of Egypt—and of the Prague spring in 1968. Any thoughts of radical reform to introduce market forces into the main eastern European economies were suppressed, though in all sorts of small and oblique ways—not least systematic corruption in the more pragmatic societies, such as Hungary—the price mechanism asserted itself in the growing cracks in the smooth face of the planned economies.

As they fell behind the West in technical progress, many tried to bridge the gap by importing Western capital goods as a basis for producing high-quality final goods for reexport. This strategy failed, partly because cheap Soviet oil and cheap Western credits, both driven by political calculations, led the eastern Europeans down a primrose path of energy waste and unmanageable debt and partly because their culture and technical training were not ready for the high-tech role of which their planners dreamed.

By 1989 the game was manifestly up, but it had been lost long before. It is not surprising that the revolt that finally overthrew Soviet communism—or at least presented a challenge that men of Gorbachev's stamp had no stomach to suppress by the methods of his predecessors—started in the eastern European satellites. They were most closely exposed to the growing contrast between how they lived and how their western neighbors lived. Some of them had modern experience of democratic and pluralistic institutions, and all of them blamed Russian oppression for their backwardness. The moment Gorbachev signaled that there would be no tanks, the dash for freedom was on; within an astonishingly brief time the whole fabric of command economics had turned to dust, long before any thought could be given to what exactly might replace it and how. The Eastern bloc became "countries in transition" in the jargon of the newly globalized institutions of the old First World they all rushed to join; the rest of their story in the final decade of the millennium became part of the story of the global economy in that period.

For Russia and the other former republics of the Soviet Union, the last decade of the millennium was to be yet another false dawn, a decade of hope deferred and dreams disappointed. But for most of the rest of the old COMECON world the dawn seemed genuine enough, though the sun of market-based economic growth rose more swiftly in some countries, like Poland and Hungary, than in the Baltic states, Bulgaria and Romania. Even so, by 1998 only Poland had actually increased its GDP significantly since 1989.[39] The average GDP of the old eastern Europe economies (including the Baltic states) was still just below 1989 levels, and that of the former Soviet Union was down 45 percent, indubitably the worst peacetime economic setback experienced by any substantial economic area since—who knows? But maybe since the Black Death.

Communism's other great experiment was in China. It had its own chronology, different from that of the Soviet bloc and the West, and its own different outcome. China came out of the war massively scarred by partial Japanese occupation and by the continuing struggle between Chiang Kai-shek's nationalists and Mao Zedong's communists. The civil war lasted until Mao's triumph in 1949 and Chiang's final flight to Taiwan (Formosa) in 1950. At the time this transformation was celebrated as a communist revolution. It is now officially remembered in Beijing as the founding of "new China."

In Chapter 7 we noted that at the beginning of the twentieth century life for the ordinary Chinese peasant could be described in much the same way that Keynes had described the lives of ordinary unskilled laborers in Europe up to 1800, as not much changed since 2000 B.C. Indeed, Michael Lipton and Martin Ravallion have recently observed that poverty showed little if any "secular trend" (e.g., tendency to decline) in Asia before 1945.[40] China, as we saw, became a carcass to be carved up by foreign banks. In this fertile political soil the Chinese Communist Party was founded in 1921, nine years after the creation of the Republic of China under Sun Yat-sen's leadership and the abdication of the last Manchu emperor. Nearly forty years of anarchy and civil war, punctuated by twelve years of expanding Japanese occupation, left China's economy almost as blasted and blighted as America in the Great Depression or Europe at the end of World War II—and much poorer than either. There was an appetite for a new beginning, for a better kind of future, and it was Mao's People's Republic of China that seemed to offer it.[41]

China's story then became, to an outsider's eye, an extraordinary sequence of advance and retreat. Hopes were high:

> Here was a conquering army of country boys who were strictly self-disciplined, polite, and helpful, at the opposite pole from the looting and warlord troops and even the departing Nationalists. Here was a dedicated government that really cleaned things up—not only the drains and streets, but also the beggars,

> prostitutes, and petty criminals, all of whom were rounded up for reconditioning. Here was a new China one could be proud of, one that controlled inflation, abolished foreign privileges, stamped out opium smoking and corruption generally, and brought the citizenry into a multitude of sociable activities to repair public works, spread literacy, control disease, fraternise with the menial class and study the New Democracy and Mao Zedong Thought. All these activities opened new doors for idealistic and ambitious youth.[42]

For the first eight years after the revolution, reconstruction and growth were the official watchwords, and what it is hard not to regard as the native genius of Chinese traders and craftsmen contributed to an almost 9 percent annual growth rate under the first five-year plan. The usual problem about communist statistics bedevils confident interpretation to this day, but agricultural output was claimed to have risen about 1.5 percent faster than the population, urban wages were said to have risen by one-third and peasant incomes by one-fifth. If these were only half true, they would have been formidable achievements compared to the long record of perpetual poverty.

At the same time this was a revolutionary communist regime, and it set about the usual agenda of expropriating and suppressing the capitalist classes in the cities and the landlords in the country. A new constitution based on the Soviet Union's 1936 model was introduced, establishing the iron grip of the central party leadership. As in the Soviet Union, this extreme form of social and economic regimentation could for a while coexist with, or even contribute to, impressive increases in production and necessary investment. But it became obvious that under Chinese conditions the principles of the first five-year plan could not be blindly extrapolated into the second.

The second five-year plan was expected to ease some of the less practical aspects of its predecessor, especially in the rural areas, where collectivization, massive state bureaucracy and a Soviet-style priority for heavy industry were restricting output and increasing China's unwelcome dependence on Soviet aid.[43] In effect, China was coming to recognize the historical truth that industrialization presupposes an agricultural transformation that can generate the food surplus that growing urban populations require. Such an agrarian change requires incentives to peasants, notably in the form of consumer goods, which come not from exclusively heavy industrial investment but from a balance of heavy and light industry.[44]

In the Introduction to this book, we referred to Jung Chang's *Wild Swans* and suggested that although (or perhaps because) it is not an economics textbook it contains extraordinary insights into the nature of man's instinctive search for material betterment and the vital influence of political conditions, for good or evil, in liberating or crushing that search. China illustrates this thesis with exceptional clarity and with unusually violent alternations between the summers and winters of official policy.

No more vivid and horrific example can be imagined than what happened in 1958, the launching of the Great Leap Forward. Among political decisions made consciously by political leaders, this may be among the absolutely worst—in its human consequences—ever made. In the league of policies that may claim to have killed people in tens of millions—leave aside Isabella of Castile's sponsorship of Christopher Columbus—probably only Stalin's and Hitler's offer serious competition.[45] Between 1958 and 1960, 20–30 million Chinese died through lack of food, the result of the chaos caused by the insane notions of a leader whose lack of understanding was harnessed to an extraordinary capacity for political mobilization.[46]

Mao was quite literally able to command a country of 650 million people to starve to death something like one in thirty of their number for the sake of a theory embodied in a slogan.[47] The theory was that underused rural labor could be galvanized by political exhortation into a gigantic effort that would accomplish simultaneously agricultural modernization and the development of light industries supplying agricultural implements and consumer goods. The modern urban economy would continue to produce exports to pay for required capital goods imports.

The ultimate madness was embodied in the slogans "Long live the Great Leap Forward," and "Everybody make steel," according to which small backyard smelters were put to work in every village to produce steel from whatever species of scrap and not-so-scrap iron, woks and all, lay to hand.[48] Meanwhile, food production was neglected, though fantastic production figures were reported by ambitious local party supplicants to Beijing; based on those reports, Beijing requisitioned what was in fact most of the food being produced. As a result the villagers were left with half or less of their normal food, and consequently they starved or became vulnerable to the diseases that batten on malnutrition.[49]

This madness abated somewhat in the early 1960s, and there was some revival of output, notably in agriculture, as the cultivation of private plots for sale in local markets was again permitted. But by 1966 this pragmatic tilt led by Deng Xiaoping and Liu Shaoqi, which inevitably tended to restore the power and control of both the central bureaucracy in Beijing and village ruling classes, had provoked Mao to reach again for the one weapon he knew, political mobilization of the rural population, to challenge these traditional authorities and, at the same time, to reestablish his own personal ascendancy in the Communist Party. The result was the Cultural Revolution, which from 1966 threw China into cruel chaos for most of the ensuing decade until Mao's death in 1976.[50]

The adverse economic consequences of the Cultural Revolution, whose main economic thrust was managerial decentralization and rural industrialization, were slight compared with the Great Leap Forward. Those who died were numbered in hundreds of thousands, not millions, and they died of direct mob action against those set in any kind of authority rather than from mass starvation. Industrial growth, spurred by heavy official investment, was reported to have averaged 13.5 percent annually between 1969 and 1976. Population, benefiting from the green revolution (better crop strains and so on) and improvements in basic public health, rose from 725 million in 1965 to 919 million ten years later.

The implausible precision of such numbers should awaken some skepticism, but most authorities seem to accept that both output and demographic growth in China were rapid in this period, notwithstanding the political and social chaos of the time. The rural population gained little from this, except in numbers, the major advantages going to new local managerial elites.[51] Moreover, the high growth in output was heavily dependent on what the World Bank calls "increasing inputs," which means mainly investment in plant and technology. There was little sign, however, that these resources were used with growing efficiency, and therefore the productivity of the factors of production—labor, land and capital—was not rising, in stark contrast with what was happening elsewhere in East Asia and was soon to happen in China itself.[52]

After Mao's death and the ensuing political struggle for succession,

China moved with extraordinary rapidity, much resembling the sudden blooming of a whole landscape held until then in the frozen grip of an Arctic winter, into what can only be called a Chinese economic miracle.[53] Deng Xiaoping replaced ideology with pragmatism, and he began to rebalance Chinese society by strengthening central and local government's delivery of law and order while reducing its influence over economic life, thus doubly improving its ability to play its proper role in support of economic progress. His program of reform—"socialism with Chinese characteristics"—began in the countryside, where the turmoil and stagnation of the Mao years were worst. Learning from the success of China's neighbors in East Asia, Deng built on well-tried and proven mechanisms, such as the family farm, market forces, consumer goods industries and external trade. Merle Goldman sums up the result:

> In the post-Mao era China was transformed from an isolated, poor, rural, and politically turbulent country into a relatively open, stable, urbanizing, and modernizing country. With an economy growing at 9 percent a year in the last two decades of the twentieth century, China became the fastest-growing economy in the world . . . faster [according to a World Bank report] than almost any other in history. In just twenty years China had evolved from a nation in which roughly six out of ten people lived below the international poverty rate of $1 a day into a nation in which per capita income virtually quadrupled.[54]

Nothing could better have illustrated Adam Smith's notion of the "progress of opulence" wherever constraints on mankind's basic curiosity, ingenuity and competitiveness are removed. Smith had himself been intrigued by China's stagnation in his own time, blaming adverse political and ecological influences. But before we are carried away in admiration of Deng's miracle as a vindication of liberal doctrines, we need to remember the democratic deficit—which Deng's China shared with the economic golden age of ancient Rome from Augustus to Marcus Aurelius—that persisted under the continuing communist monopoly of political power.

We need also to contemplate the paradox that almost simultaneously with China's miracle, Russia, as we have seen, was suffering the greatest retrogression in history, or at least since the Black Death, in apparent consequence of undergoing the same economic liberalization that inaugurated in China almost the fastest growth of any country in history. Many possible explanations proffer themselves: failure of government to perform its minimal functions, cultural differences, better or worse management and sequencing of the transition to market freedom in town and country. None seems adequate to explain the difference over twenty years between just about the best and just about the worst economic performance in modern history.

The scope for catching up that China enjoyed, as a result of both Mao's destruction and the rest of East Asia's rapid progress, doubtless explains much of China's real leap forward. But Russia, too, had huge scope for catching up with western Europe, as Poland has demonstrated, yet the "progress of opulence" seems not to have operated, perhaps because a Chinese farmer or businessman can have more confidence than his Russian counterpart that he will be free to keep and to enjoy at least a significant part of any wealth that he generates by his own curiosity, ingenuity and competitiveness, to say nothing of hard work. And that, together with appropriate fiscal discipline, which also collapsed in Russia, is a hallmark of good government.[55]

Self-government remains another matter, and in the twenty-first century China will have to grapple with the same problem that bedeviled ancient Rome and bedevils any absolutist regime: how to secure its indefinite perpetuation without any tests of popular consent and despite the mortality of each succeeding emperor. Russia, meanwhile, will need to grapple with the opposite problem, of anarchy, finding (it is to be hoped) a more acceptable remedy than the classic strongman precedent of the caesars. When it has done so, its own long-postponed miracle may at last begin. Both cases demonstrate the primary thesis of this book: the high dependency of economic performance on matters of government, neither too much nor too little nor the wrong sort, but enough and working to liberate and exploit the basic urge of the "progress of opulence."

So the postwar story of the two major communist experiments, viewed as their own versions of the global "never again" sentiment that gripped every country in 1945, ended in both cases, as also in the First World, with the abandonment of the formula in which so much hope had been invested: abandoned in the Soviet Union because its own leaders ceased to believe in it and dissolved it in favor of an alternative that by the end of the century was yet to deliver any reassuring results, and abandoned in China for the same reason, but with far more impressive consequences so far.

There was as well after 1945 a Third World, the world that was neither the industrial democracies that gathered under U.S. wings to construct a better postwar economic order, nor the communist bloc taking its lead, originally at least, from the Soviet Union. The Third World never was a "world" in any strongly coherent sense. It included Latin American countries in which deep antagonisms among populist, military and commercial parties dominated political affairs, while economic development depended on both private capital, some of it from the United States, and state investment. But there were other countries, especially newly independent former colonies in Asia and Africa, who took their lead mainly from India, set free from the British Empire and dedicated to a noncapitalist, government-led and centrally planned road to a better future.

The capital for this strategy would come not from inward private investment (which was suspect as exploitative) nor entirely, as in the communist models, from the forced savings of the home population. Official development assistance (ODA)—flows of investment funds from government to government, from the more affluent in the already industrialized North to the developing South—would square the circles of both economic development and moral duty. Meanwhile, such states would remain nonaligned in the emerging ideological and geopolitical rivalry between East and West.

The hope was that fast-track, forced industrialization would provide general employment, reduce poverty and pay for the minimum unavoidable imports. The plan failed partly because it did not go hand in hand with any matching rural development to produce the food surplus needed to feed an increasingly urbanized industrial workforce. It was hostile to trade and so denied itself the benefits of comparative advantage. Its dependence on official aid flows was constantly disappointed, and anyway such public capital brought with it few if any of the benefits of management and technology transfer that go with private international investment, especially by major corporations who for a long time were made thoroughly unwelcome in such developing economies.

And it suffered acutely from the problem of the four Is, as well as from the obvious hazards of any government-led society, namely, that the government itself may become corrupt and a conduit for sectional and other private interests in conflict with the general interests of society. Amartya Sen has written tellingly of India:

> Economic initiatives were made overpoweringly contingent on official permission; competitiveness of Indian industries was persistently sacrificed in favour of protected markets for selected businessmen; a mass of badly run public enterprises made chronic losses, drawing on—rather than contributing to—the national economic resources; and there was little attempt to facilitate India's participation in the general economic expansion that was occurring across the world.[56]

This picture applied most obviously to India itself, but the absurdities of closed economy, autarkic and industrializing strategies became even more obvious—with the passing of the colonial era at the end of the 1950s—in the much smaller economies of Africa. Their boundaries represented little but arbitrary accidents of colonial history, and their best industrial prospects, if any, might have lain in supplying by specialized mass production the specific needs of one another, where those needs diverged from the stereotypical items made and bought in the highly industrialized North (e.g., items embodying intermediate and appropriate technologies).

Efforts were constantly made, most notably by Robert McNamara as president of the World Bank beginning in 1968, to reform this process, to target it more effectively on "the poorest 40 percent" and to correct its urban bias. The green revolution was hugely important in this new drive for rural development and contributed critically to feeding the extra mouths that the uniquely rapid demographic growth of the second half of the twentieth century produced.[57] But by the early 1980s it was overwhelmingly clear that this model of economic development, whether targeted at growth or poverty reduction or both, was simply not matching the competition or delivering sufficiently rapid change or amelioration. In the twenty-five years to 1985, India's per capita GDP barely rose at all (less than 0.25 percent a year); at the same time in almost all African countries output per head of the population was falling.

But countries that came to be known as the Asian tigers—and later the tiger cubs—were achieving annual growth rates per head of 5 percent or better, and they were mostly combining this with growing equality and dramatic improvements in human welfare.[58] These impressive performances came to overshadow, if they did not absolutely dispose of, the arguments about the earlier Indian model of state-planned, import-led, ODA-financed development. The World Bank, which in the early 1990s increasingly saw the Asian tigers' performance as a paradigm for all development, observed that there was "one chance in ten thousand that success would have been so regionally concentrated" by random chance.[59]

That did not settle the arguments about the essence of successful development policies, since some attributed Asia's success to the scope offered to market forces to do their work in a large private sector, whereas others emphasized the role of governments. Taiwan and South Korea, for example, two countries that did exceptionally well in growth and reducing poverty, used the powers of government forcefully to direct economic change. Export-led strategies were fostered through devaluations and direct intervention. Landownership was radically reformed in favor of the poorer peasants. Government invested heavily in human capital(through education and health programs), and the forced savings being extracted from the peasants by government taxes and pricing strategies were, at least in part, recycled back to rural areas in the form of infrastructure investment, agroscience research and subsidies for nonfarm enterprises.[60]

The World Bank, dominated by its American intellectual climate at the time, ascribed the success—"growth with equity"—of the eight high-performing Asian economies (Japan, Hong Kong, South Korea, Singapore, Taiwan, Indonesia, Malaysia and Thailand) mainly to their adherence to sound economic fundamentals: letting markets, prices and competition work in an environment of low inflation, competitive exchange rates, investment in human capital, strong financial systems, openness to foreign technology imports and respect for the vital role of agriculture. Insofar as direct intervention in markets by industrial, trade and financial measures produced helpful results, as they clearly did in Japan, South Korea and Taiwan, this, said the bank, "was only possible because of highly unusual historical and institutional circumstances." The bank believed that the foundation of the whole operation, the strategy of "export-push," a mix of both fundamentals and interventions, need not necessarily get more difficult as the number and size of successful users of this approach increased and as the absorptive capacity of the rest of the world fell back from the seemingly exceptional levels enjoyed in the early postwar decades, because such exports still represent a very small share of the big markets of the developed North and because new opportunities are emerging for South-South trade between developing nations exploiting their respective comparative advantages.[61]

The Asian crisis of 1997–1998 seemed to knock a large dent in this confident thesis, especially the part that seemed to commend the success and strength of the financial sectors of the East Asian economies. With hindsight, the authors of the 1993 report might have preferred not to have written that

> fundamental approaches were important in all eight economies. These included . . . the creation of secure bank-based financial systems. . . . Regulation included enforcement of prudent behaviour, such as limiting speculative lending. . . . [Governments] promoted confidence in the banking system by devising rescue programmes as needed . . . [and] have also promoted bond and equity markets to increase the depth of maturing financial sectors . . . , creating specialised development banks . . . [which] furthered the growth of the financial sector by establishing procedures for project financing and monitoring that commercial banks then copied. . . . Their bad debts were usually associated with economic downturns rather than the willful default common in economies where government officials are closely involved in day-to-day management.[62]

This language sits uncomfortably with the instant retrospective diagnosis of the financial panics, exchange rate depreciations, stock market collapses and bank failures that characterized the spreading Asian crisis after the Thai devaluation in the summer of 1997. All this was suddenly explained—by the IMF, perhaps seeing an opportunity to score off its sibling organization the World Bank—by the immaturity of East Asia's financial sector, the shallowness of its financial markets and institutions and the excessively close relationship between too many of its banks and the political leadership, which stood in the way of a proper reconstruction that would have involved the bankruptcy of precisely those leaders.

But we are getting ahead of ourselves. The last decade of the century may be looked at differently from, though in the light of, the distinct stories of First, Second and Third Worlds that, for convenience, we have so far traced (or in some cases more than traced). There developed a sense in which not the division of the planet into three or more separate worlds but its integration into a single—"globalized"—economy came to dominate perceptions of economic change in the last lap to the millennium. A word needs to be said about the nature of the thing called "globalization."

A primitive model is often presented of the challenge that it presents to the nation-state and of the appropriate response to it. It implies that globalization is some sort of alien force—insidious and corrosive—a gas, perhaps, that has got loose and that man, in the form of the nation-state, needs to bring back under control, a task that can be successfully undertaken only if the nation is very strong and therefore very big.

But this is fantasy. Globalization, in the sense of the modern form of the world economy with a high degree of freedom of movement of goods, services, capital, technology and management in response to market opportunity, is our own recent creation.

It is we who through successive GATT rounds and the establishment of the World Trade Organization, including the agreement in November 1999 to include China as a member, have liberalized world trade. It is we who through the progressive implementation of the stated goals of the International Monetary Fund have liberalized world payments, established internal and external convertibility of currencies, reduced and abolished exchange controls and smoothed the path for the free movement of capital. It is we who have fostered and championed the development of great multinational and global corporations that use the best management skills and mobilize the cheapest savings and the latest technology to combine with the most effective labor in the lowest-cost base to produce the tradable goods and services that they sell in the best markets, indeed in almost all markets. And it is we who have urged and welcomed the admission of the former communist and other self-isolated economies and their huge labor forces back into the world market economy.

And we have done all these things because we, the governments and peoples of the old First World in North America, Europe and Japan, who were the architects of the postwar global economic order and the guardians of its more recent development, believe that such economic liberalism promotes economic prosperity.

If we had believed that it was a problem, not a solution, an unacceptable challenge to the nation-state, a threat to our living standards, a source of global turbulence, we need not have done it. But it is anyway an error to regret what we have done and a misconception to wish to recreate the predominant power of the autarkic nation-state in order to subdue the forces we have unleashed.

We expected it to enhance global prosperity, and it has. The opportunity to combine capital and labor, management, technology and markets in the most efficient manner no doubt accelerates the growth and improves the distribution of the prosperity of the globe as a whole.

It is perverse to wish to unwind this real leap forward, though it is also true that we need a comparable leap forward in our ability to capture environmental goods in the interplay of market forces. We need, as it were, to harness the pervasive influence of the "invisible hand" to protect and promote such goods, along with the other elements in human welfare that already enter into market forces through their influence on consumer preferences, relative prices, changing profitability and so the decisions of producers and investors.

Nonetheless, there is a globalization problem, and it is important to be clear what it is and what it is not. It is not the case that the availability of cheap labor in South and East Asia is leading to vast swathes of the world's production being transferred to these areas, with disastrous consequences for the old industrial economies and their workers. If that were so, the effects would manifest themselves in huge export surpluses in the Third World countries and impossible deficits, leading to contraction and crisis, in the First World. There are few such surpluses for the good reason that the newly emergent economies in Asia and elsewhere wish to spend their export earnings buying the luxuries, technologies and other advantages they do not yet have.

In this respect world trade has been working very much in the way that the textbooks said it should, with different economies exploiting their comparative advantages and the general level of prosperity rising as a result. But something else has happened that has caused a problem. The effective addition in a short space of time of the Indian and Chinese (and some other) workforces—self-disciplined, apt and poor—to the labor supply of the global market economy must have changed the supply and demand balance for labor and therefore the relative bargaining power of capital and labor.

In conditions of global management of companies, free movement of capital and free trade, the global labor market is more nearly a single market in which price differences are anomalies that tend to be eroded by normal arbitrage—the process technically known as factor cost equalization. There comes more nearly to be a world price for a given category of labor, where the category defines the skill level of the workers in question.

This is good news for a lot of people. It is good news for the owners of capital who can marry their savings to more cost-effective labor and earn a better return. It is good news for the owners of labor who could not previously get together with globally mobile capital to their mutual advantage. It is good news for the world's consumers, who will now be offered low prices. In other words, it is good news for rich people in rich countries: They can invest where labor is cheaper or just drive a better bargain with labor at home. It is good news for rich people in poor countries for the same reason. It is good news for poor people in poor countries because they are offered jobs and even incomes that were not previously available to them.

But it is bad news for the owners of the labor that was previously combined with capital that was effectively imprisoned in the home economy but is now free to seek new alliances wherever the most cost-effective deals offer themselves. It is potentially very bad news, that is, for poor people in rich countries. The historic high living standards of the blue-collar working class in First World countries did not rest on their special, marketable skills, though there were certain social and cultural qualities that in the opinion of many employers made some areas and even nations more attractive locations for production than others.

What made the European and even more the American working classes affluent by global standards in the twentieth century was essentially that more capital was combined with each worker in those economies than elsewhere. That in turn reflected their early successes in generating savings and discovering new continents and was combined with the unacceptable commercial and political hazards (until recently) of large-scale direct or portfolio investment outside the First World, to say nothing of direct government prohibitions against such investment.

That corset holding in the affluent world's capital has been shed, and globally minded management in international companies has stood ready to seize the opportunity, which has been reinforced by the opening up of formerly self-isolated economies such as India and China. All this has driven down the real-world price of low-skilled labor, and this has coincided with a quite different pressure on the manufacturing base of First World economies, as they were up until at least the 1960s. As the world has become more affluent, there has been a relative shift away from manufactured goods in favor of services and other forms of consumption. This in its turn seems to have coincided with an exceptionally rapid rise in productivity in manufacturing. This has doubly reduced the amount of labor required to produce the manufactured goods the world wants, which has prompted a process of deindustrialization—of the labor force, if not of the total output of the First World economies.

If this had been the only thing going on, it might have created no more than uncomfortable adjustment problems for the industrial working classes in North America and Europe. But when combined with the global deterioration in the bargaining power of low-skilled labor and the resulting fall in its real global price, it has generated the problem we know as globalization, which concretely means that in America a significant underclass is obliged to live on more or less subsistence earnings and in Europe the equivalent people, unable to earn what we think of as a "First World" standard of living in the global labor market, depend on forms of corporate and state welfare that even Germany increasingly doubts whether it can afford.

None of this means that the old First World economies are poorer in consequence of these changes than they would have been without them. For while their low-skilled labor faces a fall in its real-world price, their capital is benefiting from the opportunity to combine with cheaper labor, not only in Asia but at home, too, as a consequence of the changed bargaining power. Thus, in an extreme case the gross domestic product of such an economy might fall, relative to normal growth trends, but its gross national product, which includes investment income from abroad, might be unchanged or even enhanced.

The challenge to which this gives rise may therefore be not how to isolate the home economy from global market forces but how to recycle the income that is flooding in from the enhanced profitability of capital back to the bulk of ordinary consumers whose income as workers has relatively diminished.

To the extent that their own savings have been invested in forms that participate in the new flow of profits, this recycling may come about automatically, especially for those with private insurance and pension protection. It may also come about through the operation of both public and corporate welfare schemes financed out of the general stream of corporate profits and the general pool of taxation (what on the Continent is called the "European social model").

Or the challenge may be simply ignored, as it is to some degree in the United States, with the consequent creation of what Robert Reich, President Clinton's secretary of labor, called a "Third World" economy within America.[63]

We said earlier that the perception of a globalized economy dominated the last lap to the millennium, and so it has. But in the final straight some of the urgency of those preoccupations abated in consequence of the Asian crisis, on which we have already touched, and the threat in the summer of 1998 that that crisis might spread into a more general crisis of confidence in the ability of the world's economic and monetary authorities to prevent a general meltdown, as it was called, and possible global depression.

That did not happen, and in 1999 that shadow seemed to pass almost as rapidly as it had appeared. The U.S. economy, buoyed by a stock market whose sanguineness defied all hazards, continued to provide the locomotive drive of a world economy that refused to lie down despite an almost decade-long slump in Japan, a near recession in Europe, the recent havoc from South Korea to Thailand in Asia, horrible wobbles in Latin America and the awful agonies of Russia. By the final quarter of 1999, all these areas, even Russia, seemed to be strengthening rather than deteriorating, and still the U.S. crash was postponed.

The effect, however, of the traumas from 1997 had been temporarily to resurrect, on a basis of common commercial prudence rather than official regulation, the barriers to capital flows from the First World to emerging markets that had been a key feature of early 1990s globalization. As a result, and as cyclical conditions improved in the old First World economies, fears about globalization, both the rationally based ones described above and the more hysterical and xenophobic variety, abated. The peril appeared more remote, though the basic threat to the incomes of unskilled workers in historically rich countries remained just as real in the medium term. And to widespread surprise in America and Europe, even in the short term globalization was a contributory factor to the failure of the inflationary dog to bark even when the American boom seemed to be giving it every possible provocation.

Was this another false dawn or, as some hoped, the final beginning of the end of the search for a global political economy that would deliver prosperity for most people while discouraging conflict among them and among nations? Was the battle of ideologies, if not history itself, over? Were we at last stumbling upon a sound footing for a new century and a new millennium, which could therefore hope to be safe from the disfigurements that had made the first half of the twentieth century so hideous and that inspired the "never again" search for better answers in the second half of the century? Many dawns had proved false. Was this one any better? The answer will be known only in the future, and the question can be discussed at this stage only as speculation. This is not the historian's normal stock in trade, but in the final chapter we shall allow ourselves some speculative license.

CHAPTER TEN

Now What?

WE HAVE TOLD OUR STORY. WITHIN THE LIMITS OF SUCH A VOLUME as this, aiming to trace the key episodes in our economic course from our original lives as hunters and gatherers to our condition today, written by a layman for laymen, pretending to no academic refinement, but with the hope of vouchsafing a sufficient smattering of those moments of "Oh, I *see!*" to give intellectual pleasure to the reader, our task is done.

Yet an author would need be fastidious to the point of asceticism to lay down his pen at this point, telling himself that the future is not his province, that speculation is not history and that guesswork ill becomes the scholar or even the journalist. It is repugnant to human intelligence to survey the facts of our knowledge and experience without making some attempt to discern patterns that give us what we regard as understanding. Just to observe and record the past like stones and boulders randomly distributed across a barren landscape and to leave them so with no more than a shrug is to explain nothing, and to extol such purity of empiricism as a scholarly virtue is to cheat the natural appetite of curious minds for enlightenment, for a satisfying account not just of what happened but of why it happened, or at least how it happened.

Such an account cannot but deal in generalizations. If everything is particular, there can be no recognition of recurrent patterns. And if there are no such patterns, there can be no understanding, no explanation and certainly no prediction. However often we are reminded of the fallibility of our generalizations, we cannot learn, or bear, to live without them.

So as our calendar counts down to now, to n-year, n-day and n-hour, what should we tell our children that we have learned from our past, and what can they expect in the future? These questions we address in this final chapter, allowing ourselves more latitude of opinion and speculation than would have been tolerable before. Those for whom such stuff is odious or otiose may skip it, substituting perhaps their own musings.

A *theory* of human economic change is implied in and by the account so far given in this history of the wealth of man, if the word "theory" can be applied loosely to a set of general beliefs about people, individually and in society, and about the material world with which they interact. The first proposition is a basic proposition about what might be called man's economic nature. That proposition, baldly put, is that given half a chance he will seek to maintain and improve his material condition.

This is no more than Adam Smith's original psychological premise of his theory that human societies progress naturally toward "opulence" (a word he used in order to avoid the narrower connotation of "wealth") provided that mankind's natural curiosity, ingenuity and competitiveness are unconstrained by human predators from above or from without or by other ecological or political adversity. This "natural" disposition may be taken to include not just the mental agility to figure out answers to practical "how" questions but also the imagination to conceive of and covet forms and degrees of wealth and comfort well beyond those immediately presented to the senses. Only the human brain, both clever and greedy, seems to have continuously impelled its host species toward levels of affluence, for individuals, that are and remain quite inconceivable to other animals.

It is tempting to link this with the hypothesis we examined in Chapter 1 that some kind of fundamental physical change occurred in the operation of the brain about 60–30 kya as a result of which it became capable of feats of abstract thought that brought huge extensions of both human appetite and human skill and knowledge within the potential range of the species. It is also tempting to rely on a quasi-Darwinian presumption that humans—and human societies that gave particular scope to such humans—who displayed such capacities would have been likely to prevail in economic competition with those who did not, thereby making them more likely to survive and prosper and so over time to come to constitute a growing and ultimately dominant proportion of mankind.

A second proposition within the theory implied in these pages is that the human proclivities described above interact with more or less favorable surrounding circumstances, some of which are natural, some man-made. Where this interaction produces an increase in economic opportunity—the discovery of agriculture; the spread of settlements in villages, towns and cities; the coinages of the Aegean world; the Roman "peace"; the Islamic, Indian and Chinese civilizations; the resurrection of feudal Europe; the reconnection of the Eurasian world to the American land masses; the interconnection of almost all economic centers in a single global network of ocean routes; the surge of enterprise, invention and investment that became the industrial revolution—such increase generates predatory reflexes. These threaten both from within and without the societies enjoying the new opportunities, and the management of those challenges by government—through lawmaking and law enforcement, military action and political and diplomatic negotiation—determines how much, if any, of the original enlargement of opportunity is successfully cashed in improved living standards (or rising population) and how much is squandered in conflict. That is the theme of the waltz motif running through our story.

A third proposition in our theory is that *government matters.* To some extent this is implicit in the second proposition, because the ability of societies to prosper depends on their ability, mainly through their governance systems, to manage the predatory threats that economic success generates.

There have, of course, to be the initiating steps forward in economic opportunity, which may frequently develop with little or no input from government, indeed despite its active discouragement. But the greater the success, the greater is likely to be the target for predators, who may be nothing but the general run of citizens who are not seemingly benefiting from the latest figure of the waltz. If this provokes a direct move to preempt the new wealth and transfer it by political action, whether violent or not, whether within or between societies, then governance becomes the key issue. Can the threat be managed, and can it be managed in a way that preserves at least most of the original gain in economic opportunity to be enjoyed by someone?

Such successful management requires that any governance that seeks to regulate the balance between economic opportunity and economic order is both strong enough to overbear those predators who seek to take advantage by direct seizure rather than by production and limited enough to leave ample room for man's curiosity, ingenuity and competitiveness to continue the great work of the progress of opulence. In the search for that balance, in its all too frequent loss on one side or the other, lies much of the story of the wealth of man, as it has been experienced by most of the 80 billion or more human beings who have so far lived on earth.[1]

Good government, it may be said, allows mankind more nearly to live up to the potential of both knowledge and the existing supplies of natural resources, including land. It may further allow that potential to be extended more rather than less rapidly over longer periods. Bad government has an almost limitless downward potential and can indeed reduce material standards to the level of subsistence and below. It is perhaps unduly semantic to quibble over whether this should be construed as meaning that governments can do harm but cannot do good, other than by refraining from doing harm, or at least can do limitless harm but only limited good. What appears beyond historical dispute is that government matters and that its variable quality accounts for a huge amount of the variability of human economic experience from place to place and time to time.

A refinement of this thesis grapples with the notion that if the test of good government in its economic aspect is how conducive it is to prosperity and growth, then in the longer term the best form of governance may be one that offers a plurality of authorities, both in neighboring territories and within any particular territories, between which and with which the innovator may to some degree choose and negotiate, seeking the environment most favorable to his ideas and putting a kind of Darwinian pressure on those who lag behind to join the vanguard or vanish. Some such thought as this, offensive as it may be to tidy-minded theories of elegant and stable constitutional architecture and vulnerable as it may be to the obvious objection that that way lies chaos and conflict, has animated those historians of medieval Europe who have been impressed by its progress, in both country and town, from the ninth to the twelfth centuries and then again beginning in the fourteenth century.

The centrally orchestrated rejection by China of economic opportunities—for industrialization in the twelfth century and for global maritime and commercial dominance in the fifteenth—may seem to provide negative evidence for the pluralist case, though the twentieth-century experiences of post-communist Russia, Mao's China, Deng's China and postcolonial Africa all seem to put the emphasis back on the simpler notion of the need for good—and the perils of bad—government rather than on the subtler notion of pluralism. The fate of the Greek city-states and the glories of the Roman Antonines seem likewise to teach the conservative message of the blessings of order, whereas the ultimate fate of Rome and the modern story of Soviet communism—both ossified and denied the dynamism of competition—teach the radical message of the need for change.

Most historians struggle with the dilemma that although logic demands that theories be consistently applied—if pluralism was good for tenth-century Europe, it should be good for twentieth-century Africa—history requires respect for the particular, the concrete and, above all, the attested. To say that things work differently in different places and at different times will hardly be tolerated by natural scientists as a defense of the inconsistent application of natural laws; but historians, wherever they prefer to lie on the spectrum from chronicler to theorist, can never quite be scientists and must always seek to tell the story in ways that compel belief without the enviable sanction of repeatable experiments in the laboratory.

Postcolonial Africa, even if superficially similar as the relic of a departed empire (or empires) is like all historical periods and places unique and so uniquely different from all others, not least Dark Age and medieval Europe. It may be that the second half of the twentieth century has been the Dark Continent's dark age and that the flickering we now see of new and wiser attempts at progress for its people will in retrospect warrant analogies with Europe's awakening in the ninth or tenth century. But Africa's quest for a better century than the past three takes place in the world of modern science and technology, as well as modern weapons of war and revolt, with nearly thirty times the population of tenth-century Europe and with so many other differences that it seems absurd even to inquire whether some broad-brush formula, such as pluralistic authority, would have the same effects in both places and times.

And yet and yet . . . What is the value of such an account of medieval Europe's development if it has no consistent application elsewhere and elsewhen? So long as history is written by historians—and some of it always will be because of the insatiable demand for narrative, to know what happened—this question will remain, breathing down the neck of the author who generalizes too glibly or whose vision is through a tunnel and beckoning the more formal disciplines to encroach ever further onto the historian's patch.

This is, perhaps, little different, in logic and differentiation of function, from the coexistence in the ephemeral world of today of ever more specialized knowledge with undiminished demand for the kind of journalism that seeks to report and to explain events as they occur by reference to frequently implicit, though sometimes widely shared, assumptions about the way the world works. We cannot escape the desire to know or the need to say, whether about medieval Europe or about yesterday's news, what happened and why. Faced with stern pressure from the experts and from the people with the numbers to state a universal hypothesis or be silent, we may just have to reject the choice, to speak and to write what seems to us to be true and to confess without excessive shame that we are unable for the moment, or perhaps at all, to explain why it does not always work like that. But we may still think, and without self-contradiction, that pluralism contributed to economic dynamism in medieval Europe, whereas postcolonial Africa might have been better served by the likes of Marcus Aurelius and Deng Xiaoping.

A fourth proposition in our theory must be that the discovery of agriculture and the discovery of compound growth of economic output (otherwise known as the industrial revolution) were changes of profounder importance than any others, though of course it remains incumbent upon us to continue to delve into their own antecedent causes. Agriculture revolutionized the productivity of land, and industry revolutionized the productivity of labor. Between them they account for, if they do not completely explain, the main quantitative changes in mankind's material condition. When Steven Mithen says that "if you look at the last 100,000 years, the start of farming is the biggest transformation that has occurred and after it has happened, well, the rest just unfolds as history," he is half right.[2] The great growth in human numbers is thereby enabled. But the other half—the great growth in living standards in the industrial world over the past two centuries, the final seconds of archaeological time—is more than "just history."

Oversimplifying bravely, but not intolerably, one may say that agriculture enabled mankind to increase 1,000-fold in number over the previous 10,000 years. We saw in Chapter 1 that one hunter-gatherer needed around 10 square miles of favorable territory to survive, but with even primitive agriculture more than fifty people could live off just one square mile—though it naturally took most of the time since primitive times for the potential to be anywhere nearly fully exploited.

If we disregard new additions of favorable territory since the earliest days, we would still need only, by arithmetic, a microscopic further annual growth in agricultural land efficiency of less than 0.05 percent to provide the extra food necessary to feed the 1,000-fold increase in population that has actually occurred. In other words the discovery of agriculture enabled the population to increase 500 times, and improvements in its efficiency enabled one further doubling of that result. Actual food supply has of course increased even more than that because four-fifths of the world's population are living today at better than subsistence levels. But that extra can be ascribed to the impact of the industrial revolution on agriculture, as in the role of the tractor and the green revolution.

What agriculture did not do was greatly to raise the productivity of (farm) labor. Indeed, in Chapter 1 we saw that early farm societies worked much longer hours and lived harder lives than the hunter-gatherers they replaced. That helps to explain why the main effect of the huge increase in land productivity went, as the millennia rolled by, into growing population rather than higher living standards. The land could produce 500 times as much food and eventually 1,000 times as much. But if we disregard the extra effects of the industrial revolution on food production, we would expect it to have taken something approaching as many people to produce each hundredweight of food and therefore eventually 500 times as many people to produce the 500-fold greater full potential global food supply by 1960 (when the population was indeed 3 billion, which equals 6 million times 500).

Likewise industry, by investing in and otherwise harnessing an indefinitely expanding body of technical skill and knowledge to the task of increasing economic output in quantity and quality, gave mankind for the first time the prospect of significant output growth at compound interest for an indefinitely long future period. This growth, unlike the growth in farm production, did not require a more or less equivalent increase in human numbers to produce it. It could be produced by an increase in output *per head,* and this over two centuries delivered what D. N. McCloskey calls the "heart of the matter": . . . twelve, the factor by which real income per head now exceeds what it was in 1780 in countries that have experienced "modern economic growth." No other "episode of enrichment" approaches modern economic growth in what it has done for the living standards of those humans affected by it, just as nothing approaches what the discovery of agriculture has done for human numbers.

In this way we can reconcile Mithen's view—crudely paraphrased as saying that after the agricultural revolution it was all over bar the history—with Keynes's view that there was no significant progress in the human condition before 1700, already quoted in Chapter 6.

Keynes made his characteristically arresting and bold assertion as a premise of his reasoning that "mankind is solving its economic problem," that "the standard of life in progressive countries one hundred years hence will be between four and eight times as high as it is today" and that "assuming no important wars and no important increase in population, the *economic problem* may be solved, or be at least within sight of solution, within a hundred years" and is not therefore "*the permanent problem of the human race.*"[3] The core of his argument was "the principle of compound interest . . . that most purposive of human institutions" applied to production.[4]

Until 1700 progress was small or negligible owing "to the remarkable absence of important technical improvements and to the failure of capital to accumulate."[5] Warming to his theme, Keynes asserted that "almost everything which really matters and which the world possessed at the commencement of the modern age was already known to man at the dawn of history."[6] If the dawn of history corresponds to his 2000 B.C. (4 kya) date, this gives scant credit to such things as coins, Pythagorean and other Greek mathematics, the water mill and the windmill, the compass, paper, gunpowder, the horse collar, the heavy plow, the clock, the spinning wheel and spectacles.

Nonetheless by the end of the Sumerian period (4.35 kya) human technical skills either embraced or were within a millennium of acquiring writing, including an alphabetic script; mathematics; astronomy and primitive science; architecture; medicine and engineering as professional disciplines; standardized weights and measures and the crafts of potters, metalworkers, weavers, masons, carpenters, shipbuilders, bronzesmiths and goldsmiths, to say nothing of the Ten Commandments, supposedly inscribed on tablets of stone by about 3.3 kya.[7] The potter's wheel, kiln-fired pottery, irrigation, the plow, the sail, wheeled vehicles, copper and silk manufacturing, advanced architecture (ziggurats, temples, pyramids, palaces), baking and iron smelting and ironworking all followed, if not by the dawn of history, at least by the time it was having breakfast, say 3 kya.[8]

Keynes's point, which is not necessarily disturbed even by quite a long list of important technical improvements, was that before the Industrial Revolution there was no basis in technical change or in capital accumulation for a process of self-perpetuating, exponential growth of output. But once that basis was supplied, the consequences are astounding, in any case to those not daily familiar with the magic of compound interest. Keynes calculates, just to illustrate his point, that if the £40,000 profit Queen Elizabeth I probably made from Sir Francis Drake's depredations upon the Spanish in 1580 had been invested abroad and had earned the 6.5 percent a year that Britain's overseas investments were earning between World Wars I and II, and if even half of that had been reinvested, then it would have become £4,000 million 250 years later, just the amount of Britain's foreign investments when Keynes was writing in 1930. More to the point, he notes that "if capital increases at 2 percent per annum, the capital equipment of the world will have increased by half in twenty years and seven and a half times in a hundred years. Think of this in terms of material things—houses, transport, and the like." He argues, too, that the pace of growth is accelerating and that what has so far chiefly affected industry may soon spread to agriculture, presciently speculating on a green revolution that would produce "improvements in the efficiency of food production as great as those which have already taken place in mining, manufacture, and transport."[9]

Thus he arrives at his prospective eightfold rise in the standard of life in progressive countries, absent war and extravagant population increases. In fact, if we look at world GDP per head over the seventy years since Keynes wrote, we find that even after the world's worst-ever war and another half century of immensely destructive warlike conflict and even after a threefold rise in global population, the average has already risen by between four- and sixfold, according to how one measures it (see Chapter 8).[10] Continuation of growth at the same rate would deliver a gain of between six- and twelvefold over Keynes's century, firmly embracing his eightfold or even his "possibility of a far greater progress still." And he was thinking only of "progressive countries."[11]

Before we address Keynes's amazing suggestion that by a date that is only thirty years away mankind may have permanently solved his economic problem, we must note that an English writer as great as Keynes—there are not many—had already understood and mutatis mutandis proclaimed Keynes's optimistic message precisely a century earlier. In 1830 Thomas Babington Macaulay, the great Whig theorist of English history, wrote:

> If we were to prophesy that in the year 1930 a population of fifty millions, better fed, clad and lodged than the English of our time, will cover these islands, that Sussex and Huntingdonshire will be wealthier than the wealthiest parts of the West Riding of Yorkshire now are, that cultivation, rich as that of a flower-garden, will be carried up to the very tops of Ben Nevis and Helvellyn, that machines constructed on principles yet undiscovered will be in every house, that there will be no highways but railroads, no travelling but by steam, that our debt, vast as it seems to us, will appear to our great-grandchildren a trifling encumbrance, which might easily be paid off in a year or two, many people would think us insane. We prophesy nothing; but this we say: If any person had told the Parliament which met in perplexity and terror after the crash in 1720 [the South Sea bubble] that in 1830 the wealth of England would surpass all their wildest dreams, that the annual revenue would equal the principal of that debt which they considered as an intolerable burden, that for one man of ten thousand pounds then living, there would be five men of fifty thousand pounds, that London would be twice as large and twice as populous, and that nevertheless the rate of mortality would have diminished to one half of what it then was, that the postoffice would bring more into the exchequer than the excise and customs had brought in together under Charles the Second, that stage-coaches would run from London to York in twenty-four hours, that men would be in the habit of sailing without wind, and would be beginning to ride without horses, our ancestors would have given as much credit to the prediction as they gave to *Gulliver's Travels*. . . . To almost all men the state of things under which they live seems to be the necessary state of things. . . . Hence it is that, though in every age everybody knows that up to his own time progressive improvement has been

> taking place, nobody seems to reckon on any improvement during the next generation. We cannot absolutely prove that those are in error who tell us that society has reached a turning point, that we have seen our best days. But so said all who came before us, and with just as much apparent reason. . . . On what principle is it that, when we see nothing but improvement behind us, we are to expect nothing but deterioration before us?[12]

That is the authentic voice of the optimists of the British nineteenth century, the believers in progress as an all-but-inevitable law of history, or at least of English history after the Glorious Revolution of 1688. With a selective and Anglocentric eye it was not too difficult to trace this happy story from the monetary foundations laid by Locke and Newton, through the beginnings of England's great leap forward after 1700, taking in the midcentury geopolitical order of Lord Chatham (see Chapter 5) and celebrating the liberal ideas of David Hume and Adam Smith, all amplified and reenergized by the industrial, American and French Revolutions, culminating in the triumphs of a truly international economy by 1850. The truth was grubbier, but both Macaulay and Keynes grasped the fundamental factor and its implications, economic growth.

Together they challenge us to ask the question they asked—What can we expect for our grandchildren and our great-grandchildren?—and to explain why the next 100 years should not experience or indeed improve further upon the rate of progress of the previous century and the one before that. As in 1850, and in a far more thoroughgoing way, we live at what seems some kind of high tide of economic globalization. Barriers to everything except the mass migration of peoples are low. As Macaulay did when he was writing in 1830, we live now a decade or so after what we hope is the end of almost a century of wars hot and cold and in the early spring of a long peace. As to Keynes's other proviso—"no important increase in population"—we have really for the first time since the Black Death the prospect, according to the dominant demographic consensus emanating from the UN, of a stable world population, not admittedly at today's numbers but only about 50 percent above today's numbers. This projection is rooted in the very fact of economic growth and rising living standards, especially as they affect the decisions of women about their own fertility.

Nothing could be harder to predict with confidence than the progress of knowledge itself or of those innovations in technique and management that augment the productivity of each person and other productive factors—capital and land. In the late 1970s it was possible to hear arguments that so far as economically useful research was concerned, pure science had advanced to a point where it was scraping the barrel and that therefore future science-based economic growth might slow down. Now we are in the full throes of what we call the information technology (IT) revolution. In addition the chemistry of new materials and the life sciences, including medical science, brain science and genetics, appear to the layman and the scientist alike to be overflowing with exciting new knowledge.

Today's new technologies of information, communication, tailor-made materials and biotechnology, with new fuels and nanotechnology (the technology of producing goods out of individual atoms and molecules) on their way, all add up in the judgment of Richard Lipsey to the kind of "general purpose technologies" that transform the economic, social and political structures of whole societies, like the great pillars of the agricultural revolution (domestication of crops and animals); like the great advances of Sumer and Babylon; like the waterwheel and the windmill, the three-masted sailing ship and the movable-type printing press; like the big inventions of the first and second industrial revolutions (especially automated textile machinery, the steam engine, electricity and the internal combustion engine) and now like the computer.[13] That is a big claim, as is its corollary, that similar long periods of sustained dynamism may be expected in the economies chiefly affected, especially the United States, with economic, social, political and cultural consequences as profound as those of the industrial revolutions.

It would not trivialize the importance of the computer and its emerging role in the modern economy to hesitate just a little longer before we put it into the same hall of fame as farming, writing, global navigation, coal, iron, steam, electricity and motorized transport. Those things, as we have seen, transformed the human presence on the planet by 1,000 times in numbers and by manyfold in average wealth. The computer allows us to do a whole range of things that we have been doing for a long time more quickly (not always), more conveniently, more reliably, more efficiently, more economically and perhaps, in some more elusive sense, more democratically, as computer use spreads more widely. Such a change on so broad a front may add up in the end to something that should be regarded as completely new in its own right. And computers already enable us to do some things we could not previously do at all, for example, in the fields of very complex mathematical modeling (as in long-range weather forecasting, short-range prediction of hurricane behavior, medical diagnosis using CAT scans and air traffic control).[14]

But whatever exactly will be said by the economic historian in the year 3000 about the importance of today's technical advances, there is not the slightest plausibility in or evidence for the proposition, which would anyway be inherently unprovable, that some kind of law of diminishing returns is about to curtail economic growth in the new century. The nature of knowledge, or even of just knowledge about the physical world, suggests no analogy with other economic resources whose supply may be supposed to be finite. Knowledge could be exhausted only if it were total, and one can hardly suppose that mankind is to be so fortunate as to be confronted with that problem, even if we could attach any meaning to the notion of the exhaustion of knowledge.

Keynes's other main driver of growth is capital, the investment that turns new knowledge and ideas into productive facilities and processes. For capital, nothing is required but savings, and for savings nothing is required but income. Incomes we already have. They are on average higher than they have ever been, and that average is rising. Capital shortages may indeed arise from time to time in relation to particular challenges. But even the huge present challenges of reconstructing eastern Europe and the former Soviet Union, as well as financing the rapid transformation of vast economies like China and India, do not seem to be posing a problem of absolute capital shortage. With incomes rising, the difficulty of finding capital for investment cannot be increasing absolutely.

So can economic growth continue indefinitely, and if it does, will the "economic problem" be solved, by 2030 or any other date? There are, if we exclude threats from beyond the province of the economic historian such as a new Black Death, asteroid collision or radical instability in man's genetic composition, several kinds of threat that we may suppose could derail—some would argue is in one case already derailing—the progress of mankind, or at least a majority of mankind, toward permanent emancipation from the struggle for subsistence. This, as Keynes observed, "has been hitherto the primary, most pressing problem of the human race—

not only of the human race, but of the whole of the biological kingdom from the beginnings of life in its most primitive forms."

To escape altogether from this problem would amount to a kind of permanent suspension of Darwinian pressures uniquely for our species. Is it possible? Let us leave on aside for the moment the question whether Darwin's most familiar proposition is not at bottom a truism and, as such, incapable of suspension in any realizable world. Instead let us first note the less philosophical and more empirical clouds in the sky: population, politics and possible threats to the global and/or large regional environment.

We have already noted the comforting belief of consensus demographers that the global population is probably stabilizing and doing so at a level clearly not beyond—or anywhere near—the limits of habitable space or prospective food supplies, though we would intuitively consider alarming a 50 percent rise in what we commonly think of as our crowded planet. We need, however, to note the intellectual magnitude of any claim that the world's population might be indefinitely stable at, say, 9 billion people. Both Malthus and Darwin were deeply serious thinkers grappling with fundamental questions about the nature and dynamics of life on earth and of human population. For a whole species—and seemingly one of the most successful in evolutionary terms in the 600 million or so years of life on earth—suddenly to cease to press against the limits of the environment on which it depends would be an astonishing event. For it to do so, not because as with the Black Death some other life form has at least temporarily triumphed over it, nor because it has destroyed itself in fratricidal conflict, but simply and voluntarily because the individual members of the species no longer choose, by way of procreation and self-reproduction, to do what their ancestors in their own and other species had been doing so tirelessly and so successfully for most of biological time would indeed seem to require the natural order to be suspended.

Of course, it might so fall out for a few decades, perhaps even a century or two. There are plenty of places and times in human and indeed other zoological history where population has not immediately pressed to its theoretical limits, and we have never before lived in a time when living standards, education, knowledge and therefore choice were as high or as real as they are now for the average human being, though there are also, of course, more people living in absolute poverty, poverty that might have been recognized as such by our forebears even thousands of years ago, than ever before—probably 200 times as many as there were on the eve of the agricultural revolution. There is nothing impossible about the official UN population forecasts.

But even in the short term the recent response of people to rising living standards—to slow their own fertility down to mere replacement rates—may not be stable or permanent. There are already weak signs that even higher levels of affluence and even better systems of support for mothers are creating incentives to increase family sizes again. More broadly, one cannot but wonder how sensitive the recent slowdown may be to the cultural and social, as well as the material and economic, conditions that have encouraged it. Will societies fully embrace and continue to protect the relatively liberal attitudes that have made it practicable for women to make the decisions that their new knowledge and living standards have made possible? Or may fashions in such matters seesaw? Even in the United States primitive superstitions and ethical blindness can afflict broad swathes of an immensely affluent and educated society, not least constraining the nation's lawmakers to adopt barbaric postures.

Beyond the short term there are the basic engines of the Darwinian and the Malthusian models, in Darwin's case that the "survivors" will survive and that those who opt out of the evolutionary competition will be outflanked by those who stay in the game (as with the farmers and the hunter-gatherers in the early Neolithic period) and in Malthus's case that reproduction at any rate greater than replacement is a geometric progression while environmental support for a species—food and the rest—may increase only arithmetically or, if geometrically, only for a while before collision with the rest of nature puts a knee in the curve and so levels its growth off. To see his point, consider only that 100 barrels of annual oil use increased by 5 percent a year will overtake 100 barrels of annual oil supply increased by 100 barrels a year within less than a century (and will have cumulatively consumed more than the accumulated supply over a period of 121 years). How sure should we be that enough, as it were, dedicated Darwinians will not break from the ranks of the nice "replacement rate" majority to visit precisely such a Darwinian revenge on their demographic betters? If not sooner, then why not later? The pope, for example, may feel that it is not only the big battalions but also the laws of Darwin and compound interest that may yet be on his god's side.

This brings us in turn to the equally fundamental and perhaps slightly less intractable Malthusian question about how sure we should be that the planet can achieve—and otherwise sustain—a geometric progress of supply, either to meet the needs of an exponentially growing population or to fulfill the aspirations of a stable population for exponentially rising living standards, broadly measured by global economic production spread across all consuming heads, or some combination of the two. We have already dismissed this question in its purely economic aspect. Knowledge and investment to sustain such exponential growth may be presumed to be, in principle, in essentially limitless supply.

But what of the environment? Can we extract—or substitute for—the raw materials of production and of life itself without any limit? We need, above all, energy. We need potable water and breathable air. We need soils that we can cultivate. We need perhaps some key materials (wood, paper, metals), chemical elements and life forms (biodiversity) without which many what seem to us now indispensable processes could not get started, whether in construction, the creation of new materials or healthcare. We need other animals than ourselves and other species that in ways we cannot definitively map are deeply involved in that complex, kaleidoscopic and sometimes unstable balance of nature that underpins our own habitat. In most of these fields, beyond energy itself, water, air and soil, it becomes increasingly difficult to specify exactly what is essential. Some of the things that sound essential, like materials and biodiversity, are not so much specific items as categories of necessity that can be met in a variety of ways.

If we take a reasonably robust view of these matters, we may decide that an unknowable future is at least as likely to throw up answers to many, perhaps all, of the problems of sustainable supply as was the past to find, for example, undreamed of ways of feeding a gradually growing population even after the supply of large huntable mammals collapsed. But there is one obvious matter in which we need to dig a little deeper before we snuggle into the warm blanket of fingers-crossed self-reassurance that "it may never happen," and that is waste.

Economic activity on the scale and in the numbers we now have, and will increasingly have, generates waste, fundamentally in the form of matter and heat given off by or left over from our useful economic exertions and their products. The laws of physics require that waste energy goes somewhere, and not all of it can be successfully recycled into a stable and life-supporting ecology. Until very recently the relative size of the human species and the planet it inhabits seemed to provide a limitless capacity for absorbing, or at least accommodating unnoticed, such waste as could not be recycled into our biosphere. The oceans alone seemed boundless in this as well as in other ways.

But the planet's capacity to absorb waste without cumulatively harmful consequences for man—and for many other living organisms—no longer appears boundless. It is not beyond dispute, but it is well beyond complacent disregard, that progressively drastic changes in our physical global environment will occur within periods of time measured in decades rather than centuries, let alone millennia, if mankind continues to generate into the atmosphere emissions of the kind, on the scale and at the rate of growth currently associated with energy use in the advanced economies and in those other highly populous economies, such as India and China, who are determined not forever to be denied American and European standards of life.

Such a threat is a classic example of the economist's "external diseconomy," a damage to everyone or to the society at large that is not discouraged or protected against by any corrective feedback through market forces. The man who emits the damage—most of us as individual consumers and economic operators—may in the end face the consequences as a member of the human race, but he is under no individual economic incentive to restrain himself. His best interest is that everyone else should restrain themselves while he continues to use the planet as his free garbage disposal service. He is or aspires to be, in the language of the economist, a free rider.

This is not the place to burrow deeply into the attempts to wrestle with this problem made at successive earth summits or global conferences on climate change in Rio, Kyoto and wherever next. Nor need we join in the arguments how far some system of emission entitlements, perhaps based on the eventual goal of an equality of entitlements per head of population and perhaps linked to a secondary market in which such entitlements can be bought and sold between those who have them and those who need them, may or may not be either sufficient or workable. It is enough to note that here at least is one way in which Malthus's big idea—that if human numbers tend in the absence of war and disease to rise geometrically, something somewhere that they need will sooner or later run out, thus curbing their numbers by famine or other equivalent shortage—may still have the power to haunt us.

The numbers at the moment may be tending to stabilize, and the threat of global warming flows more from the manner and increase of our energy use than from the sheer multiplication of population. But it is still the case that now and for the first time we have a concrete sense of running up against some kind of physical limitation in the absolute capacity of our planet to absorb the kind of punishment we are dishing out. This is quite a first, especially when we reflect on the whole course of man's economic progression over ten millennia—from a few million widely dispersed and more threatened by than threatening to other species to today's billions armed with the appetites and technologies of the year 2000 and threatened only by ourselves, leaving aside the bacteria and other pathogens.

If it is true that we are approaching a real limit for the first time, that is an answer to Macaulay's challenge to the pessimists to say why we should not expect the future to be as full of progress as the past. On this view the past, or at least that part of it since 1700 that has commanded the enthusiasm of Macaulay and the optimists, has simply been using up a once-and-for-all scope for demographic and economic growth based on the generation of unrecycled and cost-free (to its creator) waste, which scope is now within sight of being fully taken up. We cannot be sure that this is wrong, even if we think with Adam Smith that "there is an awful lot of ruin in a nation" and a fortiori even more ruin in a globe. What we can do is to think about the governance problem posed by the possibility that it is right.

What sort of a world would it be in which 6 billion people, going on 9 billion, could be reasonably sure of detecting such threats in good time, devising effective countermeasures, implementing them, policing any rules that their implementation requires and doing all this before the damage had become irreversible, which may be decades before any damage at all were visible to the general public? A centralized command structure at the global level, a true world government, would be tolerated by very few and would therefore have to impose itself. This could in theory happen if those who perceived themselves to be victims, in Asia and Africa, for example, decided to turn upon the minority in Europe and

America whom they blamed for their sufferings. But manifestly that is a recipe for utter human catastrophe, a truly Malthusian denouement.

Today we are offered instead a kind of running multilateral negotiation among nation-states, with noises on and off from other interested organizations, which is at best worthy and at worst futile. It suffers from the fatal defect of the need for unanimity, at least of the significant players, which means that the default outcome is always likely to be that too little is done too late, if indeed anything is done at all. The world moves at the speed of the most recalcitrant country and in accordance with the perceptions of the most shortsighted public opinion. As a system for regulating and moderating the affairs of a species whose habitat and therefore survival may be at stake at some point, even if it is not yet, it appears designed to guarantee failure and doom, Malthus by another route.

Any escape from this dilemma, other than crossing one's fingers and hoping that it all blows over thanks to some possible but unforeseen lucky turn of events, needs to start from a recognition that politics, democratic or otherwise, is unlikely to do the job. Direct government action is prey to too many pressures other than those of the problem to be solved ever to be relied upon to adopt and implement strategies that may well require changes in private behavior by people who do not recognize or understand the need for such change. In open societies, however much the truth of the warnings is there to be read and heard freely by all, that truth may as easily be drowned out by bland reassurances feeding the natural desire to believe that all is indeed well. In closed societies consent may not be the problem, but man's posterity seems likely to lie even less securely in the hands of a Saddam Hussein than in those of a volatile public opinion practiced upon by interested manipulators.

If there are better ways, perhaps they are to be found in forms of governance that do not order private behavior by the fiat of a ruler but constrain a better correspondence of private and public interest by a less visible hand. When Adam Smith had his great revelation that "it is not from the benevolence of the butcher, the brewer, or the baker, that we expect our dinner, but from their regard to their own self-interest," he not merely unveiled an immensely fertile economic idea but also discovered a profound truth about governance: It works better when people do the right thing not because someone else tells them to but because they expect to profit from doing so.[15]

How far this mechanism can and should be extended to activities not normally and easily amenable to market procedures and so to market forces is keenly debated on both practical and equity grounds. The attempt so to bring the "external diseconomies" within the framework of costs that play upon economic agents—known in the jargon as "internalizing the externalities"—provokes strong resistance when, as with the enclosure of common lands in England in the eighteenth and nineteenth centuries, it appears to involve the transfer into private ownership of what has previously been public property. Yet it is a commonplace of our experience that that which everybody owns nobody owns and that which nobody owns attracts no protection, no maintenance, no conservation and no investment. Cows and pigs and sheep and hens, to say nothing of cats and dogs, prosper and multiply while wild species and fish stocks become endangered and extinct. So also with plant life, and so perhaps with other global commons, including the planet's available spaces—geographical and ecological—for containing our waste.

Such mechanisms could be combined perhaps with others that earmark—or hypothecate—revenue from new global sources, such as the sale of emission permits or levies on air travel or international monetary flows, for functional global bodies charged with specific global management tasks and accountable not only to national governments but also to a wider constituency of voluntary, parliamentary and business organizations. Of course starting from where we are, all such transformation of our mechanisms of global governance presupposes an initial act by the existing apparatus of national governments and their superstructure of international bodies. If they are deemed themselves to be fatally flawed, how then can they be relied upon to enact their own partial replacement in favor of other mechanisms and other bodies? One answer is to point to what may happen if they do not. Another is that it is easier to extract one supreme act of enlightenment from governments, as, for example, in the immediate aftermath of World War II, than it is to rely on them for timely and sufficient global management year in and year out from now on.

It is time to answer our own Malthusian question. How sure should we be that the planet can supply—and otherwise sustain—a geometric progress of production, either to meet the needs of an exponentially growing population or to fulfill the aspirations of a stable population for exponentially rising living standards? On our answer to that more than any other question should in turn depend our answers to Macaulay's question why we should not expect the future to deliver the same glorious onward march of progress that distinguishes the past and to Keynes's question whether we have solved the economic problem.

Our answer to the first is that it—a geometric progress of production—cannot be taken for granted as a certainty derivable from within economic science, nor as a reliable consequence of the fact that Malthusian rigors seem to have been avoided by large parts of the human race for at least a few centuries, nor yet as a certain guarantee given by the ceaseless advance of science. Maybe global population will stop rising for a while in the middle of the twenty-first century, and maybe it will not resume its growth before that century's end, though these are big maybes. But mankind's potential collision course with the limits, or at least limitations, of his physical environment will not be deflected simply by demographic stability.

The progress of opulence, as a disposition of man, will continue. GDP per head will rise, and therefore GDP will rise, whether fourfold, eightfold or twelvefold, every 100 years. And if this requires a systematic fouling of our own nest by mankind, fouling of a kind that feeds back to us as climate change, rising oceans, expanding deserts, vanishing forests and intensifying conflicts of interests between the West and the East and between the North and the South, then a growing rather than the presently falling proportion of mankind may be struggling for subsistence, finding themselves the unfortunates sandwiched between the rock of growth and the hard place of the planet's not quite limitless capacity. That is what Malthus feared was mankind's fated lot: to return however high he soared, and however long he might for a while escape from the trap, to the point where his numbers were curtailed by the privations to which at least parts of the species were subjected.

Such an outcome would obviously be the antithesis of Keynes's prediction of a final solution to the economic problem of how to subsist in a world of scarcity. Keynes's optimism was based on the formidable potential of economic growth at compound interest of the kind unleashed by the industrial revolution. He included provisos about population growth and war, but the possibility that such growth might have such an impact on our planetary environment as to damage it as a human habitat and so create a problem of subsistence for even stable numbers of people did not occur to him.

But even without that new peril there are other reasons for being sure that by 2030 we will not be suffering, as he suggested, some kind of nervous breakdown as a consequence of being deprived of the purpose for which evolution has so deeply prepared and programmed us, to sweat for our daily bread. Keynes was a creature of the Cambridge of G. E. Moore and of the Bloomsbury of Lytton Strachey and Virginia Woolf. He believed that the highest good resided not in great piles of wealth but in the best states of mind that could be enjoyed by those who had the good fortune and the ability to contemplate truth, beauty and goodness and to immerse themselves in the joys of friendship. For him, therefore, it was possible to believe in a finite level of wealth, comfortably above subsistence, beyond which mankind would be free "to return to some of the most sure and certain principles of religion and traditional virtue—that avarice is vice, that the exaction of usury is a misdemeanour, and the love of money is detestable, that those walk most truly in the paths of virtue and sane wisdom who take least thought for the morrow. We shall once more value ends above means and prefer the good to the useful."[16]

We may dream of such a world. We may admire it and hanker after it. But we cannot believe in it because it reckons without either Darwin or Adam Smith. The progress of opulence does not stop when subsistence is left behind, and those who choose the life of leisure and the pleasures of the mind, high thinking and the living standards of Cambridge in the 1930s, will be outrun and outflanked in wealth, power and survival by those who continue to obey what Keynes called "the pseudo-moral principles which have hag-ridden us for two hundred years, by which we have exalted some of the most distasteful of human qualities into the position of the highest virtue . . . those semi-criminal, semi-pathological propensities which one hands over with a shudder to the specialists in mental disease," such as "all kinds of social customs and economic practices, affecting the distribution of wealth and of economic rewards and penalties, which we now maintain at all costs, however distasteful and unjust they may be in themselves, because they are tremendously useful in promoting the accumulation of capital."[17]

Keynes's dream of subverting the bourgeois world by bursting through onto a higher plateau of affluence in which greed and thrift and toil are superfluous is unrealizable not because such levels of output are unattainable—they will be attained even earlier than Keynes surmised—but because the propensity to go on striving for yet higher peaks will continue in the breasts of enough members of the human race to ensure that it is they and not those who opt for the "economic bliss" of cultivating "the arts of life" rather than "the activities of purpose" who dominate the subsequent story.[18] In that sense Darwin always wins in the end.

But before we take our leave of speculation, there is another contemporary doctrine of "economic bliss" we must notice, and that is what is variously known as the "new economy" and the "new paradigm." This, roughly speaking, is the optimistic end of the view increasingly associated with Washington (as the headquarters of the IMF and the World Bank as well as of the U.S. government), that history as a struggle between rival ideologies is over; the good guys—in the shape of political democrats and economic liberals—have finally won; sound fiscal and monetary policies can and will indefinitely provide macroeconomic stability (low inflation, negligible business cycles); free trade, free capital flows and free money movements will foster continuing high growth and more rapid catch-up of the poorer economies; technological dynamism now offers the platform for a "long boom"; and democratic government will legitimize and give stability to the political framework within which all this takes place. The flavor of some of this thinking has recently been reflected in *The Future of the Global Economy* published by the Organisation for Economic Cooperation and Development (OECD).[19]

It is a powerful picture, and clearly there are many who believe in it, not least many of those who continue to pile into Western stock markets at prices that terrify their elders. But the economic historian, as distinct from the evangelical economic liberal from middle America, must still find it difficult to swallow what must seem to him far too mechanistic and unhistorical a view of human affairs. There have, of course, been long booms in the past, for example from the late 1890s to 1913 and from 1950 to 1973. There have been long periods of peace and stability, in classical times, in Chinese history, in Europe after 1815 and in North America for most of the time since the Civil War. It is not impossible.

But what the story so far has taught us is the profound interdependence of politics and economics. How we perform and how we are governed are inseparable. Economic success tends to feed back negatively upon itself in the form of predatory attacks from within and without. Statecraft faces a constant, perhaps impossibly difficult challenge to find enduring reconciliations between the need to police the predatory attacks and to keep opportunity open for enterprise, innovation and the general progress of opulence.

These are the shadows that lie across the threshold of the new millennium. Ancient Rome opted for security behind its natural frontiers as prescribed by its first emperor, Augustus. The predatory threat of those it saw as barbarians was held at bay, on and off, for a remarkably long time, but in the end the appetite and the vigor of those who are denied the warmer climes and the lusher pastures come to exceed the prowess and the energy of those who have the good things and would prefer to enjoy them than to fight. Today the "new economics," the Washington paradigm, denies almost entirely the one great freedom that a truly free global economy would afford, the freedom of people to move, to live and to work where they choose.

Accordingly, the European Union and the United States stare nervously from behind their own outward-facing bars as poorer people plot how to get in or otherwise to divert to themselves the wealth that they see. In these tensions, which radiate from geographical frontiers and from global negotiations on trade, the environment and monetary disorders, lies the potential for huge conflict in the coming century. One, two, three, ten crises may be managed, finessed, kicked into touch, but is there any more durable basis of agreed rules, of widely acknowledged equity and of practicable enforcement on which a confident prediction of peaceable progress can be made?

Manifestly there is not, despite all the strivings of the United Nations and other global bodies with unglamorous but useful missions. For a moment after the cold war ended, some people thought they detected a flash of a new order in which the UN would pass political judgment and coalitions of obliging nations would enforce the decision. Something like this did indeed happen in the Gulf War. But as time has gone by it has become ever more apparent that this, far from being a strong constitution of global equity and stability, is little more than a fleeting gloss on the old diplomacy of national interests and national politics. Humanitarian and other crises in other places have called forth such an uneven response that malefactors have been having themselves a ball almost wherever they choose.

Such turbulence does not by itself directly threaten global economic prospects. But it should remind us strongly that human affairs and human history are in the hands of human beings. Human beings are moved by fierce passions of national and ethnic identity. These are quickly allied to formidable hatreds and suspicions of strangers, foreigners, outsiders, aliens and those who worship strange gods or are in any other way different. Such passions can easily be exacerbated by conflicts of economic interest. At the end of a century in which such deformities have had their fullest and most calamitous scope yet to blight the affairs of our species, it would be irrational, however tempting, to take for granted that we are now at the dawn of an age in which such things will play at most a small part. That would be another form of the fallacy Macaulay derides, of expecting in the future the opposite of the past.

So what can we say? What at the end of it all is the balance sheet as we peer into the future? On the plus side are:

- the long historic progress of man's clever and greedy brain
- the genuine progress of opulence attempted and achieved
- the transformations of the agricultural and industrial revolutions
- the 1,000-fold multiplication of the species
- the twelvefold multiplication of living standards where the magic of coal, iron, steam and their successors has been translated into the miracle of economic growth at compound interest
- the prospect of an end to the struggle for subsistence
- the glimpse of new technologies promising a new transformation of society on a scale to be compared with those earlier transforming revolutions
- the grail of a stable world population at only 50 percent above its present level within half a century
- a recent escape from the deepest ideological conflicts that carried for forty years the greatest direct risk of terminal warfare

- the spreading acceptance of an economic system that has proved itself capable of digesting the challenge of change—requiring information, investment, incentive and innovation—and of regulating broad swathes of human economic activity without imposing insupportable burdens on the fallible shoulders of government

On the minus side are:

- the ecological doubt that a species that indefinitely increases its own numbers—or, if no longer its numbers, at least its calls upon the finite capacities of its environment—can escape a dreadful conclusion
- the political antithesis of the economic thesis, namely, that the greater and better the economic opportunity the fiercer and more threatening will be the challenge from those who are excluded
- the vulnerability of the new paradigm itself to all kinds of malfunction, including inflationary mismanagement of currencies, violent fluctuations in business and financial confidence and the monopolistic tendencies of a laissez-faire world in which, as in the knowledge industries, the costs of supplying an extra customer are nil and therefore the incumbent big gun, such as Microsoft, can always drive out any lesser competitor or new entrant
- the missing keystone of the arch: nobody and no thing has the job, let alone the authority and capability, of keeping the whole show on the road, of worrying about its weaknesses and deficiencies as a system and of mobilizing remedial action when failure looms. There is no hegemon

We can only expect that the waltz motif will go on, then: that economic opportunity will continue to beckon mankind on, as it does strongly at present, that he will respond in full measure to such opportunities, that the affluence this generates will attract envious glances and indignant counterclaims and that the political process within and between nations and at the level of global management will continue to struggle to arbitrate and contain these disputes. In the course of a century, it will be hard to expect that none of them will get out of control, polarizing nations and peoples in acute hostility to one another. Under such conditions a world accustomed to tell itself that the nation-state has had its day, that its budgets are exceeded by the value of mere corporations and that flows of money and information through the ether exceed and elude anything that governments can deploy or control may receive a sharp reminder that governments still have if not a monopoly, at least a predominance of force within their own boundaries, that people have to reside somewhere even if digital data does not and that when governments are backed by an aggrieved public opinion they can cause a great deal of mayhem, economic and otherwise.

To be fully convincing, any thesis of global economic optimism would need to show that its new paradigm included effective political machinery for obtaining the assent and compliance of billions of people to the rules of the game under which they are expected to play and that, however successful, will leave many of them poor and some of them destitute. In truth, politics will not be suspended for the convenience of the new paradigm, and history will not end at the behest of the new economy. If they are lucky and live in the right parts of the world, in 100 years' time our grandchildren (or our great- and great-great-grandchildren) may indeed live in states of economic bliss, variously defined as very high levels of material comfort (the kind of thing that Europeans in morose moods imagine Californians enjoy all the time) or as very large amounts of leisure or some combination of the two. The technical and economic preconditions for such a possibility already exist. But if our descendants are to enjoy it as we would wish they should, they will have to show a great deal more skill than their ancestors in managing global as well as national and local politics. And if they are unlucky or unskilled in that, or if they live in the wrong parts of the world, they may struggle to survive.

INTRODUCTION: THE IDEA OF THE BOOK

1. Fogel, 1997, p. 7; Mithen, 1996, pp. 223–247; *Cassell Atlas of World History,* 1997, pp. 1.01–1.02, 1.19.
2. See Brittan, 1998, chapter 11.
3. Tennyson, 1923, "In Memoriam A.H.H., 1850," canto 55.
4. In anthropologists' terms, these modern humans were *Homo sapiens sapiens.* Their ancestors *Homo sapiens,* included Neanderthals and were eventually replaced by *Homo sapiens sapiens* (*Cassell Atlas of World History,* 1997, p. 1.01). But note that some authorities, such as William H. McNeill in drafts of his forthcoming *Very Short History of the Whole World* (with John R. McNeill), use the term *Homo sapiens* in the more limited sense in which *Homo sapiens sapiens* is here defined.

   Cassell's atlas says these humans have been around perhaps 135,000 years (*Cassell Atlas of World History,* 1997, p. 1.01). According to McNeill (forthcoming), bones of *Homo sapiens* appeared in Africa 200,000 years ago, and *Homo sapiens* displaced Neanderthals.
5. *Cassell Atlas of World History,* 1997, p. 1.19; Livi-Bacci, 1997, p. 31.
6. Theya Molleson of the Natural History Museum, London, Department of Palaeontology, e-mail to author, 22 October 1998; Livi-Bacci, 1997, p. 31, suggests a life expectancy of only twenty.
7. Hobbes, 1969, p. 143.
8. Stavrianos, 1989, chapter 1.
9. *Guardian,* society supplement, 10 February 1999.
10. World Health Organization, 1995.
11. Darwin, 1859, chapter 3; Smith, 1812, p. 354.
12. Marshall, 1916, book 1, chapter 1, section 5, p. 10.
13. Ibid., pp. 723–724.
14. Kipling, (1906); see, for example, "Road-Song of the Bandar-Log," p. 84:

    Here we sit in a branchy row
    Thinking of beautiful things we know
    Dreaming of deeds that we mean to do
    All complete, in a minute to two—
    Something noble, grand and good,
    Won by merely wishing we could.
    Now we're going to—never mind,
    Brother thy tail hangs down behind!

    and at pp. 51–57: "'I have taught thee all the Law of the Jungle for all the peoples of the jungle—except the Monkey-Folk who live in the trees. They have no law. . . .

They are without leaders. They have no remembrance. They boast and chatter and pretend that they are great people about to do great affairs in the jungle, but the falling of a nut turns their minds to laughter *and all* is forgotten,' said the Bear. . . . 'They never go far' [Rann, the Kite] said with a chuckle. 'They never do what they set out to do. Always pecking at new things are the Bandar-log.'"

15. Marshall, 1916, p. 723.
16. Ibid., pp. 240–243.
17. On the term "survival of the fittest," see Darwin, 1859, chapter 3; Marshall, 1916, p. 240.
18. Marshall, 1916, pp. 240, 241.
19. Ibid., p. 241.
20. Ibid., pp. 243–244.
21. Ibid., p. 723.
22. Landes, 1998.
23. Marshall, 1916, p. 723.
24. Landes, 1998, pp. 14–15.
25. Marshall, 1916, p. 723.
26. North, 1981, p. 5.
27. Marshall, 1916, p. 724.
28. Chang, 1991.
29. Ibid., pp. 274–316, my emphasis.
30. Ibid., pp. 593–594.
31. Smith, 1812, 1976, 1978, 1980, 1983, 1987.
32. Smith, 1812, book 3, chapter 1, p. 300.
33. This sketch is paraphrased from lecture notes distributed by Alan Macfarlane of Cambridge University at an Institute of Historical Research seminar convened by Patrick O'Brien in the Senate House, University of London, 8 December 1998. See also Macfarlane, 2000, which examines the same questions of the relationship between political and economic development through the work of Montesquieu, Adam Smith, de Tocqueville and Gellner.

CHAPTER ONE: THE DISCOVERY OF VALUE

1. Livi-Bacci, 1997, p. 31.
2. Livi-Bacci, 1997, p. 31; McEvedy and Jones, 1978.
3. According to the *Cambridge Ancient History,* volume 1, part 1, p. 1, "complex life forms that have left abundant traces as fossils are not found in rocks older than those of the Cambrian system, which may be accepted as having been laid down about 600 million years ago." It adds that "the remains preserved in the Lower Palaeozoic systems [600–400 mya] are all of marine organisms."
4. *Cassell Atlas of World History,* 1997, p. 1.01.
5. Diamond, 1998, p. 36.
6. *Cassell Atlas of World History,* 1997, p. 1.01.
7. Mithen, 1996, p. 18; Barraclough, 1978, p. 36.
8. *Cassell Atlas of World History,* 1997, p. 1.01.
9. Diamond, 1998, pp. 36–37.

10. *Cassell Atlas of World History,* 1997, p. 1.01.
11. Ibid.
12. Ibid., p. 1.02; Mithen, 1996, p. 20.
13. *Cassell Atlas of World History,* 1997, p. 1.02.
14. Mithen, 1996, p. 171.
15. McNeill and McNeill, forthcoming, p. 9.
16. *Cassell Atlas of World History,* 1997, p. 1.02.
17. McNeill and McNeill, forthcoming, pp. 7–8.
18. Mithen, 1996, p. 171; Diamond, 1998, p. 39.
19. *Cambridge Ancient History,* 1970, vol. 1, part 1, p. 1.
20. McNeill and McNeill, forthcoming, pp. 9–10.
21. Diamond, 1998, p. 40.
22. Mithen, 1996, pp. 171–210.
23. Ibid., p. 21.
24. Ibid., p. 30.
25. Hobbes, 1969, p. 143.
26. Stavrianos, 1989, p. 24, quoting Sahlins, 1972.
27. Theya Molleson of the Natural History Museum, London, Department of Palaeontology, e-mail to author, 22 October 1998.
28. *Guardian,* society supplement, 10 February 1999, reporting on work of Dr. Larry Barham, Bristol University, at Cheddar Gorge.
29. Barraclough and Overy, 1999, p. 34.
30. McNeill and McNeill, forthcoming, pp. 13–15; *Cassell Atlas of World History,* 1997, p. 1.19; Diamond, 1998, pp. 42, 46–47.
31. McNeill, 1994, p. 30, suggests that "probably the most significant factor in blunting the initial impact of humanity upon other forms of life was the peculiar richness and elaboration of African infestations and infections—an elaboration of parasitism that evolved along with humanity itself and tended to intensify as human numbers increased."
32. Diamond, 1998, p. 47.
33. Ibid., p. 68.
34. McNeill and McNeill, forthcoming, p. 21.
35. *Cassell Atlas of World History,* 1997, p. 1.19; McNeill and McNeill, forthcoming, p. 23.
36. McNeill and McNeill, forthcoming, p. 25; *Cassell Atlas of World History,* 1997, p. 1.08.
37. Sherratt, 1997, p. 32, footnote.
38. North, 1981, pp. 78, 81–83.
39. On population growth, see Livi-Bacci, 1997, p. 31.
40. Diamond, 1998, pp. 158–174.
41. Barraclough and Overy, 1999, p. 36.
42. Sahlins, 1972, p. 34.
43. Diamond, 1998, pp. 110–112.
44. *Cassell Atlas of World History,* 1997, p. 1.03.
45. Curtin, 1984, p. 8.
46. McEvedy and Jones, 1978, p. 149.
47. Crawford, 1991, p. 10.

48. Nissen, 1988, p. 5; Crawford, 1991, pp. 29–34.
49. *Cassell Atlas of World History*, 1997, p. 1.09.
50. Crawford, 1991, p. 13.
51. *Cassell Atlas of World History*, 1997, p. 1.09, 1.10; Nissen, 1988, p. 5.
52. McEvedy and Jones, 1978, p. 149.
53. Nissen, 1988, pp. 67, 69.
54. Crawford, 1991, pp. 29–34.
55. Ibid., p. 9.
56. Barraclough and Overy, 1999, p. 52.
57. *Cassell Atlas of World History*, 1997, pp. 1.17, 1.26–1.28.
58. Crawford, 1991, p. 14.
59. North, 1981, p. 95, my emphasis.
60. *Cassell Atlas of World History*, 1997, pp. 1.11–1.12.
61. Curtin, 1984, pp. 63–64.
62. Williams, 1997, p. 16.
63. Crawford, 1991, p. 124.
64. Williams, 1997, pp. 16–19.
65. McNeill, 1994, p. 49.
66. Postgate, 1994, pp. 109–113.
67. Crawford, 1991, pp. 24–25.
68. Curtin, 1984, pp. 64–65.
69. Postgate, 1994, pp. 225–229.
70. North, 1981, p. 93.
71. McNeill, 1994, p. 47.
72. Nissen, 1988, pp. 96–97.
73. Crawford, 1991, p. 16.
74. Curtin, 1984, pp. 66–67.
75. Runciman, 1998, p. 120.
76. Curtin, 1984, pp. 67–68.
77. Ibid., pp. 68–69.
78. Barraclough and Overy, 1999, p. 56.
79. *Cassell Atlas of World History*, 1997, p. 1.17.
80. Ibid.
81. Barraclough and Overy, 1999, p. 56.
82. Ibid.; *Cassell Atlas of World History*, 1997, p. 1.18.
83. Barraclough and Overy, 1999, p. 56; *Cassell Atlas of World History*, 1997, p. 1.18.
84. *Cassell Atlas of World History*, 1997, p. 1.12.
85. Barraclough and Overy, 1999, p. 56; *Cassell Atlas of World History*, 1997, p. 1.18.
86. Ibid.

CHAPTER TWO: CITIZENSHIP

1. *Cassell Atlas of World History*, 1997, pp. 2.04 and 3.02.
2. Livi-Bacci, 1997, p. 31.
3. Alan Bowman advises that all estimates of population in the ancient world are speculative.

4. *Cassell Atlas of World History,* 1997, pp. 1.13, 1.23; Cameron, 1997, p. 33.
5. *Cambridge Ancient History,* vol. 1, part 3, chapter 36, p. 693.
6. *Cassell Atlas of World History,* 1997, p. 1.12; Austin and Vidal-Naquet, 1977, pp. 36–40.
7. Boardman et al., 1991, pp. 14–17.
8. Thucydides, quoted in Starr, 1977, p. 21.
9. Starr, 1977, pp. 27–28.
10. McNeill and McNeill, forthcoming, p. 79; Starr, 1977, p. 31.
11. *Cassell Atlas of World History,* 1997, p. 1.22; Starr, 1977, p. 25.
12. Starr, 1977, pp. 34–35; Curtin, 1984, p. 78; *Cassell Atlas of World History,* 1997, pp. 1.23, 1.24.
13. Manville, 1990, pp. 57–58.
14. Cartledge et al., 1998, p. 140.
15. Quoted in Zimmern, 1924, pp. 207–211.
16. Austin and Vidal-Naquet, 1977, p. 57.
17. Williams, 1997, pp. 23–32; Austin and Vidal-Naquet, 1977, pp. 56–58; Cameron, 1997, pp. 35–36; Finley, 1985, p. 166–167.
18. Williams, 1997, p. 25.
19. Roberts, 1980, p. 193.
20. Austin and Vidal-Naquet, 1977, pp. 147–150.
21. Williams, 1997, pp. 34–38.
22. Gibbon, 1846, vol. 1, p. 4.
23. Garnsey, Hopkins, and Whittaker, 1983, pp. xix.
24. Ibid., pp. xiv–xxi.
25. Garnsey and Saller, 1987, pp. 51–55.
26. Runciman, 1998, p. 144.
27. North, 1981, p. 109.
28. Gibbon, 1846, vol. 1, pp. 44–45.
29. Cameron, 1997, p. 39.
30. Livi-Bacci, 1997, p. 31.
31. Duncan-Jones, 1982, pp. 260–261, footnote.
32. *Cassell Atlas of World History,* 1997, p. 2.14.
33. Livi-Bacci, 1997, p. 31; Cameron, 1997, p. 39.
34. McNeill, 1994, pp. 114–115.
35. Gibbon, 1846, vol. 1, pp. 86–87, 92.
36. Finley, 1985a, p. 51.
37. Williams, 1997, p. 54.
38. Ibid.
39. Cameron, 1997, p. 41.
40. Williams, 1997, pp. 55–59.
41. Ibid., p. 59.
42. I am grateful to Alan Bowman for his comments on this period.
43. *Cassell Atlas of World History,* 1997, pp. 2.16, 3.06.
44. Ibid., p. 3.05.
45. Cameron, 1997, pp. 42–43.

CHAPTER THREE: PASSING THE BATON

1. Livi-Bacci, 1997, p. 31, McEvedy and Jones, 1978, pp. 18–21, 123–128, 170–173, 182–185, 206–213, 226–227, 270–272.
2. Deng, 1999, p. 252.
3. Ibid., passim.
4. McNeill and McNeill, forthcoming, pp. 93–94.
5. *Times Atlas of Ancient Civilizations,* part 4, p. 10.
6. McNeill and McNeill, forthcoming, p. 76.
7. Ibid., p. 94.
8. McNeill, 1991, p. 362.
9. McEvedy and Jones, 1978, pp. 18, 171, 182.
10. *Cassell Atlas of World History,* 1997, pp. 1.26, 2.22.
11. Ibid., p. 2.23.
12. Thapar, 1966, p. 148.
13. Ibid., pp. 148–150.
14. Hollingdale, 1989, p. 96.
15. Russell, 1946, p. 444.
16. Thapar, 1966, p. 155; *Times Atlas of Ancient Civilizations,* part 6, p. 10.
17. McNeill, 1991, p. 374.
18. Chaudhuri, 1990, p. 56.
19. *Cassell Atlas of World History,* 1997, p. 3.19.
20. Thapar, 1966, pp. 141–142; *Cassell Atlas of World History,* 1997, p. 2.23.
21. McNeill and McNeill, forthcoming, p. 97.
22. Cameron, 1997, p. 80; Mokyr, 1992, p. 42.
23. Chaudhuri, 1985, p. 49.
24. *Mitchell Beazley Atlas of the Oceans,* 1977, p. 43.
25. Levathes, 1996, p. 92.
26. Mokyr, 1992, p. 47; *Mitchell Beazley Atlas of the Oceans,* 1977, p. 44; Cameron, 1997, p. 80; Abu-Lughod, 1989, p. 112.
27. *Mitchell Beazley Atlas of the Oceans,* 1977, p. 43; *Cassell Atlas of World History,* 1997, p. 2.26.
28. Mokyr, 1992, pp. 41–43.
29. Mokyr, 1992, p. 42.
30. Conrad et al., 1995, p. 121.
31. Details on medicine from ibid., pp. 116–122.
32. Abu-Lughod, 1989, p. 244.
33. Ibid., pp. 221–222.
34. Al-Hassan, 1994, p. 360.
35. Conrad et al., 1995, p. 93.
36. Russell, 1946, p. 446.
37. Ibid., p. 448.
38. Audi, 1995, pp. 18–19.
39. Abu-Lughod, 1989, p. 225.
40. Ibid., pp. 227–230.
41. Ibid., pp. 214–215.
42. Ibid., pp. 230–244.

43. Ibid., pp. 242–243.
44. Ibid., p. 244.
45. Elvin, 1973, p. 54.
46. Ibid., pp. 54–55.
47. Abu-Lughod, 1989, p. 238; *Cassell Atlas of World History*, 1997, p. 3.20.
48. *Cassell Atlas of World History*, 1997, p. 3.20.
49. Deng, 1999, pp. 306–307.
50. Merson, 1989, p. 23.
51. Ibid., p. 23, citing official statistics.
52. Ibid., p. 26; Deng, 1999, pp. 302–308.
53. Merson, 1989, p. 32.
54. *Cassell Atlas of World History*, 1997, p. 3.21.
55. Elvin, 1973, p. 85; McNeill, 1982, pp. 26–27; Merson, 1989, p. 21.
56. *Cassell Atlas of World History*, 1997, p. 3.21.
57. Ibid.
58. Ibid.
59. Ibid.
60. Ibid.
61. Elvin, 1973, p. 137.
62. Ibid., p. 161.
63. Williams, 1997, p. 149.
64. Elvin, 1973, pp. 149, 159; Deng, 1999, p. 307.
65. Williams, 1997, p. 149.
66. Ibid.
67. Because of the Yin occupation in the north and the Song's move to the south, the Song is divided into northern (pre-A.D. 1127) and southern (post-A.D. 1127) periods.
68. Deng, 1999, p. 311.
69. Ibid., pp. 83–85; Welsh, 1997, p. 28.
70. Deng, 1999, pp. 311–318.
71. Ibid., p. 321.
72. McNeill, 1994, p. 154.
73. Deng, 1999, p. 326.
74. Curtin, 1984, p. 125.
75. Quoted in Curtin, 1984, p. 125, from the 1931 Benedetto translation of Marco Polo.
76. Curtin, 1984, p. 125.
77. Levathes, 1996, p. 147.
78. Ibid., passim.
79. Chaudhuri, 1985, p. 61.
80. Levathes, 1996, p. 142.
81. Ibid., p. 20.
82. Ibid., pp. 163–164.
83. Chaudhuri, 1985, p. 61.
84. Extract from Fairbank and Goldman, 1998, p. 139.
85. *Cassell Atlas of World History*, 1997, p. 4.21; Chaudhuri, 1985, p. 62.

CHAPTER FOUR: PLURALISM

1. Livi-Bacci, 1997, p. 31; McEvedy and Jones, 1978, p. 18.
2. McEvedy and Jones, 1978, pp. 23–24.
3. Moss, 1950, p. 156.
4. *Cambridge Medieval History,* 1953, vol. 1, p. 301.
5. *Cassell Atlas of World History,* 1997, p. 3.07.
6. *Cambridge Medieval History,* vol. 1, pp. 438–439.
7. Wickham, 1994, pp. 19–36.
8. Cameron, 1997, pp. 45–46.
9. Randsborg, 1991, p. 18.
10. Cameron, 1997, pp. 46–47.
11. Mokyr, 1992, p. 33.
12. Ibid.
13. Cameron, 1997, p. 53.
14. Mokyr, 1992, p. 38.
15. Miller and Hatcher, 1995, pp. 6–7.
16. Mokyr, 1992, pp. 34, 38.
17. Britnell, 1993, pp. 80–90.
18. Abu-Lughod, 1989, p. 45.
19. Cameron, 1997, pp. 56–57.
20. Davies, 1997, p. 312.
21. Abu-Lughod, 1989, p. 45.
22. Ibid., p. 47; Cameron, 1997, p. 59.
23. Cameron, 1997, p. 61.
24. McNeill, 1982, pp. 66–68.
25. Cameron, 1997, pp. 59–65.
26. Abu-Lughod, 1989, p. 47.
27. Ibid., pp. 58–59.
28. Miller and Hatcher, 1995, pp. 397–398.
29. Abu-Lughod, 1989, pp. 59–60.
30. Jones, 1987, p. 53.
31. Davies, 1997, p. 361.
32. Merson, 1989, p. 82.
33. Ibid., pp. 83–84.
34. Davies, 1997, pp. 361, 1248.
35. Merson, 1989, pp. 84–85.
36. Mokyr, 1992, pp. 44–46.
37. Ibid., p. 54.
38. Ibid., pp. 51–52.
39. Smith, cited in ibid., p. 51.
40. Mokyr, 1992, p. 52.
41. Ibid., pp. 53–54.
42. Ibid., p. 41.
43. Ibid., p. 39.
44. Ibid., pp. 39, 54.
45. Jones, 1987, p. 55.

46. Landes, 1998, pp. 47–51; Mokyr, 1992, pp. 49–51; Cameron, 1997, pp. 71–72.
47. Landes, 1998, pp. 49–50.
48. Jones, 1987, pp. 52–53.
49. Cameron, 1997, p. 63; *Cassell Atlas of World History,* 1997, p. 3.11.
50. Mokyr, 1992, p. 39.
51. Curtin, 1984, pp. 112–113; Abu-Lughod, 1989, pp. 26–27.
52. Cameron, 1997, p. 66; Abu-Lughod, 1989, pp. 116–117.
53. Abu-Lughod, 1989, p. 69.
54. Cameron, 1997, p. 67; Abu-Lughod, 1989, pp. 92–93.
55. Williams, 1997, p. 82.
56. Cameron, 1997, p. 67.
57. Williams, 1997, p. 80.
58. Cameron, 1997, pp. 66–68.
59. Ibid., p. 66.
60. Mokyr, 1992, p. 74; Davies, 1997, p. 402.
61. Goody, 1996, p. 64.
62. Quoted in Rosenberg and Birdzell, 1986, p. 127. Sombart's great study, *Der moderne Kapitalismus,* published in 1902, surveyed capitalism from medieval times.
63. Telephone conversation with John Gunnell of the accountants Morley & Scott, 4 May 1999.
64. Abu-Lughod, 1989, pp. 117–118; Rosenberg and Birdzell, 1986, p. 127.
65. Rosenberg and Birdzell, 1986, p. 127.
66. Hollingdale, 1989, p. 101.
67. Goody, 1996, p. 75.
68. Ibid., p. 101.
69. Ibid., p. 102.
70. Mokyr, 1992, p. 74.
71. Davies, 1997, p. 443.
72. Buchan, 1997, p. 64.
73. Campbell and Overton, 1993, p. 97; Cameron, 1997, p. 74.
74. Malthus, *Essay on the Principle of Population,* quoted in Livi-Bacci, 1997, p. 82.
75. Ricardo, *The Principles of Political Economy and Taxation,* quoted in Livi-Bacci, 1997, p. 81.
76. Boserup, 1965.
77. Campbell and Overton, 1993, p. 98.
78. Cameron, 1997, p. 74; Livi-Bacci, 1997, p. 47.
79. Campbell and Overton, 1993, p. 99.
80. Conrad et al., 1995, pp. 191–192.
81. Porter, 1997, p. 124.
82. Cannon, 1997, p. 754.
83. McNeill, 1994, p. 154; Herlihy, 1997, pp. 23–24.
84. Herlihy, 1997, p. 24.
85. Livi-Bacci, 1997, pp. 52–53.
86. Davies, 1997, p. 412; McNeill, 1994, p. 158; Cannon, 1997, p. 754.
87. See Chapter 2.
88. Herlihy, 1997, pp. 46–49; Cameron, 1997, p. 76; Davies, 1997, p. 412.
89. Cameron, 1997, p. 76; Anderson, 1996, pp. 15, 55.

90. Cameron, 1997, p. 76.
91. Matteo Villani, *Cronica di Matteo Villani,* quoted in Herlihy, 1997, pp. 48–49.
92. Jones, 1987, p. 60.
93. Mokyr, 1992, p. 49.
94. Herlihy, 1997, pp. 49–51.
95. Ibid., pp. 69–70.
96. Ibid., pp. 71–72.
97. Porter, 1997, pp. 125–126.
98. Davies, 1997, p. 412.
99. Platt, 1997, p. 192.
100. Cameron, 1997, p. 97.
101. Anderson, 1996, pp. 52–53.

CHAPTER FIVE: GLOBALIZATION

1. Frank, 1998, p. 52.
2. Ibid.
3. O'Brien, 1990, pp. 154–177.
4. Curtin, 1984, p. 101.
5. Tibbetts, 1971, pp. 7–41.
6. Diamond, 1998, pp. 370–371; *Cassell Atlas of World History,* 1997, p. 1.02.
7. Microsoft ENCARTA 97 WORLD ATLAS (a CD-ROM); Diamond, 1998, pp. 371–372; *Cassell Atlas of World History,* 1997, p. 3.26.
8. Diamond, 1998, pp. 372–373.
9. Ibid., p. 67.
10. O'Brien, 1990, pp. 156–157.
11. Tibbetts, 1971, pp. 1–7.
12. Chaudhuri, 1985, pp. 52–53.
13. Cameron, 1997, p. 78.
14. O'Brien, 1982, p. 4.
15. Jones, 1987, pp. 75–79.
16. Fernandez-Armesto, 1995a, pp. 104–105, 111.
17. Fernandez-Armesto, 1987, p. 169.
18. Ibid., pp. 251–252; Frank, 1998, p. 58; Pohl, 1990, p. 47.
19. Kurlansky, 1999, pp. 24–29.
20. Morison, 1971, p. 199.
21. Kurlansky, 1999, pp. 24–29.
22. Fernandez-Armesto, 1987, pp. 111–112.
23. Ibid., p. 152; Cameron, 1997, p. 100.
24. Mokyr, 1992, p. 46; Fernandez-Armesto, 1995a, p. 50.
25. Mokyr, 1992, p. 46; Fernandez-Armesto, 1995a, p. 219.
26. Fernandez-Armesto, 1995a, p. 50.
27. Morison, 1974, pp. 46–48.
28. Fernandez-Armesto, 1995a, p. 52.
29. Ibid.; Rosenberg and Birdzell, 1986, p. 81; Morison, 1974, pp. 44–48.
30. Morison, 1974, p. 45.

31. Mokyr, 1992, p. 47.
32. Hollingdale, 1989, p. 83; Mokyr, 1992, p. 47.
33. Mokyr, 1992, p. 69.
34. Landes, 1998, p. 86.
35. Tibbetts, 1971, pp. 10–11, 91.
36. *Mitchell Beazley Atlas of the Oceans,* 1977, p. 44.
37. Morison, 1974, pp. 87–88.
38. Tibbetts, 1971, pp. 314–315.
39. *Mitchell Beazley Atlas of the Oceans,* 1977, p. 44; Morison, 1974, pp. 87–88.
40. Fernandez-Armesto, 1987, p. 167.
41. Fernandez-Armesto, 1995a, pp. 278–300.
42. Morison, 1974, pp. 364, 380.
43. Rosenberg and Birdzell, 1986, p. 85.
44. McNeill, 1982, p. 81; Frank, 1998, p. 58.
45. Kennedy, 1989, pp. 25, 28.
46. Ibid., p. 29.
47. Ibid., pp. 28–32.
48. McNeill, 1982, pp. 79–116; Kennedy, 1989, pp. 20–28.
49. Kennedy, 1989, pp. 30–31.
50. Morison, 1974, p. 98; Cameron, 1997, p. 102. The Treaty of Tordesillas (1494) moved the line 210 miles to the west, greatly to Portugal's advantage.
51. Landes, 1998, p. 93.
52. Pohl, 1990, pp. 45–46.
53. Cameron, 1997, p. 105; Pohl, 1990, p. 47.
54. Diamond, 1998, pp. 80–81.
55. McNeill, 1994, p. 192; Diamond, 1998, p. 77; Livi-Bacci, 1997, p. 59.
56. Diamond, 1998, p. 75.
57. Ibid., p. 77.
58. Livi-Bacci, 1997, p. 58.
59. Ibid., p. 59.
60. Ibid., p. 56.
61. Davies, 1997, p. 512.
62. Diamond, 1998, p. 78.
63. McNeill, 1994, pp. 153, 158; Livi-Bacci, 1997, p. 31.
64. Pohl, 1990, p. 48.
65. Cameron, 1997, p. 105; Williams, 1997, p. 165.
66. Davies, 1997, p. 513.
67. *Cassell Atlas of World History,* 1997, p. 4.25.
68. Pohl, 1990, pp. 53–54.
69. Fernandez-Armesto, 1987, pp. 200–202.
70. Pohl, 1990, pp. 48–49; Blackburn, 1997, p. 163.
71. Schwartz in Drescher and Engerman, 1998, pp. 100–101.
72. Diamond, 1998, chapter 11; McNeill, 1994, chapter 5.
73. Chaudhuri, 1985, p. 66.
74. Ibid.
75. Curtin, 1984, p. 142.
76. Chaudhuri, 1985, p. 75.

77. Curtin, 1984, pp. 142–143.
78. Ibid., pp. 144–149; Chaudhuri, 1985, pp. 78–79.
79. Curtin, 1984, p. 143; Davies, 1997, p. 513.
80. O'Brien, 1990, pp. 156–157.
81. Merson, 1989, p. 77, reports that between 1573 and 1580 Drake captured treasure worth £1.5 million from Portuguese and Spanish ships. Instead of punishing him, Queen Elizabeth I attended a banquet on his ship, knighted him and used a share of his booty to pay off foreign debt.
82. Cameron, 1997, p. 122.
83. Ibid., p. 122; Keay, 1991, pp. 12–13.
84. Cameron, 1997, pp. 106–107.
85. Smith, 1812, vol. 3, pp. 59–60.
86. Ibid., pp. 60–61.
87. Cameron, 1997, p. 106.
88. Frank, 1998, pp. 163–164.
89. Ibid., pp. 158–164; Chaudhuri, 1985, pp. 218–220.
90. Cameron, 1997, pp. 135–143; Davies, 1997, pp. 529–534.
91. Cameron, 1997, pp. 155–156.
92. Cameron, 1997, pp. 153–156; Wrigley, 1988, pp. 58, 113; De Vries and van der Woude, 1997, pp. 693–694.
93. De Vries and Van der Woude, 1997, p. 383.
94. Ibid., p. 357.
95. Cameron, 1997, pp. 116–117; Tracy, 1991, p. 247; De Vries and van der Woude, 1997, pp. 355–357.
96. Cameron, 1997, pp. 116–117, de Vries and van der Woude, 1997, pp. 355–357.
97. De Vries and van der Woude, 1997, p. 403.
98. Tracy, 1991, p. 252.
99. De Vries and van der Woude, 1997, p. 403.
100. Tracy, 1990, p. 175.
101. Tracy, 1991, p. 252.
102. Tracy, 1990, p. 175; Tracy, 1991, pp. 6–7.
103. Pohl, 1990, pp. 244–245.
104. Tracy, 1990, p. 184.
105. De Vries and van der Woude, 1997, p. 384.
106. Ibid., p. 387.
107. Ibid.
108. Ibid.
109. Pohl, 1990, p. 246; Cameron, 1997, p. 123.
110. De Vries and van der Woude, 1997, pp. 376–377.
111. Pohl, 1990, pp. 246–247.
112. Milton, 1999, pp. 360–364.
113. Pohl, 1990, pp. 246–247.
114. De Vries and van der Woude, 1997, p. 412.
115. Goody, 1996, p. 116.
116. Cameron, 1997, p. 126.
117. De Vries and van der Woude, 1997, p. 385.
118. Ibid.

119. Ibid., p. 131.
120. Ibid., p. 147.
121. Ibid.
122. Ibid., p. 149.
123. Ibid., p. 692.
124. Ibid., p. 150.
125. Ibid., pp. 150–151.
126. Ibid., p. 151.
127. Ibid., p. 693.
128. Chaudhuri, 1985, p. 95.
129. De Vries and van der Woude, 1997, pp. 143, 409–410, 502–503, 693–694.
130. Cameron, 1997, pp. 133–134.
131. De Vries and van der Woude, 1997, p. 409.
132. Ibid., pp. 457–458.
133. Ibid., p. 458.
134. Ibid., pp. 462–464.
135. Ibid., p. 463.
136. Ibid., p. 502, my emphasis.
137. Ibid.
138. Wrigley, 1988, pp. 57–60.
139. O'Brien, 1996, pp. 213–249.
140. The Act of Union, 1707, united England and Scotland and created the kingdom of Great Britain—see Cannon, 1997, p. 944; *Cassell Atlas of World History*, 1997, p. 4.27.
141. Canny, 1998, pp. 482–505; Cameron, 1997, pp. 122–123.
142. De Vries and van der Woude, 1997, pp. 502–503.
143. O'Brien, 1998, p. 53.
144. Ibid., pp. 52–53.
145. Ibid., p. 54.
146. Ibid., pp. 53–77.
147. Ibid., pp. 74–75.
148. Ibid., p. 60.
149. Cameron, 1997, p. 157; Cannon, 1997, p. 373.
150. Jay, 1985, p. 41.
151. O'Brien, 1998, p. 65.
152. Jay, 1985, pp. 44–46.
153. Ibid., pp. 47.
154. Brewer, 1989, pp. 89, 91.
155. Ibid., p. 91.
156. Kennedy, 1989, pp. 102–103.
157. Ibid., pp. 103–105.
158. Brewer, 1989, pp. 119–120, citing Dickson, 1967, p. 457.
159. Brewer, 1989, pp. 124–125; Kennedy, 1989, p. 104.
160. De Vries and van der Woude, 1997, p. 152.
161. Brewer, 1989, p. 125.
162. Murphy, 1997a.
163. Ibid.
164. Ibid.; Brewer, 1989, p. 125; Cameron, 1997, pp. 171–172.

165. Murphy, 1997a; de Vries and van der Woude, 1997, p. 152; Williams, 1997, p. 182.
166. Murphy, 1997a; Williams, 1997, p. 182.
167. De Vries and van der Woude, 1997, pp. 152–153.
168. Brewer, 1989, p. 125.
169. De Vries and van der Woude, 1997, p. 153.
170. Murphy, 1997a.
171. Brewer, 1989, p. 125.
172. Murphy, 1997a.
173. Floud and McCloskey, 1994, vol. 1, p. 53; Cameron, 1997, p. 172.
174. Brewer, 1989, p. 126, quoting Dickson, 1967, p. 198.
175. De Vries and van der Woude, 1997, p. 153.
176. O'Brien, 1998, p. 63. See also Floud and McCloskey, 1994, vol. 1, pp. 180–181.
177. Frank, 1998, pp. 258–320.
178. *Cassell Atlas of World History*, 1997, p. 4.19.
179. Frank, 1998, p. 269.
180. Quoted in ibid.
181. Ibid., p. 271.
182. Ibid.
183. Smith, 1812, book 3, chapter 1, p. 300.
184. Quoted in ibid., p. 273.
185. Chaudhuri, 1985, p. 97.

CHAPTER SIX: INVENTIONS AND SURPLUSES

1. Livi-Bacci, 1997, p. 31.
2. Wrigley, 1988, pp. 47–50.
3. Keynes, 1984, pp. 322–326.
4. Floud and McCloskey, 1994, vol. 1, p. 242.
5. Ibid., p. 45.
6. Quoted in Davies, 1997, p. 764.
7. Floud and McCloskey, 1994, vol. 1, p. 47, quoting Deane and Cole, 1962.
8. Ibid., p. 45.
9. Floud and McCloskey, 1994, vol. 1, p. 247.
10. Ibid., quoting Mokyr, 1985, p. 44, and 1993.
11. Gibbon, 1846, vol. 1, pp. 525–526.
12. Floud and McCloskey, 1994, vol. 1, pp. 242–243.
13. Marshall, 1916, p. 751.
14. Ibid., p. 742.
15. Ibid., pp. 740–747.
16. Ibid., p. 748.
17. Mokyr, 1992, p. 81.
18. Ibid.
19. Adapted from the chronology by Wade E. Shilts in Floud and McCloskey, 1994, vol. 1, pp. 387–395; Mokyr, 1992, pp. 81–148; Cameron, 1997, pp. 175–184, 197–211; Dyos and Aldcroft, 1969, pp. 62–126; Cannon, 1997, pp. 125, 509, 602, 912.
20. Mokyr, 1992, p. 128.
21. Keynes, 1984, p. 323.

22. Floud and McCloskey, 1994, vol., 1, p. 267.
23. Keynes, 1984, pp. 323.
24. Ibid., pp. 330.
25. Floud and McCloskey, 1994, vol. 1, p. 269; private conversation with forum attendee John Graham, 29 November 1999.
26. Floud and McCloskey, 1994, vol. 1, pp. 242–270.
27. Floud and McCloskey, 1994, vol. 1, pp. 44–59.
28. Wrigley and Schofield, 1981, pp. 528–529.
29. Floud and McCloskey, 1994, vol. 1, p. 56.
30. North, 1990, p. 139.
31. Floud and McCloskey, 1994, vol. 1, chapter 9.
32. Floud and McCloskey, 1994, vol. 1, p. 56.
33. Ibid., p. 58.
34. Ricardo quoted in Floud and McCloskey, 1994, vol. 1, p. 58.
35. Floud and McCloskey, 1994, vol. 1, pp. 58–59.
36. Crouzet quoted in Floud and McCloskey, 1994, vol. 1, p. 54.
37. Floud and McCloskey, 1994, vol. 1, pp. 54, 59.
38. Ibid., p. 243.
39. Macaulay quoted in ibid., p. 243.
40. Floud and McCloskey, 1994, vol. 1, p. 747.
41. Ibid., pp. 54–55.
42. Ibid.
43. Defoe, 1927, vol. 2, pp. 600–601.
44. Kirzner, quoted in Floud and McCloskey, 1994, vol. 1, pp. 267–268.
45. Floud and McCloskey, 1994, vol. 1, pp. 269–270.
46. Pomeranz, 1998.
47. De Vries, 1994, pp. 249–270.
48. Wrigley, 1988, pp. 54–55.
49. Pomeranz, 1998, p. 36.
50. Landes, 1998, p. 207; O'Brien, 1990, p. 167.
51. Pomeranz, 1998, pp. 64, 68.
52. Marshall, 1998, p. 443.
53. Ibid., p. 458.
54. Ibid., pp. 441–442, 454.
55. O'Brien, 1990, p. 165.
56. Ibid.
57. Williams, 1944, p. 52, quoted in Crafts, 1985, p. 125.
58. Marshall, 1998, p. 461.
59. Ibid., p. 462.
60. Floud and McCloskey, 1994, vol. 1, pp. 371, 394; Hicks, 1950, p. 2.
61. Trevelyan, 1923, pp. 292–295.
62. Davies, 1997, p. 776.
63. Dickens, 1854, book 1, chapter 5, pp. 26–27; chapter 10, pp. 74–75.
64. Crafts, 1997b, p. 628.
65. Ibid., pp. 617–639.
66. Floud and McCloskey, 1994, vol. 1, p. 385.
67. Szreter and Mooney, 1998, pp. 84–112.

CHAPTER SEVEN: INTERNATIONAL ECONOMY AND ECONOMIC NATIONALISM

1. Cameron, 1997, p. 193. According to calculations based on the figures given by Cameron and by McEvedy and Jones, 1978, pp. 30–1, Europe's population increased by 79 million or 42.2 percent, 1800–1850; by 135 million, or 50.75 per cent, 1850–1900; and by 184 million, or 69.2 per cent, 1850–1914.
2. Cameron, 1997, p. 193.
3. McEvedy and Jones, 1978, pp. 30–31.
4. Ibid., p. 270.
5. Calculated from figures for 1850–1900 given in Cameron, 1997, p. 193.
6. McEvedy and Jones, 1978, p. 206.
7. Ibid., pp. 215–216.
8. *Cassell Atlas of World History*, 1997, p. 5.19.
9. Shepherd, 1991, p. 86.
10. Malthus, 1815.
11. Chambers and Mingay, 1966, p. 122.
12. Trevelyan, 1923, p. 205.
13. Floud and McCloskey, 1994, vol. 1, p. 312.
14. Trevelyan, 1923, p. 273.
15. Chambers and Mingay, 1966, pp. 158–210 and passim.
16. Floud and McCloskey, 1994, vol. 1, p. 313.
17. Foreman-Peck, 1995, p. 45.
18. Floud and McCloskey, 1994, vol. 1, pp. 313–314.
19. Ibid., p. 315.
20. Foreman-Peck, 1995, pp. 1–3.
21. Kennedy, 1989, pp. 193–203.
22. Ibid., p. 199, citing Shaw, 1970, p. 2.
23. Cameron, 1997, p. 206.
24. Barraclough and Overy, 1999, p. 220.
25. DeVoto, 1954.
26. Chandler, 1990, pp. 411, quoting Clapham, 1955, p. 280.
27. Cameron, 1997, pp. 207–208.
28. Ibid., pp. 208–209; Mokyr, 1992, p. 128; Foreman-Peck, 1995, p. 34.
29. Mokyr, 1992, p. 129.
30. Ibid., pp. 129–130.
31. Foreman-Peck, 1995, p. 35.
32. Mokyr, 1992, p. 124.
33. Ibid., p. 123.
34. Ibid., pp. 122–123.
35. Landes, 1969, pp. 284–285.
36. Standage, 1998, p. 138.
37. Ibid., p. 58.
38. Ibid., p. 50.
39. Ibid., pp. 60–61.
40. Mokyr, 1992, p. 123; Cameron, 1997, p. 209.
41. Foreman-Peck, 1995, p. 68.

42. Ibid., pp. 68–69.
43. Standage, 1998, p. 97.
44. Cameron, 1997, p. 209; Mokyr, 1992, p. 247.
45. Mokyr, 1992, p. 144.
46. Cameron, 1997, p. 209.
47. Mokyr, 1992, p. 144.
48. Ibid., p. 124.
49. Foreman-Peck, 1995, p. 67.
50. Landes, 1969, p. 200.
51. Ibid.
52. Ibid., p. 198.
53. Ibid. pp. 198–199.
54. Foreman-Peck, 1995, pp. 46–47.
55. Ibid. p. 64.
56. Ibid., pp. 120–139.
57. Ibid., pp. 123–126 and passim.
58. Kennedy, 1989, p. 200.
59. Cameron, 1997, p. 308; Barraclough and Overy, 1999, p. 255.
60. Barraclough and Overy, 1999, p. 255.
61. Landes, 1998, p. 366.
62. Jay, 1985, p. 47.
63. Ibid., p. 45.
64. Eichengreen, 1996, p. 12.
65. Ibid., pp. 15–18.
66. Ibid., p. 18; Cameron, 1997, p. 307.
67. Foreman-Peck, 1995, p. 173.
68. Ibid.
69. Ibid., pp. 166–169.
70. Ibid., pp. 85–86.
71. Ibid., p. 85.
72. Ibid., p. 86.
73. Ibid., p. 88.
74. Kennedy, 1989, p. 188, citing Landes, 1969, pp. 97–98.
75. Ashton, 1968, p. 129.
76. Floud and McCloskey, 1994, vol. 1, p. 242.
77. Kennedy, 1989, p. 190, citing Bairoch 1982, pp. 294, 296.
78. Kennedy, 1989, p. 203.
79. Landes, 1969, p. 230.
80. Crafts, 1998b.
81. Cameron, 1997, pp. 226–227.
82. Ibid., pp. 202–203.
83. Ibid., pp. 200–201.
84. Ibid., pp. 197–198.
85. Chandler, 1990, p. 89.
86. Foreman-Peck, 1995, p. 169.
87. Kennedy, 1989, p. 250.
88. Craig, 1981, pp. 97–98. Tariffs were introduced on grain, iron and iron-made goods.

89. Kennedy, 1989, p. 252.
90. Quoted in Kennedy, 1989, p. 252.
91. Foreman-Peck, 1995, p. 46.
92. Brogan, 1985, pp. 441, 455, 469.
93. Zimmermann, 2000.
94. Mahan, 1890.
95. Mahan, 1897, p. 52, quoted in Zimmermann, 2000.
96. Cameron, 1997, p. 231; Kennedy, 1989, pp. 255–259; Chandler, 1990, p. 4.
97. Chandler, 1990, p. 52.
98. Ibid., p. 453.
99. "The White Man's Burden" (1899), in Kipling, 1922.
100. Morris-Suzuki, 1994, p. 62.
101. Ibid., p. 72.
102. Kennedy 1989, p. 190, citing Bairoch, 1982, pp. 294, 296.
103. Morris-Suzuki, 1994, pp. 63–65.
104. Waswo, 1996, pp. 22–23.
105. Ibid., p. 17.
106. Itô Hirobumi, quoted in Morris-Suzuki, 1994, p. 73.
107. Morris-Suzuki, 1994, p. 72.
108. Ibid.; Cameron, 1997, p. 274.
109. Morris-Suzuki, 1994, p. 72.
110. Barraclough and Overy, 1999, pp. 242–243.
111. Kennedy, 1989, p. 269.
112. Morris-Suzuki, 1994, p. 72.
113. Service, 1998, p. 4.
114. Kennedy, 1989, p. 255.
115. Nove, 1992, pp. 2–4.
116. Ashton, 1968, p. 129.
117. Service, 1998, pp. 9–21.
118. Deng, 1999, p. 323; Wong, 1997, p. 155.
119. Wong, 1997, p. 155.
120. Ibid., p. 156; *Cassell Atlas of World History,* 1997, p. 5.19.
121. Kennedy, 1989, p. 190.
122. Keynes, 1984, p. 322.
123. Mani Shankar Aiyer, on "Palm and Pine," in the series *Empire,* BBC Radio 4, 26 January 1998.
124. Barraclough and Overy, 1999, p. 234.
125. Kennedy, 1989, pp. 190–191.
126. *Cassell Atlas of World History,* 1997, p. 5.16.
127. Ibid.
128. Floud and McCloskey, 1994, vol. 2, pp. 214–215.
129. Foreman-Peck, 1995, pp. 110–113.
130. Kennedy, 1989, p. 192, citing Fieldhouse, 1973, p. 178.

CHAPTER EIGHT: CUL-DE-SAC, 1910–1945

1. Livi-Bacci, 1997, p. 31; Kremer, 1993, quoted in DeLong, 1999.
2. DeLong, 1998.
3. Ibid.
4. Kennedy, 1989, p. 359; Aldcroft, 1987, pp. 14–17; Cameron, 1997, p. 346; Bullock, 1991, p. 1085.
5. Aldcroft, 1993, p. 10, quoted in Kennedy, 1989, p. 360.
6. Cameron, 1997, p. 346.
7. Kennedy, 1989, p. 361.
8. Aldcroft, 1987, p. 34.
9. Kennedy, 1989, p. 361.
10. Aldcroft, 1987, p. 45.
11. Feinstein et al., 1997, pp. 21–25; Aldcroft, 1987, pp. 30–31.
12. Service, 1999, pp. 33–39, 50–51.
13. Marx, 1977; Heilbroner, 1991, p. 162.
14. P. N. Tkachev (1844–1885), quoted in Davies, 1997, p. 839.
15. Heilbroner, 1991, pp. 141–142.
16. Service, 1999, pp. 4–8.
17. Nove, 1992, pp. 21–22.
18. Service, 1999, pp. 55–57.
19. Ibid., p. 58.
20. Barraclough and Overy, 1999, p. 256; Bullock, 1991, pp. 1085, 1087.
21. Service, 1998, p. 124.
22. Kennedy, 1989, p. 415.
23. Service, 1998, p. 197.
24. Bullock, 1991, passim.
25. Kennedy, 1989, p. 416.
26. Ibid., p. 386.
27. Ibid., p. 418.
28. Aldcroft, 1987, p. 21.
29. Keynes, 1985, p. 26.
30. Kindleberger, 1987, pp. 1–14, 288–305; Kennedy, 1989, pp. 357–358; Foreman-Peck, 1995, p. 212.
31. Cameron, 1997, p. 350.
32. Ibid., p. 352.
33. Kindleberger, 1987, pp. 17–18.
34. Foreman-Peck, 1995, p. 216.
35. Cameron, 1997, p. 352.
36. Foreman-Peck, 1995, p. 216.
37. Ibid.
38. Cameron, 1997, p. 352.
39. Ibid.
40. Kindleberger, 1987, pp. 20–21.
41. Cameron, 1997, p. 353.
42. Aldcroft, 1987, p. 136.
43. Williams, 1997, p. 237; Cameron, 1997, p. 253.

44. Cameron, 1997, p. 353; Aldcroft, 1987, pp. 20–21.
45. Kindleberger, 1987, pp. 20–21.
46. Foreman-Peck, 1995, p. 209.
47. Kindleberger, 1987, p. 15.
48. Cameron, 1997, p. 353; Kenwood and Lougheed, 1999, p. 181; Aldcroft, 1987, p. 138.
49. Foreman-Peck, 1995, p. 209.
50. Kindleberger, 1987, pp. 15–17; Aldcroft, 1987, pp. 64–67.
51. Kenwood and Lougheed, 1999, p. 181.
52. Ibid., pp. 183–184.
53. Kindleberger, 1987, p. 27.
54. Kenwood and Lougheed, 1999, pp. 182–183.
55. Feinstein et al., 1997, p. 46; Eichengreen, 1996, pp. 47–48.
56. Hume, *On the Balance of Trade* (1752), quoted in Eichengreen, 1996, p. 25.
57. Brogan, 1985, pp. 444–445.
58. Jay, 1985, p. 47; Keynes, 1984, p. 223.
59. Kindleberger, 1987, pp. 16–17.
60. Keynes, 1984, p. 223.
61. Eichengreen, 1996, pp. 48, 87.
62. Ibid., p. 48.
63. Kindleberger, 1987, p. 32; Feinstein et al., 1997, p. 48; Eichengreen, 1996, p. 59.
64. Keynes, 1984, p. 211.
65. Feinstein et al., 1997, pp. 63–64; Kindleberger, 1987, p. 42.
66. Kindleberger, 1987, p. 44.
67. Dow, 1998, pp. 161–162.
68. Ibid., p. 165.
69. Ibid.
70. Kindleberger, 1987, p. 95.
71. Available at: http://averages.dowjones.com/cgi-bin/.
72. Dow, 1998, p. 180.
73. Ibid., pp. 160–181.
74. Interview in Parkin and King, 1992, p. 90.
75. Kenwood and Lougheed, 1999, p. 228.
76. Ibid., pp. 227–228; Dow, 1998, p. 180.
77. Kindleberger, 1987, p. 116.
78. Ibid., p. 130.
79. Friedman and Schwartz, 1963.
80. Ibid., pp. 128–129; Dow, 1998, p. 173.
81. Galbraith, 1975, passim.
82. Dow, 1998, pp. 157–159; Eichengreen, 1996, p. 73.
83. Dow, 1998, p. 159.
84. Ibid., p. 137.
85. Ibid. pp. 137, 159.
86. Ibid. p. 136.
87. Floud and McCloskey, 1994, vol. 2, pp. 322–323.
88. *Economic Trends,* August 1999, series BCJE, total claimant count UK, seasonally adjusted.
89. Kindleberger, 1987, p. 170; Dow, 1998, pp. 163, 169; Barraclough and Overy, 1999, p. 265.

90. Quoted in Brogan, 1985, pp. 536–537.
91. Quoted in Bullock, 1991, p. 343.
92. Kindleberger, 1987, p. 230.
93. Dow, 1998, pp. 137, 182–183.
94. Ibid., pp. 181–182.
95. Feinstein et al., 1997, p. 104.
96. Bairoch, 1993, p. 9.
97. Feinstein et al., 1997, p. 123.
98. Ibid., p. 174.
99. Ibid., p. 175.

CHAPTER NINE: FALSE DAWNS? 1945–1999

1. *Guardian,* 23 September 1999, citing United Nations population statistics.
2. Ibid.
3. United Nations, 1999a.
4. Ibid., chapter 1, citing International Road Federation statistics (1997).
5. Livi-Bacci, 1997, p. 31.
6. United Nations, 1999a.
7. Ibid., pp. 2, 3, 15.
8. The term "iron curtain" is usually attributed to Winston Churchill, who famously declared in 1946 that "from Stettin in the Baltic to Trieste in the Adriatic an iron curtain has descended across the Continent." Speech at Westminster College, Fulton, Missouri, 5 March 1946. But the expression previously had been applied by others to the Soviet Union or its sphere of influence, for example by Ethel Snowden in *Through Bolshevik Russia* (1920), Joseph Goebbels in *Das Reich* (2 February 1945), and Churchill himself in a cable to President Harry Truman (4 June 1945). The first known use of the phrase, according to Brewer's *Twentieth Century Phrase and Fable* (1991), is in the Earl of Munster's journal, 1917.
9. Churchill, 1949, vol. 2, p. ix.
10. Gardner, 1969, p. 43.
11. Floud and McCloskey, 1994, vol. 2, p. 405.
12. *The Harper Dictionary of Modern Thought,* p. 175.
13. Gardner, 1969, p. 40.
14. Ibid., pp. 54–62.
15. Van der Wee, 1987, pp. 428–432; Kenwood and Lougheed, 1999, p. 241.
16. Van der Wee, 1987, pp. 440–443.
17. Keynes, 1936.
18. Van der Wee, 1987, p. 291.
19. Ibid., pp. 297–299.
20. Ibid., pp. 48–50; Toniolo, 1998, p. 252.
21. Van der Wee, 1987, p. 62.
22. OECD Historical Statistics, 1960–1995.
23. Dow, 1998, pp. 273–316.
24. Ibid.
25. Ibid., p. 2.
26. Ibid., pp. 32–33.

27. Sudoplatov, 1994, pp. 230–232.
28. Kindleberger, 1987, p. 355.
29. Davies, 1997, p. 1092; Kennedy, 1989, p. 556; Service, 1998, p. 356.
30. Shanks, 1961, p. 15.
31. Ibid., pp. 14–16.
32. Kennedy, 1989, p. 467.
33. Macmillan's speech in Bedford on 20 July 1957 is widely misquoted. He echoed Harry Truman's words—"You never had it so good"—from the 1952 presidential election when he sought to warn that although "most of our people have never had it so good," the new prosperity, created by expansionary economic policy, might be "too good to last" if inflation were not controlled.
34. Service, 1998, p. 361.
35. Ibid., p. 408.
36. Ibid., p. 467.
37. Aldcroft, 1993, pp. 170–171.
38. Ibid., p. 173.
39. *Financial Times, World Economy and Finance Survey,* 24 September 1999.
40. Lipton and Ravallion, 1993, p. 2554.
41. Barraclough and Overy, 1999, pp. 232–233, 260–261; Fairbank and Goldman, 1998, pp. 250–341.
42. Fairbank and Goldman, 1998, pp. 348–349.
43. Ibid., p. 359.
44. Ibid., pp. 369–370.
45. Morison, 1974, p. 42.
46. Fairbank and Goldman, 1998, p. 368.
47. Ibid., p. 371.
48. Chang, 1991, pp. 291–292; Fairbank and Goldman, 1998, pp. 370–371.
49. Fairbank and Goldman, 1998, pp. 368–374.
50. Ibid., pp. 374–382.
51. Ibid., pp. 383–405.
52. World Bank, 1993, p. 59.
53. Ibid.
54. Fairbank and Goldman, 1998, p. 406.
55. Nove, 1992, p. 419.
56. Sen, 1995b, p. 5.
57. Lipton and Ravallion, 1993, p. 2563.
58. World Bank, 1993, pp. 2–4.
59. Ibid., p. 2.
60. Lipton and Ravallion, 1993, p. 2562.
61. World Bank, 1993, pp. 347–368.
62. Ibid., pp. 350–351.
63. BBC, *Panorama,* "Age of Fear," 10 October 1994.

CHAPTER TEN: NOW WHAT?

1. Livi-Bacci, 1997, p. 32.
2. BBC, 2000, "Clever and Greedy," in the series *The Road to Riches.*

3. Keynes, 1984, pp. 325–326, his emphasis.
4. Ibid., p. 330.
5. Ibid., p. 323.
6. Ibid.
7. *Cassell Atlas of World History*, 1997, p. 1.07.
8. Cameron, 1997, p. 31.
9. Keynes, 1984, pp. 324–325.
10. DeLong, 1998, and my own calculations.
11. Keynes, 1984, p. 326.
12. Macaulay, 1843, pp. 267–268.
13. OECD, 1999.
14. Correspondence with J.C.R. Hunt, Department of Space and Climate Physics, University College, London. See also Hunt, in *Physica D 133* (1999), pp. 270–295.
15. Smith, 1812, vol. 1, p. 27.
16. Keynes, 1984, pp. 330–331.
17. Ibid.
18. Ibid., p. 332.
19. OECD, 1999.

BIBLIOGRAPHY

Abramowitz, M. 1986. "Catching Up, Forging Ahead and Falling Behind." *Journal of Economic History* 46, pp. 385–406.

Abulafia, David. 1993. *Commerce and Conquest in the Mediterranean, 1100–1500.* Aldershot: Variorum.

———. 1997. *The Western Mediterranean Kingdoms, 1200–1500.* London: Longman.

Abu-Lughod, Janet. 1989. *Before European Hegemony: The World System AD 1250–1350.* Oxford: Oxford University Press.

Adas, Michael, ed. 1993. *Islamic and European Expansion: The Forging of a Global Order.* Philadelphia: Temple University Press.

Aldcroft, Derek H. 1987. *From Versailles to Wall Street, 1919–1929.* Harmondsworth, UK: Pelican.

———. 1993. *The European Economy, 1914–1990.* 3rd edition. London: Routledge.

Aldcroft, Derek H., and Morewood, Steven. 1995. *Economic Change in Eastern Europe Since 1918.* Aldershot, UK: Edward Elgar.

Allen, Robert C. 1999. "Tracking the Agricultural Revolution in England." *Economic History Review,* 2nd ser., 52, 2, pp. 209–235.

Anderson, Michael, ed. 1996. *British Population History.* Cambridge: Cambridge University Press.

Andrews, Kenneth R. 1984 *Trade, Plunder and Settlement: Maritime Enterprise and the Genesis of the British Empire, 1480–1630.* Cambridge: Cambridge University Press.

Angell, Norman. 1912 (first published 1910). *The Great Illusion.* London: Heinemann.

Appleby, John C. 1998. "War, Politics and Colonization, 1558–1625." In Nicholas Canny, ed., *The Oxford History of the British Empire,* vol. 1, pp. 55–78. Oxford: Oxford University Press.

Ashton, T. S. 1968. *The Industrial Revolution.* Oxford: Oxford University Press.

Asian Development Bank. 1997. *Emerging Asia: Changes and Challenges.* Manila: Asian Development Bank.

Astill, Grenville, and Grant, Annie. 1988. *The Countryside of Medieval England.* Oxford: Blackwell.

Astill, Grenville, and Langdon, John. 1997. *Medieval Farming and Technology: The Impact of Agricultural Change in North-west Europe.* Leiden: Brill.

Atack, Jeremy, and Passell, Peter. 1994. *A New Economic View of American History.* 2nd ed. New York: W. W. Norton.

Audi, Robert, ed. 1995. *Cambridge Dictionary of Philosophy.* Cambridge: Cambridge University Press.

Auerbach, Jeffrey A. 1999. *The Great Exhibition of 1851.* New Haven: Yale University Press.

Austin, M. M., and Vidal-Naquet, P. 1977. *Economic and Social History of Ancient Greece: An Introduction.* London: Batsford.

Aylmer, G. E. 1998. "Navy, State, Trade, and Empire." In Nicholas Canny, ed., *The Oxford History of the British Empire,* vol. 1, pp. 445–466. Oxford: Oxford University Press.

Bairoch, Paul. 1976a. *The Economic Development of the Third World Since 1900.* Berkeley: University of California Press.

———. 1976b. "Europe's Gross National Product: 1800–1975." *Journal of European Economic History* 5.

———. 1982. "International Industrialisation Levels from 1750 to 1980." *Journal of European Economic History* 11, 4, pp. 269–334.

———. 1988. *Cities and Economic Development.* London: Mansell.

———. 1993. *Economics and World History: Myths and Paradoxes.* Hemel Hempstead, UK: Harvester Wheatsheaf.

Bairoch, Paul, and Levy-Leboyer, Maurice, eds. 1981. *Disparities in Economic Development Since the Industrial Revolution.* London: Macmillan.

Barraclough, Geoffrey, ed. 1978. *The Times Atlas of World History.* London: Times Books.

Barraclough, Geoffrey, and Overy, Richard, eds. 1999. *The Times History of the World.* London: Times Books.

Behrman, Jere, and Srinivasan, T. N., eds. 1995. *Handbook of Development Economics.* Amsterdam: Elsevier.

Berg, Maxine, and Hudson, Pat. 1992. "Rehabilitating the Industrial Revolution." *Economic History Review,* 2nd ser., 45, pp. 24–50.

Bermingham, Ann, and Brewer, John. 1995. *The Consumption of Culture, 1600–1800.* London: Routledge.

Bisson, T. N. 1994. "The 'Feudal Revolution.'" *Past and Present* 142, pp. 6–42.

———. 1997. "The 'Feudal Revolution,' Reply." *Past and Present* 155, pp. 208–225.

Blackburn, Robin. 1997. *The Making of New World Slavery: From the Baroque to the Creole, 1492–1800.* London: Verso.

Bloom, David, and Sachs, Jeffrey. 1998. *Geography, Demography and Economic Growth in Africa.* Brookings Papers on Economic Activity, no. 2. Washington, D.C.: Brookings Institution.

Boardman, John, Griffin, Jasper, and Murray, Oswyn. 1991. *The Oxford History of Greece and the Hellenic World.* Oxford: Oxford University Press.

Boserup, E. 1965. *The Conditions of Agricultural Growth.* London: Allen & Unwin.

Braudel, Fernand. 1984. *Civilization and Capitalism.* 3 vols. Trans. Siân Reynolds. London: Collins.

———. 1994. *A History of Civilizations.* Trans. R. Mayne. London: Penguin.

———. 1995. *The Mediterranean and the Mediterranean World in the Age of Philip II.* 2 vols. Trans. Siân Reynolds. Berkeley: University of California Press.

Braund, David. 1994. "The Luxuries of Athenian Democracy." *Greece and Rome* 41, 1 (April), pp. 41–48.

Brewer, John. 1989. *The Sinews of Power: War, Money and the English State, 1688–1783.* London: Unwin Hyman.

Brewer, John; McKenrick, N.; and Plumb, J. H., eds. 1990. *The Birth of a Consumer Society: The Commercialization of Eighteenth Century England.* London: Europa.

Brewer, John, and Porter, Roy, eds. 1993. *Consumption and the World of Goods.* London: Routledge.

Britnell, R. H. 1993. *The Commercialisation of English Society, 1000–1500.* Cambridge: Cambridge University Press.

Brittan, Samuel. 1998. *Essays: Moral, Political and Economic.* Hume Papers on Public Policy 6, 4. Edinburgh: Edinburgh University Press.

Broadberry, S. N. 1997a. "The Long-run Growth and Productivity Performance of the UK." *Scottish Journal of Political Economy* 44, pp. 403–424.

———. 1997b. *The Productivity Race: British Manufacturing in International Perspective, 1850–1990.* New York: Cambridge University Press.

Broadberry, S. N., and Crafts, N. 1996. "British Economic Policy and Performance in Early Post-war Britain." *Business History* 38, pp. 65–91.

Brogan, Hugh. 1985. *Longman History of the United States of America.* London: Longman.

Bronk, Richard. 1998. *Progress and the Invisible Hand: The Philosophy and Economics of Human Advance.* London: Little, Brown.

Buchan, James. 1997. *Frozen Desire: An Inquiry into the Meaning of Money.* London: Picador.

Bullock, Alan. 1991. *Hitler and Stalin: Parallel Lives.* London: HarperCollins.

Cambridge Ancient History. 14 vols. Cambridge: Cambridge University Press.

Cambridge Economic History of Europe. 8 vols. Cambridge: Cambridge University Press.

Cambridge Economic History of India. 2 vols. Cambridge: Cambridge University Press.

Cambridge History of China. 15 vols. Cambridge: Cambridge University Press.

Cambridge Medieval History. 8 vols. Cambridge: Cambridge University Press.

Cameron, Rondo. 1997. *A Concise Economic History of the World from Paleolithic Times to the Present.* 3rd ed. Oxford: Oxford University Press.

Campbell, Bruce, and Overton, Mark. 1993. "A New Perspective on Medieval and Early Modern Agriculture: Six Centuries of Norfolk Farming, c. 1250–c. 1850." *Past and Present* 141, pp. 38–105.

Cannon, John, ed. 1997. *Oxford Companion to British History.* Oxford: Oxford University Press.

Canny, Nicholas, ed. 1998. *The Origins of Empire: British Overseas Enterprise of the Close of the Seventeenth Century.* Vol. 1 of William Roger Louis, ed., *Oxford History of the British Empire.* Oxford: Oxford University Press.

Cartledge, Paul, ed. 1998. *Cambridge Illustrated History of Ancient Greece.* Cambridge: Cambridge University Press.

Cartledge, Paul; Millett, Paul; and Todd, Stephen, eds. 1990. *Nomos: Essays in Athenian Law, Politics and Society.* Cambridge: Cambridge University Press.

Cartledge, Paul; Millett, Paul; and Von Reden, Sitta, eds. 1998. *Kosmos: Essays in Order, Conflict and Community in Classical Athens.* Cambridge: Cambridge University Press.

Cassell Atlas of World History. 1997. London: Cassell.

Chambers, J. D., and Mingay, G. E. 1966. *The Agricultural Revolution, 1750–1880.* London: Batsford.

Chandler, Alfred. 1990. *Scale and Scope: The Dynamics of Industrial Capitalism.* Cambridge: Harvard University Press, Belknap Press.

Chandler, Alfred, Amatori, Franco, and Hikino, Takashi, eds. 1997. *Big Business and the Wealth of Nations.* Cambridge: Cambridge University Press.

Chang, Jung. 1991. *Wild Swans.* London: HarperCollins.

Chase-Dunn, Christopher, and Willard, Alice. 1993. "Systems of Cities and World-systems: Settlement Size Hierarchies and Cycles of Political Centralization, 2000 BC–1988 AD." Paper presented to the International Studies Association, Acapulco, Mexico.

Chaudhuri, K. N. 1985. *Trade and Civilisation in the Indian Ocean: An Economic History from the Rise of Islam to 1750.* Cambridge: Cambridge University Press.

———. 1990. *Asia Before Europe: Economy and Civilisation of the Indian Ocean from the Rise of Islam to 1750.* Cambridge: Cambridge University Press.

Chown, John F. 1994. *A History of Money from AD 800.* London: Routledge.

Churchill, Winston S. 1949. *The Second World War.* 5 vols. London: Cassell.

Cipolla, Carlo M. 1965. *Guns and Sails in the Early Phase of the European Expansion, 1400–1700.* London: Collins.

———. 1976. *Before the Industrial Revolution: European Society and Economy, 1000–1700.* London: Methuen.

———. 1976–1977. *Fontana Economic History of Europe.* 6 vols. London: Fontana.

———. 1978. *The Economic History of the World Population.* 7th ed. Harmondsworth, UK: Pelican.

Clapham, J. H. 1955. *The Economic Development of France and Germany, 1815–1914.* 4th ed. Cambridge: Cambridge University Press.

Clark, Colin. 1977. *Population Growth and Land Use.* London: Macmillan.

Clayre, Alasdair, ed. 1977. *Nature and Industrialization.* Oxford: Oxford University Press.

———. 1984. *The Heart of the Dragon.* London: Collins.

Coats, A. W. 1971. *The Classical Economists and Economic Policy.* London: Methuen.

Cohen, Joel E. 1995. *How Many People Can the Earth Support?* New York: Norton.

Colclough, Christopher, and Manor, James. 1991. *States and Markets.* Oxford: Oxford University Press.

Conquest, Robert. 1986. *Harvest of Sorrow: Soviet Collectivisation and the Terror-Famine.* Oxford: Oxford University Press.

———. 1991. *The Great Terror: A Reassessment.* Oxford: Oxford University Press.

Conrad, Lawrence I., Neve, Michael, Nutton, Vivian, Porter, Roy, and Wear, Anthony, eds. 1995. *The Western Medical Tradition, 800 BC–AD 1800.* Cambridge: Cambridge University Press.

Cotterell, Arthur. 1980. *The Encyclopaedia of Ancient Civilizations.* Leicester, UK: Windward.

Crafts, Nicholas F. R. 1983. "British Economic Growth, 1700–1831: A Review of the Evidence." *Economic History Review,* 2nd ser., 36, pp. 177–199.

———. 1985. *British Economic Growth During the Industrial Revolution.* Oxford: Clarendon Press.

———. 1992. "Output Growth and the British Industrial Revolution: A Restatement of the Crafts-Harley View." *Economic History Review,* 2nd ser., 45, pp. 703–730.

———. 1995a. "The Golden Age of Economic Growth in Western Europe, 1950–73." *Economic History Review,* 2nd ser., 48, pp. 429–447.

———. 1995b. "Macro-inventions, Economic Growth, and 'Industrial Revolution' in Britain and France." *Economic History Review,* 2nd ser., 48, pp. 591–598.

———. 1997a. "The Human Development Index and Changes in the Standards of Living: Some Historical Comparisons." *European Review of Economic History,* 1, pp. 299–322.

———. 1997b. "Some Dimensions of the 'Quality of Life' During the British Industrial Revolution." *Economic History Review,* 2nd ser.,50, 4, pp. 617–639.

———. 1998a. *The Conservative Government's Economic Record: An End of Term Report.* London: Institute for Economic Affairs, for the Wincott Foundation.

———. 1998b. "Forging Ahead and Falling Behind: The Rise and Relative Decline of the First Industrial Nation." *Journal of Economic Perspectives* 12, 2, pp. 193–210.

Crafts, N.F.R.; Leybourne, S. J.; and Mills, T. C. 1991. "Britain." In R. Sylla and G. Toniolo, eds., *Patterns of European Industrialization: The Nineteenth Century*, pp. 109–152. London: Routledge.

Crafts, N.F.R., and Mills, T. C. 1994. "The Industrial Revolution as a Macro-economic Epoch: An Alternative View." *Economic History Review*, 2nd ser., 47, pp. 769–775.

———. 1997. "Endogenous Innovation, Trend Growth, and the British Industrial Revolution: Reply to Greasley and Oxley." *Journal of Economic History* 57, pp. 950–956.

Crafts, N.F.R., and Toniolo, G., eds. 1996. *Economic Growth in Europe Since 1945*. Cambridge: Cambridge University Press.

Crafts, N.F.R., and Van Ark, B., eds. 1997. *Quantitative Aspects of Europe's Post-war Growth*. Cambridge: Cambridge University Press.

Crafts, N.F.R., and Woodward, N.W.C., eds. 1991. *The British Economy Since 1945*. Oxford: Clarendon Press.

Craig, Gordon A. 1981. *Germany, 1866–1945*. Oxford: Oxford University Press.

Crawford, Harriet. 1991. *Sumer and the Sumerians*. Cambridge: Cambridge University Press.

Cunliffe, Barry. 1988. *Greeks, Romans and Barbarians: Spheres of Interaction*. London: Guild.

Curtin, Philip D. 1969. *The Atlantic Slave Trade: A Census*. Madison: University of Wisconsin Press.

———. 1984. *Cross-Cultural Trade in World History*. Cambridge: Cambridge University Press.

Darwin, Charles. 1859. *On the Origin of Species*. London: John Murray.

Dasgupta, P. 1993. *An Inquiry into Well-being and Destitution*. Oxford: Clarendon Press.

Davies, Glyn. 1996. *A History of Money*. Cardiff: University of Wales Press.

Davies, John K. 1984. *Wealth and the Power of Wealth in Classical Athens*. Ayer: Manchester, NH.

Davies, Norman. 1997. *Europe: A History*. London: Pimlico.

Dean, Trevor, and Wickham, Chris. 1990. *City and Countryside in Late Medieval and Renaissance Italy*. London: Hambledon.

Deane, Phyllis. 1979. *The First Industrial Revolution*. 2nd ed. Cambridge: Cambridge University Press.

Deane, Phyllis, and Cole, W. A. 1962. *British Economic Growth, 1688–1959*. Cambridge: Cambridge University Press.

Defoe, Daniel. 1927 (first published 1724–1726). *A Tour Thro' the Whole Island of Great Britain*. 2 vols. London: Peter Davies.

DeLong, J. Bradford. 1998. "Estimating World GDP, One Million BC–Present." Available at http://econ161.berkeley.edu.

Deng, Gang. 1999. *The Pre-modern Chinese Economy*. London: Routledge.

DeVoto, Bernard. 1954. *The Journals of Lewis and Clark*. London: Eyre and Spottiswoode.

De Vries, Jan. 1976. *The Economy of Europe in an Age of Crisis, 1600–1750*. Cambridge: Cambridge University Press.

———. 1994. "The Industrial Revolution and the Industrious Revolution." *Journal of Economic History* 54, pp. 249–270.

De Vries, Jan, and van der Woude, Ad. 1997. *The First Modern Economy: Success, Failure, and Perseverance of the Dutch Economy, 1500–1815*. Cambridge: Cambridge University Press.

Diamond, Jared M. 1991. *The Rise and Fall of the Third Chimpanzee*. London: Radius.

———. 1998. *Guns, Germs and Steel: A Short History of Everybody for the Last 13,000 Years*. London: Vintage.

Dickens, Charles. 1854. *Hard Times*. London: Bradbury and Evans.

Dickson, P.G.M. 1967. *The Financial Revolution in England: A Study of the Development of Public Credit, 1688–1756*. London: Macmillan.

Dimbleby, David, and Reynolds, David. 1988. *An Ocean Apart*. London: Hodder and Stoughton.

Dow, Christopher. 1998. *Major Recessions: Britain and the World, 1920–95*. Oxford: Oxford University Press.

Drescher, Seymour, and Engerman, Stanley L., eds. 1998. *A Historical Guide to World Slavery*. New York: Oxford University Press.

Duncan-Jones, R. P. 1982. *The Economy of the Roman Empire*. 2nd ed. Cambridge: Cambridge University Press.

———. 1990. *Structure and Scale in the Roman Economy*. Cambridge: Cambridge University Press.

———. 1994. *Money and Government in the Roman Empire*. Cambridge: Cambridge University Press.

Dyer, Christopher. 1989a. "The Consumer and the Market in the Middle Ages." *Economic History Review*, 2nd ser., 42, pp. 305–326.

———. 1989b. *Standards of Living in the Later Middle Ages: Social Change in England, c. 1200–1500*. Cambridge: Cambridge University Press.

———. 1994. *Everyday Life in Medieval England*. London: Hambledon Press.

Dyos, H. J., and Aldcroft, D. H. 1969. *British Transport*. Leicester: Leicester University Press.

Eichengreen, Barry. 1992. "The Origins and Nature of the Great Slump Revisited." *Economic History Review*, 2nd ser., 45, pp. 213–239.

———. 1996. *Globalizing Capital: A History of the International Monetary System*. Princeton, N.J.: Princeton University Press.

Elvin, Mark. 1973. *The Pattern of the Chinese Past*. London: Eyre Methuen.

Engerman, Stanley, and Solow, Barbara. 1989. *British Capitalism and Caribbean Slavery: The Legacy of Eric Williams*. Cambridge: Cambridge University Press.

Englund, Bob, and Nissen, Hans J. 1993. *Archaic Bookkeeping*. Chicago: University of Chicago Press.

Epstein, S. R. 1991. "Cities, Regions and the Late Medieval Crisis: Sicily and Tuscany Compared." *Past and Present* 130, pp. 3–50.

Esteban, Javier Cuenca. 1995a. "British Textile Prices, 1770–1831: Are British Growth Rates Worth Revising Again?" *Economic History Review*, 2nd ser., 48, pp. 66–105.

———. 1995b. "Further Evidence of Falling Prices of Cotton Cloth, 1768–1816." *Economic History Review*, 2nd ser., 48, pp. 145–150.

Fairbank, J. K., and Goldman, Merle. 1998. *China: A New History*. Cambridge: Harvard University Press, Belknap Press.

Faith, Nicholas. 1990. *The World the Railways Made*. London: Bodley Head.

Feinstein, Charles H.; Temin, Peter; and Toniolo, Gianni. 1997. *The European Economy Between the Wars*. Oxford: Oxford University Press.

Ferguson, Niall. 1995. *Paper and Iron: Hamburg Business and German Politics in the Era of Inflation, 1897–1927*. Cambridge: Cambridge University Press.

———. 1998a. *The Pity of War*. Penguin, London.

———. 1998b. *The World's Banker: A History of the House of Rothschild*. London: Weidenfeld & Nicolson.

Fernandez-Armesto, Felipe. 1987. *Before Columbus: Exploration and Colonisation from the Mediterranean to the Atlantic, 1229–1492*. Basingstoke, UK: Macmillan Education.

———. ed. 1995a. *The European Opportunity*. Brookfield, Vt.: Variorum.

———. ed. 1995b. *The Global Opportunity*. Brookfield, Vt.: Variorum.

Fieldhouse, D. 1973. *Economics and Empire, 1830–1914*. London: Weidenfeld & Nicolson.

Figes, Orlando. 1997. *A People's Tragedy: The Russian Revolution, 1891–1924*. London: Pimlico.

Finley, Moses, ed. 1968. *Slavery in Classical Antiquity: Views and Controversies.*. Cambridge: Cambridge University Press and Heffer.

———. 1981. *Economy and Society in Ancient Greece*. London: Chatto & Windus.

———. 1985a. *The Ancient Economy*. London: Penguin.

———. 1985b. *Ancient History: Evidence and Models*. London: Chatto & Windus.

———. ed. 1987. *Classical Slavery*. London: Cass.

Fitzgibbons, Athol. 1995. *Adam Smith's System of Liberty, Wealth and Virtue*. Oxford: Clarendon Press.

Fleming, Robin. 1993. "Rural Elites and Urban Communities in Late-Saxon England." *Past and Present* 141, pp. 3–37.

Flinn, Michael W. 1981. *The European Demographic System, 1500–1820*. Baltimore, Md.: Books Demand.

Floud, Roderick, and McCloskey, D. N. 1994. *The Economic History of Britain Since 1700*. 3 vols. Cambridge: Cambridge University Press.

Fogel, Robert. 1994. "Economic Growth, Population Theory, and Physiology: The Bearing of Long-term Processes on the Making of Economic Policy." *American Economic Review* 84, 3, pp. 369–395.

———. 1997. "When Will Humanity Finally Escape from Chronic Malnutrition?" Nestlé Lecture on the Developing World, London, 20 March 1997. Available from Nestlé UK Ltd, St. George's House, Croydon, Surrey, England. ISSN 1364–4807.

Fogel, Robert, and Engerman, Stanley L. 1989. *Time on the Cross: The Economics of American Negro Slavery*. New York: W. W. Norton.

Foreman-Peck, James. 1991. *New Perspectives on the Late Victorian Economy*. Cambridge: Cambridge University Press.

———. 1995. *A History of the World Economy: International Economic Relations Since 1850*. 2nd ed. New York: Harvester Wheatsheaf.

Franck, Irene, and Brownstone, David M. 1986. *The Silk Road: A History*. Oxford: Facts on File Publications.

Frank, Andre Gunder. 1984. *Critique and Anti-critique: Essays on Dependence and Reform*. London: Macmillan.

———. 1998. *Re-ORIENT: Global Economy in the Asian Age*. Berkeley: University of California Press.

Frank, Andre Gunder, and Gills, Barry. 1996. *The World System: 500 Years or 5000?* London: Routledge.

Frederiksen, M. W. 1975. "Theory, Evidence and the Ancient Economy." *Journal of Roman Studies* 65, pp. 164–171.

French, A. 1991. "Economic Conditions in Fourth-Century Athens." *Greece and Rome* 38, 1 (April), pp. 24–40.

Friedman, Thomas. 1999. *The Lexus and the Olive Tree.* London: HarperCollins.

Friedman, Milton, and Schwartz, Anna Jacobson. 1963. *A Monetary History of the United States, 1867–1960.* Princeton, NJ: Princeton University Press.

Galbraith, John Kenneth. 1975. *The Great Crash 1929.* London: Pelican.

———. 1977. *The Age of Uncertainty.* London: BBC.

———. 1987. *A History of Economics.* London: Hamish Hamilton.

Gall, Lothar. 1986. *Bismarck: The White Revolutionary.* 2 vols. London: Allen & Unwin.

Gardner, Richard. N. 1969. *Sterling-Dollar Diplomacy.* New York: McGraw-Hill.

Garnsey, Peter. 1988. *Famine and Food Supply in the Greco-Roman World.* Cambridge: Cambridge University Press.

———. 1996. *Ideas of Slavery from Aristotle to Augustine.* Cambridge: Cambridge University Press.

Garnsey, Peter; Hopkins, Keith; and Whittaker, C. R. 1983. *Trade in the Ancient Economy.* London: Chatto & Windus.

Garnsey, Peter, and Saller, Richard. 1987. *The Roman Empire: Economy, Society and Culture.* London: Duckworth.

Gibbon, Edward. 1846 (first published 1776–1788). *The History of the Decline and Fall of the Roman Empire.* London: John Murray.

Goody, Jack. 1996. *The East in the West.* Cambridge: Cambridge University Press.

Gray, John. 1998. *False Dawn: The Delusions of Global Capitalism.* London: Granta.

Greasley, David, and Oxley, Les. 1994. "Rehabilitation Sustained: The Industrial Revolution as a Macro-economic Epoch." *Economic History Review,* 2nd ser., 47, pp. 760–768.

———. 1997. "Endogenous Innovation, Trend Growth, and the British Industrial Revolution." *Journal of Economic History,* 57, pp. 935–949, 957–960.

Greene, Kevin. 1986. *The Archaeology of the Roman Economy.* London: Batsford.

Haber, S. H. 1997. *How Latin America Fell Behind.* Stanford: Stanford University Press.

Hardach, Gerd. 1977. *The First World War, 1914–1918.* London: Allen Lane.

Harley, C. K. 1998. "Cotton Textile Prices and the Industrial Revolution." *Economic History Review,* 2nd ser., 51, pp. 49–83.

Harley, C. K., and Crafts, N.F.R. 1995. "Cotton Textiles and Industrial Output Growth During the Industrial Revolution." *Economic History Review,* 2nd ser., 48, pp. 134–144.

Harris, D. R., ed. 1996. *The Origins and Spread of Agriculture and Pastoralism in Eurasia.* London: UCL Press.

Hartwell, R. M. 1967. *The Causes of the Industrial Revolution.* London: Methuen.

———. 1972. *The Industrial Revolution in England.* London: Historical Association.

Al-Hassan, Ahmad Y. 1994. "Factors Behind the Decline of Islamic Science After the Sixteenth Century." In *Islam and the Challenge of Modernity: Historical and Contemporary Contexts.* Kuala Lumpur, Malaysia: International Institute of Islamic Thought and Civilization.

Hatcher, John. 1986. "Mortality in the Fifteenth Century: Some New Evidence." *Economic History Review,* 2nd ser., 39, pp. 19–32.

———. 1996. "Plague, Population and the English Economy, 1348–1530." In Michael

Anderson, ed., *British Population History*. Cambridge: Cambridge University Press.

Heilbroner, Robert. 1991. *The Worldly Philosophers*. Harmondsworth, UK: Penguin.

Held, David, McGrew, Anthony, Goldblatt, David, and Perraton, Jonathan, eds. 1999. *Global Transformations: Politics, Economics and Culture*. Cambridge: Polity Press.

Herlihy, David, ed. 1971. *The History of Feudalism*. London: Macmillan.

———. 1997. Ed. and with an introduction by Samuel K. Cohn Jr. *The Black Death and the Transformation of the West*. Cambridge: Harvard University Press.

Hicks, J. 1950. *A Contribution to the Theory of the Trade Cycle*. Oxford: Clarendon Press.

Hilton, Boyd. 1977. *Corn, Cash and Commerce: The Economic Policies of the Tory Governments, 1815–30*. Oxford: Oxford University Press.

Hirsch, Fred. 1977. *Social Limits to Growth*. London: Routledge & Kegan Paul.

Hobbes, Thomas. 1969 (first published 1651). *Leviathan*. London: Fontana/Collins.

Hobsbawm, E. J. 1968. *Industry and Empire*. London: Weidenfeld & Nicolson.

Hodges, R. 1982. *Dark Age Economics: The Origins of Towns and Trade, AD 600–1000*. London: Duckworth.

Hodges, R., and Hobley, Brian, eds. 1988. *The Rebirth of the Towns in the West, AD 700–1050*. London: Council for British Archaeology.

Hoffman, Philip T. 1997. *Growth in a Traditional Society: The French Countryside, 1450–1815*. Princeton, N.J.: Princeton University Press.

Hollingdale, Stuart. 1989. *Makers of Mathematics*. Harmondsworth, UK: Penguin.

Hopkins, K. 1978. *Conquerors and Slaves*. Cambridge: Cambridge University Press.

———. 1980. "Taxes and Trade in the Roman Empire, 200 BC–AD 400." *Journal of Roman Studies* 70.

———. 1983. *Death and Renewal*. Cambridge: Cambridge University Press.

Hopper, R. J. 1979. *Trade and Industry in Classical Greece*. London: Thames and Hudson.

Hosking, Geoffrey. 1998. *Russia: People and Empire, 1552–1917*. London: Fontana.

Hourani, Albert Habib. 1991. *A History of the Arab Peoples*. London: Faber.

Houston, R. A. 1996. "The Population of Britain and Ireland, 1500–1750." In Michael Anderson, ed., *British Population History*. Cambridge: Cambridge University Press.

Howgego, Christopher. 1992. "The Supply and Use of Money in the Roman World, 200 BC–AD 300." *Journal of Roman Studies* 82, pp. 1–31.

Humphreys, S. C. 1978. *Anthropology and the Greeks*. London: Routledge & Kegan Paul.

Hyam, R. 1976. *Britain's Imperial Century, 1815–1914*. London: Batsford.

Inkori, Joseph E., and Engerman, Stanley L. 1992. *The Atlantic Slave Trade: Effects on Economies, Societies, and Peoples in Africa, the Americas and Europe*. Durham, N.C.: Duke University Press.

Jackson, R. V. 1992. "Rates of Industrial Growth During the Industrial Revolution." *Economic History Review*, 2nd ser., 45, pp. 1–23.

James, J., and Thomas, M., eds. 1994. *Capitalism in Context: Essays in Honor of R. M. Hartwell*. Chicago: Chicago University Press.

Jay, Douglas. 1985. *Sterling: A Plea for Moderation*. London: Sidgwick and Jackson.

Jones, A.H.M. 1974. *The Roman Economy*. Oxford: Blackwell.

Jones, Eric L. 1987. *The European Miracle: Environments, Economics and Geopolitics in the History of Europe and Asia*. Cambridge: Cambridge University Press.

———. 1988. *Growth Recurring: Economic Change in World History*. Oxford: Clarendon Press.

Keay, John. 1991. *The Honourable Company*. London: HarperCollins.

Kennedy, Paul. 1989. *The Rise and Fall of the Great Powers*. London: Fontana.

———. 1993. *Preparing for the Twenty-first Century*. London: HarperCollins.

Kenwood, A. G., and Lougheed, A. L. 1999. *The Growth of the International Economy, 1820–2000*. London: Routledge.

Keynes, John Maynard. 1936. *The General Theory of Employment, Interest and Money*. London: Macmillan.

———. 1984. *Essays in Persuasion*. London: Macmillan.

———. 1985. *Essays in Biography*. London: Macmillan.

Killick, Tony. 1989. *A Reaction Too Far*. London: Overseas Development Institute.

Kindleberger, Charles. 1987. *The World in Depression, 1929–39*. London: Pelican.

———. 1996. *Manias, Panics, and Crashes: A History of Financial Crises*. New York: Wiley.

Kipling, Rudyard. 1906 (first published 1894). *The Jungle Book*. London: Macmillan.

———. 1922. *Rudyard Kipling's Verse, 1885–1918*. London: Hodder and Stoughton.

Kirzner, I. 1989. *Discovery, Capitalism and Distributive Justice*. Oxford: Blackwell.

Korten, David. 1995. *When Corporations Rule the World*. London: Earthscan.

Kremer, Michael. 1993. "Population Growth and Technical Change, One Million BC to 1990." *Quarterly Journal of Economics* 108, 3, pp. 681–716.

Krugman, Paul. 1992. "Toward a Counter-revolution on Development Economics." In *Proceedings of the World Bank Annual Conference on Development Economics*. Washington, D.C.: World Bank.

———. 1998a. *The Accidental Theorist*. New York: W. W. Norton.

———. 1998b. *Pop Internationalism*. Cambridge: MIT Press.

———. 1999. *The Return of Depression Economics*. London: Penguin.

Kurlansky, Mark. 1999. *Cod*. London: Vintage.

Kuznets, Simon. 1966. *Modern Economic Growth*. New Haven, Conn.: Yale University Press.

———. 1971. *Economic Growth of Nations*. Cambridge: Harvard University Press, Belknap Press.

Kynaston, David. 1999. *Illusions of Gold: The City of London*. Vol. 3: *1914–45*. London: Chatto & Windus.

Lal, Deepak. 1997. *The Poverty of Development Economics*. 2nd ed. London: Institute of Economic Affairs.

———. 1998. *Unintended Consequences*. Cambridge: MIT Press.

Lal, Deepak, and Myint, H. 1996. *The Political Economy of Poverty, Equity and Growth: A Comparative Study*. Oxford: Clarendon Press.

Lamb, Ursula, ed. 1995. *The Globe Encircled and the World Revealed*. Brookfield, Vt.: Variorum.

Landes, David S. 1969. *The Unbound Prometheus: Technological Change and Industrial Development in Western Europe from 1750 to the Present*. Cambridge: Cambridge University Press.

———. 1995. "Some Further Thoughts on Accident in History: A Reply to Professor Crafts." *Economic History Review*, 2nd ser., 48, pp. 599–601.

———. 1998. *The Wealth and Poverty of Nations*. London: Little, Brown.

Lane, Frederick C. 1973. *Venice: A Maritime Republic*. Baltimore, Md.: Johns Hopkins University Press.

Lawrence, Alan. 1998. *China Under Communism*. London: Routledge.

Leadbeater, Charles. 1999. *Living on Thin Air: The New Economy.* London: Viking.

Levathes, Louise. 1996. *When China Ruled the Seas.* New York: Oxford University Press.

Lipton, Michael. 1977. *Why Poor People Stay Poor.* London: Temple Smith.

———. 1998. *Successes in Anti-Poverty.* Geneva: International Labor Organization.

Lipton, Michael, with Longhurst, Richard. 1989. *New Seeds and Poor People.* London: Unwin Hyman.

Lipton, Michael, and Ravallion, Martin. 1993. *Poverty and Policy.* Washington, D.C.: World Bank.

Little, Lester K., and Rosenwein, Barbara H., eds. 1998. *Debating the Middle Ages: Issues and Readings.* Oxford: Blackwell.

Livi-Bacci, Massimo. 1997. *A Concise History of World Population.* Oxford: Blackwell.

Luttwak, Edward. 1998. *Turbo-Capitalism: Winners and Losers in the Global Economy.* London: Orion Business.

Lynch, Michael. 1998. *The People's Republic of China Since 1949.* London: Hodder and Stoughton.

Macaulay, T. B. 1843. *Critical and Historical Essays.* 3 vols. London: Longman, Brown, Green and Longmans.

McEvedy, Colin, and Jones, Richard. 1978. *Atlas of World Population History.* London: Allen Lane.

Macfarlane, Alan. 2000. *The Riddle of the Modern World.* London: Macmillan.

McKendrick, N. 1982. "Commercialization and the Economy." In J. Brewer, N. McKendrick, and J. H. Plumb, eds., *The Birth of a Consumer Society: The Commercialization of Eighteenth Century Britain.* London: Europa.

McLellan, David, ed. 1977. *Karl Marx: Selected Writings.* Oxford: Oxford University Press.

———. 1979. *Marxism After Marx.* London: Macmillan.

———. 1980. *The Thought of Karl Marx.* London: Macmillan.

McNeill, William H. 1982. *The Pursuit of Power: Technology, Armed Force and Society Since AD 1000.* Chicago: University of Chicago Press.

———. 1991. *The Rise of the West: A History of the Human Community.* Chicago: University of Chicago Press.

———. 1992. *The Global Condition: Conquerors, Catastrophes and Community.* Princeton, N.J.: Princeton University Press.

———. 1994. *Plagues and Peoples.* Harmondsworth, UK: Penguin.

McNeill, William H., and McNeill, John R. Forthcoming. *A Very Short History of the Whole World.*

Maddison, Angus. 1991. *Dynamic Forces in Capitalist Development: A Long-run Comparative View.* Oxford: Oxford University Press.

———. 1995a. *Explaining the Economic Performance of Nations.* Aldershot, UK: Edward Elgar.

———. 1995b. *Monitoring the World Economy, 1820–1992.* Paris: OECD.

———. 1998. *Chinese Economic Performance in the Long Run.* Paris: OECD.

Mahan, A.T. 1890. *The Influence of Sea Power upon History 1660–1783.* Boston, MA: Little, Brown and Company.

———. 1897. "Hawaii and Our Future Sea Power," in *The Interest of America in Sea Power, Present and Future.* Boston, MA: Little, Brown and Company.

Maier, C. 1987. *In Search of Stability: Explorations in Historical Political Economy.* Cambridge: Cambridge University Press.

Malthus, Thomas Robert. 1986. *The Works of Thomas Robert Malthus.* Ed. E. A. Wrigley and David Souden. London: Pickering.

———. 1815. *The Grounds of an Opinion on the Policy of Restricting the Importation of Foreign Corn.* London: John Murray.

Manville, Philip Brook. 1990. *The Origins of Citizenship in Ancient Athens.* Princeton, N.J.: Princeton University Press.

Marshall, Alfred. 1916. *Principles of Economics.* 7th ed. London: Macmillan.

Marshall, P. J., ed. 1998. *The Eighteenth Century.* Vol. 2 of William Roger Louis, ed., *Oxford History of the British Empire.* Oxford: Oxford University Press.

Marx, Karl. 1977 (first published 1875). "Critique of the Gotha Programme." In David McLellan, ed., *Karl Marx: Selected Writings.* Oxford: Oxford University Press.

Mathias, Peter. 1969. *The First Industrial Revolution: An Economic History of Britain, 1700–1914.* London: Methuen.

Meikle, Scott. 1996. "Aristotle on Business." *Classical Quarterly* 46, 1, pp. 138–151.

Merson, John. 1989. *Roads to Xanadu: East and West in the Making of the Modern World.* London: Weidenfeld & Nicolson.

Microsoft ENCARTA 97 WORLD ATLAS.

Middleton, Roger. 1998. *Charlatans or Saviours?* Cheltenham: Edward Elgar.

Miller, Edward, and Hatcher, John. 1978. *Medieval England: Rural Society and Economic Change, 1086–1348.* London: Longman.

———. 1995. *Medieval England: Towns, Commerce and Crafts, 1086–1348.* London: Longman.

Millett, Paul. 1991. *Lending and Borrowing in Ancient Athens.* Cambridge: Cambridge University Press.

Milton, Giles. 1999. *Nathaniel's Nutmeg.* London: Hodder and Stoughton.

Milward, Alan S. 1977. *War, Economy and Society, 1939–45.* London: Penguin.

———. 1992. *The European Rescue of the Nation State.* London: Routledge.

Milward, Alan, and Saul, S. B. 1973. *The Economic Development of Continental Europe, 1780–1870.* London: Allen & Unwin.

———. 1977. *The Development of the Economies of Continental Europe, 1850–1914.* London: Allen & Unwin.

Mitchell Beazley Atlas of the Oceans. 1977. London: Mitchell Beazley.

Mithen, Steven. 1996. *The Prehistory of the Mind: A Search for the Origins of Art, Religion and Science.* London: Thames and Hudson.

Mokyr, J. 1985. *The Economics of the Industrial Revolution.* N.J.: Rowman and Allanheld.

———. 1992. *The Lever of Riches: Technological Creativity and Economic Progress.* Oxford: Oxford University Press.

———. ed. 1993. *The British Industrial Revolution: An Economic Perspective.* Oxford: Oxford University Press.

Morison, Samuel Eliot. 1971. *The European Discovery of America: The Northern Voyages, AD 500–1600.* New York: Oxford University Press.

———. 1974. *The European Discovery of America: The Southern Voyages, AD 1492–1616.* New York: Oxford University Press.

Morris-Suzuki, Tessa. 1994. *The Technological Transformation of Japan: From the Seventeenth Century to the Twenty-first Century.* Cambridge: Cambridge University Press.

Moss, H. St. L. B. 1950. *The Birth of the Middle Ages, 395–814.* Oxford: Oxford University Press.

Murphy, Antoin E. 1997a. "Flawed Visionary Who Burst His Own Bubble." *Financial Times*, 1 June 1997, Weekend FT, p. iv.

———. 1997b. *John Law: Economic Theorist and Policymaker*. Oxford: Clarendon Press.

Nash, R. C. 1997. "The Balance of Payments and Foreign Capital Flows in Eighteenth-century England: A Comment." *Economic History Review*, 2nd ser., 50, 1, pp. 110–128.

Needham, Joseph. 1954–1984. *Science and Civilization in China*. 6 vols. Cambridge: Cambridge University Press.

New Cambridge Medieval History of Europe. 7 vols. Cambridge: Cambridge University Press.

New Cambridge Modern History. 14 vols. Cambridge: Cambridge University Press.

Nissen, Hans J. 1988. *The Early History of the Ancient and Near East, 9000–2000 BC*. [trans. Elizabeth Lutzeier with Kenneth J. Northcott.] Chicago: University of Chicago Press.

North, Douglass C. 1981. *Structure and Change in Economic History*. New York: W. W. Norton.

———. 1990. *Institutions, Institutional Change and Economic Performance*. Cambridge: Cambridge University Press.

North, Douglass C., and Thomas, Robert Paul. 1973. *The Rise of the Western World*. Cambridge: Cambridge University Press.

North, Douglass C., and Weingast, B. R. 1989. In *Journal of Economic History*, 49, pp. 803–832.

Nove, Alec. 1992. *An Economic History of the USSR*. Harmondsworth, UK: Penguin.

O'Brien, Patrick Karl. 1982. "European Economic Development: the Contribution by the Periphery." *Economic History Review*, 2nd ser., 35, pp. 1–18.

———. 1990. "European Industrialization: From the Voyages of Discovery to the Industrial Revolution." In Hans Pohl, ed., *The European Discovery of the World and Its Economic Effects on Pre-industrial Society, 1500–1800*. Stuttgart: Franz Steiner Verlag.

———. 1996. "Path Dependency, or Why Britain Became an Industrialized and Urbanized Economy Long Before France." *Economic History Review*, 2nd ser., 49, 2, pp. 213–249.

———. 1997. "Intercontinental Trade and the Development of the Third World Since the Industrial Revolution." *Journal of World History* 8, 1, pp. 75–134.

———. 1998. "Inseparable Connections: Trade, Economy, Fiscal State, and the Expansion of Empire, 1688–1815." In P. J. Marshall, ed., *The Oxford History of the British Empire*, vol. 2, pp. 53–77. Oxford: Oxford University Press.

O'Brien, Patrick Karl, and Keyder, Caglar. 1978. *Economic Growth in Britain and France, 1780–1914: Two Paths to the Twentieth Century*. London: Allen & Unwin.

O'Brien, Patrick Karl, and Quinault, Roland, eds. 1993. *The Industrial Revolution and British Society*. Cambridge: Cambridge University Press.

OECD (Organisation for Economic Cooperation and Development). 1999. *The Future of the Global Economy: Towards a Long Boom?* Paris: OECD.

Olson, Mancur. 1982. *The Rise and Decline of Nations*. New Haven, Conn.: Yale University Press.

———. 1996. "Big Bills Left on the Sidewalk: Why Some Nations Are Rich, and Others Poor." *Journal of Economic Perspectives*, spring, pp. 3–24.

Olson, Mancur, and Kähkönen, Satu, eds. 2000. *A Not-So-Dismal Science: A Broader View of Economics and Societies*. Oxford: Oxford University Press.

Ormerod, Paul. 1999. *Butterfly Economics*. London: Faber and Faber.

Ormrod, Mark, and Lindley, Philip. 1996. *The Black Death in England.* Stamford, UK: Paul Watkins.
O'Rourke, Kevin H., and Williamson, Jeffery G. 1999. *Globalization and History: The Evolution of a Nineteenth-century Atlantic Economy.* Cambridge: MIT Press.
Osborne, Robin. 1985. *Demos: The Discovery of Classical Attika.* Cambridge: Cambridge University Press.
———. 1996. *Greece in the Making, 1200–479 BC.* London: Routledge.
Overy, Richard. 1999. *Russia's War.* London: Penguin.
Parkin, Michael, and King, David. 1992. *Economics.* Wokingham, UK: Addison-Wesley.
Parkins, Helen, and Smith, Christopher. 1998. *Trade, Traders and the Ancient City.* London: Routledge.
Platt, Colin. 1997. *King Death: The Black Death and Its Aftermath.* London: University College Press.
Pohl, Hans, ed. 1990. *The European Discovery of the World and Its Economic Effects on Pre-industrial Society, 1500–1800.* Stuttgart: Franz Steiner Verlag.
Pomeranz, Ken. 1998. "East Asia, Europe, and the Industrial Revolution." Conference paper, Department of History, University of California, Irvine.
———. 2000. *The Great Divergence: China, Europe and the Making of the Modern World Economy.* Princeton, N.J.: Princeton University Press.
Pomeranz, Ken, and Topik, Steven. 1998. *The World That Trade Created.* London: M. E. Sharpe
Porter, Roy. 1997. *The Greatest Benefit to Mankind.* London: HarperCollins.
Postan, M. M. 1972. *The Medieval Economy and Society.* Vol. 5 of *The Pelican Economic History of Britain.* London: Weidenfeld & Nicolson.
Postgate, J. N. 1994. *Early Mesopotamia.* London: Routledge.
Price, B. B., ed. 1997. *Ancient Economic Thought.* London: Routledge.
Price, Jacob M. 1998. "The Imperial Economy, 1700–76." In P. J. Marshall, ed., *The Oxford History of the British Empire,* vol. 2, pp. 78–104. Oxford: Oxford University Press.
Randsborg, Klavs. 1991. *The First Millennium AD in Europe and the Mediterranean.* Cambridge: Cambridge University Press.
Raphael, D. D. 1985. *Adam Smith.* Oxford: Oxford University Press.
Rawski, T. G., and Li, L. M. 1992. *Chinese History in Economic Perspective.* Berkeley: University of California Press.
Ricardo, David. 1955 (first published 1817). *Principles of Political Economy and Taxation.* London, Dent Dutton.
Richards, John F. 1997. "Early Modern India and World History." *Journal of World History* 8, 2, pp. 197–209.
Richardson, David. 1998. "The British Empire and the Atlantic Slave Trade, 1660–1807." In P. J. Marshall, ed., *The Oxford History of the British Empire,* vol. 2, pp. 440–464. Oxford: Oxford University Press.
Riesman, David A. 1976. *Adam Smith's Sociological Economics.* New York: Croom Helm.
Roaf, Michael. 1991. *Cultural Atlas of Mesopotamia and the Ancient Near East.* Oxford: Facts on File Publications.
Roberts, J. M. 1980. *The Pelican History of the World.* Harmondsworth, UK: Pelican.
Rodger, N.A.M. 1997. *The Safeguard of the Sea: A Naval History of Britain.* Vol. 1: *660–1649.* London: HarperCollins.

———. 1998a. "Guns and Sail in the First Phase of English Colonization, 1500–1650." In Nicholas Canny, ed., *The Oxford History of the British Empire,* vol. 1, pp.79–98. Oxford: Oxford University Press.

———. 1998b. "Sea Power and Empire, 1688–1793." In P. J. Marshall, ed., *The Oxford History of the British Empire,* vol. 2, pp. 169–183. Oxford: Oxford University Press.

Rojas, Mauricio. 1999. *Millennium Doom.* London: Social Market Foundation.

Roll, Eric. 1992. *A History of Economic Thought.* 5th ed. London: Faber and Faber.

Ronan, Colin. 1978–1994. *The Shorter Science and Civilization in China.* 4 vols. Cambridge: Cambridge University Press.

Rosenberg, Nathan, and Birdzell, L. E., Jr. 1986. *How the West Grew Rich: The Economic Transformation of the Industrial World.* New York: Basic Books.

Runciman, W. G. 1998. *The Social Animal.* London: HarperCollins.

Russell, Bertrand. 1946. *History of Western Philosophy.* London: Allen & Unwin.

Sahlins, Marshall. 1972. *Stone Age Economics.* Chicago: Aldine Atherton.

Scammell, G. V., ed. 1989. *The First Imperial Age: European Overseas Expansion, c. 1400–1715.* London: Unwin Hyman.

Seeley, J. R. 1883. *The Expansion of England in the Eighteenth Century.* London: Macmillan.

Sen, Amartya. 1981. *Poverty and Famines.* Oxford: Clarendon Press.

———. 1983. "Development: Which Way Now?" *Economic Journal* 93 (December), pp. 745–760.

———. 1991a. *Markets and Freedoms.* London: London School of Economics.

———. 1991b. *War and Famines: On Divisions and Incentives.* London: London School of Economics.

———. 1995a. *Economic Development and Social Change: India and China in Comparative Perspective.* London: London School of Economics.

———. 1995b. *Population Policy: Authoritarianism Versus Cooperation.* London: London School of Economics.

———. 1997a. *Development Thinking at the Beginning of the 21st Century.* London: London School of Economics.

———. 1997b. *What's the Point of a Development Strategy?* London: London School of Economics.

Service, Robert. 1998. *A History of Twentieth-Century Russia.* London: Penguin.

———. 1999. *The Russian Revolution 1900–27.* 3rd ed. London: Macmillan.

Shanks, Michael. 1961. *The Stagnant Society: A Warning.* Harmondsworth, UK: Penguin.

Shaw, A.G.L., ed. 1970. *Great Britain and the Colonies, 1815–1865.* London: Methuen.

Shepherd, Robert. 1991. *The Power Brokers.* London: Hutchinson.

Sherratt, Andrew. 1995. "Reviving the Grand Narrative: Archaeology and Long-term Change." *Journal of European Archaeology* 3, 1, pp. 1–32.

———. 1997. *Economy and Society in Pre-historic Europe: Changing Perspectives.* Edinburgh: Edinburgh University Press.

Smith, Adam. 1812. (first published 1776). *An Inquiry into the Nature and Causes of the Wealth of Nations.* London: Ward, Lock & Co.

———. 1976 (first published 1759). *The Theory of Moral Sentiments.* Oxford: Oxford University Press.

———. 1978. *Lectures on Jurisprudence, 1762–63, 1766.* Oxford: Oxford University Press.

———. 1980. *Essays on Philosophical Subjects.* Oxford: Oxford University Press.

———. 1983. *Lectures of Rhetoric and Belles Lettres.* Oxford: Oxford University Press.

———. 1987. *Correspondence of Adam Smith.* Oxford: Oxford University Press.
Solow, Barbara L. 1991. *Slavery and the Rise of the Atlantic System.* Cambridge: Cambridge University Press.
Soros, George. 1998. *The Crisis of Global Capitalism.* London: Little, Brown and Company.
Speake, Graham, ed. 1994. *Dictionary of Ancient History.* Oxford: Blackwell.
Standage, Tom. 1998. *The Victorian Internet: The Remarkable Story of the Telegraph and the 19th Century's Online Pioneers.* London: Weidenfeld & Nicolson.
Starr, Chester G. 1977. *The Economic and Social Growth of Early Greece.* New York: Oxford University Press.
Stavrianos, L. S. 1989. *Lifelines from Our Past: A New World History.* Armonk, N.Y.: M. E. Sharpe.
Stearns, Peter N. 1998. *The Industrial Revolution in World History.* Boulder, Colo.: Westview Press.
Story, Jonathan. 1999. *The Frontiers of Fortune.* London: FT/Prentice-Hall.
Sudoplatov, Pavel. 1994. *Special Tasks: The Memoirs of an Unwanted Witness—a Soviet Spymaster.* London: Little, Brown.
Sylla, Richard, and Toniolo, Gianni, eds. 1991. *Patterns of European Industrialization: The Nineteenth Century.* London: Routledge.
Szreter, Simon, and Mooney, Graham. 1998. "Urbanization, Mortality, and the Standard of Living Debate: New Estimates of the Expectation of Life at Birth in Nineteenth-century British Cities." *Economic History Review,* 2nd ser., 51, 1, pp. 84–112.
Tawney, Richard H. 1936. *Religion and the Rise of Capitalism.* London: John Murray, Holland Memorial Lectures.
Teich, Mikulas, and Porter, Roy, eds. 1996. *The Industrial Revolution in National Context: Europe and the USA.* . Cambridge: Cambridge University Press.
Temin, Peter. 1997. "Two Views of the British Industrial Revolution." *Journal of Economic History* 52, pp. 63–82.
Tennyson, Alfred, Lord. 1923. *Poetical Works of Alfred, Lord Tennyson.* London: Macmillan.
Thapar, Romila. 1966. *A History of India.* Harmondsworth, UK: Penguin.
Thompson, I.A.A., and Yun-Casalilla, B., eds. 1994. *The Castilian Crisis of the Seventeenth Century.* Cambridge: Cambridge University Press.
Thurow, Lester. 1996. *The Future of Capitalism.* London: Nicholas Brealey.
Tibbetts, G. R. 1971. *Arab Navigation in the Indian Ocean Before the Coming of the Portuguese.* London: Royal Asian Society of Great Britain and Ireland.
The Times Atlas of Ancient Civilizations. London: Times Books.
The Times Atlas of Medieval Civilizations. London: Times Books.
Toniolo, Gianni. 1998. "Europe's Golden Age, 1950–1973: Speculations from a Long-run Perspective." *Economic History Review,* 2nd ser., 51, 2, pp. 252–267.
Toynbee, Arnold. 1884. *Lectures on the Industrial Revolution of the Eighteenth Century in England.* London: Rivingtons.
———. 1946. *A Study of History.* Ed. D. C. Somervell. Oxford: Oxford University Press.
Tracy, J. D., ed. 1990. *The Rise of the Merchant Empires: Long Distance Trade in the Early Modern World, 1350–1750.* Cambridge: Cambridge University Press.
———. ed. 1991. *The Political Economy of the Merchant Empires.* Cambridge: Cambridge University Press.
Trevelyan, G. M. 1923. *British History in the Nineteenth Century, 1782–1901.* London: Longman.

Tudge, Colin. 1999. *Neanderthals, Bandits and Farmers: How Agriculture Really Began.* London: Weidenfeld & Nicolson.

United Nations. 1998. *World Investment Report.* New York: United Nations Conference on Trade and Development.

———. 1999a. *Global Environment Outlook 2000.* London: Earthscan for United Nations Environment Programme.

———. 1999b. *Human Development Report.* New York: Oxford University Press for United Nations Development Programme.

———. 1999c. *World Population Prospects: The 1998 Revision.* 3 vols. New York: UN.

Van Ark, Bart. 1997. *Economic Growth in the Long-Run: A History of the Empirical Evidence.* 3 vols. Cheltenham, UK: Elgar Reference Collection.

Van der Wee, Herman. 1987. *Prosperity and Upheaval: The World Economy, 1945–1980.* Harmondsworth, UK: Pelican.

Waldrop, M. Mitchell. 1992. *Complexity.* New York: Simon & Schuster.

Wallerstein, Immanuel. 1974–1989. *The Modern World System.* 3 vols. San Diego: Academic Press.

———. 1995a. The Capitalist World-economy. Cambridge: Cambridge University Press.

———. 1995b. *Historical Capitalism with Capitalist Civilization.* London: Verso.

Ward, J. R. 1994. "The Industrial Revolution and British Imperialism, 1750–1850." *Economic History Review,* 2nd ser., 47, pp. 44–65.

———. 1998. "The British West Indies in the Age of Abolition, 1748–1815." In P. J. Marshall, ed., *The Oxford History of the British Empire,* vol. 2, pp. 415–439. Oxford: Oxford University Press.

Waswo, Ann. 1996. *Modern Japanese Society, 1868–1994.* Oxford: Oxford University Press.

Wayland Barber, Elizabeth. 1999. *The Mummies of Urumchi.* London: Gollancz.

Weber, Max. 1931. *The Protestant Ethic and the Spirit of Capitalism.* Trans. Talcott Parsons. London: Allen & Unwin.

Weizsacker, Ernst von; Lovins, Amory B.; and Lovins, Hunter L. 1997. *Factor Four: Doubling Wealth, Halving Resource Use.* London: Earthscan.

Welsh, Frank. 1997. *A History of Hong Kong.* London: HarperCollins.

Wickham, Chris. 1984. "The Other Transition: From the Ancient World to Feudalism." *Past and Present* 103, pp. 3–36.

———. 1994. *Land and Power: Studies in Italian and European Social History, 400–1200.* London: British School at Rome.

———. 1997. "The 'Feudal Revolution.'" *Past and Present* 155, pp. 196–208.

Williams, Eric. 1944. *Capitalism and Slavery.* Chapel Hill: University of North Carolina Press.

Williams, Glyndwr. 1998. "The Pacific: Exploration and Exploitation." In P. J. Marshall, ed., *The Oxford History of the British Empire,* vol. 2, pp. 552–575. Oxford: Oxford University Press.

Williams, Jonathan, 1997. *Money: A History.* London: British Museum Press.

Williamson, Jeffrey G. 1989. "Inequality and Modern Economic Growth: What Does History Tell Us?" Discussion paper, Harvard Institute for Economic Research, Harvard University.

———. 1997. *Industrialisation, Inequality and Economic Growth.* Cheltenham: Edward Elgar.

———. 1998. "Globalization, Labour Markets and Policy Backlash in the Past." *Journal of Economic Perspectives* 12, 4, pp. 51–72.

Wilson, Edward O. 1998. *Consilience: The Unity of Knowledge.* London: Little, Brown.

Wink, Andre. 1990. *Al-Hind: The Making of the Indo-Islamic World.* Leiden: Brill.

Wong, R. B. 1997. *China Transformed, Historical Change and the Limits of European Experience.* Ithaca, N.Y.: Cornell University Press.

Woods, R. I. 1996. "The Population of Britain in the Nineteenth Century." In Michael Anderson, ed., *British Population History.* Cambridge: Cambridge University Press.

World Bank. 1992. *Proceedings of the World Bank Annual Conference on Development Economics.* Washington, D.C.: World Bank.

———. 1993. *The East Asian Miracle.* Washington, D.C.: World Bank.

———. 1997. *The State in a Changing World: World Development Report.* New York: Oxford University Press for the World Bank.

———. 1998a. *Assessing Aid: What Works and What Doesn't, and Why.* New York: Oxford University Press for World Bank.

———. 1998b. *Global Economic Prospects and the Developing Countries.* Washington, D.C.: World Bank.

———. 1999. *World Development Report.* Washington, D.C.: World Bank. .

World Health Organization. 1996. *World Health Statistics Annuals, 1995 and 1996.* Geneva: WHO.

Wrigley, E. A. 1987. *People, Cities and Wealth: The Transformation of Traditional Society.* Oxford: Blackwell.

———. 1988. *Continuity, Chance and Change: The Character of the Industrial Revolution in England.* Cambridge: Cambridge University Press.

———. 1998. "Explaining the Rise in Marital Fertility in England in the 'Long Eighteenth Century.'" *Economic History Review,* 2nd ser., 51, 3, pp. 435–464.

Wrigley, E. A., and Schofield, R. S. 1981. *The Population History of England, 1541–1871.* London: Edward Arnold.

Wrigley, E. A., and Souden, David, eds. 1986. *The Works of Thomas Robert Malthus.* London: Pickering.

Wrigley, E. A.; Davies, R. S.; Oeppen, J. E.; and Schofield, R. S. 1997. *English Population History from Family Reconstruction.* Cambridge: Cambridge University Press.

Yergin, Daniel, and Stanislaw, Joseph. 1999. *The Commanding Heights: The Battle Between Government and Marketplace That Is Remaking the Modern World.* New York: Touchstone.

Yun-Casalilla, Bartoleme. 1998. "The American Empire and the Spanish Economy: An Institutional and Regional Perspective." Paper presented to the Twelfth International Economic History Congress, Seville, Spain.

Zahadieh, Nuala. 1994. "London and the Colonial Consumer in the Late Seventeenth Century." *Economic History Review,* 2nd ser., 47, pp. 239–261.

———. 1998. "Overseas Expansion and Trade in the Seventeenth Century." In Nicholas Canny, ed., *The Oxford History of the British Empire,* vol. 1, pp. 398–422. Oxford: Oxford University Press.

Zimmermann, Warren. 1998. "Jingoes, Goo-goos, and the Rise of America's Empire," in the *Wilson Quarterly,* Spring 1998. Washington, D.C.: Woodrow Wilson International Center for Scholars.

———. 2000. As yet untitled work on the origins of American imperialism. New York: Farrar, Strauss & Giroux.

Zimmern, A. E. 1924. *The Greek Commonwealth.* Oxford: Oxford University Press.

Zuckerman, Larry. 1999. *The Potato.* London: Macmillan.

ACKNOWLEDGMENTS

THIS BOOK WAS WRITTEN AT THE SAME TIME A BBC TELEVISION series, which I presented, was being created on the same subject. I have not, however, sought to homogenize the book and the series. The stories they tell, though ultimately based on the same unique human story, follow different paths, use different illustrations and at times offer different emphases (though not, I hope, too many downright contradictions). The selections, judgments and opinions in the television series were those of a team, whereas those in the book are solely mine. I say nothing important in the series that I do not think, and in the book I say many things that are not in the programs.

I owe many debts of gratitude for the help I have had. This is not the place to say formal thanks to all those in the television team who have encouraged, enabled, supported, shared in and labored on a project that has been every bit as much theirs as mine. But because of both the fundamental synergy and the superficial conflicts between the book and the television series, the author of the book cannot but proclaim his profound gratitude to the women and men of the BBC without whose goodwill, prodigious skills, generously given friendship and patient forbearance he could have completed neither the one task nor the other.

I thank Diarmuid Jeffreys, our executive producer, for daring me to attempt the impossible and for fulfilling the truest role of any great editor, getting more out of his contributors than they themselves ever believed to be possible. I thank Barbara Want, our series editor, whose eye never strayed from the steep and narrow path up the mountain of six one-hour programs and whose dedication to that mission struck therapeutic terror into the hearts of all who would obstruct her, especially the clerks and clowns in accounts who never quite gave up their hopes of hobbling the series.

I thank Adam Salkeld and Charles Bruce, who each produced two of the six programs, and David Wright and Krishna Govender, with whom I also worked as producers. Television is made, at root, by producers, and good television is made by good producers. Those with whom I worked on this series were very good indeed, delightful colleagues, superb professionals, luminously bright, tirelessly industrious, of rare skill and very kind. They alone ultimately have to bridge the perpetually threatening gap between the medium and the message, between the technique and the story, between the camera and the context. They are, and in this case were, the real program-makers. There is no higher activity in broadcasting, and I was privileged to help them. And there were many more—Ruth, Kim, Amanda, Karen, the crews, editors, overseas "fixers" and others—who worked immensely hard, contributed precious talent and skill and were fun to be with. And there was the good old BBC, still a matchless resource and a uniquely supportive platform on which to find oneself lucky enough to make programs.

The book was labored upon in a less populous vineyard. There was Rob Shepherd, and there was myself. It is to Rob that my greatest single debt is owed. He worked ceaselessly from the first day to the last, reading and inquiring widely, assembling material and texts, offering suggestions and ideas, compiling bibliographies and otherwise keeping house amid the mass of material that rose around us. Without him there would be no book. The opinions, the selections, the writing and the errors are mine, and therefore the responsibilities of author are mine alone. But if ever an author needed a colleague, I did, and Rob, by his indefatigable labors, his sharp and meticulous qualities of mind, his unfailing good humor (even when mine failed) and his ability to encourage and reassure without indulging or flattering, transcended all the duties of his engagement to the point where colleague became friend and where he will, I hope, think of the book with pride as his as well as mine.

There was one other, Ion Trewin of Weidenfeld and Nicolson. A quondam colleague at the *Times* [London] and long since distinguished head of a famous publishing house, he showed first interest, then solid support and thereafter faith and enthusiasm that carried the book from the slipways of the mind to the shelves of the booksellers and, it must be hoped, of the public. He never uttered a tiresome word, and he always overcame my own misgivings over matters great and small. If I was fortunate to have the ideal editor in Diarmuid Jeffreys, I was doubly so to have the perfect publisher in Ion Trewin. And in Felicity Bryan I had the perfect agent, always supportive, never importunate, always shrewd, never carried away, always a kind friend and more recently a warm-hearted neighbor and throughout the whole project a superb professional.

I have benefited from global history seminars of the Institute of Historical Research, thanks to the kind hospitality of Professor Patrick O'Brien. Dr. Alan Bowman of Christ Church, Oxford, provided invaluable and copious comments on Chapter 2; and Patrick Wormald, also of Christ Church, shared his insights into the breakdown, especially in Britain, of key aspects of civil society as the Roman imperium crumbled. Professor William McNeill was generous with his time both in receiving me in Connecticut and in private correspondence. Professor Alan Macfarlane generously shared his profound knowledge of Adam Smith's thought. Michael Bailey was inexhaustible in his knowledge of early railways and the fate of William Huskisson.

There are other friends and indeed relations whom I have peppered with ignorant questions about physics, mathematics, epidemiology, ancient history and many other things that journalists know little about and so rely on knowing someone who does know about them. In this category I thank in particular Professor Julian Hunt, Professor Sebastian Lucas, Sir Samuel Brittan and Martin Wolf, as well as many others who will know that they have my great gratitude. My long-standing friend Ambassador Warren Zimmermann very kindly allowed me to see drafts of certain, for me, key passages in his keenly awaited book on the origins of American imperialism. His admirable style and unfaltering good sense helped me immensely, making it as he always has a pleasure as well as an education to learn from him. My old friend John Graham has subedited and otherwise improved the whole work, and I am grateful as ever for his ever rarer qualities of literacy and erudition, as well as for his friendship and support.

It is customary to thank one's wife and children. Husbands and other, less-established partners get less of a look in, one notices. The problem about thanking one's family is that although it is often sincere and surpassingly well merited, few authors manage to bring it off without being hackneyed, mawkish, boring or all three, apart that is from those who escape into sarcasm or abuse. I know no way around this problem, which is made worse by Emma's particular fastidiousness about such yuck. But there it is. Her life and that of our three young boys has been deplorably disrupted, constrained and bereft of a functioning husband-and-father because of the book, and despite this she has given unstinting support and encouragement, frequently drawing my attention to interesting new material and commenting all too pungently on my lapses of knowledge, logic, humor, grammar and style. It is not just the book that would not be possible without her. It is me.

Woodstock, Oxfordshire
1 January 2000

THE AUTHOR AND PUBLISHERS ARE GRATEFUL FOR PERMISSION to quote the following copyright material: Colin McEvedy and Richard Jones, *Atlas of World Population History,* 1978, Allen Lane; Bertrand Russell, *History of Western Philosophy,* 1946, George Allen & Unwin, and Simon & Schuster, copyright © 1945, copyright © renewed 1973 by Edith Russell; Nathan Rosenberg and L.E. Birdzell Jr., *How the West Grew Rich,* copyright © 1986, Basic Books Inc.; Chambers, J.D., and Mingay, G.E., *The Agricultural Revolution 1750–1880,* 1966, Batsford and Salamander Books, Chrysalis Books Group; William H. McNeill, *Plagues and Peoples,* 1994, Blackwell Publishers and Penguin Books; Jonathan Williams (ed.), *Money: A History,* 1997, © the British Museum, British Museum Press; *Cambridge Ancient History,* Cambridge University Press; K.N. Chaudhuri, *Trade and Civilisation in the Indian Ocean,* 1985, Cambridge University Press; Harriet Crawford, *Sumer and the Sumerians,* 1991, Cambridge University Press; Philip D. Curtin, *Cross-Cultural Trade in World History,* 1984, Cambridge University Press; David Landes, *The Unbound Prometheus,* 1969, Cambridge University Press; Roderick Floud and D.N. McCloskey (eds.), *The Economic History of Britain since 1700,* 3 vols., 1994, Cambridge University Press; Jan de Vries and Ad van der Woude, *The First Modern Economy,* 1997, Cambridge University Press; E.A. Wrigley, *Continuity, Chance and Change,* 1988; Cambridge University Press; Winston S. Churchill, *The Second World War,* 1949, Cassell, reproduced with permission of Curtis Brown Ltd., London, on behalf of the Estate of Sir Winston S. Churchill. Copyright Winston S. Churchill; Peter Garnsey, Keith Hopkins and C.R. Whittaker, *Trade in the Ancient Economy,* 1983, Chatto & Windus; Jared Diamond, *Guns, Germs and Steel: The Fates of Human Societies,* copyright © 1997 by Jared Diamond. Used by permission of Jonathan Cape and W. W. Norton & Company, Inc.; James Foreman-Peck, *A History of the World Economy: International Economic Relations since 1850,* 1995, 2nd ed., Harvester Wheatsheaf; Jung Chang, *Wild Swans,* 1991, HarperCollins Publishers Ltd., and reprinted with permission of Simon & Schuster from *Wild Swans* by Jung Chang, copyright © 1991 by Globalflair Ltd.; Paul Kennedy, *The Rise and Fall of the Great Powers,* 1989, HarperCollins Publishers Ltd., and David Higham Associates; Roy Porter, 1997, *The Greatest Benefit to Mankind,* HarperCollins Publishers Ltd.; W.G. Runciman, *The Social Animal,* 1998, HarperCollins Publishers Ltd.; *Scale and Scope* by Alfred Chandler, copyright © 1990 by the President and Fellows of Harvard College, reprinted by permission of The Belknap Press of Harvard University Press; *China: A New History* by John K. Fairbank and Merle Goldman, copyright © 1998 by the President and Fellows of Harvard College, reprinted by permission of The Belknap Press of Harvard University Press; *The Black Death and the Transformation of the West* by David Herlihy and Samuel K. Cohn Jr., copyright © 1997 by the President and Fellows of Harvard College, reprinted by permission of The Belknap Press of Harvard University Press; Amartya Sen, "Economic Development and Social Change: India and China in Comparative Perspective," STICERD Paper No. 65, 1995, London School of Economics; John Maynard Keynes, *Essays in Biography* and *Essays in Persuasion,* 1972, Macmillan Press Ltd., and the Royal Economic Society, with the permission of Macmillan Ltd.; T.S. Ashton, *The Industrial Revolution 1760–1830,* 1948, by permission of Oxford University Press; Christopher Dow, *Major Recessions: Britain and the World, 1920–95,* 1998, by permission of Oxford University Press, Inc.; P.J. Marshall (ed., vol. 2), *The Oxford History of the British Empire,* 1998, by permission of Oxford University Press; Chester G. Starr, *The Economic and Social Growth of Early Greece,* 1977, Oxford University Press, Inc.; Janet Abu-Lughod, *Before European Hegemony,* 1989, Oxford University Press, Inc.; Joel Mokyr, *The Lever of Riches,* 1990, Oxford University Press, Inc.; Louise Levathes, *When China Ruled the Seas,* 1996, Oxford University Press, Inc.; The World Bank, *The East Asian Miracle: Economic Growth and Public Policy,* 1993, Oxford University Press, Inc.; Norman Davies, *Europe: A History,* 1997, Pimlico and Oxford University Press, Inc.; Robert Service, *A History of Twentieth-Century Russia,* 1998, Penguin; Michael Shanks, *The Stagnant Society: a Warning,* 1964, Penguin; Gang Deng, *The*

Pre-Modern Chinese Economy, 1999, Routledge; Hans Pohl (ed.), *The European Discovery of the World and its Economic Effects on Pre-Industrial Society, 1500–1800,* 1990, Franz Steiner Verlag, Stuttgart; Colin Platt, *King Death: the Black Death and its Aftermath,* 1997, University College Press; Re-ORIENT: *Global Economy in the Asian Age,* by Andre Gunder Frank, published by the University of California Press, copyright © 1998 Andre Gunder Frank; Hans J. Nissen, *The Early History of the Ancient and Near East, 9000–2000 B.C.,* University of Chicago Press; *Capitalism and Slavery* by Eric Williams, copyright © 1944 by the University of North Carolina Press, renewed (with a new introduction by Colin A. Palmer), 1994, used by permission of the publisher; Rudyard Kipling, *Road-Song of the Bandar-Log, The Jungle Book* and *The White Man's Burden,* by permission of A. P. Watt Ltd., on behalf of The National Trust for Places of Historic Interest or Natural Beauty; Tom Standage, *The Victorian Internet,* 1998, Weidenfeld & Nicolson, London.

I am grateful to the following for allowing me to see and to quote draft material for books that were due to be published after I had completed writing this book: Professor William H. McNeill who, with John R. McNeill, is writing a book provisonally entitled *A Very Short History of the Whole World,* and Professor Kenneth Pomeranz, whose *The Great Divergence: China, Europe and the Making of the Modern World Economy* is published by Princeton University Press. I am also grateful to Professor Alan Macfarlane for allowing me to see draft chapters of his book, *The Riddle of the Modern World,* published by Macmillan. Every effort has been made to trace copyright holders, but if any have been inadvertently overlooked the author and publishers will be pleased to make the necessary arrangements at the first opportunity.

INDEX

PUBLICAFFAIRS is a new nonfiction publishing house and a tribute to the standards, values, and flair of three persons who have served as mentors to countless reporters, writers, editors, and book people of all kinds, including me.

I.F. STONE, proprietor of *I. F. Stone's Weekly*, combined a commitment to the First Amendment with entrepreneurial zeal and reporting skill and became one of the great independent journalists in American history. At the age of eighty, Izzy published *The Trial of Socrates*, which was a national bestseller. He wrote the book after he taught himself ancient Greek.

BENJAMIN C. BRADLEE was for nearly thirty years the charismatic editorial leader of *The Washington Post*. It was Ben who gave the *Post* the range and courage to pursue such historic issues as Watergate. He supported his reporters with a tenacity that made them fearless, and it is no accident that so many became authors of influential, best-selling books.

ROBERT L. BERNSTEIN, the chief executive of Random House for more than a quarter century, guided one of the nation's premier publishing houses. Bob was personally responsible for many books of political dissent and argument that challenged tyranny around the globe. He is also the founder and was the longtime chair of Human Rights Watch, one of the most respected human rights organizations in the world.

. . .

For fifty years, the banner of Public Affairs Press was carried by its owner Morris B. Schnapper, who published Gandhi, Nasser, Toynbee, Truman, and about 1,500 other authors. In 1983 Schnapper was described by *The Washington Post* as "a redoubtable gadfly." His legacy will endure in the books to come.

Peter Osnos, *Publisher*